Presidential Campaign Politics
Coalition Strategies and Citizen Response

Presidential Campaign Politics
Coalition Strategies and Citizen Response
THIRD EDITION

John H. Kessel

THE DORSEY PRESS
Chicago, Illinois 60604

This book was set in Palatino by Bi-Comp, Incorporated.
The editors were Leo Wiegman, Gladys True, and Jane Lightell.
The production manager was Carma W. Fazio.
The designer was Keith McPherson.
The drawings were done by Precision Graphics.
Malloy Lithographing, Inc. was the printer and binder.

ISBN 0-256-05922-5

Library of Congress Catalog Card No. 87–70916

Printed in the United States of America

1 2 3 4 5 6 7 8 9 0 ML 5 4 3 2 1 0 9 8

Preface

While writing this book I tried to combine flesh-and-blood politics with serious analysis. An attempt to combine substance and method can be awkward and imperfect, but the alternatives are either to shift readers away from the fascinating realm of political maneuver, or to deny readers the real explanatory power of sophisticated methodology. As V. O. Key put it: "Method without substance may be sterile, but substance without method is only fortuitously substantial."

I have tried to make clear that coalition strategies and citizen choice are equally important parts of the same political process. In recent decades, there has been much more research and writing on voting behavior than on political parties. An unhappy consequence has been the appearance of many "electoral" studies that rely almost completely on voting data. Political scientists who wouldn't write a word about voting without a national sample and multivariate analysis unhesitatingly offer off-the-top-of-the-head surmises about party activities. Equally careful analyses of parties and voters are essential to understand the linkage between coalition strategies and citizen response.

I have tried to unite a concern for politics with some attention to the development of theory. I argue that *why* something happens is sometimes explained by internal structure, sometimes by external environment, and sometimes by both. *When* it happens is explained by the temporal pattern of the acting unit. This is a simple theory, but it is sufficiently flexible to be adapted to the subjects. It also permits a comprehensive treatment of presidential nominations and elections within one theoretical framework.

These were my goals when I wrote the first edition of *Presidential Campaign Politics,* and they still are. But while my goals have remained constant, two revisions have produced a book with a substantial amount of new material. Just about half of the pages in this edition are new since the first edition was published.

Analyses of the 1980 and 1984 campaigns have been substituted for accounts of earlier campaigns. The new analyses of nomination and electoral politics still follow a temporal outline, but they are a little longer. This permitted me, for example, to deal with the more complex strategic choices involved in a three-candidate race in 1980. I was also able to say something about all eight of the aspirants who entered the Democratic lists in 1984, and to follow them as the fortunes of nomination politics favored first one and then another. The probit analyses continue to serve as accurate models of vote choice. Eighty-seven percent of the Reagan-Carter choices were correctly predicted, as were ninety percent of the Reagan-Mondale decisions. In general, the 1984 analysis showed that Mr. Reagan was popular with the voters, but his policies were not.

I have also incorporated major studies by other scholars. In the second edition, I added material from the Cotter, Gibson, Bibby, and Huckshorn study of state and local party organizations. In this edition, I have been able to draw on the Miller-Jennings analysis of increasing conservatism among party elites and to include the first report of the seventeen-year socialization study by Jennings, Niemi, and Markus. In both editions, I have relied on Herbert Alexander's continuing documentation of the changing role of campaign finance. My hope is that these additions adhere to my original goal of combining flesh-and-blood politics and serious analysis in the same book.

ACKNOWLEDGMENTS

Any book such as this depends as much on the research milieu in which it is written as much as it does on the thoughts of the author. I have been extremely fortunate in having colleagues at Ohio State with strong research orientations. Those whose work is most closely related to campaign politics—Herbert Asher, Aage Clausen, and Herbert Weisberg—have been more than generous with their time and counsel when I have come to them with questions and puzzlements. Thomas Boyd, Thomas Jackson, Bruce Moon, Barbara Norrander, Stephen Shaffer, Evelyn Small, Gerald Stacy, Kenneth Town, Barbara Trish, and Steven Yarnell have all been responsible in one way or another for analyses that appear between these covers. Stephen Shaffer and Steven Yarnell made particularly important contributions to the analysis of political activists; Stephen Shaffer, Barbara Norrander, Thomas Boyd, and Barbara Trish did so for the analysis of vote choice; Thomas Boyd helped with the material on party identification.

A number of people were generous enough to lend data sets. I should like to thank Richard Hofstetter for allowing me to use his 1972 surveys of political activists and voters, Aage Clausen for the use of his congressional scales, Doris Graber for allowing me to use some of her media analyses, Jeane Kirkpatrick for access to data on convention delegates, and Herbert Weisberg for data pertaining to party identification. I should like to thank Warren Miller and Kent Jennings for giving me an advance look at their *Parties in Transition:*

A Longitudinal Study of Party Elites and Party Supporters, and allowing me to incorporate some of their principal results. Steven Rosenstone shared his data on candidates' issue positions from *Forecasting Presidential Elections,* and was more than patient in providing counsel on their proper use. I also wish to acknowledge *The New York Times'* willingness to let me use data they had assembled on attitudes of 1984 convention delegates and the general public. And data on citizen reaction came, thanks to the National Science Foundation, from the Center for Political Studies through the auspices of the Inter-University Consortium for Political and Social Research.

Having the data sets is of little use without access to data analysis capabilities. Here, too, many people have been helpful. Richard McKelvey was kind enough to send his probit analysis program, and Forrest Nelson and John Aldrich (the latter on repeated occasions) helped me understand how to use probit analysis. Herbert Weisberg helped remove a block from the OSIRIS CLUSTER program so a large input matrix could be used, rewrote a section of the CLUSTER program to assure that each case would end up in the cluster with which it was most closely associated, and coached me on the use of the MDSCAL program. The Polimetrics Laboratory at Ohio State helped me get my data in and out of the computer; James Ludwig helped me time and again when his special expertise was needed. In addition to general gratitude to the authors of the OSIRIS and SPSS programs, a special word of thanks ought to go to Norman Nie and his SPSS colleagues for the COMPUTE (and other similar) statements that allow nonprogrammers to manipulate data to meet particular needs.

As I was beginning to work on the second edition, Kristi Andersen encouraged me to begin using a computer as a text-editor. My move from a typewriter to a computer was facilitated by the Polimetrics Laboratory, and particularly by James Ludwig's willingness to provide the software and advice necessary to convert thoughts into SCRIPT files, and to get the files onto computer tape.

It is a pleasure to acknowledge financial assistance that has allowed me to collect data and analyze them. The National Science Foundation has supported my work with three grants, GS-2660, GS-35084, and SES 80-24079, to study presidential politics. Ohio State University provided time by granting me professional leave during 1980–81. The American Enterprise Institute for Public Policy Research gave me a Washington base by welcoming me as a Visiting Scholar during 1980–81, and again during the summer of 1982. And the Earhart Foundation gave me a fellowship research grant that allowed me to devote Winter Quarter 1983 to full-time writing.

Kristi Andersen, Richard Fenno, and Fred Greenstein all offered helpful reactions as this book was taking shape. Philip Converse, Richard Niemi, and Herbert Weisberg provided illuminating criticisms of the part on the Citizen in Presidential Elections. John Bibby, Stephen Brown, and Samuel Patterson read the entire original manuscript and showed me many ways it could be improved. Critical reaction and counsel on subsequent editions has come from Allan Cigler, William Crotty, Richard Fenno, Daniel Fleitas, Susan Howell, Loch Johnson, Joan McLean, Joseph Pika, Samuel Patterson, Steven Rosenstone, and Herbert Weisberg. No one named in these paragraphs is responsible for the interpretations in the book, but all should be given credit for trying to make it better.

Finally, and above all, my thanks go to Maggie for all the love and understanding she has shared with me since 1954.

John H. Kessel

Contents

PART TWO
Electoral Politics

List of Figures

List of Tables

Part One

Nomination Politics

Chapter 1

Early Days and Initial Contests

FIRST STIRRINGS

Republican Hopefuls

In the summer of 1986, Republican roads led to Michigan, and most of them veered to the right. An idea had come to Republican State Chairman E. Spencer Abraham. If, he thought, Michigan picked its delegates before any other state, presidential candidates might pay court to Michigan Republicans. Therefore, he arranged a filing deadline for May 27 and the selection of precinct delegates on August 5, a full two years before the 1988 Republican convention. Sure enough, Vice President George Bush, Representative Jack Kemp, the Reverend Marion G. (Pat) Robertson, and their delegate-recruiting political action committees all came to the party.

George Bush, a moderate candidate in 1980, was (for better or worse) a captive of President Reagan's reputation. "My view," Bush explained, "is the best thing for me to do is to support this president, which I can do enthusiastically from a philosophical standpoint and do it from my view as to how one ought to act" as vice president. Congressman Jack Kemp, who had been advocating tax cuts for more than a decade in speeches around the country, tried to take advantage of his greater independence to suggest that he ought to be regarded as Ronald Reagan's true heir. Pat Robertson, a popular television evangelist who like Bush was the son of a U.S. senator, was giving prayerful consideration to running for president. In the meantime, he was maintaining a heavy speaking schedule in the South, where his evangelical base was concentrated.

Robert Dole of Kansas and the man he had succeeded as Senate majority leader, Howard Baker of Tennessee, reacted differently to the early contest in Michigan. Dole was giving an example of his political dexterity by leading the Senate Republicans (who tended to be more liberal than President Reagan) and simultaneously edging closer to the Republican right wing. Also busy as a candidate for reelection to the Senate, he nonetheless managed to make time for some speeches in Michigan. Howard Baker, a moderate who had retired from the Senate with the thought of taking another shot at the presidency, was the only major Republican possibility to avoid Michigan. "They're going to be picking 1988 convention delegates before the 1986 election is even held," he said. "It blows my mind."

Former Delaware Governor Pierre S. Du Pont IV, former Secretary of State Alexander Haig, and former Defense Secretary Donald Rumsfeld also found their way to Michigan for speeches in early 1986. Du Pont, known as a moderate while governor, was trying to woo the right wing by calling for voluntary school prayer, a voucher system for private education, and support for freedom fighters and by opposing school busing. An admitted long shot, he had been channeling a lot of money to other Republican candidates through his GOPAC and was the first Republican to announce the formation of a presidential campaign committee. Both Alexander Haig and Donald Rumsfeld, having served as chiefs of staff to presidents, were of the opinion that they ought to be president, but it was not clear who else thought so. Finally, there were others frequently mentioned as presidential candidates: Jeane Kirkpatrick, an advocate of a resolute foreign policy; Nevada Senator Paul Laxalt, who was being urged to take the reins of conservative leadership from his friend Ronald Reagan; and New Jersey Governor Thomas Kean who was enjoying enormous popularity in his home state.

Democratic Contenders

The Democrats faced the classic problems of the out party. Lacking a visible presidential program, they needed to define themselves as a party at the same time that individuals set forth their own credentials as candidates. Roughly speaking, the Democratic field could be divided into four liberals, six who were in a liberal-to-moderate range, and three moderates.

Two of the liberals, Jesse Jackson and Gary Hart, were the runners-up from the 1984 race. Their postures were recognizable from the previous campaign. Jackson continued to give voice to the claims of his black constituency. June 1986 found him in New York City, giving a speech denouncing South African apartheid. Gary Hart chose not to seek another Senate term but hammered out ideas for his party. On June 11, 12, and 13, he delivered three foreign policy addresses at Georgetown University. Hart opposed protectionism in international trade but otherwise disagreed with the administration. He called for a test ban treaty, more diplomatic efforts in Central America, greater contributions to NATO land forces by European nations, and economic sanctions against South Africa. The third liberal was Governor Mario Cuomo of

New York, an eloquent speaker who was making a number of appearances outside the Empire State. He was said to be reaching out to a number of foreign policy experts in order to develop his own views in this policy area. Just nominated for a second term as governor, he kept presidential questions at arm's length with a series of ambiguous statements. The fourth liberal possibility was Massachusetts Governor Michael Dukakis, who had been considered for the vice-presidential nomination in 1984. Also up for reelection in 1986, he was thought more likely to run if Governor Cuomo did not.

The first member of the liberal-to-moderate sextet, Representative Richard Gephardt of Missouri, had spoken in 30 states during 1985, and by midsummer 1986 had made six trips to Iowa. A member of the House leadership as chairman of the Democratic caucus and genuinely interested in ideas, Gephardt was in perhaps the best position to make the difficult move from the House to presidential contention. Senator Joseph Biden of Delaware was another young moderate moving in a liberal direction. He had delivered Jefferson-Jackson Day speeches in New Hampshire, Oklahoma, Mississippi, Alabama, and Virginia, and had begun to recruit staff members experienced in presidential politics. Senator Bill Bradley of New Jersey was active in the Senate in 1986 in behalf of a rate-reducing, loophole-closing tax bill, and was highly regarded by his peers for these efforts. The fourth and fifth of this "middle-of-the-party" sextet were Senator Paul Simon, a political veteran from Illinois, and Senator Albert Gore, Jr., inheritor of a famous name in Tennessee. Both had just been elected in 1984, so both could try in 1988 without hazarding their Senate seats. Senator Dale Bumpers of Arkansas, was the most conservative of this middle grouping, but more liberal than most Southerners. Mentioned for some time as a presidential possibility, in 1986 Bumpers was paying more attention to being reelected to the Senate.

The three moderates included two governors, Charles Robb of Virginia and Bruce Babbitt of Arizona, and a Senator, Sam Nunn of Georgia. Robb's moderate policies had not attracted a lot of national attention until 1985 when Virginian voters chose not only the Democratic gubernatorial candidate Robb had backed but a black and a woman for statewide office as well. Speaking in 1986 as chairman of the moderate Democratic Leadership Council, Robb declared, "We need a foreign policy which neither renounces nor relies exclusively on the use of force, a policy tempered, but not paralyzed, by the lessons of Vietnam." But while Democrats were paying attention to him, Robb was telling others that they ought to consider nominating Senator Nunn. Nunn, for his part, was following a traditional Southern pattern of building Capitol Hill influence by taking thoughtful, low-key positions. He was chiefly respected for his mastery of defense issues. The only Sun Belt moderate conducting an active campaign was Governor Babbitt. Among other things, Babbitt advocated capital punishment, reducing future social security increases, and cutting federal pensions, and he could produce coherent arguments for these conservative (for a Democrat) positions.

In short, while the Republican contenders were concentrated on the con-

servative side of the GOP, the Democrats had a considerable spectrum between Jesse Jackson and Gary Hart on their left and Charles Robb, Sam
Nunn, and Bruce Babbitt on their right. Each of these contenders had some
following among Democratic activists; but in the summer of 1986, all were in
single digits in preference polls except for Gary Hart, Jesse Jackson, Mario
Cuomo—and Lee Iacocca. The presence of the Chrysler president on the list
was testimony to the formlessness of the Democratic race at this early stage
and perhaps to Democratic yearning for a nonpolitician who could draw
attention away from the gulf between liberals and moderates and lead the
party back to the White House.

Some Earlier Comparisons

Perhaps the most significant fact about the race at this stage was that it was
the summer of 1986—nearly two years before the parties' nominating conventions would meet. Some perspective can be gained by asking what was happening at this point in previous presidential nomination contests.

In late June 1982, Democrats were meeting in Philadelphia for a three-day,
midterm party conference. They listened to speeches by possible 1984 contenders: Senator Edward M. Kennedy (then still viewed as a probable candidate), former Vice President Walter F. Mondale, and Senators John Glenn,
Alan Cranston, Gary Hart, and Ernest F. Hollings. The aspirants, especially
Edward Kennedy and Walter Mondale, gave good speeches, but when the
Democrats left Philadelphia, the prospects for 1984 were much the same as
they had been. There was some speculation on whether President Reagan
would run for a second term, but the President was keeping his own counsel.

In June 1978, the news was that the consumer price index had risen .9
percent (an annual rate of 10.8 percent), and California voters had approved
Proposition 13, an initiative to cut property taxes by a little more than half. In
June 1974, Richard Nixon took two trips, a nine-day visit to the Middle East
followed by an eight-day trip to Moscow. The House Judiciary Committee
was making preparations for impeachment hearings but was not to meet until
July 24. That same month, Governor Jimmy Carter of Georgia gave a speech
on zero-based budgeting to the National Governors Conference. In June 1970,
President Nixon gave a televised speech on the problems of avoiding a recession while bringing a major war to an end. The Senate was debating the
Cooper-Church amendment, which would have forbidden any use of funds
to pay U.S. forces in Cambodia. Senator George McGovern attacked the administration's policy in Southeast Asia in a commencement address at Dartmouth College and en route persuaded Gary Hart to commute between Colorado and Washington, D.C., to begin setting up a campaign organization.

There were certainly portents here of the nomination campaigns to come,
but that's about all. No commentators, for example, told us that we should
pay attention to a senator named George McGovern or a governor named
Jimmy Carter because they were going to emerge as the Democratic nominees

for president in 1972 and 1976, nor did anyone whisper that Jesse Jackson would run for president in 1984 and Edward Kennedy would not. It was too early for that.

If there was anything unusual about the summer of 1986, it was that there was so much visible activity so early. As late as November 1943, New York Governor Thomas E. Dewey (the 1944 Republican presidential nominee) was writing to a political ally, "You and I know better than most people that this is just plain too early" for any public campaigning (Smith, 1982, p. 389). But Theodore White began chronicling the long preconvention campaigns of aspirants in 1960, and both George McGovern and Jimmy Carter were successful with campaigns that began very early. In recent decades, nomination campaigns have become longer and longer. The early selection of precinct delegates in Michigan was just the most recent indication of the lengthening of nomination politics.

THE FOUR STAGES OF NOMINATION POLITICS

Early Days

At least four stages can be distinguished in nomination politics. The first is Early Days, the period prior to the beginning of delegate selection. The initial order of business is a decision on whether or not to run for president. Barry Goldwater, for example, had not made his decision during 1963, nor had Nelson Rockefeller during 1967, the years immediately prior to the election years in which they sought the Republican nomination. Walter Mondale decided to run for president shortly after the 1972 election, actively sought support for the next two years, and then announced in November 1974 that he would not be a candidate.

If the decision to make an active bid for the White House has not been made, then the candidate spends a lot of time listening to the urgings of those who would like to see an active candidacy and a lot more time trying to figure out whether these urgings reflect the interests of the people doing the coaxing or are, in fact, grounded in genuine public support. During 1979, many people urged Senator Kennedy to become a candidate against Jimmy Carter. Did these people really want Kennedy to become president? Were they echoing the sentiments of others? Or did they just want *someone* other than Jimmy Carter at the head of the 1980 Democratic ticket?

If a decision to run has been made, then the next question is how quickly one should begin organizing. The traditional posture has been that before the midterm election, it is too early for much serious organizing. For one thing, no one can be certain who will survive the election. If a senator or governor wins by a big margin, it may set the stage for a presidential bid two years later. On the other hand, candidates rejected by the voters of their own states may not even be in a position to influence their own state delegations. Without information on the identity of the players, one can only make tentative plans.

Against the background of this traditional hesitation, some organizational steps now loom more and more important. One is the creation of an exploratory committee empowered to receive contributions. This is because of the Federal Election Campaign Act of 1974 (actually, amendments to the 1971 act) that inaugurated federal financing of presidential campaigns. This act requires a number of things. First, a candidate must raise, in each of 20 states, $5,000 in contributions of not more than $250. As national campaign expenses go, $100,000 is not a lot of money, but it does require the creation of an organization to raise money over a large area. Second, the federal fund will provide up to 50 percent of $10 million (plus an inflation allowance). Since the federal fund matches money raised by the candidate, this doubles any disparity that may result from fund-raising capacity. In other words, if Candidate A raises the minimum $100,000 and Candidate B raises $1 million, the matching funds will give Candidate B a financial advantage of $2 million to Candidate A's $200,000. These financial facts of life may lead candidates to take stands that will stimulate gifts from donors, and it does stimulate much more organized Early Days activity. Serious contenders are forced into early fund-raising, if only to keep from entering the race too far behind their competitors.

Another factor promoting earlier activity is general recognition of the importance of the early contests in providing momentum to a candidate or depriving him of it. And when delegate selection begins so very early (such as Michigan's in 1986), then candidates are forced into strategy decisions and organization building. Which primaries will be entered? What stands will the candidate take? An initial staff must be recruited. In addition to the aforementioned need for a fund-raiser, an absolute minimum requirement is someone to handle the media and someone to organize the campaign. Once these essentials are in hand, then the candidate begins making forays into those states in which the first delegates are to be chosen. These activities are intertwined with one another. The staff members are likely to take part in initial strategy discussions, and residents of early primary states who tell a campaigner how impressed they are may find themselves recruited into the candidate's state campaign organization.

The Early Days are also marked by a lack of information about the opposition. Who else will be running? Even among announced candidates, it is too soon to know how well organized they are, how well financed they will be, or how attractive they are to the voters. Given this lack of solid information, the media have considerable ability to promote or handicap a contender by just writing that Candidate A is being taken seriously or that Candidate B is lightly regarded. Such articles can be of tactical benefit to a favored candidate, as they help the candidate acquire more resources. But experienced professionals—both politicians and reporters—know that only preliminary judgments can be made about who the strong contenders will be and who will soon disappear for lack of support.

Initial Contests

The Initial Contests are, of course, the first campaigns for delegates. New Hampshire has traditionally held the first primary election, although a number of other states have scheduled early primaries in recent years. Iowa has also gained attention recently by holding the first party caucuses in which delegates are selected. Considerable attention is paid to Iowa and New Hampshire just because they are first; but the crucial point is whether or not their primaries and caucuses are being contested, especially by those regarded by the media as strong candidates. As long as New Hampshire's is first and contested, it will be an important primary; but if a New Hampshire governor were to run as a favorite son and was strong enough to keep other candidates out, attention would shift elsewhere.

The number of states in which candidates seek delegates depends on their strength and resources. If aspirants have the funds and organizations to make it feasible, they may enter a large number of primaries and seek delegates in several caucus states. With this kind of strategy, the Initial Contests phase is not so critical. Obviously it helps to win, but a defeated candidate who is confident that support can be picked up later in other parts of the country can afford to take a more detached view. For less well supported candidates, however, success in the Initial Contests is imperative. Their hope is that they can generate some enthusiasm among the voters, which in turn will produce the resources that will enable them to enter later primaries. If support from the voters is not there, the only option is to drop out.

The Initial Contests are watched very closely by the media. In 1976, the three national networks broadcast 100 stories on the February 24 primary in New Hampshire (choosing 38 delegates), compared to 30 stories on New York's April 6 primary (428 delegates) (Robinson, 1976). Whether a candidate has won or lost becomes less important in media interpretation than how the candidate's performance measures up against expectations. Needless to say, candidate organizations go to great effort to establish low expectations so they can be "pleasantly surprised" by the actual results. Reporters, however, are equally interested in establishing more objective standards. Among other things, they refer to historical standards (how well the candidate has done in the same state on previous occasions), preprimary polls, geographical proximity (whether the candidate comes from a nearby state), and the investment of time and resources made by the candidate (Matthews, 1978; cf. Arterton, 1984, pp. 174–182). If a candidate does better than expected, it is hailed as a victory, and the candidate gains precious momentum. If a candidate does about as well as expected, not too much attention is paid. If a candidate falls below expectation, then articles are written analyzing the failure of the campaign.

There have been complaints about this measurement of performance against expectation. By this logic, although he won 46.4 percent of the vote to Senator McGovern's 37.2 percent, Senator Edmund Muskie was said to have lost the 1972 New Hampshire primary because he had been expected to do better. Similarly, Congressman John Anderson got most of the headlines after the 1980 Massachusetts primary because he did so much better than expected, although George Bush got 31.0 percent of the vote to Anderson's 30.7 percent. This cost Bush an opportunity to regain the momentum he had lost to Ronald Reagan the week before in New Hampshire. This seems perverse, but in the absence of "hard" information about the progress of coalition building, the expectations developed by the media may provide better standards of comparison than the claims of the candidates.

Mist Clearing

The third phase of nomination politics is hardest to pinpoint at a particular point in time, but it usually occurs while the delegates are still being chosen. It is marked by a reduction of the uncertainty that has thus far attended the nomination process and, in this sense, is akin to the clearing of a mist that allows one to see the pine trees across a woods or cars several hundred yards down the road. Whereas vital pieces of information are missing during Early Days and subjective impressions of reporters still provide good standards for judgment during Initial Contests, Mist Clearing allows one to know how many serious contenders there are for the nomination and what their strengths are vis-à-vis one another. Some candidates who have failed to gain much support may remain in the race to give voice to a point of view (or to collect federal matching funds to pay off campaign debts), but effective campaigning will be carried on only by the serious contenders for the nomination.

During the 1980s, several changes in the primary calendar increased the possibility that Mist Clearing could occur very early. In 1980, the Carter coalition moved the Georgia and Alabama primaries into early March to coincide with Florida's, thereby balancing expected demonstrations of Kennedy strength in New England with the likelihood of a good Carter showing in the South. Then, in 1984, the Democrats "front-loaded" their primary calendar by reducing the time between Iowa and New Hampshire and moving Rhode Island from "Super Tuesday" in June to a new Super Tuesday in March. In 1988, South Dakota moved to a new February primary. And in a much more important development, most of the other southern and border states moved their primaries to March 8, joining Florida, Georgia, and Alabama, to create a southern regional primary. So a 1988 calendar emerged with the Michigan Republican conventions in January, the Iowa caucuses and New Hampshire and South Dakota primaries in February, the Vermont primary on March 1, and the southern regional primary (plus Massachusetts and Rhode Island) on March 8.

What this did was to open the possibility of someone winning a very large number of delegates on March 8. Proponents of the southern regional primary imagined that it would benefit a moderate Democrat. There were, of course, other possibilities. A candidate who gains momentum in Iowa and

New Hampshire might do very well, as Gary Hart did in 1984. Or a Jesse Jackson might gain a number of plurality victories if the white vote was split among several contenders (Broder, 1986). Therefore, it is *possible* for Mist Clearing to take place quite early, but it was not certain this would happen.

In the transition from Initial Contests to Mist Clearing the principal shift in campaigning is from a desire to create an impression of movement to a prevailing concern with the acquisition of delegates. A shift from the first 20 delegates to, say, 200 delegates implies a change in the method of campaigning as well as a more complex campaign organization. Whereas the earlier appeal had to be on the grounds that the candidate was the most attractive among half a dozen or more declared aspirants, the appeal now can be that while the candidate may not be ideal, he is the one who comes close to the stands the delegates would prefer *and* has a real chance of winning. If a candidate has already attracted 200 delegates, then there is a coalition in existence. The groups of delegates who make up the coalition do not all have identical views, and a certain amount of organizational effort is needed to hold the coalition together while additional groups of delegates are being recruited.

Relationships between the candidates and reporters are also rather different in this phase of nomination politics. Early on, the candidate is anxious to create news and make himself available to the few reporters who take the trouble to cover the campaign. By the Mist Clearing stage, the candidate's success makes him a prime news source, so he has a much larger press entourage. This shift gives the campaign staff a better opportunity to control the news by rationing the candidate's time among the greater number of reporters who want to see him. On the other hand, whatever the candidate says is now subject to much greater scrutiny. When he was one of several candidates during Initial Contests, not much space could be devoted to his issue statements or to those of any one candidate. Now that he is one of two or three who may be a major party nominee, statements on foreign policy or economics or whatever are more carefully analyzed.

During this phase, there is sometimes a flurry of activity on the part of a late entrant into the race. (Pennsylvania Governor William Scranton did not declare his candidacy until June 1964; New York Governor Nelson Rockefeller did so in May 1968, after having announced earlier that he would not run; Governor Jerry Brown of California and Senator Frank Church of Idaho made their decisions in March 1976, but the first contests they were able to enter did not take place until May.) The late entrant is likely to get a fair amount of media attention; the new candidacy enlivens what may be an all but decided contest. But the late entrant is likely to be giving voice to different attitudes than those held by the probable winning coalition, or he may be simply attracting publicity with an eye to a future campaign. Unless there are very unusual circumstances, there are just too few delegates remaining to be chosen to give the late entrant any real chance of building a winning coalition.

The Convention

In recent decades, conventions have ratified earlier decisions by nominating the leading presidential candidate on the first ballot. The last multiballot conventions were in 1952 for the Democrats and in 1948 for the Republicans. The last truly deadlocked conventions were in 1924 for the Democrats and in 1920 for the Republicans. It is always possible that we might see another multiballot convention, especially if there are two strong coalitions, each powerful enough to keep its rival from winning but without the leverage necessary to pick up the few additional votes needed to achieve victory. The dominant pattern, though, is one of first-ballot nominations. The wide publicity now given to primaries and caucuses in which the delegates are selected gives ample indication of the likelihood that one candidate or another will win. The tests of strength that took place on early ballots at multiballot conventions are no longer essential to provide clues about this.

Even so, the Convention is a consequential stage in the nominating process. Before the nomination of the presidential candidate, a series of decisions is made by the conventions voting to approve (or reject, or amend) reports from several committees. The first is a Committee on Credentials, which makes recommendations as to which delegates are to be seated. The second (used only by the Republican party) is a Committee on Permanent Organization, which suggests permanent officers to replace the temporary officers who have guided the convention in its opening sessions. Next comes a Committee on Rules, which proposes rules to govern the present convention, authorizes a national committee to transact party business during the next four years, and in the Republican party sets forth the procedure for calling the next convention. Finally, a Committee on Resolutions (Platform Committee in the Democratic party) presents the party platform for adoption.

These are important decisions. Credentials, permanent organization, and rules are important in the short term of the convention itself. By seating certain delegates—for example, McGovern delegates rather than Humphrey delegates from Illinois and California in 1972—one can create a majority in favor of one candidate. The rules may favor one side or another; Kennedy supporters claimed that Rule F3(c), binding delegates to be faithful to the candidate in whose behalf they had been elected, gave the Carter forces an advantage at the 1980 convention. And the permanent chairperson may enforce the rules so as to give an advantage to one of the contenders. Rules and the platform have long-term consequences as well. Both parties adopted rules at recent conventions that have mandated reforms in the composition or procedures of future conventions. In each of the last five conventions, the Democrats created commissions to review the procedures to be used for delegate selection in the next convention, most recently at the 1984 convention when a Fairness Commission was created to placate Gary Hart and Jesse Jackson. And a careful study of party platforms over a 34-year period has shown that 75 percent of the pledges were implemented by the party winning the White House (Pomper & Lederman, 1980, chap. 8).

Convention votes also play a role in the contests over the presidential nominee. What happens in any particular convention depends on the strength of the contending coalitions. Let's say there is a winning coalition that does not have too many votes to spare, and at least one reasonably strong challenging coalition. This has been a fairly common situation in recent conventions. In these circumstances, the challenging coalition will try for a test vote on an issue that will maximize its strength. It may come on the adoption of a rule that the challenging coalition thinks will be attractive to uncommitted delegates, or it may come on a platform plank that will tend to split the winning coalition. Whatever the topic, the object is to pick an issue that will attract more votes than the challenging coalition can muster on behalf of its candidate. The winning coalition, on the other hand, will be more interested in the presidential roll call to come and may just accept the proposed change as long as it feels it can live with it. If the winning coalition is in a very strong position, it will have the votes to beat back any challenges. In these circumstances, motions challenging credentials, rules, or platform are likely to be made only by those who feel very strongly about the issue as a matter of principle.

In view of the possibility of contests on a number of issues, the coalition leaders must have some way of communicating with their groups of delegates. When the convention is not in session, the delegates will be lodged in hotels all over the city. Some person will normally be designated as the contact for a coalition's delegates from each state, though communications are awkward when delegates are spread all over a large metropolitan area. On the convention floor, the key coalition leaders will usually be in some central location (often in a trailer parked outside the convention hall), which provides telephone or walkie-talkie communication with the state delegation leaders. This allows rapid dissemination of a decision to try to beat back a challenge, to accept it, or to take no position on it.

Finally, the Convention stage is both the conclusion of nomination politics and the beginning of electoral politics. Nomination and electoral politics differ in fundamental ways. The prime objective of the former is to attract enough delegates to win the nomination; the prime objective of the latter is to convince voters to support the candidate in November. But the conventions are widely reported by press and television, and while the delegates are listening to speeches and casting votes, citizens are making up their minds about the coming general election. A quarter of presidential voting decisions in the elections since 1948 have been made during the conventions.

There have been conventions—such as the 1964 Republican convention, when Governor Rockefeller was booed while addressing the delegates, and the 1968 Democratic convention, with a bloody confrontation between Chicago police and demonstrators protesting the war in Vietnam—that seriously handicapped the parties in the fall campaign. And even without events as dramatic as these, the identity of the nominee, the vice presidential candidate he selects, and the issues that are stressed are important considerations in the citizen's own presidential choice.

The Temporal Pattern

These four phases—Early Days, Initial Contests, Mist Clearing, and Convention—blend into one another. At times, the overlap is marked. The Michigan precinct delegate selection (the beginning of Initial Contests) has been moved far ahead into the Early Days time frame. The other campaign forays of Early Days and the skeleton organizations that are set up in Iowa, New Hampshire, and elsewhere set the stage for the Initial Contests. Victory in the Initial Contests provides pledged delegates, and delegates continue to accumulate until the genuine strength of one or more coalitions becomes apparent in the Mist Clearing phase. And while appointments to the convention committees are not formally made until the convention opens, decisions about who is going to be involved are made well in advance, and preliminary meetings of the Platform Committee (or at least of a drafting subcommittee) take place while the competing coalitions are still seeking delegate support.

Still, it is useful to consider these phases separately. Each can be distinguished on the basis of characteristic behavior patterns. To see this, we shall review four recent nomination contests as they passed through these stages. Two of the contests were essentially two-person struggles that lasted from Early Days on through the Convention. The other two races are typical of those in which there are several potential nominees during Early Days and the eventual winner gradually pulls away from the field.[1] The 1976 Ford versus Reagan and the 1980 Carter versus Kennedy races represent the two-candidate fights, and the contests won by Governor Reagan in 1980 and former Vice President Mondale in 1984 give us an idea about the dynamics of multicandidate races.

EARLY DAYS

Ford versus Reagan, 1976

Gerald Ford

There had been talk for some time about a Ronald Reagan candidacy in 1976, but Gerald Ford's advisors did not seem to believe it. In common with many organization Republicans, Ford advisors were worried about the harm conservative ideologues could do to the party in a general election but seemed to

---

[1] These are two of the three modern patterns of nomination. The third pattern is that in which the identity of the probable nominee is known from the outset, as with Lyndon Johnson in 1964, Richard Nixon in 1972, or Ronald Reagan in 1984. The selection of an obvious nominee hardly requires any analysis.

think that if enough gestures were made in their direction, they would stop acting as ideologues and support moderate candidates in the interest of party unity.

Ford's first gesture—coming at about the same time as his summertime announcement of candidacy—was the appointment of former Army Secretary Howard (Bo) Callaway to head the President Ford Committee. Callaway had achieved some success in Georgia politics (a term in Congress, a near-miss for the governorship), but he had no national experience and at once began talking about the possibility that Vice President Rockefeller would be dropped in 1976. The eventual result was that Rockefeller departed from the ticket, but conservatives kept right on supporting Ronald Reagan.

In other respects, the Ford Early Days posture was a classic strategy for an incumbent: Try to demonstrate to any potential opponent that the president has enough support in his party to make opposition impractical. Some moves in the service of this strategy were important. Republican parties in large states—Ohio, New York, Pennsylvania, and Michigan—endorsed the President for reelection, as did several prominent California Republicans. Two important personnel appointments were made in the fall. Professional campaign manager Stuart Spencer and newspaperman Peter Kaye, both long active in California Republican politics, were brought in as director of organization and as press secretary of the President Ford Committee, respectively. Spencer also lacked national campaign experience but brought real expertise to the committee. He at once turned to the task of creating a good New Hampshire organization along with Congressman James Cleveland (Witcover, 1977, chaps. 4,6).

Ronald Reagan

The serious conversations about a Reagan candidacy took place between the governor and several advisors—Lyn Nofziger, Michael Deaver, Peter Hannaford, and others—who had been close to him in his California administration. In 1974, they expanded their group by recruiting a campaign director, John P. Sears. Sears, a lawyer who had gained delegate-hunting experience in the successful 1968 Nixon campaign and who had opened a Washington law office after a brief stint on the White House staff, was an able and resourceful tactician.

With a new Republican president in the White House, Ronald Reagan was not at all sure he wanted to run. His personal decision was not made until the spring of 1975; even then, he delayed any public announcement. Sears and Nofziger started letting conservatives know that Reagan would run, recruited Nevada Senator Paul Laxalt as national chairman, and put together a New Hampshire committee headed by ex-Governor Hugh Gregg. When Reagan was ready to announce in November, his manner of doing so showed the strength of the challenge he was to make. The night before, he answered questions in New Hampshire, then flew to Washington's National Press Club for the announcement itself, then went on for press conferences in Florida,

North Carolina, and California. Ronald Reagan was a highly articulate conservative, and three of the early primaries (New Hampshire, Florida, and North Carolina) were to be held in states where a conservative should garner a lot of Republican votes.

Carter versus Kennedy, 1980[2]

Jimmy Carter

There was never any doubt in Jimmy Carter's mind about running for reelection, and preparations for that began with the creation of a Carter-Mondale Committee early in 1979. Senior White House officials, such as Hamilton Jordan, kept in close touch with the group led by Tim Kraft, who had been put in charge of these early operations. The Carter leaders did not know if they would face primary opposition but simply went ahead with their plans. "We're not going to make the same mistake Ford made with Reagan in 1976," one of them explained. "They spent the bulk of their time in 1975 worrying about whether Reagan would run instead of raising money and preparing for him if he did run" (Smith, 1979, p. 28).

The Carter coalition did get on with the business of raising money, but they also attended to the equally important business of adjusting the rules so as to favor the President. The minimum statewide vote required before proportional representation went into effect (and each candidate got his proportionate share of the delegates) had been set at 15 percent.[3] This meant that no one but a strong challenger could take delegates away from President Carter. One could not get a few delegates simply by entering and picking up, say, 11 percent of the primary vote.

The Carter coalition also altered a number of primary dates. The Alabama and Georgia primaries were moved ahead to March 11 to coincide with the Florida primary and create a block of delegates Carter could be expected to win. On the other hand, the Maine caucuses were not moved; they were scheduled early, and the Carter leaders reckoned that they would be able to win them.

While this organization work was going on in his behalf, Carter's public

---

[2] This analysis of the 1980 Democratic contest as a two-candidate race ignores the role of California Governor Jerry Brown. The reason is that the essential dynamics of the campaign followed the two-candidate mode. Brown contested only two primaries (New Hampshire and Wisconsin) and ended up with only one delegate.

[3] These rules had been set by the Winograd Commission, appointed by the Democratic National Committee. Carter supporters (and others) wanted to set a high threshold to keep the vote from being splintered among too many candidates. Those who wanted an open process favored a low threshold. The compromise reached by the commission was that the threshold for caucus states and delegates elected statewide could be set by each state at any point between a minimum of 15 percent and a maximum of 20 percent. The threshold for district delegates was to be found by dividing 100 by the number of delegates in each district. Thus, if a district had four delegates, the threshold for that district would be 25 percent.

support was ebbing rapidly. By June, Carter's Gallup Poll "approval rating" among Democrats fell to 34 percent, the lowest rating in history for a president among his own party members. Inflation and gasoline lines were cutting into the limited support the administration still enjoyed. Pollster Pat Caddell had argued in a memorandum that "this crisis is not your fault as President. It is the natural result of historic forces and events that have been in motion for 20 years." Accepting this thesis, the President's response was the July 15 "malaise" speech. This speech was more than politics; it was an effort at national leadership.

But some of the subsequent events were pure politics. One of the things the President said was that he wanted to get away from the "island" of Washington and make more contact with the people. The following month, the Carters took a vacation cruise on the Delta Queen—which began in Minnesota, an early caucus state, and ended in Iowa, the very first caucus state. Between July and December, he visited 24 states, all but 6 of which were going to hold early primary elections.

The week following the malaise speech saw major cabinet changes. Whatever virtues the departed members may have had, their replacements showed a clear White House interest in constituency politics: Patricia Roberts Harris, a black woman, was promoted to Health and Human Services; two Roman Catholics, Benjamin Civiletti and Moon Landrieu, became Attorney General and HUD Secretary; and two Jews, Philip Klutznick and Neil Goldschmidt, took over the Commerce and Transportation Departments. The administration had a good deal of discretionary funding that could be distributed, and much of this money went to cities whose mayors had seen the wisdom of supporting Jimmy Carter. Ultimately, the mayors of New York City, Los Angeles, Detroit, San Francisco, Baltimore, Atlanta, Miami, St. Louis, Pittsburgh, Denver, Salt Lake City, and Seattle all endorsed the President.

Two symbolic events that summer seemed to be inconsistent. One was a story about President Carter defending himself with a boat oar against a rabbit that was said to have attacked him while he was fishing. The other was a presidential boast that if Senator Kennedy did run against him, he (Carter) would "whip his ass." How could a president so weakened that he was vulnerable to attack by rabbits hope to defeat the popular Massachusetts Senator? One answer is that a great deal of solid political work had been done, even though its effects were not yet visible.

Edward Kennedy

Throughout the spring of 1979, Edward (Ted) Kennedy answered all questions about 1980 politics with his expect-expect-intend formula: "I expect the President to be renominated, and I expect him to be reelected, and I intend to support him." These words reflected the Senator's real feelings; but even as he spoke them, events were carrying him into opposition. Every time polls appeared that showed Carter to be unpopular and Kennedy the preferred alternative (and Kennedy was leading Carter by 62 to 24 percent in early

June), other Democrats would seek out Senator Kennedy and urge him to run to prevent a Democratic defeat in 1980.

Much of this was private, but there were some public signs. For example, five Democratic congressmen—Richard Ottinger of New York, Richard Nolen of Minnesota, John Conyers of Michigan, Fortney Stark of California, and Edward Beard of Rhode Island—announced a campaign to draft Kennedy. "There is tremendous unhappiness with Carter's policies," said Ottinger. "Also, I think the public's perception of Carter's performance is not high, and we'd like to see a Democratic victory next year."

At least some of the pressure was self-generated. Senator Kennedy regarded himself as one of the most consistent supporters of the Carter administration in the Senate, yet he was unsatisfied with the trend of Carter policies in health care, foreign policy, energy, and the economy. President Carter's malaise speech was another crystalizing point in Kennedy's thinking. "That speech," Kennedy later recalled, "was so completely contrary to everything I believe in that it upset me" (White, 1982, pp. 270–271). So the Senator returned to Hyannisport. There, sometime during August, he reached his own decision to challenge Jimmy Carter for the 1980 nomination.

What the Senator brought to the campaign was a deserved reputation as a better legislator than either of his brothers had been and a belief that the Kennedy skill in politics would allow him to prevail. But the political skill that brought the 1960 nomination to his brother John had been exercised against relatively unsubstantial opposition, and Ted Kennedy was challenging an incumbent president. Furthermore, at the point when Senator Kennedy's decision to run was made, President Carter's campaigners had been busy planning, fund-raising, and organizing in the early states for a good six months. It wasn't going to be enough for Kennedy to be a good campaigner. He had to be better.

All of the planning and organizing that normally occupy Early Days had to be done in a very short time. What issues could Kennedy stress that would both distinguish him from President Carter and make him a viable candidate? Which primaries should be entered? In the states where he did enter, how were organizations going to be created that could compete with the already existing Carter organizations? What national staff would coordinate activities across the country? How would funds be raised to pay for all this?

That the answers to all of these questions could not be found easily was apparent in the ragged start of the Kennedy campaign. For example, when Roger Mudd asked him on CBS television about reports linking him to other women, he said: "I'm . . . I'm married; I care very deeply about my wife, and my children, and we've . . . we have a rather special set of circumstances which is . . . perhaps somewhat unique." In a speech in Philadephia, he used the words *lead, leadership,* or *led* some 17 times. This just wasn't good enough.

Senator Kennedy did find noble phrases when he announced his candidacy at Boston's Faneuil Hall on November 7.

For many months, we have been sinking into crisis. Yet we hear no clear summons from the center of power. Aims are not set. The means of realizing them are neglected. . . . Surely the nation that came back from the Depression half a century ago can roll back the tide of inflation. . . . The most important task of presidential leadership is to release the native energy of the people. The only thing that paralyzes us today is the myth that we cannot move.

These lines were well written and well spoken, but they were not the lead item on the news that evening. Three days earlier, a group of Iranian students had overrun the embassy in Teheran, and American diplomats had been taken hostage.

Reagan, 1980

Ronald Reagan

There are multicandidate races in which an unheralded candidate shows unexpected strength. George McGovern's nomination victory in 1972 and Jimmy Carter's in 1976 are examples of this. In 1980, however, many observers thought Ronald Reagan would be the strongest Republican candidate. Reagan had harbored presidential ambitions for a long time and nearly won the nomination in 1976. There were in existence a solid Reagan constituency and a core group of experienced campaign organizers. Given the level of support, the 1980 nomination was probably Reagan's unless he lost it. Therefore, his central strategy question was how to hold on to the support he already had. To answer this, two things had to be determined. First, should Governor Reagan stress conservatism in order to fire up his workers and strengthen his hold on his natural constituency, *or* should he moderate some of his positions in order to broaden his appeal within the Republican party and be better positioned for the general election? Second, on the assumption that his constituency would stay with him unless he did something to upset them, should he limit his activities and statements *or* should he continue to campaign much as he had in the past?

The Reagan coalition adopted the posture favored by John Sears, who was then in charge of the campaign. Issues were stressed that aimed at gaining additional Republican support in the primaries and Democratic votes in the general election. The importance of strong leadership was stressed—in conscious counterpoint to President Carter's emphasis on malaise. And when he announced, Reagan called for a North American accord to improve the quality of life in Canada, the United States, and Mexico. Organizationally, Sears built up a network of 18 field offices across the country. Most importantly, he reached to the Northeast for support that had been let go to Ford by default in 1976. To this end, he enlisted such talent as Drew Lewis, who had led the Pennsylvania Ford campaign four years earlier.

The Reagan posture was explained by California pollster Mervin Field: "The strategy is to run him as an incumbent—with set speeches, and as few as possible. It's ball control. What he wants is a fast ticking of the clock until the convention." There were tensions within the Reagan core group that were not unrelated to these choices. Over the course of 1979, longtime Reagan aides Lyn Nofziger, Michael Deaver, and Martin Anderson all departed from the Reagan campaign. Some of these resignations grew out of personal struggles as Sears reached for greater and greater power within the Reagan organization, but Nofziger and Anderson certainly preferred an unabashed conservatism.

Conservative Alternatives

Each of the other Republican aspirants hoped to present himself as *the* alternative to Reagan. Three competed with Reagan for the votes of conservative Republicans: Congressman Philip Crane of Illinois, Senator Robert Dole of Kansas, and former Governor John Connally of Texas. Crane and Dole both saw themselves as younger alternatives to Reagan, although Dole (the 1976 vice presidential nominee) could claim a good deal more national visibility. John Connally brought to the campaign two formidable assets: a dominant personality and access to great corporate wealth. The former Treasury Secretary's strong personality was seen as the means of distinguishing him from Reagan. The Connally campaign had two unusual features. First, Connally declined federal matching funds. (This meant more fund-raising but also freed Connally from certain restrictions on how the money could be spent.) Second, rather than going into specific states to build bases for Initial Contests, the Connally campaign strategists hoped that national exposure would build up their candidate.

Moderate Alternatives

Contesting for the position of the moderate alternative to Reagan were two Republicans: Howard Baker and George Bush. Senate Republican leader Baker had the advantages of electability, leadership experience, and a posture as a party unifier. He had been elected to the Senate three times from a competitive state and was, in the judgment of David Broder, "the most principled and skillful Republican leader in the Senate since Robert Taft."

The Senate leadership post was both an advantage and a disadvantage to Baker (much as it had been for Lyndon Johnson when he sought the Democratic nomination in 1960). On the one hand, it guaranteed him a degree of prominence; on the other, Senate responsibilities kept him in Washington and away from the campaign trail. The developing SALT II debate was also a challenge and an opportunity. Republican conservatives, already suspicious because Baker had supported the Panama Canal treaty, were alert to any further hints of liberalism. But if Baker were to oppose a treaty that was in the best interests of the country, he could lose his reputation for responsibility. Baker himself looked to the debate as an opportunity to demonstrate his leadership on a major issue. Unfortunately, the debate never came.

Even costlier to Baker's chances was a tendency to put off organizational decisions. By the time he got around to setting up a field organization, he found that many of his natural supporters had already been recruited by others, especially George Bush.

George Bush had held a number of positions, but two of them were particularly important to his presidential bid. As a former chairman of the Republican National Committee, he was well known to Republican activists. And as an unemployed millionaire, he could afford to devote the time needed for a long primary campaign. Bush surrounded himself with a number of experienced organizers, including James Baker, Gerald Ford's 1976 campaign director (after he had gotten a go-ahead from Ford); Robert Teeter, who had done Ford's polling; and David Keene, who had worked the South for Ronald Reagan in 1976. In December 1978, George Bush and James Baker decided on the classic strategy of concentrating on Iowa and New Hampshire, and hoping for enough momentum from those races to carry Bush through the other early primaries. They assumed that by the March 18 Illinois primary, the race would be down to two candidates, Bush and Reagan.

A Liberal Alternative

The most liberal of the Republican aspirants was Illinois Congressman John Anderson. Anderson's intelligence was well known in Washington though not to the general public. He was chairman of the House Republican Conference but had not been a viable candidate for the top Republican leadership position because he was something of a loner and his positions were too liberal for many Republican congressmen. With more limited finances and less of an organization than any other Republican aspirant, Anderson hoped to "stay alive" in the New England primaries and thought he might do better when the race got to his native Illinois and adjacent Wisconsin.

Mondale, 1984

Walter Mondale

On January 20, 1981, Walter F. Mondale's Washington, D.C., neighbors organized a Welcome Home party on his return from the Vice President's official residence. The intimation was that he was going to resume the life of an ordinary citizen. But Mondale was already running for president in 1984. He had abandoned a presidential bid in November 1974 out of a distaste for the begging involved in seeking political support. Now, after a dozen years in the U.S. Senate and four as vice president, there was no more hesitation. Mondale was sure that he wanted to be president and had begun to build toward that end.

1982 was a year of steady building. Mondale's political action committee (PAC), the Committee for the Future of America, raised and spent $2 million. It not only financed Mondale's own campaigning but contributed some $224,000 to candidates for the House and Senate. When Mondale went to the

Democratic midterm conference in Philadelphia in June, he took along enough staff to fill an entire hotel floor with typewriters and telephones. Mondale himself appeared in 42 states in 1982, campaigning in behalf of 95 House candidates, 15 Senate candidates, and 18 aspirants for governorships.

The pace did not slacken in 1983. The candidate made repeated trips to Iowa and New Hampshire, though not to the exclusion of other states. The efficient Mondale fund-raising operation raised an estimated $9.5 million. The former Vice President also received endorsements from major organizations. The AFL–CIO, seeking to reverse a decline in its political influence, decided to endorse a candidate in the early stages, and its support went to Mondale. Mondale picked up formal endorsements from the National Organization of Women (NOW) and the National Education Association, many of whose members had been delegates to recent Democratic conventions.

These endorsements brought resources with them; union dollars and union workers meant that other Mondale resources could be concentrated elsewhere. But they also carried a danger that Mondale would be seen as a captive of special interests. He rejected warnings about this. Mondale consciously "chose not to distance himself from interest groups. . . . He would act as a staunchly partisan Democrat, build a traditional organization, and seize the nomination by force of organization" (Orren, 1985, p. 57).

Edward Kennedy

During 1981 and 1982, most observers assumed the coming contest would be a two-candidate race dominated by Mondale and Kennedy. Both had the visibility and resources for presidential races. The activities of the Hunt Commission (heavily influenced by Kennedy, Mondale, and organized labor), lent credence to the supposition of a two-candidate contest.

The Hunt Commission, one of a series of Democratic rule-reforming commissions, met from mid-1981 through early 1982 and took two steps that were to affect the 1984 selection process. First, they set aside 568 seats (14 percent of the total) for "superdelegates," elected officeholders and party officials who would be able to attend the convention without declaring in advance whom they supported. This presumably would strengthen the role of party professionals, giving those who would share the task of governing a greater say in the selection of the presidential candidate. Second, they front-loaded the selection process, reducing the time between the Iowa caucuses and the New Hampshire primary to a single week and concentrating the primaries and caucuses so that 40 percent of the delegates would be selected by late March and a majority picked by mid-April.

Taken together, these changes would favor those who were highly regarded by party professionals and whose organizations were strong enough to support them in the Initial Contests (Price, 1984, chaps. 6–7; Orren, 1985; Shafer, 1983a, 1983b). Assuming that Mondale and Kennedy were equally strong (and that no other strong candidate emerged), they should split most of these delegates between them. This would have made it difficult for anyone else to catch up, and either Mondale or Kennedy—who would have been equally acceptable to organized labor—should have emerged as the eventual nominee.

This two-man race was not to be. Senator Kennedy thought carefully about 1984. The prospects were attractive, especially in the immediate aftermath of Democratic gains in the 1982 elections. But Kennedy was also concerned about his family, and on December 1, 1982, he called a press conference. In his opening statement, he said:

> The political case for my becoming a candidate is a strong one. But for me, any decision about 1984 inevitably involves more than public consideration or political calculation. For the members of my family, the 1980 campaign was sometimes a difficult experience. And it is very soon to ask them to go through it again. In addition, the decision that Joan and I have made about our marriage has been painful for our children as well as ourselves. For these reasons I believe that my first and overriding obligation now is to Patrick and Kara and Teddy. I will not be a candidate for the presidency of the United States in 1984.

With these words, a prospective two-man race was transformed into an *n*-candidate race in which Walter Mondale had the greatest resources. The question was who would provide the competition.

Reuben Askew

There were Democratic voices saying the party had become too liberal; that if the party wanted to regain the White House and certainly if it wanted to gain Southern support, a more moderate nominee would be needed. One such was Reuben Askew. He had been regarded as an effective governor of Florida, and some of his fellow governors thought he would have been a more effective president than Jimmy Carter. He favored free trade, opposed labor union endorsements, and favored abortion only in case of a threat to the mother's health or rape or incest—all relatively conservative positions for a Democrat. Askew campaigned frugally and quietly. He hoped to conserve money for a big media drive in the Initial Contests. Askew's strategy was to do better than expected in Iowa and New Hampshire, then pick up real momentum with a victory in Florida and impressive showings in Georgia and Alabama on Super Tuesday, March 13.

Ernest Hollings

Another moderate possibility was Senator Ernest (Fritz) Hollings of South Carolina. Hollings, slightly more conservative on domestic issues than other Senate Democrats, and slightly more liberal on foreign issues, was respected within the Senate for his knowledge of budget and defense issues. When he announced, he said, "The Democratic party lost the 1980 election because we lost the faith of the American people. Every time a special interest appeared, we responded. Every time a problem arose, we offered a single solution—spend more money." For his part, Senator Hollings called for an across-the-board budget freeze to spread sacrifice equally among all segments of society. He emphasized education and felt a change of attitudes was needed on the part of business, labor, and government to restore America's international competitiveness. Hollings did not, however, have name recognition outside of the Senate and, in spite of articulateness and genuine wit, was unable to expand his reputation during Early Days. He raised just enough money to travel and maintain a small staff but seemed to have no strategy beyond the hope that voters would notice him in some of the early primaries.

John Glenn

Senator John Glenn of Ohio had no problem with name recognition. As the first American to orbit the earth, Glenn was an authentic hero. The resulting reputation gave Glenn private wealth (through Royal Crown Cola and hotels) and—after a couple of false starts—carried him to the U.S. Senate in 1974. That reputation gave presidential candidate Glenn both a guarantee and a problem. The guarantee was that he would start with a level of public attention other politicos labor years to develop; the problem was how to develop his reputation *beyond* that of an ex-astronaut.[4]

Glenn's voting record in the Senate was liberal except on agricultural issues,[5] but his campaign rhetoric was relatively moderate.

> I'd ask for strong medicine in the fiscal area. I have said that we have get back on a pay-as-you-go system. That in itself is strong medicine with a 10 percent surtax devoted solely to deficit reduction. Doing away with indexing or deferring indexing is another one. Those two things would gain us some $80 billion a year by 1988.

Glenn also emphasized education, stressed the importance of basic research, and called attention to his expertise in military affairs. As things turned out, though, Glenn's issue positions were less important than the lack of an adequate organization.

John Glenn was a thoroughly likable man but without experience in nomination politics. Some of the staff members recruited for the Glenn campaign could have compensated for this with their own campaign experience. But the key position was held by a Columbus lawyer named William White who had been with Glenn since 1974. White knew even less about nomination politics than Glenn and was not disposed to let anyone else exercise real authority.

---

[4] Glenn's problem coming into 1984 was analogous to Ronald Reagan's coming into 1980. In 1980, the public knew two things about Reagan: that he had been a movie actor and that he was a conservative. In 1984, the public knew one thing about Glenn: that he had been an astronaut.

[5] John Glenn was unpopular with some liberals because of his presumed hawkishness. In fact, his voting record cast him as a member of a small group of Senate Democrats (including Robert Byrd, Daniel Patrick Moynihan, and Joseph Biden) that was seen as a bit more conservative on defense matters. But the issue that distinguished this group from other Senate liberals was agriculture—not defense.

The cost of Glenn's organizational difficulties can be seen in two surveys by Dom Bonafede of the *National Journal*. In midsummer, Bonafede contacted Democratic leaders in all 50 states. Mondale was leading in 11 states, Glenn in 11; in 26 more, there was either insufficient evidence or a toss-up between Mondale and Glenn. At the time, Glenn was not too far behind Mondale in opinion polls and in financing. The nomination was not Glenn's for the asking, but the opportunity was clearly there. When Bonafede checked back at the end of the year, though, an eastern leader said, "I was one of the first chairmen to come out for Glenn. But they never responded; they never asked me to do anything. . . . Glenn had a leg up on everybody, and he blew it." From Alabama he heard, "The potential is there but he hasn't gotten off the ground." And in Illinois, the report was, "Mondale's people are working all over the place and beating the pants off Glenn. I'm surprised, but Glenn seems not to have taken off." The Ohio Senator, Bonafede concluded, "may have mortally injured his chances" (Bonafede, 1983a, 1983b).

Gary Hart

Senator Hart of Colorado had made his principal mark in the Senate on military reform, arguing for more smaller, simpler weapons rather than expensive weapon systems. He also felt that economic growth—stimulated by more research, aid to small business, and so forth—was preferable to government spending per se. When Senators Hart and Glenn were reelected in 1980, both emerged as presidential prospects.[6] Unlike John Glenn, however, Gary Hart knew a great deal about nomination politics. He had managed the McGovern campaign in 1972 and knew what had to be done to move from a long-shot candidacy into serious contention.

Hart gathered a small staff about him. As things were to develop, his most important appointment was Jeanne Shaheen who was given charge of the New Hampshire campaign and drew on her own excellent network to develop a first-rate field organization for Hart (Goldman & Fuller, 1985, pp. 132–33).

Within the Hart campaign, there was discussion about a campaign theme. Advisor John Holum drew the various strands together and in August 1983 wrote a memo proposing a single central theme: "Senator Gary Hart represents the next generation of leadership—uniting old values with new perspectives and ideas" (Goldman & Fuller, 1985, p. 397). This emphasis came naturally to Hart. A decade earlier, he had concluded his book on the McGovern campaign by saying: "New ideas must be found to solve old problems. . . . The Democratic party . . . must bring forward a new generation

---

[6] Senators Hollings and Cranston were also reelected that year, but a number of well-known liberal Democrats—George McGovern, Birch Bayh, Frank Church, Warren Magnuson, John Culver, and Gaylord Nelson—were all defeated.

of thinkers who are in touch with the real world and a new generation of leaders who can inspire enthusiasm, hope, and energy in the people" (Hart, 1973, pp. 329–330). And when he had run for the Senate in 1974, his slogan had been, "They had their turn. Now it's our turn" (Broder, 1984a; Maraniss, 1984). It was to be Hart's good fortune that others who might have spoken for the rising generation (Senators Dale Bumpers and Joseph Biden, for example) chose not to enter the presidential sweepstakes. Gary Hart was alone with his claim of new ideas for a new generation.[7]

In 1984, all of these factors—Hart's knowledge of campaign politics, the strong organization Jeanne Shaheen put together for him in New Hampshire, and his identification with a new generation—were to play important roles in the Hart campaign. But the Early Days were a lonely and frustrating time. Hart's public support was very limited. The press lumped him in with the "other contenders" when it mentioned him at all. And as a consequence of the lack of support and attention, money was very difficult to raise, and the campaign was badly in debt. In October 1983, the Hart campaign had only $6,000 on hand and owed $714,000.

Alan Cranston

"Why," asked one of Senator Cranston's television spots, "vote for a 69-year-old man who they say is not charismatic, who's bald?" Why, indeed? And what persuaded this man that he ought to run for president? The answer is that Alan Cranston was as ambitious as the other candidates we have been discussing. Furthermore, he had two real political advantages: He was a proven vote getter in California, a state that would send 20 percent of the delegates needed for nomination. Also, as the whip, he was a leader of the Democratic party in the Senate.

Cranston's strategic problem was the same as Hollings': he was not well known outside his home state and the Senate. He used two devices to try to separate himself from the pack of "other contenders." One was the straw poll, which had been used to advantage by Jimmy Carter in 1975. Cranston won the first straw poll in California in January 1983. This was discounted because it was his home state. But he came in third in Massachusetts in April and then surprised everyone by winning in Wisconsin in June.[8] Cranston's other stratagem was to identify himself completely with one issue: the nuclear freeze movement. The Senator felt deeply about this issue, but it also served as a source of volunteers and gave him some recognition as the "antinuclear" candidate. Beyond this, the Cranston campaign was sustained by the hope that he would do well in the early primaries, or that Mondale would stumble and liberals would turn to him as an alternative, or that *something* would happen to sustain his candidacy beyond the Initial Contests.

---

[7] Jesse Jackson was four years younger than Hart, but he had a different message to deliver.

[8] The Mondale organization put a lot of resources into the next straw poll in Maine and won handily.

George McGovern

All of the preceding candidates had planned to run for some time. In fall 1983, they were joined by two more contenders, George McGovern and Jesse Jackson. George McGovern, out of office after losing his South Dakota Senate seat, seemed to yearn for the political spotlight once again. There were those who were unenthused (reportedly including his wife), but as he said when he announced in mid-September, "You have to do what you have to do." His positions seemed to have been lifted from his 1972 script, with some small changes. For example, where he had earlier pledged to end all American involvement in Vietnam, he now said "As president, I would end all United States military involvement in Central America." But he did have some real advantages. As a former nominee, he did not have to struggle to establish name recognition. And, a dozen years older, he was a good deal more relaxed.

Jesse Jackson

Jesse Jackson was the last to announce his candidacy for the presidency. Jackson's decision was different from the others and in many ways more difficult. For all his rhetorical skill and two decades in the civil rights movement, there were reasons for him not to run. There were other civil rights activists who did not like him and on whose support he could not depend. Jesse Jackson's talents lay much more in theater, in making the dramatic move, than they did in administration or finance. And whereas all the other Democratic candidates had held *major* political offices, Jesse Jackson had never held *any* elective office.

There were political dilemmas as well as personal considerations. The argument in favor of his candidacy was that black registration and black turnout were lower than white registration and turnout, that the pride generated by a Jackson candidacy would increase black registration and turnout, and that this would increase black political power.[9] The argument against was that Jackson would take black votes away from liberal white candidates, who would have a better chance to get elected and actually implement the policies that many blacks preferred. A Jackson candidacy might lead to the election of a more conservative candidate and thus diminish black political power.

Furthermore, there was an important split between two groupings of black political leaders. Many of those opposing Jackson's candidacy were established black politicians. Some, such as Mayors Thomas Bradley of Los Angeles and Wilson Goode of Philadelphia, were already committed to Walter Mondale and would therefore find a black candidacy very embarrassing. Even if they weren't committed, established black leaders wanted to be free to

---

[9] Another argument was that someone with Jackson's platform skill could use the publicity of a presidential campaign to give voice to black positions on issues. It was rarely mentioned that Shirley Chisholm had already done this in 1972. Jackson supporters viewed the Chisholm candidacy as having been "only symbolic" whereas the Jackson candidacy was "real."

take such action as they saw fit. Those favoring a Jackson candidacy, on the other hand,

> were mainly more locally-based politicians; the more peripheral, less well known, less well supported national civic leaders; and a variety of individuals, politicized by Reagan administration policies and encouraged by recent victories in Chicago and by the mood of political awareness in numbers of black communities across the country. . . . For these more ideological black leaders, the leverage exerted by the existing national black leaders is irrelevant because it is insufficient to produce the kinds of broad-based, sweeping change needed to alter the subordinate condition of the black community. Political legitimacy, they believe, grows out of the closeness of the relation between leaders and local communities. (Barnett, 1983, pp. 490–91)

When Jackson did announce his candidacy, he called for a "Rainbow Coalition" of "blacks, Hispanics, Indian and native Americans, Asians, women, young people, poor people, old people, gay people, laborers, small farmers, small-business persons, peace activists and environmentalists." However much he may have wanted to expand his base beyond blacks, though, he tended to rely on the advice of experienced black politicians such as Mayor Richard Hatcher of Gary, Indiana, and Arnold Pinkney, former president of the Cleveland Board of Education. And alone among the candidates, he did not look to Iowa and New Hampshire to give life to his presidential bid. Not only did these states have tiny black populations but Jackson's late entry allowed too little time to do anything in these already overorganized states. Jackson looked to Deep South states and heavily black congressional districts in the North as his natural base.

The Ideological Lineup

With Jackson's entry, the field was complete. Particular issues would be cited later as evidence that one candidate or another was relatively liberal or conservative, but Jackson was clearly farthest to the left.[10] On the basis of their Senate voting records, Hart, Mondale, McGovern, and Cranston could all be regarded as members of the large group of Senate liberals. John Glenn was close to them, save on agricultural issues. Fritz Hollings had a slightly more conservative voting record but was distinctly closer to the liberal Democrats than to any Republican. If Reuben Askew had been in the Senate, his record would probably have been similar to Hollings'. In short, only Jackson on the left and Hollings and Askew on the right could really be distinguished ideologically among the eight candidates. And, again with the exception of Jackson, the strategies of all called for them to do well in the Initial Contests. Since that was impossible, the field would shortly be less crowded.

---

[10] One could say that Jesse Jackson was articulating issues important to blacks, but this is the same thing as saying that Jackson was much more liberal. If one analyzes attitudes by race, blacks are significantly more likely to favor neoisolationist positions in foreign policy, and government spending and benefit programs at home.

INITIAL CONTESTS

Ford versus Reagan, 1976

In this 1976 battle, as is usually the case in two-person contests, the structure of competition was evident from the beginning. It was moderate versus conservative, although it wasn't quite a straight ideological contest. Gerald Ford won some support from conservatives because he was the President, and Ronald Reagan had some appeal to middle-of-the-road Republicans because of his platform skill. Still, both camps placed great importance on the Initial Contests, and both tried to rob the opponent of credibility. The Ford campaign sought to depict Ronald Reagan as given to irresponsible ideas, and the Reagan campaign tried to show that President Ford was not an effective leader.

Many early polls in New Hampshire gave Reagan a lead, and the Reagan campaign tried to hold this lead with "citizens' press conferences," in which members of the audience (rather than experienced reporters) asked questions. In his replies, Reagan did not attack Ford directly but placed himself on the side of "the people" as opposed to "the government." Defense spending? "Well, here again is where I believe a president must take his case to the people, and the people must be told the facts." Angola? "The government has left the American people in complete ignorance." He stressed that he was an outsider, "not part of the Establishment in Washington, and therefore not part of that buddy system that goes on." Reagan spent 15 days in the state, and the applause lines from the citizens' press conferences were used in television commercials.

Reagan was unable to hold his lead over Ford. This was partly due to an improvement in the economy, which helped the incumbent, and partly due to the skill of Ford campaigners, especially Stuart Spencer. In September, Ronald Reagan gave a speech in Chicago that included the claim that "transfer of authority in whole or in part [in welfare, education, housing, food stamps, medicaid, community and regional development, and revenue sharing] would reduce the outlay of the federal government by more than $90 billion." Not much attention was paid at the time, but it caught Stuart Spencer's eye, and he had some research done on its implications. Peter Kaye, the press secretary, made arrangements for the New Hampshire Speaker of the House and the Senate President to hold a press conference denouncing the plan on Reagan's first trip into New Hampshire, and the issue dogged Reagan throughout the campaign. Later, Reagan made a comment about investing social security funds "in the industrial might of the country," and Commerce Secretary Elliot Richardson promptly interpreted that as a suggestion to risk social security funds in the stock market (Witcover, 1977, chap. 25). The improvement in the economy and television ads showing Gerald Ford at work in the Oval Office made the incumbent look a little better; questions raised about Ronald Reagan's proposals made him look a little less responsible. New Hampshire voters gave the President 50.6 percent of their vote.

The Florida primary was another in a conservative state that was won by the moderate Mr. Ford. Three things helped Ford here. First, Stuart Spencer hired the other half of the Spencer-Roberts campaign management firm, William Roberts, and placed him in charge of the Florida campaign. Second, the President, having won New Hampshire by however narrow a margin, seemed stronger; this impression was strengthened by uncontested victories in Vermont and Massachusetts. Third, Ford began to remind people he was the head of the federal government, announcing such things as a missile contract award and the completion of an interstate highway. On primary election night, the President had 53 percent of the vote, and the next day the *New York Times'* R. W. Apple wrote that Reagan's loss had drastically reduced his chances. "With only two contestants, a consistent loser soon finds himself without the funds and the campaign workers to keep him fighting."

Carter versus Kennedy, 1980

The political fortunes of President Carter and Senator Kennedy changed almost the moment that Kennedy announced his candidacy. While the Iranian hostage crisis was ultimately to prove costly to the President, at the outset it helped him. The proportion approving Carter's handling of his job jumped from 32 percent in early November to 61 percent a month later. In early January, he withdrew from a scheduled debate with Senator Kennedy, pleading the need to remain in the White House to deal with the hostage crisis. In fact, a good deal of attention was being devoted to Iowa. Rosalynn Carter, Walter Mondale, and other administration luminaries were out campaigning, and President Carter spent hours telephoning Iowa Democrats. One made news by refusing to take the President's call because she was watching television and because he was calling so many people that it was becoming commonplace.

The other change that took place was that the focus of public opinion shifted from President Carter's record to Senator Kennedy's character. For example, a Des Moines lawyer was quoted as saying: "Carter may have done a lot of things that were not as well thought out as they might have been. But he comes across as sincere. That's not true for Senator Kennedy. I'm suspicious of his motives." For his part, Kennedy knew that Carter was far ahead in Iowa but, being aware of the importance of Initial Contests, felt he (Kennedy) had to campaign in Iowa in the hope of attracting enough support to get off to a reasonably good start. This didn't happen. The Iranian crisis, very effective constituency politics, and Senator Kennedy's own difficulties resulted in a 2 to 1 margin for the President.

Kennedy's Iowa defeat resulted in two important changes. One was a major financial crisis that was to last throughout the nomination contest. Not only did the Senator give up his chartered plane and lay off paid staff, but the finances severely limited the number of primary elections that Kennedy could contest. The other change was to resolve a debate within the Kennedy coalition on whether to take relatively moderate positions to expand Kennedy's appeal or more liberal positions to solidify existing support. The Senator gave a speech at Georgetown University on January 28, saying:

> The 1980 election should not be a plebiscite on the Ayatollah or Afghanistan. The real question is whether America can afford four more years of uncertain policy and certain crisis, of an administration that tells us to rally around their failures, of an inconsistent nonpolicy that may confront us with a stark choice between retreat and war. These are the policies that must be debated in the campaign.

In the speech, Kennedy also opposed draft registration and called for a six-month wage-price freeze. The decision had been made to nail down the liberal constituency.

New Hampshire was seen as critical by many observers. Senator Kennedy was thought to be on stronger ground because he was from neighboring Massachusetts. The Carter coalition tried, with some success, to plant the story that Kennedy had to win in New Hampshire in order to remain as a viable candidate, while they were pouring resources into the Granite State to make sure that he lost. On election day, Kennedy did get the votes of liberals who agreed with him on economics, but only 29 percent of New Hampshire Democrats described themselves as liberals, and Carter beat Kennedy 47 percent to 37 percent.

His home state of Massachusetts provided better news for the Senator.[11] He did well with all categories of voters, especially among the wealthy, the elderly, Roman Catholics, and moderates. The proportion that thought he was lying was only half as large as it was nationally, and he gained a lot more support because of his economic positions. Jimmy Carter did relatively well among conservatives and actually had a majority among Protestants, but he lost 65 percent to 29 percent.

In important respects, the Carter primary strategy was built around an understanding of proportional representation. This method of selecting delegates gives each candidate approximately the same ratio of delegates as he receives votes, as long as the candidate gets more than a minimum vote. This minimum level was set at 15 percent in 1980. The Alabama, Georgia, and Florida primaries had all been scheduled for March 11, a week after the Massachusetts primary. The Carter coalition poured resources into these primaries, not because they were in any danger of losing any of them but because they wanted to keep Senator Kennedy below 15 percent and thus deprive him of delegates. Edward Kennedy was too strong for the Carter forces to do this in Florida; but he was held to 13 percent in Alabama and to a mere 8 percent in Jimmy Carter's native Georgia.

Of the seven Initial Contests, Edward Kennedy won only in Massachu-

---

[11] Anticipating this, Hamilton Jordan directed that a serious Carter effort be made in the same-day Vermont primary, and Carter won Vermont by 73 percent to 26 percent. This affected the way newspaper stories were written the following day.

setts. It was clear that President Carter had shown himself to be much the stronger candidate. What was not clear was whether Senator Kennedy won in Massachusetts only because it was his home state or whether Massachusetts happened to be the first contest in the urban, industrial East, where Senator Kennedy could be expected to do very well.

Reagan, 1980

The relative strength of the candidates coming into the Iowa caucuses on January 21 was largely a consequence of the strategies they had been following. John Connally's strategy of campaigning nationally through the mass media had not proven successful. Connally made some last-minute, state-oriented efforts—for example, hiring a bus to campaign for 40 hours across Iowa—but they were inadequate.[12] Senator Howard Baker had waited too long to begin his campaign and had no real organization in Iowa. The Baker coalition did spend a good deal on media. Given their competition with George Bush for the moderate vote, they felt it was essential to beat Bush; a last-minute media campaign was their only hope of doing so. George Bush had been campaigning for a very long time in Iowa, and a poll of county chairpersons showed that he was running neck and neck with Reagan. Governor Reagan, in keeping with John Sears' ball control strategy, chose not to take part in a widely publicized debate among Republican candidates[13] and also limited his own campaigning to a few brief appearances. The precinct caucuses gave Bush 33 percent, Reagan 27 percent, Baker 14 percent, and Connally 10 percent.

The Iowa results brought major changes to the Reagan campaign. The most immediate was that the Governor went back on the road, devoting almost full time to appearances in New Hampshire, Florida, and South Carolina. Ronald Reagan as a campaigner was the best asset the Reagan coalition had, an asset that hadn't been used in Iowa. Another change was the firing of John Sears as campaign director, along with invitations to longtime Reagan aides Michael Deaver, Lyn Nofziger, and Martin Anderson to rejoin the campaign. This was not just because of the Iowa defeat. (It actually took place on the day of the New Hampshire primary.) In part, Sears had provoked Governor Reagan by reaching for more organizational power at the expense of other Reagan associates. In part, the Sears-led campaign, while grandly conceived,

---

[12] The two other conservative candidates, Robert Dole and Philip Crane, were also unable to establish themselves as alternatives to Ronald Reagan in spite of very hard campaigning.

[13] All of the Republican candidates in this debate acquitted themselves well, but John Anderson drew particular attention to himself by his candor. Whereas other candidates could not recall anything they wished they had done differently in their public lives, he said he wished he had voted against the Gulf of Tonkin resolution. When asked how one could balance the budget, reduce taxes, and increase defense spending all at the same time, he responded, "It's very simple. You do it with mirrors." This performance did not have any impact on the Iowa outcome, but it did catch the eye of voters and journalists elsewhere.

was also very expensive. By the time of New Hampshire, three quarters of all available funds had been spent. This left the Reagan campaign quite vulnerable to any strong challenge.

The Iowa results also dramatically changed the attention being paid to George Bush. Among Republican and independent voters, he had been behind Ronald Reagan by a margin of 38 percent to 6 percent as recently as November. After Iowa, he was suddenly ahead 32 percent to 29 percent. Ignored earlier, Bush was now on magazine covers. The difficulty was that while the Bush leaders had longed for just this kind of attention, they had no strategy to take advantage of it. Bush talked about "Big Mo," which sounded preppy, rather than being able to give solid reasons why his new supporters should stay with him.

George Bush enjoyed a slight lead in New Hampshire until a Manchester debate in which Ronald Reagan joined the six candidates who had debated in Iowa. Traveling reporters weren't too impressed with this debate, but subsequent polls showed that it gave the lead back to Reagan. This lead was solidified at a two-candidate debate in Nashua, where Reagan protested the exclusion of four other Republican candidates. Reagan gained 50 percent of the February 2 vote, a long way ahead of Bush's 23 percent, Baker's 13 percent, and Anderson's 10 percent.

The Bush campaign was looking past New Hampshire to the Massachusetts primary the following week. This was foresighted. Bush won the Massachusetts primary, drawing votes from all socioeconomic groups and making effective use of his claim to experience. Moreover, Senator Baker withdrew the following day, leaving Bush as the candidate of the moderate conservative Republicans. Unfortunately for Bush, Congressman John Anderson also emerged as the object of much media attention in the Massachusetts primary. Anderson ran barely behind Bush in Massachusetts, barely behind Reagan in the same-day primary in Vermont, and demonstrated great strength with independents and well-educated voters. George Bush had defeated Howard Baker, the man he had to get by in order to take on Ronald Reagan in a head-to-head race, only to see the emergence of another rival for media attention and moderate-to-liberal Republican votes.

John Connally played a very small role in these New England Initial Contests because he was concentrating on the South Carolina primary. Having made a belated decision to try to build state strength and competing with Reagan for conservative support, he needed to show that he could beat Reagan somewhere. South Carolina was small enough to be affected by Connally's ample resources and conservative enough to be a good testing ground for him. Governor Connally had the support of Senator Strom Thurmond, but even so, Reagan got 55 percent of the vote to Connally's 30 and Bush's 15. Three days later, Ronald Reagan's southern strength was further demonstrated with votes of 73 percent, 70 percent, and 55 percent, respectively, in Georgia, Alabama, and Florida. But by then, John Connally was no longer in the race.

Mondale, 1984

By any measure, Walter Mondale was out in front as the Initial Contests stage began. A mid-January *New York Times*/CBS poll found Mondale the preference of 44 percent of the Democrats surveyed nationwide. Glenn and Jackson were tied for second with 14 percent each. McGovern had 4 percent, Askew 3 percent, and Cranston, Hart, and Hollings 2 percent apiece. Mondale had raised much more money than any of his rivals. And a *Newsweek* cover story was headlined: "Mondale's machine is simply the biggest and best in the history of U.S. politics."

The problem of the other candidates, of course, was how they were going to attack the former Vice President. John Glenn had a particular need to do so. He was second in the polls and in the amount of money raised; but the preceding June, Mondale and Glenn had been almost tied in the polls, and Glenn needed a way to turn the "two-man race" into a real two-man race. His strategy was to hit Mondale almost head-on and tie him to the Carter administration. In the meanwhile, Pat Caddell (having failed to persuade other young Democrats to run) had attached himself to the Hart campaign.[14] He urged that Hart emphasize his generational message by lumping Mondale and Glenn together with Reagan as part of the past (Orren, 1985, p. 58; Goldman & Fuller, 1985, pp. 98–99).

The first highly publicized event was a debate between the eight contenders at Dartmouth on January 15. The strategies being followed were evident in some of the exchanges. Mondale had just finished explaining his plans for reducing the deficit. Glenn responded:

> Let me point out that it's the same vague gobbledegook of nothing we've been hearing all through this campaign. . . . I'm disgusted and tired of all the vague promises. I wish the former Vice President would get some figures down so they can be compared with what the rest of us are proposing.

Mondale, who had been attacking Glenn for voting for the Reagan budget in the Senate,[15] came back:

> Baloney. . . . Mr. Glenn voted to create those $200 billion deficits that we're suffering from. He wants to add the B–1 bomber, he voted for poison nerve gas, and he tries to attack my specific proposals that would reduce the federal deficit by more than half.

---

[14] Caddell's role in 1984 is interesting. Without a presidential client of his own, he attached himself first to Gary Hart in the primaries and then to Walter Mondale in the fall. Because of his prior work as a campaign pollster, Caddell had been friendly with Hart since the 1972 campaign and with Mondale since the 1976 campaign. He was not gladly received by many of those who had already been in the Hart and Mondale coalitions, but he brought both ideas and experience, rare and valuable commodities in presidential campaigns.

[15] Mondale had made particularly sharp comments about Glenn in Iowa in October. On Glenn's vote for Reagan's budget, he said, "That would have been a good time for a Democrat to stand up against the special interests and vote no" (Germond & Witcover, 1985, p. 109).

Gary Hart began his attack on both Mondale and Glenn by using Ronald Reagan's line from his 1980 debate with Jimmy Carter:

> Fritz, John, there you two go again. The fact of the matter is, this party will not regain leadership so long as the leaders of the past continue to debate whose policies of the past are the worst. . . . What I bring to this race is unique, and that is new leadership and new proposals to address the new generation.

The sniping between Glenn, Mondale, and Hart led both Jesse Jackson and George McGovern to ask for more decorum. At one point, Jackson intervened, saying that "we have to conduct . . . this business in a serious vein. That's important." And toward the end of the debate, McGovern admonished his colleagues; "I think that it's fine that we air our differences here, but all of us are jumping on the front-runner. I didn't expect to come here today to defend Fritz Mondale, but sometimes front-runners get nominated."

Mr. Mondale did not appear to have been hurt by the debate in the initial selection of delegates. In 1984, this was not in Iowa but rather the "superdelegates" selected by the House of Representatives. Of the 164 selected, 75 were for Mondale as compared to 47 for all the other candidates put together.[16] The results in Iowa also showed the strength of the Mondale candidacy. The former Vice President came close to getting an absolute majority of the caucus votes, ending up with 45 percent. (By way of comparison, Jimmy Carter "won" Iowa with 28 percent in 1976.)

The problem for Mondale was that in nomination politics, interpretation rests on *departure* from expectations. A January poll in the *Des Moines Register* had predicted he would receive 45 percent, and this is exactly what he got. The departures from expectations focused attention on Glenn and Hart.[17] Glenn's organizational difficulties[18] were a particular handicap because a caucus vote depends much more on an organization's ability to get supporters out than does a primary election. Further, since Glenn's organizational problems were not known to the general public, people expected him to do rather well.

After some false starts, Hart workers had managed to put together a reasonably effective, low-cost, low-visibility campaign in Iowa. For a long time, they didn't have resources to spend; when a little money became available in January, it was used to buy television time in Boston (for New Hampshire) and Iowa (Germond & Witcover, 1985, pp. 127–35). In his personal campaign-

---

[16] Since superdelegate selection was not a designated event on the mass media calendar, this was not widely reported. But Mondale's strength with the superdelegates was to be critical in his eventual success.

[17] Hollings and Jackson wrote off the state. Except for Askew, the other candidates relied on a combination of personal campaigning and television. Askew emphasized his antiabortion position in the hope of attracting volunteers. (See Hershey, 1984, chap. 7.)

[18] William White had been removed as campaign manager in late January, but a last-minute shift of this kind is more likely to be a sign that a campaign is in deep trouble than an effective reorganization.

ing, Hart continued to sharpen his image as a new-generation candidate. In Council Bluffs, he said:

> The election of 1984 is . . . a choice between the past and the future. It must not become a choice between two different forms of reaction—between those in the Republican party who have taken us back to William McKinley and those in the Democratic party who would return us to the old programs, old patterns and outworn appeals. (Goldman & Fuller, 1985, p. 400)

As things turned out, Hart got the largest portion of the non-Mondale vote. Hart got 15 percent; McGovern 13 percent; Cranston 9 percent; Glenn 5 percent; and Askew 3 percent.

The post-Iowa stories gave some attention to Mondale's real triumph but paid more attention to the new developments: Hart's rise from the also-rans to finish second and Glenn's fifth-place finish. The consequence was that voters paid real attention to Hart for the first time. (He had been at 2 percent in national polls.) The New Hampshire primary was only a week away, and New Hampshire was the one state in the country where there was an effective Hart organization in place. On the morning of the New Hampshire primary, the *New York Times* published a new survey under the headline, "Mondale Lead over Nearest Rival in Poll Sets Nonincumbent Record." But this was a national survey, and when the New Hampshire vote came in that evening, the results were Hart 38 percent; Mondale 28 percent; Glenn 12 percent; Jackson 5 percent; McGovern 5 percent; Hollings 4 percent; Cranston 2 percent; and Askew 1 percent. Surveys for both Mondale and Hart had shown that Hart support was building very rapidly, but no one had expected him to move that fast. What happened was that Hart's message had resonated with young voters, college graduates, and independents, all of whom were found in unusually large numbers in New Hampshire, and the strong organization created by Jeanne Shaheen had maximized Hart's strength at the polls. Furthermore, Hart won the Maine caucus vote the following Sunday. Suddenly, Gary Hart was not only the new face who was speaking to a new generation, but he had the appearance of being a winner as well.

With the New Hampshire results, the field became less crowded. On February 29, Senator Cranston said, "I know the difference between dreams and reality" and the next day, Governor Askew and Senator Hollings dropped out as well. Senator McGovern, with the serenity he had been exhibiting in 1984, said that he wanted to wait for the vote in Massachusetts (the one state he had carried in 1972). He received a very respectable 21 percent; but once that vote came in on March 13, he abandoned his race.

The next decision point was Super Tuesday, March 13, with five primaries—Massachusetts and Rhode Island in New England and Florida, Alabama, and Georgia in the South—and four western caucuses. As they began their campaigning for those delegates, all four candidates were vulnerable. John Glenn had long believed that his relatively moderate positions would have more appeal in the South. With Hollings and Askew now out of the race, he had a chance to present his case to a more sympathetic electorate. However, his poor showings in Iowa and New Hampshire had undercut his claim to be the candidate to challenge Mondale, and his campaign was now subsisting on money borrowed from Ohio banks. If he had a chance in the South, it was clearly going to be the last chance of his presidential campaign.

Jesse Jackson had not conducted serious campaigns in Iowa or New Hampshire. His candidacy so far had existed largely in the media, with favorable attention when he won the release of Lt. Robert Goodman from Syrian captivity and negative attention coming from his reference to New York City as Hymietown. There was a question whether the Jackson organization, underfinanced and relying on contacts made through black churches, could reach enough people to produce Jackson votes. In the upcoming southern primaries, he had an opportunity because of the substantial numbers of black voters—but if he was going to become anything more than an asterisk in the Democratic race, he had to show he could win votes.

Foreseeing a strong showing by Gary Hart in New Hampshire, Pat Caddell had written a memo three days before on how to exploit the resulting momentum:

> We must be bold—We must go all out everywhere, to finish off Mondale, using momentum as a substitute for money, organization, etc. We must move to broaden and deepen the Hart image. . . . We must fill in themes—We need to broaden and deepen our message with major speeches that fill in the specifics of ideas, visions and program. . . . We have no choice but to go all out. The key is to ride the momentum into a national free media campaign that exploits the breakthrough before the Mondale campaign and its establishment allies can regroup and counterattack. (Goldman & Fuller, 1985, pp. 403–4)

The key elements were the references to the need to broaden and deepen the message (Hart was becoming identified with his call for new ideas, but it was not clear what these new ideas were) and the lack of organization. In dramatic contrast to Hart's earlier poverty, money was now gushing in. But there was no organization to conduct a campaign, and because of the lack of an organization, the Hart staff could not even absorb and spend money very efficiently. The Hart strategy was switched from selective campaigning to campaigning everywhere. (In fact, none of the Hart strategists was arguing that he should continue to campaign selectively. Since Hart was now the front-runner, the consensus was that he no longer had the luxury of being able to choose particular primaries.) What this new mode of campaigning meant was flying from one airport news conference to the next, hoping that frenzied activity could compensate for organizational weakness.

As we have already seen, the primary schedule had been front-loaded to give a strong candidate an opportunity to build up a substantial number of delegates during the Initial Contests. That presumably would be the well-financed, well-organized Mondale, who, after entrenching his coalition with a large delegate base early on, could turn his attention to President Reagan.

After New Hampshire, Mondale strategists had to confront the possibility that Gary Hart would be the one to profit from the front-loaded schedule.

In a meeting two days after the New Hampshire primary, Peter Hart reported that his surveys showed a tidal wave for Hart. It would be impossible to beat him in Massachusetts on Super Tuesday; the only possibility would be in the South, where Alabama still looked good and Georgia was a question mark. There were those who felt that they ought not to change their preset strategy, but Walter Mondale thought that they should counterattack Hart just as they had earlier struck back against Glenn and that they should project *their* image of Gary Hart before he had a chance to do so himself (Goldman & Fuller, 1985, p. 139). This was a chancy strategy. The Mondale coalition had good ties to southern Democratic organizations, but Mondale no longer seemed to be the annointed candidate. Also, with Jesse Jackson in the race, Mondale would have to split the black vote with him. But they had no choice.

An important turning point came in a televised debate in Atlanta on the Sunday evening preceding the election. Gary Hart began an answer with his now familiar claim, "I've made quite an issue out of the need for a new generation of leadership." When he finished, Walter Mondale replied, "When I hear your new ideas, I'm reminded of the ad: 'Where's the beef?' "[19] "Fritz, if you'd listen just a minute, I think you'd hear," Hart continued, but Mondale had found a short slogan to suggest that there weren't many new ideas being offered by Hart.[20]

When the votes came in, Hart won the primaries in Massachusetts, Rhode Island, and Florida and the caucus votes in Oklahoma, Nevada, and Washington. Mondale was second in these states but came in first in Georgia and Alabama. Hart and Glenn had very little black support, and Jackson had very little white support. That Mondale alone was able to draw substantial support from both races was critical in Georgia and Alabama.[21]

The Super Tuesday results reversed the impact of the Iowa caucuses. By virtually any test,[22] Hart had done better, winning six of the eight states being contested. But the predominant media reaction, with a *lot* of help from the Mondale campaign staff, focused on Mondale's comeback (Germond & Witcover, 1985, pp. 196–200). Mondale had truly won in Iowa, and Hart had

---

[19] The idea for this line came from a television commercial for Wendy's Hamburgers. In the commercial, an elderly customer walks into a rival establishment and is served a very small hamburger on a very big bun, at which point she loudly demands, "Where's the beef?"

[20] Another effective attack on Hart was based on voter concern about whether he had enough experience to handle a foreign-policy crisis. A television commercial showed a red telephone ringing, while a voice intoned, "The most awesome, powerful responsibility in the world lies in the hand that picks up this phone" (Germond & Witcover, p. 201).

[21] In Georgia and Alabama, the white vote was split between Hart, Mondale, and Glenn, in that order. The black vote was divided 50 percent for Jackson to 47 percent for Mondale in Alabama and 61 percent for Jackson to 31 percent for Mondale in Georgia.

[22] Mondale did somewhat better in terms of delegates won, because the Mondale coalition had been well enough organized to file full delegate slates.

been the beneficiary. Hart had truly won on March 13, and Mondale had been the beneficiary.

These southern results were also critical for John Glenn and Jesse Jackson. There had been southern support for Senator Glenn. His 21 percent in Alabama and 18 percent in Georgia were much better than he had done anywhere else. But a bare second place in Alabama was also the best he had done out of all the primaries and caucuses he had entered. This wasn't good enough to sustain his candidacy. His withdrawal statement three days later showed why so many people were fond of John Glenn as a human being. There was no finger-pointing, only "Annie and I . . . have traveled from one end of this nation to the other. We'll never forget the genuine affection and friendship we received all across this great land of ours."

Jesse Jackson, remembering full well his early life as a poor black, had demonstrated convincingly that he could not only bring pride to black citizens but earn their votes as well. Just as Walter Mondale had first found his constituency of traditional Democrats, union members, and older voters in Iowa and Gary Hart had demonstrated his appeal to younger, relatively affluent, relatively well educated independents in New Hampshire, Jesse Jackson proved that he had a constituency in Alabama and Georgia. These votes meant he would be a candidate to be reckoned with wherever there was a sizable black electorate.

Jackson's Georgia vote (21 percent of the total) was critical in another respect. By getting over 20 percent of the vote, he reestablished his eligibility for federal matching funds.[23] These funds are, of course, important to any campaign; to the underfinanced Jackson campaign, they were absolutely vital.

SUMMARY

In this chapter, we have reviewed the first two stages of the nominating process: Early Days and Initial Contests. Both are necessary preludes for the activity that is going to take place, but neither provides any certain knowledge about the outcome.

For instance, as early as 1985, it was evident that Republicans including George Bush, Jack Kemp, Pat Robertson, Robert Dole, and Pete DuPont and Democrats such as Gary Hart, Jesse Jackson, Richard Gephardt, Joseph

---

[23] The rule was that a candidate lost his certification for federal matching funds if he failed to get at least 10 percent of the vote on two consecutive primary days. (If there was more than one primary on the same day, the candidate's highest vote counted.) If a candidate fell under the 10 percent criterion on two consecutive days, he had to get 20 percent of the vote in a succeeding primary to reestablish his eligibility for funding. There was also a 30-day grace period before funding actually was cut off. If a candidate reestablished his eligibility during that time, there would be no interruption of funding (Wilcox, 1985). Since the black vote was usually a small proportion of a statewide vote, Jackson was constantly threatened by a cutoff of federal funding throughout the 1984 primaries.

Biden, and Bruce Babbitt were giving speeches, organizing PACs, and otherwise behaving as presidential contenders. But predicting what would happen as 1988 nomination politics developed was another matter. Who could guess that Mario Cuomo would not run, that Gary Hart would drop out after charges of womanizing, or that Howard Baker would become President Reagan's chief of staff? Would others being discussed but who were not yet committed, such as Republican Paul Laxalt and Democrat Sam Nunn, actually run? Would there be a Republican conservative or a Democratic liberal strong enough to gain most of the support of these party factions, or would these votes be split among several candidates in 1988? Would George Bush—the runner-up the last time he had sought his party's nomination—prove to be attractive enough to command greater support this time?

During Early Days, the questions are evident, but the answers are not. During this stage, we know only that potential candidates are maneuvering to be in a position to take advantage of whatever opportunities come to them. But we can not know what these opportunities are going to be.

A similar point can be made about the Initial Contests. There is now more information about the structure of competition. In this stage we know who has decided to enter the lists and who is remaining on the sidelines. But Initial Contests may be either revealing or deceptive. For example, the Iowa caucuses accurately foretold Jimmy Carter's eventual success in 1976 and 1980, but George Bush did not go on to win the Republican nomination in 1980. Success in Iowa proved to be an accurate precursor of Walter Mondale's eventual victory in 1984, but it was some time before that became evident.

Two kinds of conclusions can be drawn after the Initial Contests. One, the weaker candidates in a multicandidate race are forced out for lack of support. Two, if there are two strong candidates with support across the country and both do reasonably well in the Initial Contests, then it is likely (but not yet certain) that there will be a relatively stable two-candidate race that will last through the Convention stage. For more than this, we have to wait for Mist Clearing, and it is to this stage of nomination politics that we now turn.

Chapter 2

Mist Clearing and the Convention

MIST CLEARING

Ford versus Reagan, 1976

Ronald Reagan's campaign did not look too strong after his defeat in the Initial Contests, and Gerald Ford sympathizers began to urge Reagan to drop out of the race. There was one meeting between John Sears and Rogers Morton, the new President Ford Committee chairman, about conditions under which a withdrawal might take place (Witcover, 1977, p. 413).

Three things, however, combined to revive the Reagan campaign. First, Ronald Reagan began to focus on three international issues—détente, the proposed Panama Canal treaty, and Secretary of State Kissinger—on which pollster Richard Wirthlin's surveys had uncovered a fair amount of criticism of the Ford administration among Republican activists (Moore & Fraser, 1977, p. 46). Second, there was a nationally televised speech by Governor Reagan that brought in contributions at a time when the campaign was badly in debt. Third, many of the later primaries were scheduled to take place in states where conservatives were quite strong.

Reagan's campaign began to work in North Carolina, where last-minute decision making carried him to victory. This quickly ended calls for him to abandon his candidacy. Mist Clearing really came, though, in early May.[1] In

---

[1] There had been only two primaries during the whole month of April. Ford beat Reagan in Wisconsin, and Reagan was not on the ballot in Pennsylvania.

the Texas primary on May 1, Ronald Reagan carried every congressional district and picked up 96 delegates. Even Texas Senator John Tower, running as a Ford delegate, was defeated. In the Alabama, Georgia, and Indiana primaries on May 4, Ronald Reagan got 130 delegates to Gerald Ford's 9. This brought the strength of the Reagan coalition to 313 delegates to 241 for the incumbent President.

These figures did not reflect the large New York and Pennsylvania delegations, formally uncommitted though likely to support Ford; but with many remaining primaries in conservative states, it was clear that this was a contest between two strong coalitions. It was not clear which would win.

Carter versus Kennedy, 1980

Illinois was important to Democrats in 1980 for two reasons. First, there was the question about whether Senator Kennedy could win in another big, industrial state besides Massachusetts. Second, the Illinois primary had long been identified as crucial by the Carter coalition.[2] Not only was it "neutral" (that is, neither New England nor southern), but Illinois did not use proportional representation. And just as the Carter leaders had been alert to earlier opportunities to keep the Kennedy delegate total down by working hard in Alabama and Georgia, they were alert to an opportunity to run up the Carter delegate total by making a special effort in Illinois. The Carter campaign emphasized "character" and "trust," not too subtly calling attention to Chappaquiddick and Senator Kennedy's marital problems and thus undercutting his appeal to Chicago's rather conservative Roman Catholic voters.

As things turned out, Kennedy lost Chicago, the Catholic vote, the labor vote, and the blue-collar vote. More important, Jimmy Carter won 165 of Illinois's 179 delegates. When added to the delegates won in previous primaries, that meant President Carter already had 38 percent of the votes needed to nominate. Conversely, for Senator Kennedy to get the nomination, he would have to win 61 percent of the delegates remaining to be chosen. In other words, Jimmy Carter's renomination was a virtual certainty.

The Illinois results also seemed to imply that Kennedy's victory in Massachusetts had been a home state phenomenon, but this turned out to be false. If Edward Kennedy was not popular in Illinois, Jimmy Carter was even less popular in New York. There were indications of loss of support for the President in preelection polls, and the Carter coalition's worst fears were confirmed on election day. Senator Kennedy beat President Carter by 3 to 1 among Jews, 3 to 2 among Hispanics, and 5 to 4 among blacks and Roman Catholics. Jews had been angered when United Nations delegate Donald McHenry cast an anti-Israeli vote and then was repudiated by the White House; but the New York vote was not a specific response to one incident. It was a general protest against the administration, with attitudes about infla-

---

[2] In much the same way, they had anticipated the decisiveness of the Pennsylvania primary in 1976.

tion having the greatest impact on the vote. Senator Kennedy received 59 percent of the vote in New York, and carried all six congressional districts in neighboring Connecticut.

The pattern was now set. There were three general circumstances that affected the results of the remaining primaries. One was organization. President Carter was able to contest every single primary. The Kennedy coalition was so short of resources that it could only afford to challenge the Carter forces in selected primaries. The second was geography. Speaking generally, Senator Kennedy won in the industrial Northeast, and President Carter won almost everywhere else.[3] Finally, there was the question of the dominant issue in the campaign. Whenever the election focused on Senator Kennedy's character, Carter won. Whenever the election focused on President Carter's achievements in office, Kennedy won.

The last consideration—essentially that the ability of either candidate to win depended on the weakness of the other—affected relationships between the two camps. From Senator Kennedy's point of view, there were serious issues that needed to be debated.[4] When the Carter campaign attacked Kennedy, as in Pennsylvania, with television ads with citizens expressing their doubts about Kennedy ("I don't believe him." "I don't trust him." "Between Kennedy and Carter, I would definitely go with Carter myself. I trust him."), this seemed to Kennedy partisans to be a deliberate evasion of a much needed discussion of issues.

But from President Carter's point of view, he deserved to be the Democratic nominee because he had dealt with tough issues in the White House; and given the arithmetic of the delegate count, he was going to be the nominee. Therefore, when Edward Kennedy urged a crowd in Philadelphia to "No more hostages, no more high inflation, no more high interest rates, *no more Jimmy Carter*," Carter partisans saw this as deliberately undercutting the Democratic party's chances of retaining the White House in the fall.

Finally, we should note the effect of proportional representation on a two-candidate contest such as this. President Carter's strength was not simply a result of proportional representation. Organizational strength, a decision to enter every primary, and other factors that we have discussed all contributed to Carter's lead. But the Carter camp's tactical use of proportional representation, as in their Alabama-Georgia effort to keep Kennedy from getting any delegates and the Illinois work to get more Carter delegates, certainly augmented the number of Carter delegates. On the other hand, since Kennedy was strong enough to get more than the 15 percent cutoff, he was going to

---

[3] Finally, on Super Tuesday, June 3, Kennedy beat Carter in California, New Jersey, Rhode Island, New Mexico, and South Dakota. Carter won in Ohio, Montana, and West Virginia. The Kennedy victories in California, New Mexico, and South Dakota signaled a low point in Carter fortunes.

[4] In May, Senator Kennedy offered to release his delegates if President Carter would agree to a debate. The view of the Kennedy campaign within the Carter core group was so negative at that time that the offer was not seriously explored.

pick up delegates in almost every primary. Even if he can't win, *a reasonably strong second candidate aided by proportional representation is going to have enough of a delegate base to mount a serious challenge:*[5] Thus, the Democrats' situation in the spring of 1980. The rules helped maintain two viable coalitions, and relations between the leaders of the two coalitions were very bad.

Reagan, 1980

On the surface, the Republican structure of competition looked very clear as the Illinois primary approached. Ronald Reagan, who was appealing to conservative voters, had 167 delegates; George Bush, whose ideological position was less distinct but who was appealing to moderate conservatives, had 45; John Anderson, appealing to moderates and liberals, had 13. (Illinois Congressman Philip Crane, a determined conservative who still hadn't withdrawn, didn't have any delegates.)

At the same time, none of the three candidates was very secure. The Reagan coalition, having spent most of their money, would be all right as long as they kept on winning, but they were not in a position to defeat any strong challenge. The Bush campaign was still struggling to get into a one-on-one posture against Reagan but was losing conservative support to Reagan, and moderate to liberal support to Anderson. John Anderson's positions were appealing to independents but made it very difficult for him to attract support from conservative voters in Republican primaries.

Reagan was helped by a debate between the candidates. Bush and Crane were quite direct in their attacks on Anderson; Bush attacked him as a liberal masquerading as a Republican. Reagan showed a much lighter touch, asking "John, would you really prefer Teddy Kennedy to me?" When the Illinois vote came in, Ronald Reagan had a 3 to 1 margin among conservatives. John Anderson had a small lead among moderates and a 4 to 1 lead among liberals. But there were so many more conservatives voting that this translated into an overall vote of 47 percent for Reagan, 37 percent for Anderson, and 11 percent for Bush.

George Bush managed to get back on his feet the following week in Connecticut. Feeling that their chances of winning in Illinois were rather bleak and that they *had* to win in Connecticut, where Bush's father had been a U.S. senator, the Bush coalition concentrated on that New England state. The short-of-resources Reagan coalition decided that they could afford to lose Connecticut and didn't put on much of a campaign there. The results gave some pleasure to all the candidates. With 39 percent, Bush could point to his first victory since Massachusetts. With 34 percent, Reagan could claim some support and more delegates (and a lot more the same day in New York) to add to his growing total. With 22 percent, Anderson could point to another "strong showing."

---

[5] If two candidates were of roughly equal strength, as Eisenhower and Taft in 1952 or Ford and Reagan in 1976, proportional representation could produce a very even contest.

The expectations coming into Wisconsin were much the same as they had been in Illinois. It was assumed that there might be a chance for Bush and Anderson because Wisconsin permitted crossover voting (in which Democrats could vote in the Republican primary and vice versa). It was further assumed that this was a state where John Anderson *had* to win because there was no other primary coming along where conditions would be as favorable. There was a crossover vote, and Anderson did get the largest share of it. The crossover vote, however, was split among all the candidates, and the overall result was 40 percent for Reagan, 30 percent for Bush, and 27 percent for Anderson. Shortly thereafter, John Anderson abandoned his race for the Republican nomination and began his "National Unity" third-party effort. He had gained a number of "moral victories" but had not won a single primary, and he had few delegates to show for his efforts.

The Illinois, Connecticut, and Wisconsin primaries provide good illustrations of the differences between multicandidate and two-candidate nomination contests. Since Reagan was regularly winning most of the conservative vote, Bush and Anderson were competing for the nonconservative vote and splitting it with each other. Suppose that there had been a single moderate candidate. Given the results of the three-candidate races, it is likely that Reagan would have won in Illinois, while "Bush-Anderson" would have won in both Connecticut and Wisconsin.

There is also a more subtle distinction. A multicandidate race makes it more difficult for candidates to exceed expectations (Aldrich, 1980a, 1980b). In both Connecticut and Wisconsin, a moderate Republican might have been expected to win. Relatively liberal Republicans have done well in Connecticut, and such candidates can attract independent support in Wisconsin. Measured against an expectation of victory, Anderson did not do well in Connecticut, and neither Bush nor Anderson did well in Wisconsin. Falling below expectations makes it harder to raise funds for further primaries. Since a larger number of candidates means that more of them will fail to meet expectations, this also increases the likelihood that there will be a larger proportion of dropouts in a multicandidate race.

After the Mist Clearing primaries, the capacities of the Bush and Reagan coalitions were evident. Bush could beat Reagan by outspending him in large industrial states, and Reagan could win the nomination. Bush did win in Pennsylvania on April 22 and in Michigan on May 20. He also showed real strength in Texas, holding Reagan to a victory margin of 51 percent to 47 percent. By remaining in the race and demonstrating political strength, Bush was safeguarding his political future; but his continuing efforts had less and less to do with the 1980 Republican nomination. On May 26, Bush conceded to Reagan.

The Reagan coalition was guided during this phase by a remarkably far-sighted memorandum written in late March by pollster Richard Wirthlin.

> With over a third of the 998 delegate votes needed now locked into the Governor's column and with his best states only now starting to come up on the

primary calendar, the general election campaign, from our point of view, starts today. . . . We must position the Governor, in these early stages [of the *general election* campaign] so that he is viewed as less dangerous in the foreign affairs area, more competent in the economic area, more compassionate on the domestic issues, and less of a conservative zealot than his opponents and the press now paint him to be.

Wirthlin went on to point out the importance of expanding the Reagan coalition by gathering additional support from less conservative elements of the Republican party, including supporters of the now defeated aspirants, and concluded, "Plans should be prepared now to garner the full and active support of George Bush, once he realizes that his candidacy has lost its viability. . . . His support and resources should be absorbed by our campaign fully and enthusiastically" (Drew, 1981, pp. 351–55).

Mondale, 1984

In retrospect, the outlines of 1984 nomination politics were clear in the aftermath of the Super Tuesday primaries in mid-March. Once John Glenn and George McGovern departed, the structure of competition was set, and each of the remaining contestants had located his core constituency. But it was not yet clear if Mondale could reestablish himself as the front-runner and if the Hart and Jackson constituencies would be large enough, and dependable enough, to sustain their candidacies until the Convention. Answers to these questions emerged in the Illinois (March 20), Connecticut (March 27), and New York and Wisconsin (April 3) primaries.

The campaign tactics were of some consequence here. Essentially, Hart seemed to shift position about some television ads. This gave some credence to Mondale charges that Hart lacked the experience and stability for the presidency. But in a larger context, these four primaries were all of a piece. Mondale won the industrial states of Illinois and New York and in fact carried constituencies (suburban, college educated, independent) that had been producing Hart majorities elsewhere. Hart won in the relatively affluent, relatively well educated state of Connecticut and won a nonbinding primary in Wisconsin.[6] And Jackson did even better with blacks in Illinois and New York than he had done in Alabama and Georgia.

There were several patterns to the Democratic race in the spring of 1984. The structure of competition was skewed in a liberal direction. None of the relatively moderate candidacies—Glenn or Hollings or Askew—had proven to be viable. Two liberal candidates, McGovern and Cranston, had been forced out. But even allowing for Jackson's more pronounced leftward tilt, Mondale, Hart, and Jackson were taking similar policy positions. There-

---

[6] The Wisconsin delegates were chosen in caucuses, and Mondale won 48 to Hart's 25.

fore, the candidates emphasized issues and symbols to appeal to different constituencies even more than is usually the case.

Once the Initial Contests were over, the nature of the contest itself changed. The race had been a dynamic eight-person race, with candidates dropping out as, inevitably, some did more poorly than expected and with individual candidates, first Mondale and then Hart, being propelled ahead of the field as they exceeded expectations. Now it suddenly became a rather stable three-person contest. It was easy to miss this stability if one read the headlines the morning after each primary—"Mondale Surges Ahead" or "Hart Surprises Again" or "Jackson Does Well." But *over time*, each candidate won whenever a primary or caucus took place where there were enough of his constituents. And this allowed each to amass a respectable number of delegates.

Jesse Jackson

At the heart of the Jackson campaign was the question of what constituted a respectable number of delegates. A case could be made that the Jackson coalition did not need many delegates to succeed; the argument being that pride motivated Jackson himself and that the pride he communicated to his followers added significantly to their dignity and sense of personal worth.

Jesse Jackson was able to reach his constituents as did no other candidate. While Mondale got 45 percent of the union vote and Hart 41 percent of the vote of college graduates, Jackson got 77 percent of the black vote (Clymer, 1984, pp. 52–53). Further, Jackson was protected against normal political attacks because the Democrats (who had failed to get a majority among white voters in every presidential election since 1968) desperately needed black support in the fall.[7] From this perspective, the Jackson candidacy succeeded simply by being.

But if Jackson was not seen simply as a unique black candidate, then he needed delegates. Jesse Jackson was not the first candidate to present himself as a spokesperson for new claimants to political power. (There was a striking similarity between Jackson's assertion that "Our time has come" and Hart's 1974 slogan, "They had their turn. Now it's our turn.") But the strength (hence, legitimacy) of any such claim is judged on the number of delegates acquired, and Jackson was not helped by the rules. He received 19 percent of the vote cast in primaries but only 10 percent of the resulting delegates (Orren, 1985, p. 35). Jackson protested this repeatedly, both to the Democratic National Committee and in campaign speeches.

---

[7] There was also considerable pressure on blacks to support the Jackson candidacy and not raise embarrassing questions. For example,*Washington Post* reporter Milton Coleman, who had revealed Jackson's use of the word *Hymietown* felt compelled to "explain why a black reporter would, as my critics have charged, 'do' this to another black man who is making a historic and inspiring presidential bid" (Coleman, 1984, p. 8; Curry, 1984).

The rules that led to this were not aimed at Jackson. As we have already seen, the rules were adopted by the Hunt Commission at a time when nobody was thinking about a possible Jackson candidacy.[8] But the rules were designed to benefit a well-organized insider—and Jackson was an outsider.[9]

Gary Hart

The Hart candidacy was not without problems either. There was some doubt among voters as to what Hart stood for. In part, this was because the Hart and Mondale positions on issues were very similar; in part, it was because Mondale was more successful in putting Hart on the defensive than the other way around; in part, it was because Hart was prone to gaffes,[10] and when he made one, the media would concentrate on that rather than on his positions on issues. There was also a good deal of infighting among Hart's senior advisors.

Given both image problems and staff wrangling, it is not surprising that there was a continuing staff dispute over how Hart should modify his strategy. The argument was whether the campaign should emphasize negative aspects about Mondale or put greater emphasis on positive themes concerning Hart. At the same time, there were Hart strengths. One of these was money. Because he did not have a large Washington staff, Hart was able to channel into state races more of the funds that became available after New Hampshire. In major primaries after Mist Clearing, Hart outspent Mondale in Illinois, Connecticut, New York, Wisconsin, Pennsylvania, Texas, Ohio, Indiana, New Jersey, and California (Orren, 1985, p. 50). And every now and then, things would fall into place—decent organization, good media, and a sympathetic electorate—and Senator Hart would win.

Walter Mondale

Walter Mondale's great strength was the support of traditional Democrats and his nationwide organization. The organization gave his candidacy resilience and the ability to reach into a number of states at the same time. Since the emphasis after Mist Clearing shifts from creating an impression of success to the accumulation of delegates, the ability to reach into many states (especially large states) meant that the Mondale coalition was doing very well during this stage. Beginning in mid-March, Mondale had won caucuses in Michigan, Minnesota, Kansas, Wisconsin, Missouri, and Texas. In these

---

[8] There is some irony here. Jackson supporter Richard Hatcher was a vice chair of the Democratic party and therefore was involved in writing the delegate selection rules. If he had cared about the principle before it became an important tactical issue to the Jackson forces, it is possible he could have done something about it.

[9] Other factors besides rules, of course, contributed to the limited number of Jackson delegates—for example, the concentration of black voters in certain congressional districts.

[10] For example, when asked in the Atlanta debate what he would do if a Czech airliner invaded American airspace, he replied that he'd instruct American fighter pilots to look inside and see whether they had military uniforms on.

states alone, Mondale accumulated 316 delegates. And since Mondale primary victories had come in large states—Illinois, New York, and Pennsylvania—Mondale delegate strength was growing significantly. By March 16, the Super Tuesday of the southern primaries, Mondale had 301 delegates, 15 percent of the number needed to nominate. By May 1, the Mondale coalition had grown to 1236 delegates, 63 percent of the size needed to win (Pomper, 1985, Table 1.1).

This combination of experience and organizational strength had been planned to create an impression of an inevitable Mondale nomination. With the string of Hart victories during Initial Contests, inevitability had to be postponed for a while. But the Mondale coalition was approaching majority size much more rapidly than either the Jackson or Hart coalition.

The Remaining State Contests

The strengths of the three coalitions were evident in the Ohio primary on May 8. Jesse Jackson ran well with blacks, carrying Louis Stokes' Cleveland congressional district. Walter Mondale carried traditional Democratic counties with relatively high unemployment. Gary Hart carried white-collar and rural areas and won the state with 42 percent to Mondale's 40 percent and Jackson's 16 percent.

Several things happened to produce the Hart victory. There were a total of five states being contested (Texas the preceding Saturday and North Carolina, Maryland, Indiana, and Ohio all on May 8), and Hart had targeted Ohio, spending a lot of time in the state. There was a good deal of last-minute deciding, and this favored Hart. A "jobs" message had been tailored for Ohio. "First, we must put Ohioans back to work," read a Hart broadsheet. "Second, we must have a long-term economic agenda for Ohio to guarantee jobs for our future and our children's future." There was an effective Hart organization in place. And not only did Hart carry Ohio, he also won Indiana as well. All this allowed Senator Hart to say, "the message is very clear, and that is that the Democrats of this nation are not prepared to have this contest and this debate end at this time."

But once the superdelegates were counted, Walter Mondale actually had majorities in both the Ohio and Indiana delegations to go with the majorities he had won in North Carolina and Maryland. The net of the day was to move the Mondale coalition from 63 percent of a convention majority to 74 percent (Pomper, 1985, Table 1.1).[11] The inevitability of a Mondale nomination may have been postponed once again, but the odds were growing shorter all the time.

The last big contest came on June 5, Super Tuesday II, with very important primaries in New Jersey (122 delegates) and California (345 delegates) and

---

[11] It was at this point that Mondale's nomination could be predicted on the basis of a gain-deficit rule devised by Stanley Kelley and his colleagues to detect the critical point when a bandwagon gains enough speed to carry it across the finish line (Broder, 1984b).

smaller primaries in West Virginia, South Dakota, and New Mexico. The period between Ohio and Super Tuesday II saw Hart victories in the West. During that time, there were two caucuses (Colorado and Idaho) and two primaries (Nebraska and Oregon), and Senator Hart won all four.

Of the two big primaries scheduled for June 5, polls conducted for both Mondale and Hart suggested that demographic characteristics made New Jersey a better state for Mondale and California a better state for Hart. Candidate standings showed Mondale with a wide lead in New Jersey, and a tight race between the two in California. If there had been any chance that Gary Hart might win New Jersey, it vanished with a joke told in California. Introducing his wife, Hart said, "The good news for her is that she campaigns in California and I campaign in New Jersey." After his wife mentioned that she got to hold a koala bear, Hart added that he got to hold "samples from a toxic waste dump." Walter Mondale won one of his biggest victories in New Jersey, doing well with almost all segments of the electorate and getting 115 delegates to Jackson's 7 and 0 for Hart.

The results in California were very different. For example, while Hart got only 38 percent of the college-educated vote in New Jersey, he got 44 percent of the much larger college-educated vote in California. Statewide, Hart got 41 percent to Mondale's 37 percent and Jackson's 20 percent. And this was one instance in which Walter Mondale was handicapped by the rules for determining the number of delegates. The California rules, originally written to benefit Alan Cranston, gave Gary Hart a much larger share. Votes were cast directly for delegates in each of the state's 45 congressional districts, and Hart got 205 to Mondale's 72 and Jackson's 29.[12]

There were two news conferences on the morning of June 6. At 11:59 A.M.—the time at which the Mondale campaign had been claiming the race would be finished—Walter Mondale congratulated his opponents and continued, "Today I am pleased to claim victory, and I will be the nominee of the Democratic party. As of 11:59 this morning, central daylight time, over 2,008 delegates had pledged their support to me." This statement came after a morning of frantic phone calls to as yet unpledged delegates to make up for the unexpected shortfall in California (Germond & Witcover, 1985, pp. 317–25; Goldman & Fuller, 1985, pp. 198–99). Gary Hart began his news conference by saying, "Welcome to overtime." He was wrong. It wasn't overtime. It was over.

THE CONVENTION

Ford versus Reagan, 1976

As the convention neared, Ford was in the better position. The Reagan forces had mounted the strongest challenge to an incumbent president in over half a

---

[12] In the other primaries, Mondale won in the East (West Virginia) and Hart in the West (South Dakota and New Mexico).

century, but when the last delegate was selected, the *Washington Post* delegate count showed Ford with 1,093, Reagan with 1,030, and 136 uncommitted. With 1,130 needed to nominate, Ford stood a much better chance of getting the uncommitted delegates that he needed. Furthermore, almost all of the ideological conservatives were already supporting Reagan. There was no other available move that would please his conservative supporters and impress uncommitted delegates. "What we direly needed," John Sears said later, "was some way to carry the fight, to get maneuverability again. At this particular juncture, the perception was growing that if things stayed as they were, we were going to get counted out of the race" (Moore & Fraser, 1977, p. 48). What John Sears proposed, and Ronald Reagan accepted, was the announcement that if Reagan were nominated, moderate Pennsylvania Senator Richard Schweiker would be tapped as his running mate. As things turned out, this did not gain additional delegates for Reagan; and the unhappiness it caused, specifically in the Mississippi delegation, ultimately led to an advantage for Ford.

John Sears selected a rules proposal as the vehicle for the Reagan coalition's principal tactical challenge. The proposal, known as Rule 16–C, would have required that presidential candidates make their vice presidential choices known before the balloting for president. There were two reasons for this selection. First, the uncommitted delegates were not ideological conservatives and so might be more easily persuaded to support a "neutral" procedural point. Second, it was hoped that Ford's choice (if he could be forced to make one) would cause enough unhappiness within his coalition so that some Ford delegates could be wooed by Reaganites. This proposal was rejected on a 59 to 44 vote within the Rules Committee itself, but the decisive vote was to come on the convention floor. At the end of that roll call, the vote stood 1,041 in favor of Reagan's 16–C motion and 1,112 against. Neither side had the 1,130 votes for a majority. Then Florida, where Ford had won an early primary, cast 28 votes for and 38 votes against; Mississippi, the object of intense effort by the Ford leaders ever since the Schweiker ploy, cast 30 votes against. The principal Reagan challenge was turned back.

There were more votes to come. There were some determined conservatives, such as North Carolina Senator Jesse Helms, who were not responsive to the Reagan leadership. They thought it would be better to have the decisive vote on a "red meat" conservative policy issue, and presented a "Morality in Foreign Policy" amendment to the report of the Platform Committee. This was intended to symbolize conservative belief in moral purpose, as opposed to the realpolitik of Secretary of State Henry Kissinger; but the amendment was stated in very general language, and the Ford leaders decided not to oppose it.

Ford received 1,187 votes on the presidential roll call to Reagan's 1,070. The regional nature of their support was quite apparent. President Ford got 73 percent of the votes cast by eastern and midwestern delegates. Governor Reagan got 72 percent of the votes cast by southern and western delegates.

Reagan agreed to a meeting with Ford afterward on condition that he not be offered the vice presidential nomination. Ford mentioned other persons he was considering, and Reagan said he thought Senator Robert Dole would be acceptable. The others who were given the most serious consideration—both before the convention and in an all-night meeting between Ford and his advisors after he was nominated—were former Deputy Attorney General William Ruckelshaus, Senator Howard Baker, and Anne Armstrong, the ambassador to England. None of these three was a liberal, but each would have broadened the ticket. In the end, it came down to Dole. Ford was comfortable with him; he was popular within the party; his nomination could get through a conservative and unpredictable convention. In a sense, the selection of Dole was comparable to Carter's selection of Mondale and Reagan's of Schweiker. In each case, the presidential contender was reaching out for a representative of the other wing of the party. The difference was that when Carter (a moderate Democrat) picked a liberal Mondale or when Reagan (a conservative Republican) said he would choose Schweiker, the tickets' chances in the general election were strengthened. But when Ford, a moderate conservative from the Midwest, chose Dole, a conservative from the Midwest, the appeal of the ticket was not expanded.

Carter versus Kennedy, 1980

The 1952 and 1976 Republican conventions were the culminations of classic two-candidate contests. Both Eisenhower and Taft in 1952 and Ford and Reagan in 1976 came to their conventions with enough delegates to make the nomination of either candidate entirely plausible. The 1980 Democratic convention was a variant on the classic two-candidate Convention. President Carter had an 8-to-5 advantage in pledged delegates. Therefore, Senator Kennedy was in the position of a very strong challenger rather than a likely nominee. Even so, the fates of Kennedy and Carter were bound together by the dynamics of a two-candidate struggle.

What were Senator Kennedy's major goals? The odds were against his nomination, and his only hope lay in a rules change that would free Carter delegates of their pledges to vote for the President. If the Kennedy coalition was successful in this first instance, then a debate on issues *might* create a momentum that *might* create a possibility of a Kennedy nomination. Failing that unlikely sequence, Kennedy needed a way of rationalizing support for the President in the fall. If there were a debate on issues, then perhaps Senator Kennedy could claim that "enough" of his views had been accepted for him to support the President he had been opposing for nine months. Given Senator Kennedy's oratorical skills, such a rationalization could best be presented in a prime-time television address. The problem with all this was that the Carter majority controlled the rules, the platform, and access to the podium. The Kennedy coalition's goals could be reached only with the acquiescence of the Carter coalition.

What were the goals of the Carter coalition? As the probable nominee, Jimmy Carter could not take more-liberal positions without risking a vote loss to Ronald Reagan. The Carter coalition did not want a debate in which the Carter administration was subject to additional criticism. And President Carter wanted to emerge from the convention with the support of all Democrats, especially Edward M. Kennedy. These were things the Kennedy coalition could prevent. They could offer platform amendments that were popular enough with Democrats to be approved by the convention but that Carter could not accept without the specter of still more deficit spending. They could criticize the Carter administration at length, and, of course, they might choose to "sit out" the fall election. Thus, both coalitions, bitter rivals for some months, were dependent on each other to achieve their goals.

Senator Kennedy and President Carter met after the last primary. This meeting was inconclusive, but the lines of communication stayed open. Further contact between the candidates' aides led to four meetings between Carter and Kennedy representatives. In a series of one-for-one trades (the Carter coalition gave up something when the Kennedy coalition gave up something), these negotiators worked out understandings about the conduct of the convention. The sequence they arrived at—rules votes on Monday night, platform votes and a prime-time Kennedy speech on Tuesday night—was one in which both the Carter and Kennedy coalitions could pursue their central goals. This was confirmed in an agreement signed by Hamilton Jordan (for Carter), Paul Kirk (for Kennedy), and Democratic national chairman John C. White.

The rule chosen by the Kennedy coalition for its first tactical challenge was F3(c), which stated, "All delegates to the national convention shall be bound to vote for the presidential candidate whom they were elected to support." There were strong logical arguments on both sides. The Carter coalition, favoring the rule, declared that the delegates ought to keep faith with the voters who had elected them to support a particular candidate. The Kennedy coalition's explicit argument was that the delegates ought to be free to vote their own consciences. Their implicit argument was that President Carter was no longer as popular as he had been in the early primaries and that to nominate him was to risk defeat. Behind the logical arguments lay Senator Kennedy's need to free the delegates of this obligation if he was to have any chance of the nomination, and the determination of the Carter coalition to use this vote to demonstrate that they were in control of the convention. When the vote was taken, the rule was supported 1,936.4 to 1,390.6. The Carter coalition had been only 30 votes off in their vote estimate; the Kennedy coalition had been 500 votes off. Shortly thereafter, Senator Kennedy announced that his name would not be put in nomination.

The Kennedy coalition, now fighting over issues, was on much stronger ground during the platform debate on Tuesday night. They were supporting four minority economic planks. One called for wage and price controls; the second prohibited any action that would result in a significant increase in unemployment; number three favored a $12 billion job-creation program endorsed by the AFL–CIO; the fourth said that high interest rates and unemployment should not be used to fight inflation. These were popular with the liberal convention delegates. Moreover, the labor unions were working hard for these planks, and they were able to reach a number of Carter delegates. The Kennedy leaders wanted roll-call votes on all four of the minority planks. The Carter leaders felt they could not accept a roll-call vote on wage and price controls. This would be too much of a handicap in the fall campaign. So agreement was reached on a roll-call vote on the $12 billion jobs program and voice votes on all the rest.

The roll-call vote became impossible because of Senator Kennedy's speech. It had been written so it could be used as the Kennedy finale, whatever the circumstances happened to be. His delivery made this one of the historic moments in convention speechmaking. When he reached his conclusion—"For me, a few hours ago, this campaign came to an end. For all those whose cares have been our concern, the work goes on, the cause endures, the hope still lives, and the dream shall never die"—the delegates erupted in a demonstration that House Speaker Tip O'Neill, the permanent chairman of the convention, could not gavel to a close. Finally, he gave up the idea of a roll-call vote and called for voice votes on all four amendments. On wage and price controls, he announced that the nays had it: on the three other amendments, he declared that the ayes had it. If O'Neill's judgments did not accord with those of other observers, it was simply because he was enforcing the agreement that Kennedy and Carter leaders had reached earlier.

All else was anticlimax. The minimum goals of both coalitions were realized. Senator Kennedy lost the nomination but was able to force some changes in the platform, and his speech was the high point of the convention. President Carter was duly renominated. Criticism of the Carter administration was limited, the worst damage in the platform was averted, and the cooperation between the Carter and Kennedy leaders set the stage for Kennedy campaigners to work for the President in the fall.

Reagan, 1980

To an unusual degree, the 1980 Republican National Convention was part of the general election campaign. There were two scripts that had been written for it, one approved by the Reagan strategy group and the other constructed by the Republican National Committee, which had the formal responsibility for organizing the convention. In late April, Richard Wirthlin, aware that the nomination was effectively in hand, put political scientist Richard Beal to work on strategy for the general election. Beal, in concert with others at Decision/Making/Information (Wirthlin's polling firm), worked throughout May and began writing a plan in early June. Once a draft was ready, it was reviewed by Edwin Meese, William Casey, Peter Dailey, and William Timmons.[13] By the Fourth of July, 10 days before the convention began, it had been approved and was in effect.

The plan focused on the larger states, whose votes would be needed to put together an electoral college majority. Therefore, California, Texas, and Florida (considered to be part of Reagan's base) and several target states around the Great Lakes were regarded as particularly important. The plan also assumed that Governor Reagan would move toward the political center as he sought support of swing voters in those states.

No essential conflict existed between this plan and the goals of William Brock. As Republican national chairman, Brock had built up the organizational muscle of the party. His plans were based on a November 1979 study conducted by Robert Teeter of Market Opinion Research. This showed that economic issues were going to be decisive in 1980 and that there was a large bloc of nonvoters under 40 whom Brock hoped to attract (*Republican National Committee Chairman's Report*, 1980).

When the identity of the candidate is already known, three things in a convention provide opportunities to attract voters: the platform, the selection of the vice presidential candidate, and the acceptance speech. The first two of these were to be affected by things that weren't in either the Reagan or the national committee script—the attitudes of conservative zealots on the Platform Committee and the negotiations with Gerald Ford over the vice presidential nomination—but otherwise, the convention proceeded according to plan.

The platform struggles were between different shades of conservatism: organized conservatism as reflected in the leadership of the committee and a more zealous version exhibited by individual committee members. Senator John Tower of Texas was the chairman; Representative Trent Lott of Mississippi was vice chairman.[14] Roger Semerad (the executive director, who supervised the committee's operations) and Michael Baroody (the editor, who did much of the actual writing) both came from the Republican National Committee. Thanks to Baroody, the platform was organized around a series of themes: the individual, the family, the neighborhood, jobs and the workplace, the nation, and peace and freedom. (Three of these—the family, the neighborhood, the workplace—reflected thinking about mediating institutions through which the individual is associated with the larger society.) The Reagan coalition was represented by Richard Allen and Martin Anderson. Anderson was much in evidence once the nomination was securely Reagan's.

---

[13] The composition of this strategy group itself marked an expansion of the Reagan coalition to include other Republicans. Meese and Wirthlin had been associated with Reagan for some time. Casey, Dailey, and Timmons had worked for other Republicans before 1980.

[14] The conservative nature of the leadership can be better grasped from the identity of the subcommittee chairs. These included Senators Dole and Roth and Representatives Michel, Stockman, Holt, Rousselot, Edwards, and Kemp. Senator Dole and Representatives Michel and Heckler occasionally had moderate thoughts. All the rest were determined conservatives.

In Detroit, these organization conservatives came up against such committee members as Donald E. White of Alaska, a supporter of the Moral Majority; Guy O. Farley, a leader of the New Right in Virginia; and the vocal Glenda Mattoon of Oklahoma. They had come to Detroit to write their views into the platform and were unmoved by grander goals such as electing a Republican president.

Perhaps the most sensitive issues were the Equal Rights Amendment (ERA) and abortion. The difficulty with ERA was that the Republican party had been the first party to endorse it (and had done so in every platform since 1940) but was about to nominate the only major aspirant in either party who opposed its ratification. The platform drafters therefore wrote straddling language saying that the party "did not renounce" its historic commitment to equal rights and equality for women. Additionally, the National Federation of Republican Women prepared a rather lengthy bill of rights for women, which had been cleared with Reagan. After a good deal of maneuvering in subcommittee and the full committee, the platform "acknowledged the legitimate efforts of those who support or oppose ratification" of ERA, "reaffirmed" the historic commitment to equal rights, and contained part of the women's bill of rights. Neither the New Right nor pro-ERA activists were happy with this compromise, but neither side was being read out of the party.

Abortion was not compromised. The drafters had tried to straddle this one, too, saying that it was a "difficult and controversial" question on which Republicans could disagree. This was changed into endorsement of a constitutional amendment protecting "the right to life for unborn children," opposition to use of tax funds for abortions, and a call for the appointment of judges who respected "traditional family values and the sanctity of innocent human life." Supporters of ERA and family planning had to accept these changes, since they did not even have enough strength to force a debate on the convention floor (Malbin, 1981).

As is almost always the case, the *bulk* of the platform was endorsed exactly as it had been written. But the debate over these social issues drew the attention of the media.[15] This was hardly what the convention scripts had anticipated. The Reagan strategy wanted to move the candidate toward the center, not draw attention to an area where he was undeniably conservative. And the national committee plan called for emphasis on vote-producing economic issues, not party-dividing social issues.

Another opportunity to broaden (or narrow) the base of the Reagan coalition came in the selection of the vice presidential nominee. The possibilities were Representative Jack Kemp of New York, Senator Paul Laxalt (Reagan's close friend from Nevada), former Treasury Secretary William Simon, Repre-

---

[15] Unable to do anything with the platform, ERA supporters had organized a parade outside the convention. Some 17 pro-ERA Republican women also met with Governor Reagan. These events conveyed the idea that some Republicans were not as conservative as the Platform Committee, but they also kept attention on social issues.

sentative Guy Vander Jagt of Michigan, Senator Richard Lugar of Indiana, former Defense Secretary Donald Rumsfeld, former Ambassador Anne Armstrong of Texas, George Bush, and Senator Howard Baker. By selecting one of those at the beginning of the list, such as Kemp or Laxalt, Reagan would have gladdened the hearts of conservative delegates but not moved toward the political center. Selecting someone from the end of the list, such as Bush or Baker, would have produced the opposite result.

Reagan strategists had been using the preconvention period to study the situation, and Richard Wirthlin had been polling to determine what differences vice presidential candidates would make. These polls showed that only one name would significantly improve Reagan's chances: Gerald R. Ford. Therefore, Reagan decided to explore this possibility before making any other choice.

The negotiations with Ford lasted from Tuesday morning until late Wednesday evening. The former President was disinclined to run but, under pressure to do so, was willing to explore whether the office of vice president could be enhanced enough to make it worthwhile. Ford aides (among them Henry Kissinger and Alan Greenspan) and Reagan aides (including Edwin Meese and William Casey) attempted to work something out. By midday on Wednesday, their discussions reached the point of augmenting the vice president's role by placing the National Security Council and Office of Management and Budget under his direction.

Several things happened to prevent an agreement being reached. First, Reagan leaders got the impression that Kissinger and Greenspan were to be part of a Reagan-Ford administration. Second, Reagan was startled to hear Ford answer, when Walter Cronkite asked him on CBS television about a *co-presidency* (a term that had not been used in the negotiations), "That's something Governor Reagan really ought to consider." Finally, when all the television networks were announcing that Ford was going to be the vice presidential nominee, Reagan sent word that he had to have an answer. As it happened, Ford had nearly made up his mind not to run anyway, and Reagan's request crystallized his refusal. Much has been written about what caused the breakdown in these negotiations. Perhaps the most crucial factor, though, was that even if all other barriers could have been surmounted, there would have remained the very difficult constitutional question of how the powers of the presidency could be shared.

Governor Reagan immediately called George Bush and offered him the nomination, thus expanding his coalition as John Kennedy did in 1960 by offering the vice presidential nomination to Lyndon Johnson and as Jimmy Carter did in 1976 by picking Walter Mondale. Bush had shown an appeal to suburban voters in Texas and Florida, two of Reagan's base states, and he had carried both Michigan and Pennsylvania, two of the target states in the Reagan strategy. Also, as Charles Jones has pointed out, the negotiations with Ford had the side effect of making the Bush selection a good deal more palatable to conservatives. Bush seemed not to have been Reagan's first choice, and the attention that was devoted to the Ford possibility kept conservatives from putting together a campaign for someone more to their liking (Jones, 1981, p. 95). The Ford negotiations were not designed to distract, but they did produce this unplanned bonus.

With his acceptance speech on Thursday night, Ronald Reagan could finally go back to what was in the scripts. From the first paragraph that echoed the organizing concepts of the platform:

> I am very proud of our party. We have shown to all America a party united, with positive programs for solving the nation's problems; a party ready to build a new consensus with all those across the land who share a community of values embodied in these words: family, work, neighborhood, peace, and freedom.

to a call for a moment of silent prayer at the end, Governor Reagan was able to say what he wanted to say to the large television audience attracted by the closing hours of the convention.

Mondale, 1984

To understand Walter Mondale's actions, it is useful to recall the position of the Mondale coalition within the Democratic party, Mondale's position vis-à-vis President Reagan, and the decisions that were open to him. Within the Democratic party, leading a prospective winning coalition didn't confer too much power. As Austin Ranney put it, "Right now the Democratic party is to a political party what the United Nations is to a government. It has a lot of the trappings and appearance, but it is really a collection of independent, sovereign powers. They negotiate with each other, but they don't feel any strong loyalty to each other" (Dillin, 1984, p. 34).

Also, in view of the positions taken by the Hart and Jackson coalitions, the Mondale group had to be careful whenever it did negotiate. Both Hart's and Jackson's foreign policy positions were quite different than Mondale's. Domestically, Hart's affluent supporters wanted somewhat less reliance on government spending and regulation, while Jackson's core suppporters wanted more government welfare programs. Many initiatives that would win favor with Hart supporters would lose support with Jackson backers, and vice versa.

On the eve of the Democratic convention, Walter Mondale was in a very weak position compared to Ronald Reagan. The President had a lead of about 15 points in the polls. A majority of Americans were giving him a positive approval rating as president, while nearly as many persons had negative views of Mr. Mondale as had positive views. Some measure of Mondale's weakness can be seen in a *New York Times*/CBS survey that showed him with only 65 percent of the *Democratic* vote. Mondale was running *behind* with such historic Democratic voting blocs as organized labor and the South. In the face of figures such as these, there was a plausible argument for a high-risk strategy. A low-risk strategy might be safer, but if Mondale only gained a couple of percentage points thereby, the election was still out of reach.

What kinds of things could Walter Mondale and his lieutenants do at the convention? The list is standard: the normal convention reports (rules, credentials, platform), selection of the vice presidential candidate, appointment of party and campaign officials, and speeches directed to the huge television audience. All these have the potential to divide but also may possibly expand the winning coalition, depending on the skill with which the moves are made. There is a difference, however, in their visibility. The selection of party leaders and fights (or negotiations that avoid them) over rules, credentials, or the platform are both likely to be meaningful primarily to the activists who are personally involved. The selection of the vice presidential candidate and the speeches (if they happen to be good enough) have more potential to make an impression on the mass of voters.

Between the last primaries and the convention, Walter Mondale devoted considerable time to his vice presidential choice. Given the progress of civil rights in recent decades and the precarious condition of the Mondale candidacy, there was a basic choice between a traditional white male and a nontraditional female or minority nominee.

Just as Jimmy Carter had brought prospects to Plains, Georgia, in 1976, Walter Mondale invited those he was considering to North Oaks, Minnesota. The list included two blacks (Mayors Thomas Bradley of Los Angeles and Wilson Goode of Philadelphia), three women (Governor Martha Layne Collins of Kentucky, Mayor Dianne Feinstein of San Francisco, and Representative Geraldine Ferraro of New York), a Hispanic (Mayor Henry Cisneros of San Antonio), and two white males (Senator Lloyd Bentsen of Texas and Governor Michael Dukakis; the latter was not brought to North Oaks but was seriously considered). As always, the choice involved decisions about the geographic and ideological emphases for the fall campaign and consideration of the talents and liabilities the nominee would bring to the ticket.

Southern Democrats, worried about the difficulty of campaigning for a too liberal ticket, had been urging balancing the ticket with a Southerner. Of the three southern possibilities, their preference was Senator Bentsen, who had been reelected by a wide margin in 1982 and who therefore could bring strength to efforts to win Texas's 29 electoral votes. Neither of the other Southerners would be as much help in the South as a relatively conservative white male. Mayor Cisneros' appeal to Hispanic voters would be of more help in Sun Belt states west of Texas. The Hispanic vote was exceedingly small in the old Confederacy. Governor Collins represented a compromise between feminists, who wanted a woman on the ticket, and those who were urging a southern candidate.

Selection of either of the California candidates would have represented a risky choice to challenge Ronald Reagan in his home state. Diane Feinstein, coming from the Bay Area, would have augmented Mondale's strength in an area where he was already strong. Mayor Bradley was a respected figure in the southern part of the state where Reagan was quite strong. If either had represented a real threat to Reagan in California, it would have added to their attractiveness, but California (as almost all of the West) had voted for Republican presidential candidates ever since 1968.

There were three Eastern candidates. Mayor Goode of Philadelphia had supported Mondale in the Pennsylvania primary, although many of his constituents favored Jesse Jackson. Representative Ferraro, a three-term legislator from Queens, had been put on the House Budget Committee and had been tapped to chair the 1984 Democratic Platform Committee, a clear sign that she was taken seriously by Democratic leaders. Governor Dukakis was in his second (nonconsecutive) term in the Bay State. He was regarded as liberal, although he had been associated with frugal spending in Massachusetts. Selection of one of these Easterners, especially Goode or Ferraro, would have reinforced Mondale's strength in New York, New Jersey, and Pennsylvania, where he had run his strongest primary races.

In alphabetical order, the four candidates most seriously considered were Cisneros, Dukakis, Feinstein, and Ferraro (Germond & Witcover, 1985, pp. 362–67; Goldman & Fuller, 1985, pp. 208–14). This list said a good deal about the choice that was going to be made. The attractiveness of shaking up the odds with a nontraditional choice was more important than seeking out the best person (after Mondale) to be president of the United States. All of the finalists were younger; all would bring some excitement to the campaign; all were liberal. The Democrats were abandoning a 30-year practice of selecting a well-known U.S. Senator,[16] as well as the New Deal–Fair Deal tendency to balance a liberal Northerner with the selection of a southern or border state vice presidential candidate.

Walter Mondale announced his historic choice on July 12 in the Minnesota State Capitol, where he had declared his own candidacy. In her remarks, Representative Ferraro said:

> When Fritz Mondale asked me to be his running mate, he sent a powerful signal about the direction he wants to lead our country. American history is about doors being opened, doors of opportunity for everyone, no matter who you are, as long as you're willing to earn it. These last few hours, I've got to tell you, I've been on the phone talking with friends and supporters around the country. There's an electricity in the air, an excitement, a sense of new possibilities and pride. My good friend, Charlie Rangel, the congressman from Harlem, said to me, "Gerry, my heart is full." So is mine.

This was a day of triumph for all who had sought the nomination of a woman for major office and a day of excitement for all who welcomed the development. But in ideological terms, when liberal Walter Mondale picked liberal Geraldine Ferraro, it was equivalent to moderate conservative Gerald Ford

---

[16] Beginning with Senator Harry Truman in 1944, the only time the Democrats did not nominate a senator for vice president was in 1980 when Vice President Mondale was renominated. The vice presidential nominee who was closest to Geraldine Ferraro in experience was Republican Richard Nixon in 1952. He also had just six years of congressional experience (two House terms and the first two years of a Senate term) and was regarded as a comer in his party.

picking conservative Robert Dole in 1976. The Mondale coalition had not been expanded at all.

If the argument for an acceptable-to-the-South vice presidential nominee had been rejected, another opportunity came in the selection of the Democratic national chairman.[17] The choice was Georgia state chairman Bert Lance. Lance was highly regarded by Mondale (and campaign chairman James Johnson) for his loyalty when the Mondale campaign was in feeble condition prior to the Georgia and Alabama primaries, for the amount of money he had raised for them, and as a useful contact with Jesse Jackson. Lance himself was only mildly positive about the idea and specifically warned James Johnson not to do anything during convention week (Germond & Witcover, 1985, p. 388). The Mondale core group, exhausted at the end of a long nomination struggle and out of touch with other Democrats,[18] went right ahead without consulting anyone. On Friday night preceding the convention, the *Atlanta Constitution* and the *Los Angeles Times* both carried stories that Lance was to replace Californian Charles Manatt as national committee chair.

The Lance announcement caused immediate problems. The minor problems involved protocol. It is customary for an incoming nominee to replace the national chairman, but not until *after* the national convention, and Manatt was being displaced during a convention in his home state. The major problem was that the Lance appointment emphasized links to the Carter administration and tied the Mondale campaign to the banking irregularities that had forced Lance's resignation as director of the Office of Management and Budget in 1977. Many delegates thought this was stupid and were not bashful about telling the Mondale core group. The Mondale leadership backed down. The face-saving solution was that Manatt remained as Democratic National Committee head, longtime Mondale aide Michael Berman would become executive director, and Lance would be appointed "general chairman" of the campaign (a position from which he rather quickly departed). But while all this was happening, the headlines dwelt not on Ferraro and the daring choice to put a woman on the ticket but on Lance and intraparty controversy. Walter Mondale had made his historic move and then, just as quickly, shifted public attention away from it.[19]

What about the Hart and Jackson coalitions (which together included 1,630 delegates)? Negotiations had been going forward with Gary Hart since the

---

[17] The appointment of the national committee chair is not always used in this way, but there are precedents. For instance, when John F. Kennedy picked a Southerner (Lyndon B. Johnson) for vice president in 1960, he asked Senator Henry Jackson of Washington, who had also hoped to run for vice president, to be Democratic national chairman.

[18] The principals were in Minnesota focusing on the vice presidential selection. From there, they headed to Lake Tahoe for what was intended to be a rest stop before the convention itself.

[19] The Lance appointment did not help in the South at all. Lance was not that popular with many southern Democrats, so his appointment probably would not have given Mondale that much of a boost. And as things worked out, Mondale lost more ground because Lance's friends thought he had been shabbily treated.

end of the primaries and were crystallized through the intercession of Edward Kennedy in late June (Goldman & Fuller, 1985, pp. 219–22; Weinraub, 1984a). Essentially, Hart agreed not to press his credentials case against so-called tainted Mondale delegates in return for some concessions on rules that would be important to Hart in 1988. Hart's name would be placed in nomination, but he would not make statements that might damage Mondale in the fall. At the convention, a Fairness Commission was created to look into rules to which Hart (and Jackson) objected. There were a number of concessions to the Hart coalition within the platform committee, and the Mondale coalition agreed to vote for the one plank (imposing more explicit limits on a Democratic president's use of military force) that the Hart forces had brought to the convention floor. These agreements were a little grudging but also relatively easy to reach. Mondale needed to unite the party, and Hart (looking to another possible run in 1988) could not afford to play a divisive role. Whatever their personal feelings, both men understood this.

Reaching an accord with the Jackson coalition was more difficult for several reasons. Jackson was sensitive about his position as the black spokesperson at the convention, all the more so because most establishment blacks were supporting Walter Mondale. (There were, in fact, more black delegates pledged to Mondale than to Jackson.) Even if Jackson himself had been disposed to compromise, his supporters (being relatively inexperienced in politics) seemed to feel that concessions should be made to the Jackson coalition simply because Jackson had run. Many were unaware that their limited numbers placed them in a poor position to make demands.[20] And when Jackson was explicit about his wishes, they were often so far to the left that agreeing to them would have severely handicapped the Mondale campaign in the fall. As things developed, Jackson was promised some representation in the Mondale campaign leadership and some concessions within the platform committee. Mondale leaders also agreed to a slightly stronger affirmative action plank on the floor. But Jackson planks on no first use of nuclear weapons, cutting defense spending, and elimination of the second runoff primary (a common practice in the South) were all defeated. On the latter two, the Hart coalition joined with the Mondale coalition to swamp the Jackson supporters.

If the Convention stage is where nomination politics blends into election politics, the speeches are perhaps the aspect of the convention that gives the greatest opportunity to reach the voters.[21] Most conventions have at most one memorable speech, such as Barbara Jordan's in 1976 or Edward Kennedy's in 1980. The 1984 Democratic convention got three: Mario Cuomo's, Jesse Jackson's, and Walter Mondale's.

---

[20] It is worth recalling that John Glenn and Jesse Jackson did about equally well in the primaries that both entered, but Glenn dropped out because of poor performance.

[21] William Adams has pointed out that in 1984, "three-quarters of the registered voters told pollsters that they watched the conventions on television at least one night, and from one-fifth to one-third have said that they make their candidate choices during the late summer convention periods" (1985, pp. 18-19).

New York Governor Mario Cuomo's keynote address focused not on the popular president's personality but on issues. Speaking rhetorically to President Reagan, he said:

> In fact, Mr. President, this nation is more a "Tale of Two Cities" than it is a "Shining City on a Hill." Maybe if you went to Appalachia, where some people still live in sheds, and to Lackawanna, where thousands of unemployed steel workers wonder why we subsidized foreign steel while we surrender their dignity to unemployment and welfare checks; maybe if you stepped into a shelter in Chicago and talked with some of the homeless there; maybe, Mr. President, if you asked a woman who'd been denied the help she needs to feed her children because you say we need the money to give a tax break to a millionaire or to build a missile we can't afford to use—maybe then you'd understand.

He had no sooner finished speaking than commentators began discussing Cuomo as a presidential possibility in 1988. But this had been a Democratic speech, not a Mondale speech (Mondale had not been mentioned once by name.); and as soon as the speech was over, Governor Cuomo left San Francisco, pleading the press of business elsewhere.

Senator Gary Hart had an opportunity to play the role of the gallant loser but only sounded determined and so was less impressive. "We will never give up. . . . If not now, someday we must prevail. If not now, someday, we will prevail." But Jesse Jackson, about whom Mondale leaders had been keeping their fingers crossed, gave a stunning display of penitence and theatricality. "If in my low moments . . . I have caused anyone discomfort . . . that was not my truest self. . . . Charge it to my head, so limited in its finitude; not to my heart, which is boundless in its love for the entire human family. I am not a perfect servant. . . . Be patient. God is not finished with me yet."

Walter Mondale had worked as long and as hard on his acceptance speech as he did on the selection of the vice presidential candidate, and Geraldine Ferraro's acceptance speech gave him a dramatic introduction. He meant to speak plainly to the American people about himself and his positions.

> Here is the truth about the future: We are living on borrowed money and borrowed time. . . . Whoever is inaugurated in January, the American people will have to pay Mr. Reagan's bills. The budget will be squeezed. Taxes will go up. And anyone who says they won't is not telling the truth. I mean business. By the end of my first term, I will cut the deficit by two thirds. Let's tell the truth. Mr. Reagan will raise taxes, and so will I. He won't tell you. I just did. . . . That's my plan to cut the deficit. Mr. Reagan is keeping his a secret until after the election. That's not leadership; that's salesmanship.

The speech was well delivered and was one of the best of Walter Mondale's political career. But in attacking Mr. Reagan on economics and leadership, he was aiming his thrust straight at the incumbent's strongest issue and most popular personal trait.

THE STRUCTURE OF COMPETITION

How did we end up with these two candidates? Can't America do better than Reagan and Mondale? Or Ford and Carter? Or whoever the major party nominees happen to be in 1988? This question is asked constantly during election years. It reflects dissatisfaction with the quality of the nominees, but it may also reveal a lack of understanding of what the nominees represent.

Our president is a symbol for the country. He is treated with respect; we speak of his wife as the First Lady. There is an implication here that he should be the best among all Americans. This isn't necessarily so. The best person, depending on the context, may be a path-breaking scientist, a skillful surgeon, an accomplished musician, or someone who has demonstrated great talent in any of dozens of different pursuits. What we need from a president is not talent or virtue measured on some absolute scale, but political leadership. Specifically, he should advocate policies that are acceptable to a majority of citizens and should have the competence to get these policies accepted and implemented. It follows that a presidential nominee should represent policies acceptable to a majority of the members of the nominee's political party and that the party members think this person can do the job.

Acceptable policies and personal competence are not unrelated to winning the nomination, but they are not directly tested by the candidate's ability to win delegates. As we have seen, the ability to win delegates is very much affected by the structure of competition. Suppose there had been a moderate midwestern governor in 1976 who split the moderate Democratic vote with Jimmy Carter in Iowa and New Hampshire. This would have meant that Birch Bayh would have gotten the most delegates in Iowa and that Morris Udall would have won in New Hampshire. Or suppose that John Anderson had not run in 1980 and that George Bush had therefore gotten the moderate votes that went to Anderson. This would have meant Bush victories in Vermont and Wisconsin and much larger Bush margins in Massachusetts and Connecticut. We can't be sure of these "might have beens," but we can be certain that winning or losing a presidential nomination does not depend on the intrinsic merit of an aspirant. *Success in nomination politics depends on both the strategy that is followed and the structure of competition.*

Frank Mankiewicz, Senator George McGovern's 1972 campaign director, compared the success of the McGovern strategy to bidding a grand slam in bridge. "You get to the point where your partner puts his cards down and you see it can be won, but only if the trumps break right, if the queen is where you want it, and all the finesses work" (Lydon, 1972). The 1972 structure of competition had McGovern and New York Mayor John Lindsay on the left, Senators Hubert Humphrey and Edmund Muskie at center-left, Senator Henry Jackson and Congressman Wilbur Mills (long time chair of the Ways and Means Committee) at center-right, and Governor George Wallace on the right. McGovern was stronger on the left than Lindsay (who dropped out after Wisconsin), and Wallace was more popular in the South than Mills. The Muskie campaign collapsed midway through the primaries, and Jackson did not prove to be a strong candidate. Consequently, the final structure of competition had McGovern on the left, Humphrey center-left, and Wallace on the right. There were votes on the right but not enough to nominate Wallace; and given the 1972 delegate selection procedures (Lengle & Shafer, 1976), McGovern got more delegates than Humphrey. Did this prove that George McGovern was the best Democrat who could have been nominated in 1972? Not at all. It is simply another illustration that winning the nomination means that the candidate's strategy has been successful in view of the structure of competition in the party that year.

A second major point we have seen in this chapter is that *there is a fundamental difference between a multicandidate structure of competition and a two-candidate structure of competition.* We have seen multicandidate structures of competition in the cases of the 1980 Reagan and 1984 Mondale nominations and two-candidate structures of competition in the cases of the 1976 Ford and 1980 Carter nominations. In the first two instances, it was not at all clear during Initial Contests who would emerge from the nomination process. Indeed, after George Bush won the Iowa caucuses in 1980 and after Gary Hart won the New Hampshire primary in 1984, there was some reason in both cases to think they would be the eventual nominees. Once Reagan and Mondale did emerge during Mist Clearing, though, the odds were against anyone being able to mount a successful challenge against them. In the Ford-versus-Reagan and Carter-versus-Kennedy cases, the structure of competition remained about the same from Early Days on through the Convention itself. Ford, Reagan, Carter, and Kennedy were strong candidates when their races began, and all came to their respective conventions with substantial delegate support.

John Aldrich, who developed a formal model of the nomination process (1980a, 1980b), found that a multicandidate structure of competition tends to be unstable. He reasons that all candidates (and the reporters covering them) develop expectations about how well they should do. If they do better than expectations, they develop positive momentum. If they just meet expectations, then there's a "that's what they were expected to do" reaction. If they do less well, then their campaigns are in trouble. "The larger the number of candidates," Aldrich writes, "the greater the number who cannot possibly meet . . . expectations" (1980b, p. 664). Therefore, early in the race, we should expect the field to be "winnowed down" to a much smaller number of viable candidates. In other words, Fred Harris, Sargent Shriver, Birch Bayh, and Morris Udall could not possibly get the same liberal Democratic votes in 1976, and Howard Baker, George Bush, and John Anderson could not get the same moderate Republican votes in 1980.

In a two-candidate contest, on the other hand, both coalitions could have legitimate expectations of getting about half of the delegates over the long run. These expectations have a better chance of being borne out, as they were with Ford and Reagan in 1976, in which case the structure of competition can remain stable from Early Days on through the Convention.

A third conclusion about the structure of competition is that *the four stages of nomination politics can be understood in terms of increasing information about the structure of competition.* During Early Days, we do not even know who all the competitors will be. Some plausible candidates may consider making the race, then decide not to do so. When Initial Contests begin, we know who the candidates are and who is likely to be fighting for liberal, centrist, and conservative votes, but we do not yet know which of the candidates will be successful in attracting this support. By Mist Clearing, information about the delegate strength of the surviving coalitions can be added to the left-right positioning of the candidates. This gives much more substantial information about the structure of competition than earlier guesses based on the momentum that a candidate is thought to have established. Finally, test votes at a convention provide nearly complete information about relative coalition strength. Even the absence of a test vote may suggest that a winning coalition is in too strong a position to be challenged.

COALITION STRUCTURE

Knowing the structure of competition leads to a more important general point. Structure is important. What we have seen in these sketches of four nominations is the gradual organization of a winning coalition around the successful candidate. These coalitions have both *internal structure*, which depends on their composition, and *external structure*, which includes those activities the coalition must carry out to reach audiences whose support is necessary and those activities that are shaped by the context in which the coalition finds itself. Both internal structure and external structure change as the coalition moves through the four stages of nomination politics. The internal structure becomes more complex, and the external stucture varies as the context changes. To see this, we shall look at internal structure and external structure in a little more detail.

Internal Structure

The idea of internal structure follows from an observation made in 1952 by Herbert Simon (who won the Nobel Prize in economics for his work on decision making).

> Complexity in any body of phenomena has generally led to the construction of specialized theories, each dealing with the phenomena at a particular 'level.' Levels are defined by specifying certain units as the object of study, and by stating the propositions of theory in terms of intra-unit and inter-unit behavior. (Compare the sequence of elementary particle-atom-molecule in physics and the sequence: gene-chromosome-nucleus-cell-tissue-organ-organism in biology)." (pp. 1030–31)

Levels of analysis may thus be understood as nested concepts. The unit on any particular level of analysis is made up of smaller components from a less inclusive level. The same unit is also contained within a larger unit on a more inclusive level. Atoms are made up of elementary particles and are contained within molecules. Similarly, groups are made up of individuals and are contained within coalitions.

For our purposes, a coalition will be understood as having three analytical levels, each with its own set of attitudes and behavior. At the first level, there is the *activist*, a citizen who is active in politics. The activist's attitudes are a set of valenced cognitions about political objects; and the set of behaviors includes those appropriate to nomination politics, electoral politics, or whatever form the activist is engaged in. The next level is the *group*, which is defined as a set of activists. The group attitudes are shared attitudes on such topics as the group's goals, norms, and environment; the group's behaviors are those that fall into a reasonably stable pattern of interaction. Finally, *coalition* is composed of a set of groups. The most important coalition attitudes are those that fall into the intersection of the sets of attitudes of member groups. Coalition behaviors need not be overtly coordinated, but the member groups are dependent on each other for achievement of the coalition goals.

The social sciences have developed rich theories of individual behavior, group behavior, and coalition behavior; the above definitions follow from these theories. Also, implications about politics flow from the definitions. A coalition is not just a collection of individuals. Rather, one must consider the groups to which the activists belong, understand how the shared attitudes of groups modify individual behavior, and consider which coalitions could be constituted from the existing groups. For example, in both the 1976 and 1980 Republican conventions, there were groups of delegates responsive to the leadership of Senator Jesse Helms and thus unwilling to cooperate with the platform strategies suggested by Reagan leaders. And what about black delegates to the 1984 Democratic convention who had committed themselves to Walter Mondale before Jesse Jackson decided to run? Surely their views of the contest between the Mondale and Jackson coalitions were different than those of white delegates. Thinking this way about the composition of a coalition suggests where tensions are apt to develop and thereby helps to understand coalition behavior.

How does the internal structure of a coalition develop in the four stages of nomination politics? Until the candidate decides to seek the nomination during Early Days, there isn't any meaningful distinction between internal and external structure. At most, there are groups of potential supporters. There is likely to be a tiny group of close advisors with whom the candidate takes counsel and who may perceive a possible candidacy when it is invisible to everyone else. The group of Georgians who began thinking about the possibility of a Carter candidacy is an example of this. There may also be enthusiasts without any close ties, such as liberal Democrats who were anxious for Edward Kennedy to run when Jimmy Carter seemed so weak in mid-1979.

Depending on the skills contained within the candidate's core group, they may constitute all the structure there is for a while, or they may recruit a few key persons, such as a press aide and/or a fund-raiser. The next groups likely to be created are those that will run the campaign in states where the Initial Contests will take place. If the campaign does not meet expectations, the structure—and the candidacy itself—may collapse at this point. Otherwise, an initial group of delegates is acquired, and coalition building begins.

The first groups of delegates are likely to admire the candidate and to be in close agreement with him on policy questions. By the Mist Clearing stage, this may not be so. Assuming the candidacy is still viable, two closely related things are likely to have happened. The appeal of the candidate is likely to have changed from "Our governor is the perfect candidate for you" to "Our governor may not be the *perfect* candidate for you, but he's certainly better than any of the other candidates, and he stands a real chance to win." Morris Udall used a version of this argument in the spring of 1976, when he said he was the only horse the liberal Democrats had to ride. The related change in Mist Clearing is that the candidate is going to attract different groups of delegates—groups whose first choice was some other contender and who are in less than full agreement with the candidate on policy questions. Therefore, coalition management becomes more of a priority because of the greater number of groups in the coalition and the increasing diversity of the groups.

By the time of every recent convention, a winning coalition has emerged. This means, of course, that the leaders of the winning coalition need to stay in touch with all of their member groups and keep them on board. Leaders of challenging coalitions want just the opposite, so appeals will focus on those groups thought to be unhappy for one reason or another and on those issues to which these groups might be responsive. Thus, the Ford coalition began to woo Mississippi delegates just as soon as Ronald Reagan announced that he was going to tap Richard Schweiker as his vice presidential nominee. And on the night of the crucial 16–C vote, when a story appeared in the *Birmingham News* headlined, "Ford Would Write Off Cotton South?" President Ford himself called Mississippi chairman Clarke Reed to deny that such a strategy was being considered. Similarly, when the Kennedy coalition wanted to challenge the Carter coalition at the 1980 Democratic convention, they offered platform amendments dealing with potential unemployment and picked up votes from groups of Carter delegates who were also labor union members.

The composition of the coalitions has a great deal to do with the policies endorsed by the convention when the platform is adopted or a candidate is nominated. In 1968, for example, James Clarke and John Soule found that 85 percent of the Democratic delegates and 90 percent of the Republican delegates said that the most important attribute for a presidential candidate was agreement in principle between the candidate and the delegate (Clarke, 1970). In 1972, Jeane Kirkpatrick reported that 90 percent of the Democratic delegates and 81 percent of the Republican delegates said that a chance to influence the party on policy was either an extremely important or a very important reason for their participation in politics (1976, p. 101). The extremely conservative 1984 Republican platform and the liberal 1984 Democratic platform certainly reflected the views of the coalitions at those conventions.

Not only are policies important, but there is some consistency over time in the states that join liberal and conservative coalitions. A study of five contested Democratic conventions between 1952 and 1976 found that the states with the most liberal voting records were Wisconsin, Oregon, Arizona, New Hampshire, Michigan, Massachusetts, Iowa, South Dakota, Vermont, and New York; those with the most conservative voting records were South Carolina, Louisiana, North Carolina, Texas, Delaware, Arkansas, Florida, Kentucky, Missouri, and Georgia. A parallel study of six Republican conventions between 1940 and 1976 shows that the states with the most moderate voting records were Connecticut, New York, New Hampshire, Oregon, Vermont, Maine, New Jersey, Michigan, Massachusetts, and Maryland. The state delegations with the most conservative voting records were Texas, Mississippi, California, Alabama, North Carolina, Idaho, Louisiana, Ohio, New Mexico, and Oklahoma (Costain, 1978, Appendix 2).[22]

The Republican coalitions have been a little more stable over time than the Democratic. There has been a strong tendency for southern Republicans to be conservative and for the East plus Michigan, Minnesota, and Oregon to end up in moderate coalitions. Still, comparison of these findings with an earlier study (Munger & Blackhurst, 1965) indicates that recent coalitions are less regional in character. The left coalition in the Democratic party includes groups from all regions except the South. The right coalition in the Republican party has included groups from all regions of the country except the East; and in 1980, the Reagan coalition reached into Pennsylvania, New York, and New England for support. Increasingly, Democratic conventions are ending up as contests between left and nonleft coalitions and Republican conventions as struggles between right and nonright coalitions (Costain, 1978). Hence, the change in internal structure from Early Days to the Convention is apt to be a growth from a single group composed of the candidate and his closest advisors to a coalition whose groups have been drawn from all parts of the country.

External Structure

Each coalition exists in a specific institutional context, and each institution has certain functions. In order to carry out these functional requirements, the coalition must be able to attract the attention and support of specific audi-

---

[22] It should also be remembered that there is considerable turnover in delegates from convention to convention. From 1944 through 1968, 65 percent of Republican delegates and 64 percent of Democratic delegates were attending their first conventions (Johnson & Hahn, 1973, p. 148). Therefore the same state may have quite different groups of delegates attending conventions at different points in time. For example, the California Republican Assembly whose hero was Governor Earl Warren in 1952 was very different from the California Republican Assembly of 1976 and 1980, whose hero was Governor Ronald Reagan.

ences. For a nomination coalition to succeed, it must be able to gain delegates. To do this, the coalition must be able to reach *reporters, voters in the primary election states,* and the *delegates* themselves. Its chances of successfully doing so are affected by the *structure of competition,* the *legal requirements that set the dates and conditions of delegate selection,* and the *convention rules.* In nomination politics, external structure is focused on these half-dozen elements. More generally, it embraces the structured activities carried on to reach audiences whose support is essential, and those constraints that delimit the coalition's ability to do so.

In truth, it should be added that external structure is much harder to define satisfactorily than internal structure. Referring to our earlier discussion, a coalition is put together from the less inclusive levels of analysis. So long as one knows which activists are included in which groups and which groups are included in which coalition, the internal structure is completely specified. But looking outward from the coalition, virtually everything can be considered as part of its environment. The number of elements must be limited somehow, or external structure would include so many things that it would be useless as a concept. Our way of limiting it will be to focus on those activities necessary for a coalition to carry out its institutional functions and on the constraints that facilitate or inhibit it from doing so.[23]

We have already looked at one very important element of external structure—the structure of competition—in some detail. Clearly it makes a difference whether a candidate is the only one who is appealing to a segment of party support or is one of four fighting for the same votes. What other connection is there? From the time of the Early Days decision to enter until at least through the Initial Contests, perhaps the most important element of external structure is the media. There are two phrases used to refer to the traveling press corps: "surrogate audience" and "alternate audience." The former refers to the reporters' view of themselves; the latter to the politicians' view of the reporters (Arterton, 1984, p. 28).

The view of the reporters as surrogates implies that they are substitutes for citizens who are busy elsewhere and that the reporters' task is to ask questions on behalf of the general public. The national political reporters who travel with the candidates during Early Days and prior to Initial Contests are quite conscious that they constitute a screening committee that plays an important part in the winnowing process (Broder, 1970, pp. 11–14). They carefully consider problems in reporting past campaigns—such as neglecting long-shot candidates who turn out to do quite well, putting too much attention on the "horse race" aspects of the campaign, not providing enough information about candidates so readers can make judgments about their character, not examining issues in enough detail—and they do their best to

---

[23] External structure corresponds to what has been variously called contextual or institutional properties, or environmental constraints, except that temporal effects are separated out from external structure for distinct treatment.

prevent these problems from recurring (Matthews, 1978). The reporters' goal is to bring the public solid information about the serious candidates.

The campaigners, however, treat the reporters as an alternate audience—that is, one to be treated differently from the voters to whom candidate images and issue positions are being projected. The coalition leaders observe that the media give greater coverage to "serious" candidates; therefore, they spend a great deal of time trying to convince the press that their candidate is serious. Part of this is done by arranging the schedule of the candidate or campaign spokespersons or both so that they can spend time with the press. Part of it is done by trying to manipulate press expectations so the candidate will meet them. For example, as part of his standard itinerary in any community, Jimmy Carter met with newspaper editorial boards. Also, in New Hampshire in 1976, the Carter entourage consistently talked of that state's Democratic primary as a race between Carter and Udall, thus drawing attention away from the structure-of-competition advantage Carter had as the only center-conservative candidate in New Hampshire.

The most advantageous thing that can be done, of course, is to be available at a time when there is hard evidence that the candidate has met the expectations of a serious candidate. Thus, instead of leaving to campaign in Massachusetts and Florida, Jimmy Carter stayed in New Hampshire in 1976 to be available to the press when favorable returns came in. The result was that he was on all three television networks and on the covers of *Time* and *Newsweek*.

When the Mist Clearing stage arrives, the surviving candidates have a changed relation with the press. First, they are now indisputable news sources, and they will receive coverage without having to make special arrangements to be available to reporters. For example, from the week of the Nebraska primary (just after the Texas, Indiana, Georgia, and Alabama primaries, when he had done very well) until the end of the 1976 primaries, Ronald Reagan received more coverage in the *Washington Post* than Gerald Ford (Aldrich, Gant & Simon, 1978). Second, the size of the traveling press corps increases, and there are more requests for information and interviews. This requires additional staff to handle the reporters. These two developments, the greater prominence of the candidate and the increasing number of reporters, give the candidates more control over what is written.

At the same time, the statements of an aspirant viewed as a likely nominee may be scrutinized more closely. For example, in the spring of 1980, newspaper articles began to appear with headlines such as "Reagan Economic Views Still Show Few Specifics" and to say such things as economic "generalities persist, even when unresolved contradictions lurk beneath them." And in the spring of 1984, the Mondale and Hart positions on governmental support of failing industries (such as the federal loan to Chrysler) began getting a more detailed examination from the press. This closer scrutiny after Mist Clearing means that a candidate may have more difficulty with issue positions than heretofore.

Another change in external structure at the Mist Clearing stage is greater concern with the acquisition of delegates. Obviously, there has been some concern with this all along, but so few delegates are at stake in the early primaries that impressions of probable success are more important. Impressions, however, cannot move a candidate from the 200 or 300 delegate votes that establish him as a formidable contender to the 1,500 needed to nominate.[24] In the 1980 New York primary, for example, Senator Kennedy got 59 percent of the vote to President Carter's 41. The *New York Times* story began, "Senator Edward M. Kennedy decisively defeated President Carter in the New York and Connecticut primaries yesterday." But because of greater attention to the task of delegate acquisition, President Carter got 129 delegates, 46 percent of New York's total and, in defeat, moved 8 percent closer to the number of delegates needed for renomination.

Delegate acquisition also means that the coalition must be able to work state (and district) conventions and put on primary campaigns. In 1984, the proportion of Democratic delegates elected or bound by primaries dropped from 74 percent to 53 percent, the first decline in the popularity of primaries since 1968. The proportion of Republican delegates so chosen dropped from 74 to 61 percent. (Ranney, 1985, Appendix F). Even with this decline, the ability to put on a primary campaign that impresses the voters in a state remained slightly more important than the capacity to bargain with state political leaders who are presumably influential in conventions. This, in turn, calls attention to another feature of external structure in nomination politics: the rules that specify how votes are to be cast and how delegates are to be allocated to one candidate or another.

Votes are presently cast under a system in which each voter casts a single ballot for the preferred candidate. This is an important reason why the structure of competition is so important in multicandidate contests. In 1980, a moderate Republican in New Hampshire had to decide whether to cast that single vote for Bush or Baker or Anderson. In 1984, a liberal Democrat in New Hampshire had to decide whether to vote for Jackson or Mondale or Cranston or McGovern or Hart. Among other things, this requires that voters decide which candidate they prefer among several who are advocating very similar policies and (even more difficult) that they figure out which candidates have the best chance of surviving so their votes aren't "wasted" on candidates who are about to be winnowed out.

Steven J. Brams has suggested an alternative called *approval voting*, in which the voters are allowed to cast votes for as many candidates as they choose but cannot cast more than a single vote for each candidate.[25] Brams has shown that approval voting has a number of desirable properties—for

---

[24] These numbers are simply illustrative. The actual numbers vary from convention to convention. The Democrats had 3,008 delegates in 1976, 3,331 in 1980, and 3,933 in 1984. There were 2,259 Republican delegates in 1976, 1,994 in 1980, and 2,235 in 1984.

[25] There are other voting schemes: negative voting, in which one can cast negative votes for candidates one dislikes; cumulative voting, where one can cast multiple votes for candidates one particularly likes; and so forth.

instance, it eases the burden for the voter, and it favors the strongest candidate—but the most important property for our present concern is that it is insensitive to the number of candidates in multicandidate races. Voters can cast ballots for the candidates they favor whether there are two or seven or any other number running (Brams & Fishburn, 1978, 1983). In an exit survey at the time of the 1980 New Hampshire primary, ABC News asked voters whom they would have supported if they had been able to vote for as many candidates as they chose. Recall that the election results were Reagan 50 percent; Bush 23 percent; Baker 13 percent; and Anderson 10 percent. The "approval voting" results were Reagan 58 percent; Bush 39 percent; Baker 41 percent; and Anderson 26 percent. Reagan continued to be the most popular candidate; but with support from moderate Republicans no longer split, the votes for the moderate candidates increased dramatically. If adopted, approval voting would tend to reduce the importance of the structure of competition and slow down winnowing so that multicandidate races would be more stable.

Election results are used in three basic ways to divide delegates among candidates: a winner-take-all system, in which the candidate with the largest number of votes gets all of that state's delegates; a proportional scheme, in which each candidate who gets more than some threshold share of the vote receives a proportionate share of the state's delegates; and a district plan, in which the division of delegates among candidates depends on who gets how many votes within congressional districts. The rules vary from state to state, but each state has some variation of these basic forms.

The effect of the actual rules, the hodgepodge used in a given year, has been studied by comparing the actual delegate count with what would have resulted if some alternate form had been used. Senator McGovern would have had the largest number of delegates using any of the three pure forms in 1972 (Pomper, 1979), but if winner-take-all rules had been in effect, Senator Hubert Humphrey would have gone into the California primary with substantially more delegates than McGovern (Lengle & Shafer, 1976).

Similarly, Gerald Ford and Jimmy Carter would have had the largest number of delegates in their respective parties in 1976 under any of the three pure systems (Gerston, Burstein & Cohen, 1979; Pomper, 1979). But if pure proportional representation had been in effect in 1976, Carter's rivals would have been in a stronger position; and if winner-take-all rules had been in effect, Carter would have obtained a decisive lead even more quickly. On the Republican side, if pure proportional representation had been in effect, Ford would have led Reagan after the Pennsylvania primary by a ratio of 1.3 to 1. If winner-take-all rules had been in effect, Ford would have led Reagan in delegates by a ratio of 5.4 to 1. Ford actually led at this point (ignoring the New York and Pennsylvania delegations, as do the above figures) by a ratio of 3.2 to 1.

If pure proportional representation had been in effect in the 1984 Democratic contest, Walter Mondale would have ended up nearly 400 votes short of the 1,967 required for nomination, and Hart and especially Jackson would have been in stronger positions (Orren, 1985, pp. 39–41).

In other words, the effect of a different set of delegate allocation rules in the cases above would have been to change the strategic situation at important junctures during the nomination contest. Would Hubert Humphrey have won in California if he, and not George McGovern, had come in as the front-runner? Would Ronald Reagan have dropped out if Gerald Ford had had five times as many delegates as he did? Would Hart and Jackson have been able to block Mondale's nomination in 1984? Obviously, we don't know; but the rules on delegate allocation do affect the perceived strength of a candidate. The strength of a coalition, in turn, affects its ability to acquire resources, and this certainly *could* affect the outcome of subsequent primary elections.

The Convention stage has the most elaborate set of rules. A convention organizes itself by receiving a series of committee reports: credentials, permanent organization, rules, and platform. In recent decades, there have been battles waged over three of these: credentials, rules, and platform. The last big credentials fight came in 1972 when the Democrats voted to seat McGovern delegations rather than rival delegations from California and Illinois. There were rules fights in both 1976 and 1980. Rule 16–C, which would have required prior announcement of the vice presidential nominee, was the major tactical battle at the 1976 Republican convention. And Rule F3(c), which would have released delegates from their obligations to support particular candidates, was contested at the 1980 Democratic convention. Platform fights were features of the same two conventions. Each of these contests was initiated because a coalition (usually a challenging coalition) thought they would get some tactical advantage if they were able to win. But the contests also say that coalition leaders think credentials, rules, and platform are important in shaping the outcome of the convention.

One group of delegates—members of Congress—is favored because the convention proceeds under the rules of the House of Representatives. The House rules are designed to allow business to be transacted in a large body, and this of course is what a national convention is. But the House rules are different from the more familiar *Robert's Rules of Order*, and representatives who know which motion is proper enjoy a real advantage in a hotly contested floor fight. The platform has less impact on the convention itself than do the rules but has been shown to have real consequences for the actions of the executive and legislative coalitions to come (Pomper & Lederman, 1980, chap. 8).

Internal Structure, External Structure, and Time

Some actions taken by a coalition are due to its internal structure, to the activists who belong to the coalition, and to the groups into which their shared attitudes and behavior patterns assemble them. Other actions of a coalition are compelled by its external structure, by the activities necessary to gain the support of those who will allow it to achieve its goals, and by the constraints fixed by the rules of the game.

The levels of analysis within a coalition (activist-group-coalition) remain constant across institutions (although *who* is recruited into the coalition may vary). But the external structure will differ from one institutional domain to another. In nomination politics, internal structure grows more complex as one moves from Early Days to the Convention, and external structure is different from stage to stage depending on the context.

The actions of a coalition must be consistent with the demands of both internal structure and external structure. Perhaps the best example of this dual need was Ronald Reagan's selection of Richard Schweiker as a prospective vice presidential candidate in 1976. This was perfectly consistent with external needs—specifically, the need to gain additional delegates among the uncommitted moderates, and the desirability of broadening the appeal of the ticket in the fall. But this was inconsistent with the shared attitudes of some groups within the Reagan coalition, most particularly the Mississippi delegation.

The view of a political party taken in this book is based on what we can observe: a specific coalition in a specific institutional setting. There are other definitions—party as a unifying symbol, for example—but we want to explain what a party does. The principal activity we want to explain, to understand, is the strategy adopted by a party, and for this purpose, the coalition-in-institution is what we have to consider. Our general argument will be that *why* a coalition takes a particular action will be explained sometimes by its internal structure, sometimes by its external structure, and sometimes by both. *When* it takes a particular action will be explained by the temporal pattern of the institution in question.

SUMMARY

Substantively, this section of the book has covered the two principal patterns of contested presidential nominations: the relatively stable two-candidate race, in which two strong contenders struggle from Early Days on through the Convention itself, and the unstable multicandidate contest, in which one candidate tends to pull away from the field. We have seen two examples of both of these. Ford versus Reagan in 1976 followed the classic two-candidate pattern, and Carter versus Kennedy in 1980 approximated this. Reagan in 1980 and Mondale in 1984 are examples of races in which one candidate was able to do so well that he was established as the probable nominee by the Mist Clearing stage. There are, of course, variations from one nomination to another; but these are the two basic patterns in contested nominations.

Conceptually, this chapter has set forth the ideas of internal structure, external structure, and time. In nomination politics (as in other institutional domains), the internal structure of a coalition is made up of activists who are aggregated into the groups that make up the coalition. The external structure of a nomination coalition consists of the activities necessary to reach voters, reporters, and delegates; the structure of competition; the rules that state how and when votes will be cast and delegates allocated between candidates; and the rules and procedures of the convention. The four stages of the temporal pattern are Early Days, Initial Contests, Mist Clearing, and the Convention. These concepts should enable us to understand the strategies employed by those seeking presidential nominations.

Part Two

Electoral Politics

Chapter 3

Time and Internal Structure

Substantial differences exist between nomination politics and electoral politics. Nomination coalitions are made up of those groups willing to give their all for a particular candidate, whereas electoral coalitions are usually made up of all groups in the party. Nomination campaigns are aimed at getting delegates; electoral campaigns are aimed at winning votes.

Primary elections begin in February and last until early June. The general election takes place in every single state on the same day in November. The planning and organization for nomination politics begin at least a couple of years before the convention. All of electoral politics is compressed into the few months between the convention and the general election. In brief, *electoral politics is partywide, nationwide, and short.*

Some hints of the nature of electoral politics occur in the closing hours of the national convention, when the nomination has been captured and electoral politics has begun. After the acceptance speeches, division is put aside, and the assembly is transformed into a victory rally. The presidential candidate is joined by the vice presidential candidate, and both are joined by their families: the Mondales and Ferraros, and the Reagans and Bushes in 1984. The cheers continue, and the traditional pictures are taken.

Other party leaders—those who have held key positions and others who have sought the nomination themselves—make appearances to symbolize the partywide support to be given the nominees. In 1976, after considerable public coaxing, Governor Reagan joined President Ford, Vice President Rockefeller, and vice presidential nominee Dole at the Republican rostrum. At the 1980 Democratic convention, the demonstration was prolonged by inviting numerous Democratic leaders—national chairman John White, HHS Secretary Patricia Roberts Harris, Mayor Thomas Bradley of Los Angeles, Mayor Dianne Feinstein of San Francisco, and so on—until Senator Edward Kennedy finally appeared on the platform. In 1984, the Mondale and Ferraro families were first joined by Gary Hart and Jesse Jackson. Then George McGovern and John Glenn were added. Next came 1984 noncandidate Kennedy and, finally, black and Hispanic leaders, including Mayor Bradley of Los Angeles.

In part, this demonstration of unity is aimed at the millions of voters watching on television across the nation. While coalitions are struggling for the nomination, citizens are making tentative voting decisions. From 1948 through 1984, an average of 40 percent reported they had made their presidential choices before the conventions. Another 24 percent said they had made up their minds during the conventions (Flanigan & Zingale, 1983, p. 150; 1984 National Election Study). The remaining third of the electorate includes many who have only a minimal interest in politics. The faces on the convention stage constitute the image the party will present as it strives to gain the attention and win the support of these voters by November.

It would be a mistake, though, to think of this victory rally as *only* a public show. There is an affective unity—an emotional sense of belonging akin to that felt by a team of athletes—within a political party during an election campaign. The cheers of the delegates help to cement this feeling. Those who have supported the successful candidate get the thrill of seeing him as the party nominee. Those who worked just as hard for an unsuccessful aspirant get the chance for a few personal cheers when he comes to the stage. This common experience helps unify the party and set the stage for the campaign to come. After all, there is a great deal of work to be done by the party activists, and the time is very short.

THE TEMPORAL PATTERN

The Stern Limits of Time

The first thing mentioned by Gary Hart in his discussion of the differences between nomination politics and a general election campaign is that the latter "is a much briefer, more compact experience" (1973, p. 249). Of the various forms of politics, electoral politics has the most truncated time frame. Depending on when the national convention is scheduled, there may be as much as three and one-half months or as little as two months between the convention and the general election. The limits within which one must work vary, but even if the party opts for an early July convention, more must be accomplished in less time than in any other political setting.

It might seem that the campaign strategists would look ahead to this situation and try to prepare for it by making plans for the election campaign. But this overlooks what the candidate and his closest advisors are doing prior to the convention. For a good many months, winning the nomination itself is the goal to which their actions are directed. It may be that there are real questions about winning the nomination. How would the credentials fight turn out in the 1972 Democratic convention? Would McGovern get the disputed California delegates, or would he have to split them with Humphrey, making things much closer? Would Ford be able to withstand the 1976 Reagan challenges on convention rules, and would his very narrow margin in delegate support hold up?

Even if the candidate appears to have a large enough nomination coalition to win, obtaining these delegates is the focus of attention of the coalition strategists for a long enough time that they are likely to continue to organize their thinking around the imperatives of nomination politics. Questions about how the nomination is going to be ensured (for example, do you have good communications to the delegates on the floor?) occur to them a good deal more quickly than questions about what is going to be done in an ensuing fall campaign.

There are, of course, some presidents who can look forward to their own renomination.[1] In this case, however, their attention may well be focused on the imperatives of executive politics. If they have a foreign policy crisis on their hands or if the economy is shaky, they are going to give more attention to the troublesome policy area than to the relatively distant fall campaign.

The implication is that the only candidates who can "expand" the time available for electoral politics are those who can manage to assemble a winning nomination coalition early on and who are themselves free from the responsibilities of office. In recent years, this would be only Nixon in 1968, Carter in 1976, Reagan in 1980, and Mondale in 1984. The work done in advance of the conventions in three of these cases—the careful selection of Walter Mondale as Jimmy Carter's running mate in 1976, the attention Mondale devoted to the selection of Geraldine Ferraro in 1984, and especially the selection of George Bush and the extensive strategic planning done for Ronald Reagan in 1980—was important to the conduct of the general election campaigns. Still, such advance planning requires special circumstances. Most modern electoral coalitions are not able to focus on the fall campaigns until after the convention. The normal pattern forces them to work within tight, fixed time limits.

The sense of working within a very short time period is reinforced by polls that repeatedly announce the candidates' standings; these serve as reminders that only so many weeks remain until the election. In certain campaigns, these tidings were particularly ominous for one candidate or the other. In 1964, 1972, and 1984, the challengers began their campaigns far behind incumbent presidents; and while their campaigns made progress, they could

---

[1] A number of incumbents do not enjoy this prospect. Some cannot seek another nomination because of the 22nd Amendment; others are subject to a serious challenge from within their own party.

not close gaps of such magnitude. The first postconvention poll in 1964 gave Goldwater all of 31 percent. This rose only to 39 percent by election day. In late August 1972, the Gallup Poll gave McGovern only 30 percent, and he too ended up with 39 percent in the election. Immediately after the 1984 Democratic convention, Walter Mondale's support got up to the 40 percent level, and it did so again right after the first debate. But for most of the campaign, the survey estimates of his support remained in the high 30s.

In 1968 and 1976, candidates of the out party had commanding leads at the beginning but then watched them dissolve as the campaigns progressed. On Labor Day weekend in 1968, Richard Nixon had 43 percent of the vote to 31 percent for Hubert Humphrey and 19 percent for George Wallace. On election day, Nixon received 43.4 percent of the vote, while Humphrey got 42.7 percent. After the 1976 Democratic convention, the Gallup Poll gave Jimmy Carter a 62 to 29 percent lead over Gerald Ford; in the election, Carter received just a shade over 50 percent while Ford got 48 percent.

The 1964, 1972, and 1984 challengers—Goldwater, McGovern, and Mondale—were trapped by time. The election was only a short way off, and in spite of their best efforts, there seemed to be little they could do to convince the voters to move in their direction. In the 1968 and 1976 campaigns, supporters of the candidate whose lead was evaporating felt that the election was too far away. Still, all they could do was hope that the front-runner's lead would hold up until election day. From the Humphrey and Ford viewpoints, of course, the hope was that they would be able to gain fast enough to pass their rivals. But regardless of their position, all had their eyes on the calendar, and all knew that the season of passionate appeal to the electorate would be short.

One often hears pleas that American election campaigns be further shortened. The basis of this argument is that, especially after protracted nomination contests, the candidates are exhausted, campaign debts have been run up, and the voters are bored. There is something to this, and such an argument often is made by a weary campaign manager or a journalist who has gotten up at 6:00 A.M. time and again to cover another full day of campaigning. What the argument for a shorter electoral period overlooks is the number of things that must be done to conduct a presidential campaign on a subcontinental scale. Just as is true of nomination politics, there are a number of stages to a typical campaign, and it is hard to see how any of them could be omitted.

Organization and Planning

Organization and planning go on more or less simultaneously in the weeks following the national convention. The first question is who is going to fill the top jobs in the campaign organization. Frequently, more people feel they ought to be given top jobs than there are top jobs to fill. In 1964, for instance, Barry Goldwater decided that his longtime friend Denison Kitchell would be "head honcho" and that Dean Burch would chair the Republican National Committee. But F. Clifton White, who played an important part in rounding up delegates, very much wanted to be national chairman, and something had to be done about him. He was persuaded to accept the chair of Citizens for Goldwater-Miller. In 1972, George McGovern promised three people—Jean Westwood, Lawrence O'Brien, and Pierre Salinger—that each would chair the Democratic National Committee. It took some time to find assignments that O'Brien and Salinger were willing to accept after Westwood got the job.

Selection of a national chairperson is only the beginning. As we will see in Chapter 4, there are four principal activities that must be carried on by a campaign staff: campaign operations, public relations, research, and finance. Individuals must be recruited who have the skills and contacts to handle each of these responsibilities. And once the national appointments are made, the head of the campaign division must locate regional coordinators, each of whom will handle the campaign in several contiguous states. The regional coordinators, in turn, must tap state coordinators.

The staff needed to run in successive primary campaigns is much smaller than the nationwide organization required for the general election campaign. As Hamilton Jordan recalled the 1976 Carter campaign: "Early on, we had three very talented people that we just rotated in the primary period from Iowa to Massachusetts to Ohio to Florida to Wisconsin to Maryland and then to New Jersey. Of the 45 to 50 state coordinators [in the general election campaign], only 5 or 6 had been involved in our campaign previously" (Moore & Fraser, 1977, p. 132). Where do the other 40-odd state coordinators come from? Some have been involved in the nomination campaigns of losing aspirants. Some have been identified in the course of spring contests, especially if the nominee entered the primary in that state. Some come from other states. (The Kennedy organization in 1960 and the Carter organization in 1976 picked their state chairpersons from states other than those for which they had responsibility.) Perhaps the most fertile sources of leaders for the state campaigns are the regular party organizations in the state. Wherever the state chairpersons come from, the appointment is cleared with the state party organization unless the circumstances are very unusual.

Finally, the state leaders have to recruit county leaders (or town leaders in New England). As we will see later in this chapter, the heads of the presidential campaigns at the county level are largely Republican or Democratic activists who have been involved in previous presidential campaigns.

The organization of the campaign committees from nation to region to state to county has two consequences. First, there is a progressively greater overlap between the presidential campaign committees and the regular party organizations as one moves from the national to the county levels. While the headquarters of the Republican National Committee and the Reagan-Bush '84 Committee were some blocks apart in Washington, D.C., the chairmen of the Republican party and the Reagan-Bush '84 Committee in Franklin County, Ohio, were well known to each other.

Second, and more germane to our concern with the temporal pattern of electoral politics, all this organization takes time. The national chairperson has to pick a campaign director; the campaign director has to pick regional coordinators; the regional coordinators have to pick state directors; state directors have to tap county leaders. Assignments have to be made in research, public relations, and finance as well. Since each person selects subordinates in consultation with other party leaders, this process goes on sequentially. Finally, all those who are selected have to get to know one another and establish working relationships. It takes just as much time for a collection of individuals to become a functioning organization in electoral politics as in any other sphere of life. *There is no way of rushing the creation of a nationwide campaign organization.*

Planning begins as soon as individuals know their responsibilities in the campaign. This involves decisions about geographic concentration, positions to be taken on issues, media use, how the candidate is going to be portrayed, how the opposition candidate is to be attacked and by whom, what themes will tie all this together, and so on. Some of these things may not be worked out in detail in advance, but they are going to be decided *somehow*.

A key decision may be made when a reporter asks a question and the candidate answers off the top of his head because he thinks an answer is required, thus going on record with an issue statement or a characterization of his opponent. A partial plan may be thrown together hurriedly, as Joseph Napolitan did once Hubert Humphrey won the Democratic nomination in 1968. "I'm writing the campaign plan," he told Theodore White. "Do you know there isn't *any* campaign plan? I have to get this ready tomorrow" (White, 1969, p. 338). Or the plan may be quite comprehensive. The basic Reagan campaign plan in 1980 filled two bulky notebooks, and there were in fact more than 20 plans that were written for specific circumstances as they arose in the course of the campaign.

There is considerable variation here. What is improvised in one campaign is systematically planned in another. Over time, systematic planning is becoming more frequent; but in one way or another, decisions will be made.

The Organization and Planning stage is not very visible to the general public. After the 1976 campaign, Hamilton Jordan was asked why the Carter people let so much time go by after the Democratic convention without active campaigning. He replied: "Carter was in Plains most of the time with an occasional trip out, but we were busting our ass to put the fall campaign together. Tim Kraft and Phil Wise assembled a first-rate field organization, and we got control of our budget. Rafshoon was working on the media, and Pat Caddell started doing surveys in critical states. The time was well spent" (Moore & Fraser, 1977, p. 130). He might have added that the Carter coalition had time to do this because the 1976 Democratic convention was held in the first half of July. When a convention is held in late August, the Organization and Planning stage is forced into the early weeks of the campaign proper. Whenever it comes, though, and however thoroughly or hastily it is handled, Organization and Planning is a necessary prelude to the rest of the campaign.

Grand Opening

In the Grand Opening stage of the campaign, the efforts that follow from the plans made during the preceding stage first become visible to the public. This stage *includes all activities designed with an eye to sustaining and increasing the candidate's standing with the voters.* Just as the grand opening of a commercial venture is intended to bring customers to the establishment, and just as the opening night of a play is intended to spur lines at the box office, so the Grand Opening of a campaign should maintain a front-runner's lead in the polls or allow an underdog to catch up.

Grand Opening certainly includes the initial major speeches and the first campaign swings. For instance, Democratic candidates often have given their first speeches in Cadillac Square in Detroit on Labor Day and then have gone on about the country. Jimmy Carter chose to open his 1976 campaign on Labor Day with a speech at Franklin Roosevelt's "Little White House" at Warm Springs, Georgia, and then began a 10-state swing that took him to the Deep South, New York, Connecticut, the Midwest, and Florida. Walter Mondale and Geraldine Ferraro made a number of campaign appearances during August but began their formal campaign by marching in a Labor Day parade in New York City.

Incumbent presidents often stay close to the White House during the Grand Opening. Gerald Ford followed this pattern during September 1976, when he made any number of Rose Garden appearances. These were designed to keep the media spotlight on challenger Jimmy Carter and to permit Ford to be presidential when he did appear on newscasts. Ronald Reagan, a more confident incumbent, began his 1984 Grand Opening in California, speaking of the buoyant economy and of still better things to come in a second term.

How long the Grand Opening lasts depends on whether the campaign strategy appears to be leading toward the hoped-for results. Essentially, this stage of the campaign lasts as long as it is successful. Occasionally, a Grand Opening goes so well that it lasts for most of the campaign. Such was the case with the 1972 Nixon campaign. Even if the hopes of the campaign strategies are not being met, Grand Opening usually lasts for much of September. It takes at least that long to discover that things are not going well, and to devise an acceptable substitute course of action.

Campaign Adjustments

The next stage of a campaign occurs not at a specific point in time, but when the need for an adjustment becomes obvious. There are two general types of alteration: Tactical Adjustment and Strategic Adjustment.

Tactical Adjustment is much the simpler of the two. It is a response to some development. This may be a news bulletin that calls attention to a policy area and therefore suggests the desirability of the candidate's competence to deal with the question. It may be some troubling development within the campaign organization or an awkward statement by the candidate himself, such as Gerald Ford's reference in the second debate in 1976 to there not being any Soviet domination in Eastern Europe. The tactical adjustment in this case included a public statement by the President that he knew there were divisions of Russian troops in Poland, a telephone call to the president of the Polish-American Congress, and some meetings with ethnic group leaders. *A Tactical Adjustment is focused on the original development, is contained in time, and does not involve any general changes in campaign strategy.*

An *attempted* tactical adjustment involved the "meanness" issue that developed in the 1980 campaign when President Carter was viewed as making unnecessarily vindictive statements about Governor Reagan. Carter made an appearance on a Barbara Walters television interview, where he promised to "do the best I can to refrain from any sort of personal relationship with Mr. Reagan so far as criticisms are concerned." The attempt was unsuccessful because, two days later, President Carter said, "Reagan is not a good man to trust with the affairs of this nation." The suggestion that Governor Reagan was untrustworthy was enough to revive the "meanness" issue in the press.

A Strategic Adjustment is a somewhat more serious matter. It suggests that the campaign may be in real difficulty. If a projection of poll results shows a probable election loss, then groups in the electoral coalition are going to make their unhappiness known. If there is enough expression of discontent, then the campaign strategists are likely to try some new approach. This is in part because they can see the same difficulties as the members of the supporting coalition and in part because they need to do something to convince workers that an effort is being made to extricate the campaign from its difficulties. For example, in late September 1984, Walter Mondale's tax plan, which had been very prominent in his Grand Opening, quietly disappeared from view.

A Strategic Adjustment cannot be devised very quickly. It takes some time for complaints to work their way up through the campaign structure, and it takes more time for the strategy group to realize that the Grand Opening (in which they have some psychological investment, since they approved it) is not bringing about the desired results. It requires still more time for the strategy group to agree on the nature of the adjustment. The Grand Opening probably represented the satisficing agreement (that is, one acceptable to all group members) that they could reach most easily, and some time is required to discover an alternative approach that is acceptable to coalition members and has some promise of persuading voters. In fact, *enough time is needed to realize that a Strategic Adjustment is called for and then to figure out what to do, that not more than one or two real Strategic Adjustments can occur in a campaign.*

Time's Up

The last stage of a campaign is usually referred to by the media as the final drive or the climax of the campaign. It would be more accurate to call it the Time's Up stage. It is one of the ironies of electoral politics that the period just before the election is the time when the candidates have a chance to reach the largest possible audience because of the intense preelection coverage and is also the time when the strategists have the least control over what is happening. The meaning of Time's Up is that it is too late to make any more television commercials, too late to buy any more television time, too late to implement any new campaign emphases, too late to do the necessary advance work to prepare for more campaign appearances—too late, in sum, to do much more than carry out the plans that have already been made and hope that these efforts will be rewarded when the voters reach the polls.

The manifest tone of the campaign in the Time's Up phase depends on the probable outcome of the election. If the candidate is far in front, then his public appearances will have the aura of triumph. Other candidates will jostle for the honor of appearing at his elbow. The candidate may be weary, but the adrenalin stimulated by being at the top of a career in politics is enough to keep him going through the final days. If the candidate is far behind, we are likely to hear some bitter comments about the voters' failure to understand or his coalition's inability to work hard enough. He is tired, knows that he has done what he can, and needs to steel his ego against the bruises of defeat. If the race is close, then extra physical effort is put forth.

It is hard to say where the reserves of energy come from that allow this. The extra bit of energy expended on the campaign means that the candidate's voice sometimes fails and he is bone weary. But *in the Time's Up stage, it is too late to make any further plans or implement any new strategies.* And since the extra bit of effort may make the difference, he gives it willingly.

Summary

Of all the major forms of politics, electoral politics has the shortest time span. The limits vary from three and one-half months to a little more than two. Organization and Planning, Grand Opening, Campaign Adjustments, and Time's Up stages follow one another in rapid succession. The hope that the nominees bring from their convention triumphs leads to electoral glory for one and weary defeat for the other.

INTERNAL STRUCTURE OF ELECTORAL COALITIONS

Who are the activists involved in electoral politics? To which groups do their common attitudes lead them? How do these groups coalesce? Asking these questions calls our attention to a series of important political questions. How long have the activists been involved in politics? Are they more interested in patronage or in the direction of public policy? Are their issue preferences representative of the communities where they live, or are they closer to the preferences of fellow party members? Do the activists' shared attitudes make it more appropriate to think of parties being made up of issue groups or of demographic groups? Do the coalitions that are formed by the issue groups tend toward the center or toward the ends of the political spectrum?

The answers to these questions lead to very different kinds of political parties. If, for example, the activists are more interested in their own jobs, are simply spokespersons for their own communities, share attitudes with others in the same demographic categories (that is, union members, farmers, and so on), and form coalitions that tend toward the center of the political spectrum, then we have sluggish political parties that offer moderate alternatives to citizens. If, on the other hand, we have activists who are interested in issues, combine with others taking similar positions, and tend to form liberal or conservative coalitions (depending on the party), then the citizens are being presented with choices between quite diverse policies.

Core Groups and Strategy Groups

The most important strategists are those who belong to the *core group* and the *strategy group*. The core group consists of the candidate's own confidants, persons he has known well or worked closely with for some years. In the 1980 Reagan campaign, some members of the California "kitchen cabinet" were core group members, as were longtime associates Edwin Meese, Michael Deaver, and William Clark. In Walter Mondale's 1984 effort, the core group consisted of John Reilly, a political veteran and law partner, campaign chairman James A. Johnson, Robert Beckel, a former Carter staff member who was as earthy and aggressive as Johnson was buttoned down and brittle, and Michael Berman, who had been close to Mondale ever since Berman's student days at the University of Minnesota Law School. If the candidate's wife is interested in politics, she would obviously be a member of this core group. Rosalynn Carter and Nancy Reagan were among the most important of their husbands' political confidants; Pat Nixon apparently was somewhat less involved.

The strategy group is made up of those persons who are making the basic decisions about the campaign. Its membership is quite restricted, and it should not be confused with a publicly announced "strategy committee," some of whose members are likely to be key decision makers while others are included because their status calls for some kind of recognition. There is likely to be at least a partial overlap between the core group of confidants and the strategy group of decision makers. If the candidate himself is not present when the key decisions are being made (and he may be off campaigning somewhere), there must be persons present who know the candidate well enough to speak for him.

There are also likely to be members who have important operating responsibilities but who *may* not be as well acquainted with the candidate. These opposite tendencies were nicely illustrated by the two 1976 strategy groups. The Carter strategy group, was virtually an extension of the core group. Attorney Charles Kirbo, Hamilton Jordan, and Jody Powell were members, as were media consultant Gerald Rafshoon, pollster Pat Caddell, attorney Robert Lipshutz, and issues specialist Stuart Eizenstat. This strategy group was almost totally Georgian and, with the exceptions of Caddell and Eizenstat, completely lacking in national campaign experience.

The principal members of the Ford strategy group, on the other hand, consisted of White House Chief of Staff Richard Cheney, President Ford Committee chair James Baker, Ford Committee organization director Stuart Spencer, media consultant John Deardourff, and pollster Robert Teeter.[2] Neither Cheney nor Baker had been through a national campaign before, but Robert Teeter had considerable experience in political polling with the Detroit firm of Market Opinion Research, and Stuart Spencer and John Deardourff were two of the best professional campaign managers in the country. Between them, they could put together about 50 years of campaign experience. Where the Carter strategy group was unusual in being composed almost entirely of persons who knew Carter for some time, the Ford strategy group was unusual in its professional orientation.

Similar tendencies were evident in 1984, although the Mondale strategy group was more experienced than Carter's in 1976 by virtue of having gone through two vice presidential campaigns. The major Mondale decisions were made by longtime associates Reilly, Johnson, Beckel, Berman, and not too many others. The 1984 Reagan strategy group was led from the White House by James Baker and was composed of a White House contingent (including Mike Deaver, Richard Darman, David Stockman, and Paul Laxalt) and a campaign contingent (including Stuart Spencer, Bob Teeter, Richard Wirthlin, Ed Rollins, and Lee Atwater).

While core groups and strategy groups are fundamental, they are no more than the essential beginning of a campaign organization. The strategy groups make decisions about campaign emphases, but they cannot carry them out themselves. And they certainly are not a partywide coalition capable of reaching a national constituency.

Activists

Of all political activists, delegates to national conventions have been among the most extensively studied (McClosky, Hoffman & O'Hara, 1960; Niemi & Jennings, 1969; Soule & Clarke, 1970; Johnson & Hahn, 1973; Sullivan, Press-

---

[2] Robert Teeter provided a very nice description of the Ford strategy group. "The week spent at Vail (Ford's vacation home in Colorado) right after the convention was the key to the development of the fall campaign. . . . We came out of the Vail meeting a small group of men who got along, who knew and understood each other, who had a strategy in mind for the campaign. . . . Jim Baker, Dick Cheney, Stu Spencer, John Deardourff, and I were five people who got along as one unit and had a strategy in mind for what we were going to try to accomplish in the campaign" (Moore & Fraser, 1977, p. 123). Teeter did not use the formal language of group theory, such as David Truman's. "These interactions . . . because they have a certain character and frequency, give the group its moulding and guiding powers." From "interactions in groups arise certain common habits of response, which may be called norms, or shared attitudes. These afford the participants frames of reference for interpreting and evaluating events and behaviors" (1971, pp. 24, 33). But his reference to five individuals "who got along as one unit" is precisely why group theory is a useful way to analyze politics.

TABLE 3–1

Comparison of 1984 Convention Delegates and Ordinary Citizens

Characteristic	Democratic Delegates	All Democrats	All Republicans	Republican Delegates
Age				
18–29	8%	26%	32%	4%
30–44	45	26	26	27
45–64	38	31	24	60
65 and older.	6	17	18	9
Family income				
Less than $25,000	15	57	45	10
$25,000–50,000	43	38	44	33
More than $50,000	42	5	11	57
Education				
High school or less	11	72	60	12
Some college	18	16	19	25
College graduate	71	12	21	63
Ideology				
Liberal	50	25	12	1
Moderate	42	45	44	35
Conservative.	5	24	40	60

Source: *New York Times* and CBS Polls, *New York Times*, August 24, 1984, p. 10. Copyright © 1984 by The New York Times Company. Reprinted by permission.

man, Page & Lyons, 1974; Soule & McGrath, 1975; Kirkpatrick, 1976; Farah, 1982; Farah, 1984; Miller & Jennings, 1986; and many others). Republican convention delegates differ from Democratic convention delegates, and both sets of delegates differ from average citizens.

Table 3–1 presents some information about 1984 convention delegates, comparing them to ordinary members of their own parties. Republican activists tended to be a bit older than Democrats. The average age of a Republican delegate was 51 compared with 45 for a Democrat. Republican delegates were also wealthier than Democratic delegates. Democratic activists, however, were better educated than Republican activists. Fifty-one percent of the Democratic delegates had attended graduate or professional schools as compared to 35 percent of the Republicans. But while Republican delegates were older and wealthier and the Democratic delegates were better educated, *both* sets of delegates were wealthier and better educated than their respective partisans. American party activists are drawn disproportionately from the upper socioeconomic strata.

The significance of this is a matter of perspective. On the one hand, politics is a complicated business. To keep track of the various motions being voted on at a national convention, run a county campaign, stay in touch with workers, coordinate activities with state and national organizations, and so on, organizational and communication skills are necessary. These are most often associated with higher education and white-collar jobs. Moreover, college educations and professional status are increasingly common in modern American society. On the other hand, persons who have these advantages are less likely to have faced unemployment or the problems of feeding their family on food stamps. Since they lack the personal experience of making ends meet on a very limited income, they *may* be less sensitive to issues affecting poor people.

Another striking characteristic of activists is their greater emphasis on ideology. The Democratic tendency to liberalism and the Republican tilt toward conservatism can be seen clearly enough among ordinary party members. Table 3–1 shows about twice as many liberals among Democrats as among Republicans and five conservatives among Republicans for every three among Democrats. But compare the ideological contrast among activists. Fifty percent of the Democratic delegates declared their liberalism as compared to only 1 percent of the Republicans, and 60 percent of the GOP delegates said they were conservative as contrasted with only 5 percent of the Democratic delegates.

The greater polarization of national convention delegates is a very familiar finding. The principal variation from one presidential year to the next is which party is least in touch with its constituents. In 1956 and 1964, the Republican delegates were much more conservative than the persons they were nominally representing. In 1972 and 1976, the Democratic delegates were much more liberal than the average Democrat. In 1980 and 1984, there was considerable ideological distance between both sets of delegates and the citizen members of their parties. But the constant element was that Democratic delegates were more liberal than the average Democrat, and Republican delegates were more conservative that the average Republican.

Does this polarization mean that activists are interested in issues? Data collected by Richard Hofstetter in 1972 allow us to address directly this topic and several other important subjects as well.[3] Half a dozen questions in the Hofstetter study dealt with the activists' attitudes about engaging in or avoiding certain types of party activity. Two of the questions concerned the importance of issues, two tapped the importance of prior party service in candidate

---

[3] This study of campaign activists was conducted as part of a broader investigation of television coverage of the Nixon-McGovern campaign (Hofstetter, 1976). The persons to be interviewed were selected the same way the leaders themselves were chosen: by nomination downward. The names of state campaign directors were obtained from the national offices of the Committee to Re-Elect the President and the McGovern-Shriver Committee. The state leaders were then asked to supply names of the persons in charge in counties that were part of a national sampling frame. One hundred ninety-seven Democrats and 204 Republican county leaders were contacted and interviewed. One series of questions dealt with the activists' backgrounds, motivations, and activities. Another dealt with their issue positions, their perceptions of the candidates, and their perceptions of the preferences of voters in their counties. (This latter series of questions was identical to questions being put to citizens who lived in the same counties.) The first set provided information about the county leaders' attitudes and activities; the second set told us how representative these leaders were.

TABLE 3–2
Activists' Feelings of Obligation about Party Work

Activity about Which Attitude Is Held	Difference Score*	
	Democrats	Republicans
Hold strong personal beliefs about a number of different issues	72.3	54.4
Select nominee strongly committed on variety of issue positions	73.0	46.5
Weigh party service very heavily in selecting candidate for nomination	3.2	23.0
See that those who work for party get help in form of job and other things, if needed	6.5	23.2
Keep elected officials strictly accountable to party organization	4.4	13.2
Follow decisions of party leaders even when you disagree	−9.4	0

* Higher scores mean greater obligation to engage in activity. For details, see Appendix A–3.1.
   Data source: 1972 Hofstetter study.

selection or patronage, and two dealt with discipline that ought to apply to party leaders or to the activists themselves.

An analysis of the responses to these queries about party norms appears in Table 3–2. The higher the difference score for a given item, the greater the obligation the activists felt to engage in that behavior. There were noticeable differences between the parties. Issues were more important to the Democrats, both in their belief that they ought to have strong views themselves and in their belief that the nominee ought to be committed on a number of issues. (To some degree, the greater Democratic emphasis on issues probably reflects the interests of McGovern supporters in 1972.) Republicans were more likely to emphasize organization. This is reflected in the higher scores for the consideration of party work in candidate selection and patronage. The activists of both parties were in close agreement on the inappropriateness of party discipline as it applied to themselves.

Important as these party differences are, the similarities between the parties are more consequential. As you read down either party column in Table 3-2, it is clear that much more emphasis is placed on issues than on any other activity. The next most important party norms, those concerning party service and patronage, come a long way back of the issue items. Most electoral activists have a strong interest in the policies followed by the government once they are in office. It would be too much to say that an interest in issues draws them to politics in the first place. The activists are likely to speak of their motivations in global terms; they are attracted to politics per se. But it is also clear that an interest in issues is an important component in their attraction to politics and in the way they participate once they are involved.[4]

Issue Groups

Republicans

In choosing concepts to analyze the internal structure of coalitions, we have assumed that groups composed of activists with shared attitudes would be important. When we put this assumption together with the finding that issues are central to the thinking of presidential activists, it follows that issue groups composed of persons with shared attitudes on public policy ought to be a useful way to understand electoral parties. The characteristics of such groups should tell us what the party is agreed upon, what questions divide it, and something of the dynamics by which the party determines its positions on issues that cause internal division.

Issue groups of this kind have been isolated by means of a cluster analysis. The details of this procedure are set forth in Appendixes A–3.2 and A–3.3, but the essential point is that individual activists are assigned to the issue group with which each has the highest average agreement. An activist who does not meet the stipulated level of agreement with any group is treated as an isolate. Thus we can be sure that we have groups whose members share common outlooks on questions of public policy, and a number of activists who do not belong to any group because their own views are unique.

There were four Republican issue groups and seven Democratic groups in 1972.[5] The sizes and *approximate* locations of the Republican groups with respect to each other are depicted in Figure 3–1. The word *approximate* is stressed because the issue space is multidimensional.

There are four policy areas. International involvement concerns the extent of American involvement overseas: foreign commitments, defense spending, foreign aid, and (in the late 1960s and early 1970s) Vietnam. Economic management deals with the use of the federal government to direct the economy: the level of spending, the use of economic controls, and views of the power of the federal government. Social benefits includes those programs that shelter individuals from adverse circumstances: health care, social services, education, and so forth. Civil liberties deals with civil rights, police power, busing, and lifestyle questions.

Since there are four policy areas, one group might agree with a second on international involvement but disagree on economic management, and agree

---

[4] Of the many types of local politicos reported in the literature, these electoral activists most closely resemble the citizen politicians in western cities such as Los Angeles and Tucson (Marvick, 1973; Arrington, 1975). Here, too, one finds an emphasis on issue politics and a relative disinterest in patronage.

[5] This analysis of group characteristics is based largely on a memorandum written by Stephen D. Shaffer.

FIGURE 3–1
Republican Issue Groups

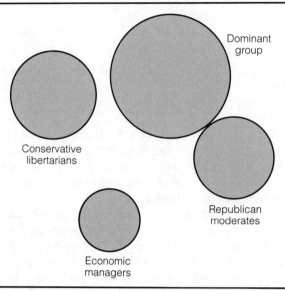

The size of the circles corresponds to the size of each group. The location suggests the *approximate* location of each with respect to the others in issue space. For details, see Appendix A–3.4.

with a third on international involvement and economic management but disagree on civil liberties. Therefore, no *two*-dimensional analysis (such as Figure 3–1) is going to be able to depict all of the relationships between the issue groups. The positions of the issue groups in all four policy areas are summarized in Table 3–3.

All four Republican issue groups took moderate positions on public-policy questions. The dominant group was poised on the boundary between moderate and moderate conservative. Within this group, there was likely to be disagreement on individual questions relating to international involvement and economic management. For example, about a quarter of the members—a larger proportion than any other GOP group—were willing to entertain the idea of bringing some American troops back from overseas. As with other Republican groups, there was some disagreement on social benefits and considerable consensus on civil liberties. This high rate of agreement on civil liberties, an agreement that tends slightly in a conservative direction, may reflect the large number of southern Republicans in this group. Half of the southern Republican activists belonged to the dominant group. This was the *only* case in *either* party where a majority of those from *any* region could be found in a single group.

TABLE 3–3
Republican Issue Groups: Varieties of Moderation

Group	Position in Policy Area*				Percent of Activists in Group
	International Involvement	Economic Management	Social Benefits	Civil Liberties	
Dominant group	Moderate (3.5)	Moderate (3.6)	Moderate (3.5)	Moderate conservative (3.2)	29.8%
Conservative libertarians	Moderate conservative (3.2)	Moderate conservative (3.3)	Moderate conservative (2.7)	Moderate (3.8)	14.9
Economic managers	Moderate (3.8)	Moderate liberal (4.9)	Moderate (3.5)	Moderate conservative (3.3)	7.7
Republican moderates	Moderate (4.1)	Moderate (3.7)	Moderate (4.3)	Moderate conservative (3.3)	11.6
Isolates	Moderate (4.4)	Moderate (4.1)	Moderate (3.6)	Moderate (3.5)	35.9

* The figures in parentheses are median positions on scales that vary between 1 and 7. In general a high score (7) represents a dove position in international involvement and a willingness to use government power and resources in the domestic policy areas. A low score (1) represents the opposite.

The convention followed for substantive interpretation of the scale scores was: values from 1 to 2.4, conservative; 2.5 to 3.4, moderate conservative; 3.5 to 4.5, moderate; 4.6 to 5.5, moderate liberal; 5.6 to 7, liberal. This classification is nothing more than an aid to understanding and should not be taken as a precise denotation. Note, for example, that if the upper boundary of moderate conservative had been moved from 3.4 to 3.5, there would have been 10 moderate conservative scores rather than 6.

Data source: 1972 Hofstetter study.

The conservative libertarians [6] had slightly more conservative positions on international and economic matters and much more conservative preferences on social benefits. On civil liberties questions, though, they depart from the other Republican groups in a liberal direction. The conservative libertarians were much more skeptical about the wisdom of increasing police authority and were much more in favor of open housing. It was in this group that one heard the strongest echo of the historic Republican position in favor of civil rights.

The economic managers were the smallest Republican group and departed

---

[6] The names I have given these issue groups can only suggest their policy tendencies, not serve as complete descriptions. With four different policy areas, a name that stated a group's full set of preferences would be too long to be useful. The problem is the same as with your family name. Your genetic inheritance comes equally from all four grandparents, but for the sake of convenience, your paternal grandfather's name is used as your family name.

from the dominant group's issue profile primarily on economic questions. They were slightly less in favor of cutting spending and were far more willing to use federal means to regulate the economy than any other Republican group. Not only did they provide the single example of a Republican group taking a moderate liberal position, but the economic managers were less worried about the power of the federal government than any *Democratic* group.

The Republican moderates were close to the dominant group's positions on economics and civil liberties but took more liberal positions with respect to international involvement and social benefits. The Republican moderates were much more in favor of foreign aid than any other Republican group. It was the only GOP group in which a majority were open to the idea or supportive of increasing welfare payments and the only one that was united in favor of a social security increase.

The isolates were also essential to an understanding of the internal structure of the Republican party. Consider the information in Table 3–3. More Republicans were isolates than fit into any one of the Republican groups. Furthermore, their policy preferences were moderate in all four policy areas. Since the isolates were more numerous and relatively liberal, it would *seem* that they ought to have been able to move the Republican party somewhat to the left. Yet they weren't. Why not?

One explanation was that the isolates were not members of any group. The workings of the computer program through which these groups were found are such that if only two activists had agreed with each other (at a stipulated level), they would have been joined in a two-person group. Therefore, we know that these persons tended to be isolated from each other as well as from the groups. Lacking allies, it was hard for them to move their party in any direction. Here is a reason for the political impotence of the Republican liberals. Not only were they outnumbered, but they disagreed among themselves.

Democrats

The Democratic issue groups are portrayed in Figure 3–2, and their issue preferences are summarized in Table 3–4. The issue space is again multidimensional, but because Democratic disagreements in 1972 were focused on international questions and economic matters, it is possible to think of the vertical dimension as being related to international questions and the horizontal dimension as being related to domestic matters. This analogy should *not* be pressed very far; some groups are out of place with respect to some other groups in certain policy areas. But the upper left-hand group (liberal pacifists) was the most dovish and the most liberal on domestic questions, and the group farthest to the right (coercive individualists) tended to be hawkish and conservative.

FIGURE 3–2
Democratic Issue Groups

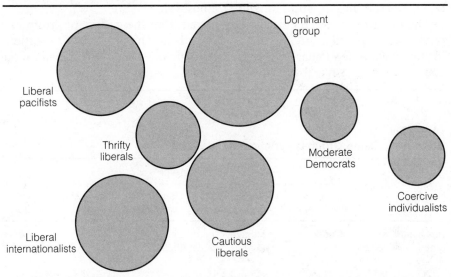

The size of the circles corresponds to the size of each group. The location suggests the *approximate* location of each with respect to the others in issue space. For details, see Appendix A–3.4.

The dominant group in 1972 took prototypical Democratic positions. It was united in favor of both social benefits and protecting the civil liberties of minorities. On foreign policy, it opposed defense spending but was divided on questions of foreign aid and keeping American troops overseas. On economic matters, it contained some skeptics about continued reliance on the federal government and showed real division on federal spending.

The liberal pacifists and liberal internationalists both took even more liberal positions on social benefits, but these two groups departed from the dominant group in opposite directions on international matters. The liberal pacifists wanted to bring American troops back home, did not want to spend for defense, and had doubts about foreign aid.[7] This group represented a tradition in the Democratic party that goes back to Henry Wallace and William

---

[7] In our coding decisions, we called these dovish positions "liberal," and the positions taken by the liberal internationalists were called "moderate." In so doing, we followed the usage of most commentators on the 1972 election. These coding decisions had no bearing on the group structure that we found. However we had decided, there would have been one Democratic group departing from the dominant group in the direction of more overseas participation and one in favor of withdrawing.

Jennings Bryan. The liberal internationalists were solidly in favor of defense spending and foreign aid. This group followed the tradition of John F. Kennedy, Dean Acheson, and Franklin D. Roosevelt.

The other Democratic groups all departed from the dominant group in a conservative direction in one or more issue areas. The profile of the cautious liberals was quite similar to that of the dominant group but a shade more conservative on several items. The cautious liberals were more willing to

TABLE 3–4
Democratic Issue Groups: Varieties of Liberalism

Group	Position in Policy Area*				Percent of Activists in Group
	International Involvement	Economic Management	Social Benefits	Civil Liberties	
Dominant group	Moderate liberal (5.1)	Moderate (4.4)	Liberal (5.8)	Liberal (6.5)	22.0%
Liberal pacifists	Liberal (6.1)	Moderate liberal (5.0)	Liberal (6.4)	Liberal (6.5)	14.3
Liberal internationalists	Moderate (4.3)	Moderate (4.5)	Liberal (6.2)	Liberal (6.5)	14.8
Cautious liberals	Moderate liberal (4.8)	Moderate (4.5)	Liberal (5.7)	Moderate liberal (5.2)	14.3
Thrifty liberals	Moderate liberal (4.6)	Moderate conservative (3.3)	Liberal (5.7)	Liberal (6.3)	7.1
Democratic moderate	Moderate liberal (5.1)	Moderate conservative (3.4)	Moderate (4.5)	Moderate liberal (5.1)	5.5
Coercive individualists	Moderate (4.0)	Moderate conservative (3.2)	Moderate liberal (4.6)	Moderate (3.8)	6.0
Isolates	Moderate (4.1)	Moderate (4.3)	Liberal (5.9)	Moderate liberal (5.0)	15.9

* The figures in parentheses are median positions on scales that vary between 1 and 7. In general a high score (7) represents a dove position in international involvement and a willingness to use government power and resources in the domestic policy areas. A low score (1) represents the opposite.

The convention followed for substantive interpretation of the scale scores was: values from 1 to 2.4, conservative; 2.5 to 3.4, moderate conservative; 3.5 to 4.5, moderate; 4.6 to 5.5, moderate liberal; 5.6 to 7, liberal. This classification is nothing more than an aid to understanding and should not be taken as a precise denotation. Note, for example, that if the upper boundary of moderate had been moved from 4.5 to 4.4, there would have been 12 moderate liberal scores rather than 9.

Data source: 1972 Hofstetter study.

spend for military purposes, much more divided on the wisdom of national health care, and perceptibly more favorable to the police. It was this last difference that moved the cautious liberals from "liberal" to "moderate liberal" on civil liberties.

The thrifty liberals took positions similar to the dominant group except on economic questions. Here their difference was quite pronounced. For example, the dominant group was split on the question of cutting government spending. All the thrifty liberals thought that government spending ought to be reduced.

The Democratic moderates were the smallest Democratic group. While they had similar international positions to the dominant group, they took more conservative positions in all the domestic policy areas. Along with the thrifty liberals, all the Democratic moderates favored a reduction in government spending. They were also less enthusiastic about social programs and protecting minority rights than the dominant group. As a matter of fact, a majority of this group opposed any increase in welfare payments.

The coercive individualists, so called because they wanted the government to let them alone but were quite willing to use the police at home and the military abroad to intervene in the lives of others, marked the Democrats' conservative perimeter. The coercive individualists were about as hawkish as the liberal internationalists and opposed foreign aid as well. They were almost as opposed to federal spending as the thrifty liberals and more resistant to a strong federal government. Some 55 percent of this group opposed national health care, whereas only 20 percent of the moderates did so. And the coercive individualists were the only group of Democratic activists who maintained that the police should be given increased authority. In every single policy area, the coercive individualists took the most conservative Democratic position.

The Democratic isolates were mirror images of the Republican isolates. Both held minority views within their own parties. The Republican isolates were relatively liberal; the Democratic isolates were relatively conservative. Neither set of isolates was very influential, because of lack of agreement among themselves or with any of the issue groups. The major contrast was that the Democratic isolates were less important to an understanding of the Democratic structure because there were so few of them.

Organizational Groups

The members of an issue group do share common attitudes. Since they are active members of the same national campaign organization, they are also tied together in a common communication network. But the members of these groups are spread out across the country. The Republicans in Boston and Birmingham and Boise who are all "economic managers" do not talk with each other and then act collectively as a unit. Their political actions are taken in their own communities, along with other members of their local campaign organizations. The same is true of Democratic "liberal internationalists" in Trenton and Toledo and Tacoma. Consequently, if we want to understand the positions the parties take on various policies, we need to see how the issue groups combine into issue coalitions (and we shall do so presently). But a full understanding of campaign activities also requires that we look at *organizational groups* such as those of the formal party committees.

There are important distinctions between the presidential parties and the formal party committees. Most of the presidential activists are also members of state or local committees. Five eighths of the Republican campaign activists and half of the Democratic campaign activists held some party office in 1972, and 76 percent of the Republicans and 69 percent of the Democrats had held some party position in earlier years. These figures probably underestimate the extent of involvement of presidential activists in formal party activities, since one can be active without being elected to party office.

While most presidential activists have been involved in the formal party organization, the reverse is *not* true. There are quite a few party committee members who have not been active in presidential campaigns. As we saw in the discussion of the Organization and Planning phase, a presidential campaign is organized downward. Regional chairs pick the state chairs, who in turn pick the county chairs. And most people who have organized states in presidential campaigns can think of at least *one or two* county chairs they have been cautioned to stay away from, either because these county chairs' reputations would harm the presidential campaign, or because their activity level was so close to zero that there was no hope of getting them to do any work. Of course, there are also county leaders who do excellent jobs. Ray Bliss and John Bailey, for example, both built strong local organizations in Akron, Ohio, and Hartford, Connecticut, respectively, before either one became state chairman and then national chairman of his own party. Since there is so much variation in capacity and vigor among state and county leaders, an effort is made to select individuals who have the capacity to put on an effective presidential campaign. Considering all this, it is important to know something about state and county committees in order to understand activities carried on at that level, but we should not think of the presidential parties and the formal party organizations as identical.

Until very recently, we knew everything and nothing about state and local party organizations. We knew a great deal because there has been a long tradition of careful studies of party organizations. Harold Gosnell's classic *Machine Politics: Chicago Model* and David H. Kurtzman's detailed *Methods of Controlling Votes in Philadelphia* both date from the mid-1930s, and there are many analyses from still earlier periods. At the same time, we knew rather little because it has been almost impossible to generalize from individual studies. What was found in Los Angeles was not found in Detroit. The motive patterns discovered in Massachusetts and North Carolina conflicted with motive patterns found in Oklahoma and Illinois, and neither set of findings seemed to apply in St. Louis.

As long as we were dependent on studies in particular localities, we could not tell whether there was a national pattern with some local exceptions, or regional patterns, or one pattern for the majority party and another for the minority party, or just what. All we knew was that things differed from one locality to another. Fortunately, a good nationwide study of state and local party organizations was recently conducted by Cornelius P. Cotter, John F. Bibby, James L. Gibson, and Robert J. Huckshorn.[8] They gave us some carefully researched answers to these questions about general patterns, and I am relying on their study in the discussion that follows.

County Committees

Almost everywhere in America, the local units of political parties are county committees. There are some exceptions (such as the town committees in New England) in areas where counties are less important political units, but county committees are by far the most common. The county committees are stable volunteer organizations led by longtime community residents. There are few paid staff members on the local level, but the vast majority of the committees (90 percent for the Democrats, 80 percent for the Republicans) do have full sets of officers. Chairing a county organization is a part-time job; the median number of hours worked each week during a campaign is 12. The average chairperson has lived in the community for about 30 years and is 49 years old, 10 years older than the average county leader in a presidential campaign. Both age and length of residence reflect the stable nature of these committees (Gibson, Cotter, Bibby & Huckshorn, 1982, pp. 15–16).

The county committees essentially have three clusters of activities. The first has a campaign focus and involves staying in touch with the candidate organizations (such as those supporting the presidential candidates) and carrying on their own campaign activities. More than three quarters of the county committees distribute campaign literature. Roughly two thirds raise funds and distribute money to candidates, organize campaign rallies, conduct telephone campaigns, and publicize candidates through newspapers, posters, and yard signs. About half send press releases to the media and mailings to voters and conduct registration drives and door-to-door canvassing. A third of the committees buy radio or television time, and relatively few use opinion surveys or buy billboard space. Democratic committees are more likely to conduct registration drives; Republicans are more likely to give money to candidates, send out mailings, and use opinion surveys. Otherwise, the activity levels of the two parties are virtually identical.

---

[8] Three of these principal investigators—Bibby, Cotter, and Huckshorn—were National Committee fellows during the 1960s under a program sponsored by the National Center for Education in Politics, and they maintained an active interest in politics thereafter. Because of their firsthand knowledge, they had reason to be suspicious of claims made by other academics that parties were disappearing.

The other activity clusters of county committees are both organizational. One is a fairly common set of election-period behaviors, such as bimonthly meetings and having a formal budget. The other is a much less common activity cluster involving organizational maintenance between election periods through such means as a year-round headquarters and having a telephone listing (Gibson et al., 1982, pp. 20–21, Tables 3, 5).

Neither the Democratic nor the Republican party had stronger county committees. In fact, both parties' county committees were strongest in the East, next strongest in the West, next in the Midwest, and weakest in the South. Since both had the same regional pattern of strength and weakness, this seemed to reflect traditional local ways of doing things rather than party organizational efforts. Both parties had much stronger county committees in the most populous counties (Gibson et al., 1982, pp. 24–28).

Finally, the investigators found no evidence that county committees were declining in strength. To the extent that there was change, it was in the direction of stronger local parties. Fifty percent of Democratic chairs and 58 percent of Republican chairs said that their county organizations were stronger than had been the case 5 to 10 years earlier. When the records of specific party activities in the same counties were compared with Paul Beck's analysis of 1964 data, (Beck, 1974), by far the most common pattern was no change. In other words, the county committees that were conducting registration drives or distributing literature or whatever in 1964 were still doing so in 1979–80. Where there was change, it was in the direction of increased activity (Gibson et al., 1982, Tables 10, 12).

State Committees

Whereas almost all the county committees are part-time volunteer organizations that become dormant between campaigns, this is no longer true of state committees. As recently as the early 1960s, four fifths of the state committees curtailed their staff operations between campaigns. Now only half of them do so, and 90 percent have a permanent headquarters location. The role of the state party chair depends on which party controls the governorship. The out party (that is, the party that does not control the governorship) is always led by what Huckshorn calls an out-party independent. In the case of an in party, the chair may be either a political agent—a designee of the governor who normally follows the governor's lead—or an in-party independent, whose own power base is independent of the governor (Huckshorn, 1976, ch. 4). Regardless of the chair's relationship with the governor, over 90 percent of the state parties have either a full-time chair or an executive director. The average state party has a staff of just over seven employees and a budget of $340,000.

State committee activities may be divided into institutional support (those activities that benefit the entire party) and candidate support. Institutional support involves such things as voter identification, registration, and get-out-

TABLE 3–5

Organizational Strength of State Parties, 1975–1980

Organizational Strength	Number of State Parties		
	Republican	Democratic	Total
Strong	8	2	10
Moderately strong	27	11	38
Moderately weak	9	26	35
Weak	1	6	7
Total	45	45	90*

* Data were available for 90 of the 100 state parties.

Source: John F. Bibby, Cornelius P. Cotter, James L. Gibson, and Robert J. Huckshorn, "Parties in State Politics," in Herbert Jacob and Virginia Gray, eds., *Politics in the American States* (Boston: Little, Brown, 1983).

the-vote drives, as well as polling. More than two thirds of the state parties are engaged in voter mobilization activities, and more than half do polling. Both of these figures have been stable since the early 70s. About half of the state parties are also involved in issue development. Voter mobilization and polling are, of course, also of benefit to candidates running for office. In addition, nearly 90 percent of the state committees conduct seminars in campaign methods, many offer research assistance, and about half of the state parties make contributions to candidates. The proportion of state committees making candidate contributions has dropped a bit in recent years (Gibson, Cotter, Bibby & Huckshorn, 1981, pp. 22–28).

There are important variations in the strength of the two parties at the state level. To begin with, the Republicans have a decided advantage in organizational strength. Table 3-5 shows the results obtained when a robust index of party institutionalization[9] was used to categorize the strength of the state parties. Seventy-eight percent of the Republican state committees fell into the moderately strong or strong categories; 71 percent of the Democratic state committees fell into the moderately weak or weak categories.

Both parties had their strongest organizations—by far—in the Midwest; but thereafter, the regional patterns were different. The next strongest Democratic parties were in the West, then in the East, and the weakest Democratic parties were in the South. The second strongest Republican party organizations were in the South, the third strongest in the West, and the weakest were in the East (Gibson et al., 1982, pp. 24–25).

---

[9] The success of the research team in devising indexes in a substantive area that has long resisted quantitative analysis is likely due to the happy combination of long familiarity with political parties (Bibby, Cotter, and Huckshorn) and technical skill (Gibson).

The research team also had state data from five time periods since 1960, and this allowed them to investigate directly whether state parties were declining, as some writers alleged.

> Party organizations scored substantially higher on organizational strength measures at the close of the 1970s than in the early 1960s. In terms of the generally accepted thesis of party decline, these data have startling implications: the year in which *The American Voter* appeared (1960) marked the beginning of a decade or more of growth for party organizations. (Cotter, Gibson, Bibby & Huckshorn, 1984, p. 33)

National Committees

A few points should be made to facilitate comparison between local, state, and national committees (the latter covered in some detail in the next chapter). To begin with, when one moves from the state to the national level, there is a continuation of the shift that we saw between the local and state levels from part time to full time and from volunteer to paid staff. The national committees have been organized for a longer time, have larger staffs, and differ from state committees in the same ways that state committees differ from local committees.

A major difference between the state and national committees is that a state chair may be either a political agent of the governor or an in-party independent, but the national chair of the in party is always the designee of the president regardless of the strength of the chair's political base. This practice had a strong test when President Nixon wanted to replace Republican national chairman Ray C. Bliss. Bliss had been given widespread credit for rebuilding the party after 1964, and members of the Republican National Committee made it abundantly clear that they wanted him to keep the chair. Nonetheless, when Nixon sent an emissary to Bliss to ask for his resignation, Bliss obliged.

In partial consequence of this presidential dominance, the major organizational developments in both national committees have taken place when the party was out of office. In theory, a president could pay attention to party organization. In practice, presidents have been so busy with affairs of state that they have had little time to concern themselves with party organization. (The recent president most interested in his party was Gerald Ford. The Republican National Committee made real progress under Mary Louise Smith when he was in office.) Consequently, national Democratic party building took place under Paul Butler in the late 50s and under Robert Strauss between 1973 and 1977. Some has been taking place under Charles Manatt and Paul Kirk since the Democrats left office in 1981. The Republicans benefited from major developmental periods under Ray Bliss from 1965 to 1969 and under William Brock from 1977 to 1981.

The net of these party-building efforts has left the Republican National Committee in a far stronger position than the Democratic National Committee. Part of this is due to the considerable skill of the two most recent Republican out-party chairmen, Ray Bliss and William Brock. Part of it is also due to the greater neglect of their national committee staffs by the two most recent Democratic presidents, Lyndon Johnson and Jimmy Carter. Both were from the South, where the Democrats have their weakest state and local parties, as we have seen. Whether lack of experience with strong party organizations contributed to their neglect of the Democratic National Committee, we cannot be sure. What is clear is that in the 1980s, the Republican National Committee enjoyed a substantial organizational and financial advantage.

Issue Coalitions

Republicans

In our discussion of activists and issue groups, we saw that issues were important to electoral activists and that the Republican and Democratic activists could be regarded as belonging to issue groups with different sets of policy preferences. What kinds of coalitions can be formed by these groups? The fundamental answer is that in electoral politics, the dominant group ends up in a key position in the dominant coalition formed in each policy area. This hardly sounds surprising, but that's because we have been calling these groups "dominant." So far we haven't said why they should be so regarded.

The dominant Republican group is the largest Republican group, and this makes it easier for other groups joining with it to form a majority coalition. But one could construct a case to show why other groups would form coalitions among themselves rather than with the dominant group. The dominant group is the largest, but it includes fewer than 3 out of 10 Republican activists. Moreover, the median positions of the dominant group are more conservative than the median positions taken by all Republicans in each policy area. Why shouldn't the Republican activists who prefer more liberal postures form coalitions to move the party toward the center?

The reason for the strength of the dominant group lies in its ability to recruit allies whose policy preferences are closer to its own than to moderate opponents. The issue coalitions differ from one policy area to another, but the dominant group ends up as a member of each winning coalition. The Republican moderates take a more liberal position in international involvement, but the dominant group can form a coalition with the conservative libertarians and the economic managers. The economic managers prefer a more liberal posture with respect to the federal government's role in fiscal affairs, but the dominant group can join with the Republican moderates and the conservative libertarians. The situation with regard to social benefits is the same as for international involvement. In civil liberties, the conservative libertarians would prefer a more moderate posture, but the dominant group can form a coalition with the Republican moderates and the economic managers. Thus, there are three different coalitions in the four policy areas, and each one tends in a conservative direction.

The strength of the dominant conservative group lies both in its relative size and in its ability to find partners. The weakness of the Republican moderates, conversely, lies not only in their minority status but also in their difficulty in finding groups with which they can combine.

Democrats

The internal issue structure of the Democrats is somewhat more complex than that of the Republicans, but the process of coalition formation is essentially a mirror image of the Republican process. There are more issue groups in the Democratic party; there is greater issue distance between the most liberal and the most conservative Democratic groups, and the coercive individualists take relatively conservative positions in every policy area. But the dominant Democratic group (just as the dominant Republican group) is the largest and has the easiest time finding policy partners.

In international involvement, the dominant group faces opposition in one direction from the liberal pacifists and in the other direction from the liberal internationalists and the coercive individualists. But they can form a moderate liberal coalition in company with the moderate Democrats, the cautious liberals, and the thrifty liberals. There is pronounced division among Democrats on economic matters. But a majority coalition can be formed by the dominant group, the cautious liberals, the liberal internationalists, and the liberal pacifists. In social benefits, a winning coalition can be formed by the dominant group, the cautious liberals, the thrifty liberals, and the liberal internationalists. On civil liberties, the views of the dominant group, the liberal pacifists, the liberal internationalists, and the thrifty liberals are so similar that the process of coalition formation is almost automatic.

There are differences between the parties in the degree of exclusion. In the Republican party, the conservative libertarians and the economic managers are members of the dominant coalition in three of the four policy areas, and the Republican moderates are in two. In the Democratic party, the Democratic moderates are part of a winning coalition only on international questions, and the coercive individualists are never part of a winning coalition. In the Republican party, the more conservative groups are always members of the dominant coalition. In the Democratic party, the most liberal group (the liberal pacifists) is included only twice. But in both electoral parties, the dominant group is a member of the dominant coalition in all four policy areas.[10]

---

[10] There are two ways these predictions about coalitions can be checked. One is to take the between-group agreement scores (which may be found in Appendix A–3.5) that are calculated across all the policy areas and to assume that the two groups with the highest agreement scores

Differences between the Parties

The processes of coalition formation have consequences. Some of the most important can be seen in Table 3–6. In every policy area, the median policy preferences of the dominant Republican coalitions are more conservative than those of all Republican activists. In every policy area, the median policy preferences of the dominant Democratic coalitions are more liberal than those of all Democratic activists. Thus, the process of coalition formation in the electoral parties has a tendency to polarize the alternatives presented to the voters rather than move them toward the center of the political spectrum.

The polarization is more pronounced in the dominant Republican coalition, for a couple of reasons. For one thing, the more conservative Republican groups are always members of the dominant Republican coalitions, while the most liberal Democratic group is not part of the dominant Democratic coalition in international involvement or social benefits. For another, the policy preferences of the dominant Republican group are all more conservative than the median preference of all Republican activists, whereas only in civil liberties are the policy preferences of the dominant Democratic group distinctly more liberal than the Democratic median. Hence, the dominant Republican coalitions are noticeably more conservative in every instance, while the dominant Democratic coalition is equally far away only in civil liberties.[11]

The data in Table 3-6 also suggest the nature of the choice the electoral parties presented to the citizen in 1972. The choice was most pronounced with respect to social benefits and civil liberties. In these areas, Democratic policies were liberal, and Republican policies were moderate conservative. In international involvement, the citizen's choice was between moderate liberal and moderate conservative policies. A tendency toward the center was most notable in economic management, where Democratic policies were moderate liberal and Republican policies were moderate.

To understand party differences, one should also consider intraparty consensus. The consensus scores for all Republican activists and all Democratic

---

will form an initial protocoalition. At that point, agreement scores are recalculated between that protocoalition and the remaining groups, and the process is repeated until a winning coalition is formed. The second way to check the process of coalition formation is to use the cluster procedure by which the issue groups were isolated and gradually to lower the criteria for admission until the equivalent of a multigroup coalition is found. There are variations in detail in what one observes, but essentially these procedures verify the existence of the issue coalitions that we have just discussed.

[11] This should remind us of two very important general points. First, these results—that the coalitions tend to be polarized and that there is greater difference between the dominant Republican coalition and Republican activists than between the dominant Democratic coalition and Democratic activists—occur because we began with a *particular* set of groups. Different groups could lead to different coalitions. Second, it is important to specify carefully just how attitudes aggregate at each level of analysis. The often-made assumption that the policy preferences in any complex institution will lie at the central tendency of the preferences of the individual members is apt to be wrong because it neglects the manner in which the preferences are aggregated.

TABLE 3-6
Comparison of Issue Coalitions with All Party Activists

	Position in Policy Area*			
Group	International Involvement	Economic Management	Social Benefits	Civil Liberties
Dominant Republican coalition	Moderate conservative (3.4)	Moderate (3.5)	Moderate conservative (3.2)	Moderate conservative (3.2)
All Republican activists	Moderate (4.0)	Moderate (3.8)	Moderate (3.6)	Moderate (3.5)
Dominant Democratic coalition	Moderate liberal (5.0)	Moderate liberal (4.6)	Liberal (6.0)	Liberal (6.5)
All Democratic activists	Moderate liberal (4.9)	Moderate (4.4)	Liberal (5.9)	Liberal (6.0)

* The figures in parentheses are median positions on scales that vary between 1 and 7. In general a high score (7) represents a dove position in international involvement and a willingness to use government power and resources in the domestic policy areas. A low score (1) represents the opposite.

The convention followed for substantive interpretation of the scale scores was: values from 1 to 2.4, conservative; 2.5 to 3.4, moderate conservative; 3.5 to 4.5, moderate; 4.6 to 5.5, moderate liberal; 5.6 to 7, liberal. This classification is nothing more than an aid to understanding and should not be taken as a precise denotation. Note, for example, that if the upper boundary of moderate had been moved from 3.4 to 3.5, there would have been five moderate conservative scores rather than three.

Data source: 1972 Hofstetter study.

activists, respectively, in the four policy areas are international involvement, .57, .31; economic management, .62, .48; social benefits, .44, .66; civil liberties, .61, .73. The consensus scores have a value of 1.0 when everyone takes the same position and a value of 0 when agreement is no greater than would be expected with an equal distribution, so these consensus scores tell us where we can expect strains and disagreements to show up within the parties.[12] The Republicans are least agreed about social benefit programs, but the similar sizes of the four consensus scores imply that Republican disagreements are spread rather equally across the four policy areas. In the Democratic case, however, disagreements are concentrated on foreign policy and economics. Democrats are united in favor of liberal positions on social benefits and civil liberties.

---

[12] See Appendix A-3.6 for an explanation of how these consensus scores are calculated.

Campaign Implications of Issue Coalitions

The activists' issue preferences affect the conduct of both local and national campaigns. In the midst of a presidential campaign, groups of activists are not free to devise campaign strategies of their own. If the presidential candidate is giving speech after speech promising to cut spending, for example, activists in the party are hardly free to claim that he will increase spending once he is in the White House. But they can choose which issues they are going to emphasize in their own localities. In some cases, the choice is forced on them. If they are printing their own campaign pamphlets, they must decide which material about the presidential candidate they are going to include. If they are embarking on a doorbelling campaign, they must decide what they are going to tell voters about the candidate. The activists' attitudes are also reported upward to coalition leaders. The policy preferences of leaders in a single county are hardly going to determine national strategy, but as these reports are aggregated, they indicate the policy preferences of the coalition to the strategy group. These coalition preferences are taken into account.

It is possible to verify the campaign implications of group and coalition preferences. In the case of the issue groups, data are available on the intensity of their feelings (whether they feel strongly or not), the extent of consensus (whether or not the members agree with each other on the issue), and whether or not the issue was emphasized. As you might expect, the intensity of group feelings has been significantly related to the emphasis placed on the issue. That is, the more strongly they felt for or against a question, the more likely they were to stress that issue in their local campaigning. The Pearsonian correlation, r, was .32. (If you have not encountered bivariate correlation before, you might want to consult the box on that topic in Chapter 8.) But in addition, consensus is related to issue emphasis ($r = .17$). This can be understood because of the group dynamics of reinforcement and sharing. Consensus is a vital property of a group and therefore related to group behavior.

There is also a strong relationship between coalition emphases and candidate emphases. The coalition emphases can be determined from the data set we have been using, and we know the candidate emphases from a content analysis of their speeches (Kessel, 1977). The correlation (r) between Senator McGovern's emphases and those of the Democratic coalition is .36. That between President Nixon and the Republican coalition is .57, and if one excludes natural resources (which Nixon barely mentioned), the correlation goes up to .84. [13] Data on the candidate's personal policy preferences are not available for Senator McGovern, but good estimates of Nixon's personal preferences are available from members of the White House staff who could

---

[13] One must be cautious in interpreting these relationships. The relevant data from the content analysis are the frequencies of reference to the six policy areas (the four used in this chapter plus natural resources and agriculture). A correlation resting on six data points is hardly reliable.

observe Nixon at close range (Kessel, 1975). Here again there was a strong relationship ($r = .56$) between the mean policy preferences of the coalition and those of the candidate.

The linkage between coalition and candidate flows in both directions. The candidate learns of coalition preferences through reports collected by the campaign organization. The coalition members learn of the candidate's positions from his many public statements as well as from communications that come through party channels. The coalition cannot prevent a candidate from taking a position about which he feels strongly. Nor can the candidate force the coalition to emphasize issues on which its members think he is taking an unwise stand. But there are forces that work toward mutual accommodation. The candidate doesn't want to get too far away from his supporters, and the coalition members can work most effectively for their candidate through a faithful representation of his positions.

A NEW VIEW OF POLITICAL PARTIES

The characteristics of the activists, the issue groups, and the issue coalitions they form point to three conclusions about American political parties. American parties are no longer held together primarily by demographic considerations. Instead, their common bonds are shared attitudes about the desirable course of public policy. While American politicians claim to be speaking for their constituents, they are more often advocating policies *they* prefer. And our presidential parties are continually evolving. This evolution takes place very gradually, as each party absorbs a new cohort every four years. To the extent that these findings challenge commonly held views about American political parties, the views need to be updated.

The Passing of Demographic Organization

The character of the issue groups is clear. They may be understood in terms of their size, the moderate-to-conservative positions taken by the Republican party, and the moderate-to-liberal positions taken by the Democratic groups.

This is a different picture of party groups than is usually offered. The standard interpretation, especially of the Democratic party, has been that the party is made up of demographic groupings. For example, Robert Axelrod (1972) named the Democratic groups as the poor, blacks, union members, Roman Catholics, Southerners, and central-city residents. Andrew Greeley wrote that the political party "is comprised of voluntary associations (such as trade unions), interest groups (civil rights organizations), strictly political groups (Cook County Democratic party), and major portions of population groups (blacks, Catholics, or Jews)" (1974, pp. 172–73). I (1968) have said that the normal Democratic coalition was made up of Southerners, Westerners, urbanites, union members, and blacks.[14] In other words, the Democratic party is usually seen as a coalition of minorities.

Why shouldn't we follow this time-honored line of analysis instead of seeking groups with distinctive attitudes in policy areas? The most direct answer is that activists who fall into the traditional categories do not have shared attitudes from which we can infer probable behavior. Therefore, it is much less useful to attempt to interpret parties this way.

Two tests were used to try to find attitude groups that corresponded to the traditional classifications. In the first, a mean agreement score was calculated for all activists who fit into the category. (These agreement scores, you will recall, represent the extent of agreement beyond that to be expected by chance.) The data are presented in Table 3–7. The extent of agreement among activists in the categoric groupings is much less than in the issue groups. The average scores (grand means) for the groupings in Table 3–5 are .29 for the Republicans and .29 for the Democrats. The average agreement scores for the issue groups are .48 for the Republicans and .50 for the Democrats. The average agreement scores among all activists are .29 for Republicans and .30 for Democrats. In other words, the demographic groupings do not provide any information beyond what we already have by just knowing whether the activists are Democrats or Republicans. The issue groups are much more distinctive.

The second test—a cluster analysis of all those who fell into the traditional categories—attempted to see whether each set of activists (black Democrats, eastern Republicans, or whatever) would form groups. The data resulting from this test also appear in Table 3–7. In most cases, either multiple groups were formed—which means that the members of each group had different attitudes—or no groups were formed—which means that the activists were isolates who didn't agree with anyone.

Three fifths of the time, multiple groups were formed. The most extreme cases were the urban Democrats, the southern Democrats, and the liberal Democrats. These categories all contained large numbers of Democratic activists. Their potential influence is limited, however, because they would have the Democratic party move in three or four *different* directions. In a couple of instances—liberal Republicans and black Democrats—no groups were formed. These categories were made up entirely of isolates. In three of the four cases in which a single group was formed, a majority of the members of the category remained outside the group. In only one instance, Republicans

---

[14] I did classify Republican groups on the basis of their attitudes on issues. Warren Miller and Teresa Levitin's (1976) classification of voters as "Silent Minority," "Center," and "New Liberals" is also a move in this direction. Other analyses of the Democratic party have been based on demographic groupings (see Ladd & Hadley, 1978; Nie, Verba & Petrocik, 1976, chaps. 13–14; and Rubin, 1976). These are but examples. Many scholars have used demographic classifications of one kind or another.

TABLE 3-7
Agreement and Clusters Formed within Categoric Groupings

Category	Mean Agreement* Score	Number of Clusters	Percent Unclustered
Republicans			
Blacks†	—	—	—
Roman Catholics	.25	2	42.2%
Urban	.27	2	47.3
East	.25	1	53.9
Midwest	.26	1	50.8
South	.34	2	31.4
Deep South	.45	1	33.3
Self-identified liberals	.14	0	100.0
Self-identified conservatives	.32	2	32.9
Democrats			
Blacks	.31	0	100.0
Roman Catholics	.24	1	69.0
Urban	.27	3	26.7
East	.25	2	45.2
Midwest	.37	2	31.5
South	.24	3	34.5
Deep South†	—	—	—
Self-identified liberals	.34	4	23.1
Self-identified conservatives†	—	—	—

* The higher the agreement score, the greater the agreement between members of the category.
† Too few cases for analysis.
Data source: 1972 Hofstetter study.

from the Deep South, is there a high agreement score and a group that includes a majority of the activists in the category. As we have already seen, southern Republicans also provide the *only* case in which a majority of the activists from a single region belong to one attitudinal group.[15]

There was a time when a demographic classification of party groups was reasonably exact. Not too long ago, Arthur Holcombe could write:

> The Democratic party, since the great realignment of parties in the course of the struggle over slavery, has consisted of three principal factions: the cotton and tobacco planters and associated interests in the South, a substantial part of the grain growers and cattlemen and associated interests in the North and West,

---

[15] This was the dominant group in the Republican party. Even in this case, it is not very useful to think of the issue group in regional terms. Fifty-four percent of the members of the dominant Republican group came from outside the South, and 80 percent came from outside the Deep South.

and a diversified group of urban interests in the same sections, in which since the Al Smith campaign of 1928 labor interests have been growing more important. (1950, p. 122)

Any such classification rested, of course, on an assumption of regional (or occupational or ethnic or whatever) homogeneity. Southerners, for example, were assumed to have sufficiently similar attitudes so a group of Southerners would act coherently within a political party.

V. O. Key, foresighted on this as on so many matters, pointed out that "for 50 years changes in both the North and South have been undermining southern solidarity" (1964, p. 239). These changes have continued apace. National media, mobility from one section of the country to another, and many other forces have eroded sectional and ethnic homogeneity. For some years, we have had a national culture. Southerners and Westerners, Irish-Americans and Polish-Americans, and all the other once distinctive categories are best understood as having subcultures that incorporate most of the features of the national culture.

In a similar way, our national political culture may be thought of as having a moderate political tone. Democrats tend toward the liberal side; Republicans to the conservative side. Democrats and Republicans are best analyzed by finding groups in which these liberal or conservative tendencies vary across particular policy areas. In this way, we achieve more precision than when we use demographic categories of fading utility.

This does not mean that we can afford to abandon all references to southern Democrats, eastern Republicans, or other demographic groupings. While an analysis that uses issue groups is more powerful, the data that allow us to do this come (so far) from a single year. Therefore, we have no choice but to use the more general ideological or demographic references in other circumstances.

Advocacy Parties

When the attitudes of activists were compared with those of their constituents, it turned out that electoral activists agreed with their party colleagues to a greater degree than they agreed with their constituents. This was rather a surprising finding, since parties are often regarded as representative institutions that articulate the preferences of less-involved members of the public. Party activists have been assumed to be persons with distinctive skills in knowing what their constituents want and in being able to assemble these preferences in packages that win votes at election time. Yet the data indicate that this was *not* what these electoral activists were doing.

There are two ways in which activists might represent their constituents. One is what Aage Clausen calls "involuntary representation," a process through which the personal attitudes of the party leaders happen to coincide with those of their fellow citizens. The party leaders have the same attitudes, presumably through living in the same community and being exposed to the same influences, but the process is as unconscious as other involuntary processes, such as breathing. The other type of representation does not call for any such coincidence between the leaders' attitudes and those of their fellow citizens but does assume that the leaders are able to perceive their constituents' attitudes accurately.

One of the advantages of the Hofstetter study was that voters living in the same counties as the party activists were also interviewed, thus presenting the opportunity to address parallel questions to both sets of respondents. By calculating agreement scores,[16] it was possible to determine the coincidence of attitudes between activists and constituents and the extent to which the activists' perceptions coincide with constituents' attitudes. When this was done, it became evident that neither one of these possible modes of representation was working very well. Considering both parties together, involuntary representation was working a little better. The scores reflecting attitudinal agreement were 17 percent better than one would expect by chance, and the scores reflecting perceptual accuracy were only 2 percent better than chance.

The average agreement score for similarity of attitudes was .22 for Republicans and .12 for Democrats. (This means 22 percent better than chance for Republicans and 12 percent better than chance for Democrats.) The average agreement scores for perceptual accuracy were 0 for Republicans and .05 for Democrats (Yarnell, 1975). The similarity of attitudes between activists and constituents is not impressive, and the political leaders' presumed competence at knowing what their constituents prefer is nonexistent.

In contrast, the average of agreement scores among all Republican activists was .29, and that among all Democratic activists was .30. These figures are almost identical for both parties and denote agreement among activists about 30 percent beyond what one would expect by chance. Even more important, the scores tell us we can know more about activists' attitudes by learning whether they are Republicans or Democrats than by knowing anything about attitudes in the communities from which they come.[17] The implication is that they are not giving voice to their constituents' views. Rather, they are urging policies that their colleagues think wise. American parties are not representative entities but *advocacy parties.*

---

[16] Agreement scores indicate the degree to which two persons take the same positions. If both persons give the same answer to every question they are asked, they will have an agreement score of 1.0. If their agreement is no better than chance, the agreement score will be 0. Thus, the agreement score between two political activists (or, in this case, between a county leader and the average response of citizens in that county) represents the extent of agreement beyond what would be expected by chance. For further details, see Appendix A–3.2.

[17] Notice, however, that this conclusion is based on lack of agreement between Democrats and residents of their counties in 1972. The agreement score between Republicans and citizens of their communities in 1972 was .22, and the agreement score among all Republicans was .29. This difference is not great, and the results might be different in some future year.

Constant Stability, Constant Evolution

Parties as Residues of Past Campaigns

It has been known for some time that political parties are marked by a constant turnover in personnel. New activists are constantly being recruited, while some of the former activists are leaving party work (Eldersveld, 1964, chap. 7). The parties are, of course, affected by the rate at which this takes place. If wholesale turnover occurs in a short time period, there will be little institutional memory, and there may be rapid shifts in party positions. If turnover takes place at a relatively slow rate, the implications run in the opposite direction.

A high proportion of the presidential activists began their political careers in past presidential campaign years. Two thirds of the Republicans and 72 percent of the Democrats began in such a year. The years are portrayed in Figure 3-3. The activists who were working in behalf of George McGovern and Sargent Shriver included significant numbers who had been brought into politics during the campaigns of Lyndon Johnson, John Kennedy, Adlai Stevenson, Harry Truman, or Franklin Roosevelt. The Committee to Re-Elect the President (Richard Nixon) included those who had rallied to the banners of Dwight Eisenhower, Thomas Dewey, Wendell Willkie, or even Herbert

FIGURE 3–3

Presidential Parties as Residues of Past Campaigns: Proportions of Electoral Activists with First Experience in Presidential Campaign Years

Democratic		Republican
16.9%	1972	10.3%
20.9	1968	4.9
6.4	1964	10.9
14.1	1960	9.2
0.6	1956	8.7
7.3	1952	9.2
2.8	1948	7.6
0.6	1944	0.5
2.8	1940	1.1
0	1936	1.6
0	1932	1.1
0	Pre-1932	1.6

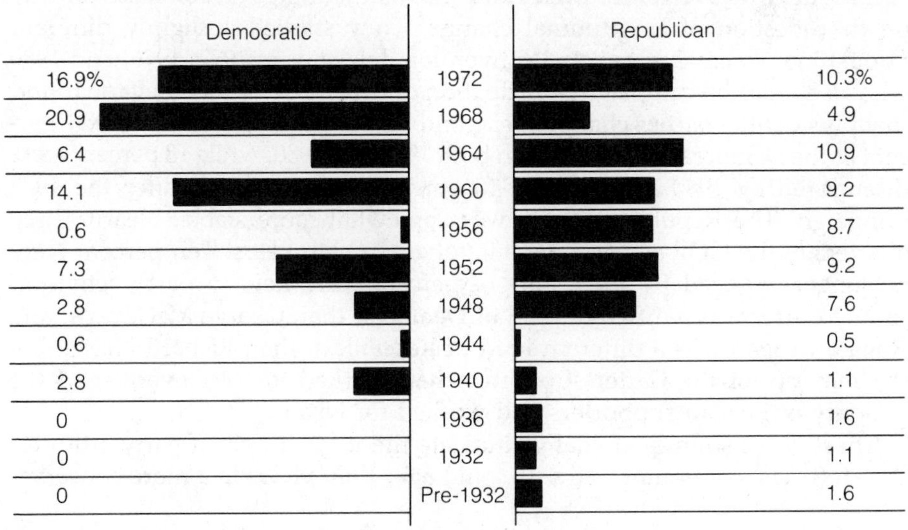

Hoover. In fact, the activist with the longest campaign experience who turned up in the sample had begun his political career working for Charles Evans Hughes over half a century earlier. This slow turnover points to a conclusion of some significance: *A presidential party at any time is a residue of its past campaigns.*

Conversely, we can see limits to the hopes of groups who want to "go back" to the party that existed before a particular campaign. These would include such groups as the moderate Republicans who hoped to return to "normal" pre-Goldwater politics after 1964 and the "Coalition for a Democratic Majority," which wanted to repudiate the "New Politics" of George McGovern after 1972. *A presidential party is never completely taken over by the new arrivals who come into politics in a given campaign.* Personnel turnover takes place at much too slow a rate for that. On the other hand, *a party never goes back to what it was before a particular campaign* either.

This slow evolution also tells us how much we can trust the 1972 data. We can be certain that the activists working for the Committee to Re-Elect the President and for the McGovern-Shriver Committee were not wildly atypical of Republicans and Democrats in previous campaigns, because 90 percent of the Republicans and 83 percent of the Democrats had begun in earlier campaigns. At the same time, we know that the parties in 1988 will be different because of subsequent changes. Since some of the 1972 activists have dropped out and the post-1972 parties have absorbed new cohorts in 1976, 1980, 1984, and 1988, the 1988 party incarnations should be altered to some degree. The question is how much.

A Drift to the Right, 1972–1980

A fine study by Warren E. Miller and M. Kent Jennings (1986) bears directly on the question of longitudinal change. They studied a slightly different population of activists: national convention delegates in 1972, 1976, and 1980 who also reported campaign participation during those years. They too found that presidential parties change their composition relatively slowly. Sixty percent of the Democrats were active in both 1972 and 1980, while 18 percent were disengaged by 1980 and another 18 percent were recruited after the 1972 campaign. The Republican party was somewhat more stable. Nearly three quarters of the GOP activists were involved in both years. Ten percent were no longer engaged by 1980, and 14 percent were new to party activity.[18] Jimmy Carter was a different kind of Democrat than George McGovern, and Ronald Reagan was a different kind of Republican than Richard Nixon; but the majority of the Carter supporters had worked for McGovern, and the majority of Reagan supporters had worked for Nixon.

These three sources of change indicate the ways in which party attitudes can shift. The continuing activists could alter their views in a more conserva-

---

[18] Small fractions in both parties were active only in 1976.

TABLE 3–8
Liberal-Conservative Self-Placement of
Party Activists*

Category	Democrats	Republicans
Continuously active		
1972 cohort	31.9	68.9
1980 cohort	34.2	74.4
Disengaged	33.7	64.8
Newly mobilized	39.6	74.1

* The cell entries are the mean scores for each category, based on a scale in which 0 is the most liberal self-placement and 100 is the most conservative self-placement.
Source: Warren E. Miller and M. Kent Jennings, *Parties in Transition: A Longitudinal Study of Party Leaders and Party Supporters* (New York: Russell Sage Foundation, 1986), Tables 7–1, 7–2.

tive or more liberal direction. Those who drop out might have distinctive views from other party members. If so, their departure would lead to a net shift in party attitudes. Similarly, the newly recruited cohorts might have more conservative or more liberal views than those already active in the party. Any one of these three possibilities could lead to a net shift in party attitudes, as long as simultaneous shifts (such as more conservative activists leaving and more liberal activists joining) do not cancel each other out. If, on the other hand, the continuing activists do not change their minds or if the departing activists or the newly engaged have attitudes that match the central tendency within their parties, no net change would occur.

The principal data base used by Miller and Jennings was a quasi panel, data gathered at one time point (1981) but analyzed on the basis of years in which the respondents reported activity. The data on liberal-conservative self-placement in Table 3–8 suggest the flavor of their findings.[19] Republicans active in both 1972 and 1980 were, on the average, more conservative by 1980 than they had been eight years earlier. Democrats active in both campaigns, however, showed little change.

Miller and Jennings present stronger evidence on this point by using data gathered in 1972 and comparing them with data gathered nine years later. An index of attitudes toward political groups (business, liberals, blacks, and so forth) shows a conversion effect for Republicans of six points (on a 100-point scale) but a shift of only a single point among Democrats. The Republican drift to the right was accelerated by the departure of activists from the moderate wing of the party. As Table 3–8 shows, the average score of the departed

---

[19] Miller and Jennings' analysis was much more complex, employing multiple indicators and dealing with many other topics besides the longitudinal change that concerns us here.

activists was more liberal than the mean scores of other Republicans. In the Democratic case (and in spite of a perception that the 1972 McGovern campaign had been a liberal aberration), the dropouts' attitudes were not distinctive.

Finally (and again, in spite of a perception that the Republican party had been taken over by a new conservative movement in 1980), the newly mobilized Republicans were a hairline less conservative than those who had been active since 1972. This was not the case with the Democrats. In 1980, the newly mobilized Democrats were more conservative than either the continuing activists or the disengaged. Hence, their attitudes moved the Democratic party somewhat to the right.

In sum, both parties were more conservative in the 1980s than they had been in the early 70s, but the reasons for the attitude changes were quite different. The perceptible rightward movement of the Republican party was caused by the increasing conservatism on the part of continuing activists and the departure of a disproportionate number of moderates. With the Democrats, it was the addition of relatively conservative new activists.

While these changes were visible (especially with the Republicans), they did not indicate "any sea changes in the ideological locations of the party elites" (Miller & Jennings, 1986, p. 158). The rightward drift of both parties has altered the tone of political discourse and the strength and composition of the issue groups that make up the party coalitions. But if both parties have moved in a conservative direction, compare the difference *between* the parties. The rightward movement has shifted the Republicans from a moderate posture to a more conservative one and the Democrats from liberalism to greater moderation—but the Republicans remain the right-of-center party and the Democrats the left-of-center party.

SUMMARY

The electoral parties consist of activists who have been recruited through one or another of the presidential campaigns through which the party has passed. The activists are middle class, interested in issues, and more likely to agree with their fellow partisans than with residents of their own communities. Their attitudes on issues allow them to be combined into groups. In 1972, there were four generally moderate groups in the Republican party and seven generally liberal groups in the Democratic party. These nationwide issue groups tell us more about the parties than do the traditional demographic categories. When these particular groups are aggregated, the resulting issue coalitions are more conservative in the Republican party and more liberal in the Democratic party. The policy preferences of the groups correspond to the issues they emphasize, and the issues emphasized by the coalitions correspond to the issues stressed by the presidential candidates. Thus the internal structure of the electoral parties does affect their campaign strategies.

Substantively, we have seen that parties are better understood by focusing on the coalitions' characteristic attitudes than by conceiving of them as made up of demographic groupings. Activists are more likely to advocate policies *they* prefer than to express the views of their constituents. And parties change very slowly. At any time, a party is a residue of its past campaigns.

The more general argument, of course, is that the reasons *why* a coalition behaves as it does depend on its internal structure and external structure, and the reasons for taking action *when* it does are to be found in the temporal pattern. In this chapter, we have focused on the temporal pattern and the internal structure of electoral politics. We saw a hint of external structure in our discussion of the organizational groups on the local, state, and national levels. Now it is time to turn directly to those outward-looking activities that arise from the need of the electoral coalitions to reach the voters.

Chapter 4

External Structure

A useful distinction can be drawn between primary and secondary audiences in politics. Primary audiences are those whose support is essential for success in a given institutional domain. Secondary audiences are those whose political reactions are consequential but come (often later) in another institutional domain. Thus voters whose ballots will not be cast until the general election are a secondary audience for nomination politics but become a primary audience for electoral politics.[1]

To a greater degree than is true of any other kind of politics, electoral politics is aimed at one primary audience: the voters. Hundreds of persons are engaged in the four types of activities necessary to reach this audience—

---

[1] There are some secondary audiences for electoral politics. If a candidate (or someone in his core group) is unusually reflective or if he is running so far ahead as to be regarded as almost certain of election, there may be concerns for how his positions on issues are going to be viewed by the bureaucracy and Congress and for how this is going to affect the candidate's ability to accomplish things in executive or legislative politics if he is elected.

Thus, in 1960, Senator John Kennedy asked two advisors to draft reports on what should be done. In 1972, ideas were sought for a possible McGovern administration. In 1976, Jimmy Carter set up a staff that worked separately from the campaign staff to make plans for a possible transition. Plans for the Reagan transition began to be laid in November 1979. Preparations were relatively detailed but on a low-key basis to avoid distracting anyone from the campaign. Planners were separate from the campaign staff but reported through campaign chief of staff Edwin Meese, thereby avoiding some staff rivalries.

An incumbent president who is also a candidate for reelection is simultaneously engaged in electoral politics and executive politics. The primary audiences for executive politics are likely to pay attention to the president's campaign statements to see if they signal any switch in administration policy. The president is aware of both executive and electoral audiences and has, of course, extensive structures to link him to both.

campaign operations, research, public relations, and finance. In this chapter, we shall want to explore these activities in some detail. Before doing so, though, we ought to review two general points about campaign organizations: their growth and development and the division of authority.

CAMPAIGN ORGANIZATIONS

Development of Campaign Staffs

The staffs that carry on the functions of electoral parties are 20th-century developments, as is the staff that serves the modern presidency. Until the 1920s, national parties largely disappeared between elections. The national chair of the incumbent party was frequently appointed postmaster general, a post from which party affairs could be conducted.[2] For example, Will Hayes was appointed postmaster general during the Harding administration. One looked in vain, though, for any substantial party headquarters. Party activity was so sporadic that most of it could be taken care of from the personal office of whoever happened to be the party chairman at the time.

For both parties, the beginnings of professional staffing came in the wake of major defeats. After the 1928 election, in which Herbert Hoover received 444 electoral votes to Al Smith's 87, Democratic national chairman John Raskob hired talented phrasemaker Charles Michelson. Michelson's publicity helped to ensure that Hoover's popularity was short lived, and in the happier year of 1932, the publicist was joined by (among others) Emil Hurja, a mining engineer who introduced Democrats to systematic analysis of voting data (Herring, 1940, pp. 208, 265; Michelson, 1944).

The beginnings of modern Republican organization came after the election of 1936, in which Franklin Roosevelt carried 46 states while Kansas Governor Alf Landon carried only Maine and Vermont. John D. M. Hamilton, Republican national chairman during the ensuing four years, appears to have been the first full-time salaried national chairman. He gave the GOP some staff to work with and envisioned a corps of party civil servants with lifetime careers and a pension plan. Hamilton also took steps toward regular party financing with a system of state quotas and sustaining memberships (Cotter & Hennessy, 1964; Lamb, 1966).

From these beginnings, party headquarters grew from "two ladies occupying one room in a Washington office building," as Franklin Roosevelt described Democratic headquarters in the 1920s (Key, 1964, p. 322), to institutions that employ scores of persons during noncampaign years and even

---

[2] The movement from appointing party leaders as postmaster general (Will Hayes, James Farley, Robert Hannegan) to making them attorneys general (Herbert Brownell, Robert Kennedy, John Mitchell, Edwin Meese) was a sign that patronage involving U.S. attorneys and federal judgeships was becoming more important in running national campaigns than the appointment of postmasters and rural mail carriers. This change took place during the Truman administration, when Howard McGrath was appointed.

more during the campaign proper (Bone, 1971, p. 170). Parallel growth has taken place on the state level, although the development of staff is even more recent. Robert Huckshorn reports that during 1962–63, when he visited some 18 Republican state parties, 7 still did not have a permanent headquarters (1976, pp. 254–55). As we saw in the last chapter, 90 percent of the state parties now have a permanent headquarters.

Another surge of Republican organizational activity took place after 1976. National chairman Bill Brock was concerned about the future of the party, which at the state level was about as weak as it had been following the defeats of 1936 and 1964. Brock supplied organizational directors for all state parties at a cost of $1 million and put together a staff of 15 regional political directors to provide liaison between the national committee and the state committees. A local-election campaign division, with 15 staff members working directly in local election campaigns (especially those for state legislatures), was particularly important. The Brock program of assistance to party organizations was unprecedented in the history of American political parties (Bibby, 1980).

In 1981, the Democratic National Committee began to do some of the things the Republican National Committee had been doing: fund-raising through mass mailings, candidate recruitment, publicity efforts, and so forth. They had a long way to go. For example, Democratic National Committee receipts rose from $15.4 million in 1980 to $16.5 million in 1982 while Republican National Committee receipts were rising from $77.8 million to $84.1 million (Ornstein et al., 1984, Table 3–9).[3]

The Democrats made some progress through 1984. They closed the Republican's fund-raising advantage from nearly 7 to 1 to under 5 to 1. Between 1984 and 1985, however, Democratic fund-raising dropped from $22.4 million to $7 million, and the GOP once again enjoyed an advantage of better than 6 to 1 (Edsall, 1986). Emulating the Republican initiative of the late 1970s, Democratic national chairman Paul Kirk announced that $3 million would be devoted to state parties and candidates, either in the form of services or direct cash contributions. But it remained to be seen whether the funds could be raised to sustain the program.

Division of Authority

Division of authority in political organizations is hardly a recent development. History tells us of many struggles for the ears of ancient monarchs, and various bases of power exist in all forms of politics. Similarly, there are

---

[3] It is important to remember that these are only the funds raised by the national committees. The total amount raised (from party contributions, from PACs, and by the candidates themselves) was $94.6 million for all Democratic Senate candidates in 1982 and $96.3 million for all Republican Senate candidates (Ornstein et al., 1984, Table 3–8). There is not a great difference between the two parties in total funds available to House and Senate candidates. There is a considerable difference in the ability of the party committees to provide funds for their candidates.

organizational features that tend to fragment authority in electoral politics, and we need to know what these are.

As we have just seen, the national committees in recent decades have developed staffs capable of conducting national campaigns. Increasingly though, candidates have chosen to work through their own organizations, such as the Reagan-Bush '84 Committee and the Mondale/Ferraro Committee Inc. in 1984. A candidate organization does the same things as a national committee staff: speech writing, media contact, and the like. But the existence of a candidate organization separate from the national committee staff means that there are at least two campaign chairpersons and two rival sets of division heads.

Furthermore, the candidate is not part of either organization. Most of the time, he is off campaigning and therefore physically separated from both headquarters. The candidate has some staff, often including some of the core group, traveling with him. This creates a third headquarters or, at the very least, a third point at which many executive decisions about the campaign are made.

All of the arguments for responsibility, efficiency, and economy would seem to go against multiple centers of authority and duplicate senior staffs. So why do they exist? The most important reason is that the national committee is, by tradition, neutral in nomination politics. There are good reasons for this. The national committee is charged with making the arrangements for the national convention. Given at least two candidates, if the national committee were to facilitate the chances of Candidate A, Candidate B would have every reason to be angry. So the national committee is neutral. It takes no action to harm Candidate A or Candidate B, nor does it promote the candidacy of any one at the expense of other aspirants.

As we have already seen, the staff needed for nomination politics is much smaller than what is needed for a general election campaign. Still, to be nominated, a candidate must have speeches written, press releases distributed, polls taken, funds raised, and so on. In the course of a quest for the nomination, close working relations develop between the senior members of this staff and the candidate. Many become members of the candidate's core group. At a minimum, the candidate knows what senior members of this staff can do and how well they can do it.

Once the nomination is in hand, there are two prospective campaign staffs in being: the candidate's own staff that has taken him through the convention and the national committee staff. Rivalries separate these staffs. The national committee staff members have had experience in previous presidential campaigns, experience often in short supply on the candidate's own staff. They have been in touch with the state party organizations. If there is a split in the state party in Montana, for example, they know just who is on which side. They know which state organizations can get things done on their own and which state organizations are going to need close supervision to accomplish essential campaign tasks.

The candidate's staff members, of course, think that they have the more essential knowledge: how to do what the candidate wants done. The national committee staff, which has been occupied with routine activities while the candidate's staff has been out winning primary elections, seems stuffy and slow to react. And while others were skeptical early on, the campaign staff has seen its leader triumph in nomination politics. They feel they have earned the right to conduct the fall campaign.

In short, after the convention, there are two rival staffs; and—especially if the convention has been held in late summer,—there is little time to deal with this dilemma.

Multiple Headquarters

With a good many variations, two basic organizational patterns have existed in electoral politics. The first is to merge the two staffs and conduct a unified campaign through the national committee staff. The second and now much more common pattern is to allow the existing candidate organization to conduct the campaign and have the national committee staff take care of "other party business." The advantage of the former is that you can utilize an experienced staff and have established lines of communication into every state, whether the candidate was involved there in the springtime or not. The advantage of the separate approach is that there is a working organization in being and separateness allows the candidate to stress his independence from other politicians. Thus, when Adlai Stevenson wanted to underscore his independence from an unpopular Truman administration, he had his headquarters in Springfield, Illinois; and when Jimmy Carter wanted to emphasize that he was not part of the Washington scene in 1976, Carter headquarters was kept in Atlanta.

Many proponents of a unified campaign point to that of Franklin Roosevelt in 1932 as an example of how a campaign should be run. Dwight Eisenhower in 1956, Adlai Stevenson the same year, John Kennedy in 1960, Barry Goldwater in 1964, Lyndon Johnson the same year, and Hubert Humphrey all conducted their campaigns from national committee headquarters. Adlai Stevenson in 1952 and Richard Nixon in his three campaigns maintained separate campaign headquarters, as has every candidate since 1972 (Cotter & Hennessy, 1964, pp. 122–27; Ogden & Peterson, 1968, chap. 5). A minimum requirement for a unified campaign is someone who can exercise unquestioned control over the merged staffs and who has the complete trust of the candidate. Robert Kennedy played this role at the Democratic National Committee in 1960. Even so, it was difficult to overcome some of the rivalries among other staff members.

Having separate candidate organizations was given a powerful push by the Federal Election Campaign Act of 1974. The act stipulates that federal funds will go to a separate candidate organization during the primaries. There is an option under which the candidate may designate the national committee as the agent to spend federal funds in the general election campaign; but no candidate has exercised this option as yet. By the time this choice is made, all the accounting and reporting procedures have been set up in the candidate organization. Gerald Ford wrote that he wanted to run his 1976 campaign through the Republican National Committee but apparently was told (erroneously) that he could not do so (Ford, 1979, p. 295).

Regardless of where the headquarters offices are located or how many of them there are, there is another campaign headquarters wherever the candidate happens to be. This used to be "the train"; now it is "the plane."[4] Not only does the physical presence of the candidate signify the location of "the campaign" as far as most media representatives are concerned, but there are certain things that can be done from "the plane" (or sometimes from a motorcade en route to a campaign event) and nowhere else. The candidate is moved on jet aircraft, not only to respond to as many requests for candidate appearances as possible but also to appear in as many media markets as he can between sunrise and sunset and thus generate broader coverage in the local press. Speeches must be ready for each stop. And there are likely to be over a hundred reporters flying along, most of them in a press plane, whose needs must be borne in mind and whose questions require answers.

A reasonably large staff must accompany the candidate. Senior speech writers need to be close at hand to alter speeches to take account of late-breaking events and to work with the candidate during in-flight time. A press secretary is needed to handle the traveling press and those encountered along the way. Often persons close to the candidate travel along so there will be a few familiar faces among the blur he sees moving from airport to airport, and to help provide background for reporters. Usually there is a very senior staff person who goes along to organize all this. Governor Sherman Adams of New Hampshire rode Eisenhower's campaign train in 1952 to provide liaison between the train and other campaign leaders. H. R. Haldeman was in charge of Nixon's campaign plane in 1968. Both ended up as chiefs of staff once the candidate was in the White House.

In theory, basic decisions are made when the candidate is available to meet with his strategy group or the candidate delegates authority to others to act in his name. In practice, unexpected developments—a foreign crisis, a charge by the opposition—require instant response from "the plane." This is frustrating to those in the headquarters. Although they supposedly have instant radio communication with "the plane," sometimes they are out of touch with the traveling party. Gary Hart recalled the situation in the 1972 McGovern campaign:

> Generally, the communications between the traveling party and the headquarters were good. . . . But occasionally, some momentous decision would be made by the Senator which we would find out about only third-hand, hours

---

[4] "The plane" appears in quotation marks because the phrase has a variety of meanings in conversations at campaign headquarters. It may refer to a "rival" headquarters, or the traveling party, or the present geographic location of the aircraft.

after the fact. That sprang from a feeling which one gets traveling on the plane with the candidate, traveling staff, and reporters, that the entire campaign is there and that everything else is at best secondary and will follow along, like the camel's body following its nose wherever it is led. (1973, p. 300)

Frustrating though it is, this situation is likely to continue.

Multiple Leaders

Since a campaign is being led from at least three sources—the national committee, the candidate's personal staff, and "the plane"—there is considerable fragmentation of authority. It is also not uncommon for two or more people to believe that they have been promised the leadership position in a campaign. In the 1960 Nixon campaign, former Republican national chairman Leonard Hall was given the title of campaign chairman, and Robert Finch, a close friend of the candidate from Los Angeles, was called campaign director. In the 1972 McGovern campaign, Gary Hart, Frank Mankiewicz, and Lawrence O'Brien (who had been recruited in that order) all had titles suggesting they were in charge of that campaign. And in 1984, John Reilly got along perfectly well without benefit of any formal title at all. Each of these persons was, in fact, playing an important role in these campaigns, and that role varied according to the background and skills of the particular individual. Who was in charge? That question was deliberately left unresolved by the candidate, who wanted to use all these people in the campaign.

Multiple Groups and Multiple Bases of Expertise

Different points of view arise as one person or another acts as a spokesperson for one of the groups in the candidate's supporting coalition. As we have seen, each issue group has a different set of policy preferences, and its members attempt to persuade the candidate to move closer to their position. Finally, the different types of expertise needed in a campaign—speech writing, fund-raising, and so on—give rise to a functional division of authority. The regional directors in campaign operations feel that the speech writers don't have a feel for how the campaign is moving out in the country; the speech writers think that the regional directors don't understand the issues; the finance people think that the other groups are spending money faster than they can possibly raise it. Since each of these actors is expert in one area, each has a basis on which to speak.

The division of responsibility between the few at the apex of the campaign and those with specific responsibilities is not unlike that in Congress between the floor leaders and committee chairmen. Nonetheless, this is a source of tension within a campaign organization. One of the reasons given by F. Clifton White for Barry Goldwater's defeat in 1964 was not that the Senator was a candidate of a minority party who took policy positions somewhat removed from the majority of the American people. Rather:

> The really important decisions of the campaign were . . . hammered out in the so-called "Think Tank" on the third floor of an office building at 1625 I Street in downtown Washington. There Denison Kitchel, Bill Baroody and their stable of speech writers and research experts held court. It was a court that was notably unreceptive to ideas from outside its own circle. (White, 1967, pp. 415–16)

White happened to be the director of Citizens for Goldwater-Miller. In this quote, he was expressing his unhappiness with the research division. But the quote could just as easily have come from an ad agency person whose favorite slogan had been rejected or from a regional coordinator who felt that others just didn't understand New England.

Multiple headquarters. Multiple leaders. Multiple groups. Multiple bases of expertise. How seriously do these affect the progress of the campaign? One of the most important determinants is the candidate's standing with the voters. If the candidate is popular and running well ahead of his opponent, then organizational problems are not too serious. Staff members' morale is high, and visions of White House offices dance in their heads. If the contestants are in a tight race, there is anxiety; but along with the anxiety, there is some extra effort put forth because it might make a difference in the election. But if the candidate is running behind, then organizational tensions are felt. Reluctant to believe that the candidate is unpopular or is saying the wrong things about issues, there is a tendency to blame improper tactics or some organizational defect. It is easy to think that it is *someone else's* fault that the party is running behind; and with responsibility so divided, there are many scapegoats close at hand.[5]

The structure of campaign staffs is certainly not the same for different candidates and elections. It does not retain the same institutional form from one campaign to another. Division titles change. Activities found in one organizational unit in a given campaign may have been assigned to another unit four years earlier. Fortunately, we are not interested in who has which title or in what an organization chart would look like. We are interested in what the campaign organization *does*. For our purposes, we can think of four clusters of activities: campaign operations, research, public relations, and finance. Each is needed to reach the voters, and each will be carried out by persons located somewhere within any campaign organization.

CAMPAIGN OPERATIONS

Where to Campaign?

Of all the decisions taken in a campaign, those which concern geographic concentration have the most extensive implications for what the campaign

---

[5] One could argue that a losing campaign is the best to study. There are likely to be just as many organizational problems in a winning campaign organization, but the euphoria that goes with victory tends to hide these problems from participants and observers.

organization does. Many things that will affect the outcome of an election—voters' attitudes at the outset of a campaign, the positions set forth by the opposition candidate—are beyond the control of the campaign managers. They can make decisions, though, about the use of the resources they control. Essentially, this refers to where the candidate will campaign, where money will be spent, and what organizational efforts will be made. Given finite time and finite resources, which cannot be expended everywhere, there are obvious incentives to use them where there will be the greatest return in votes.

As long as we continue to elect our presidents through the Electoral College and as long as the states cast all of their electoral votes for the candidate receiving a plurality in the state,[6] these decisions are going to be geographic. The decisions are likely to be made at the highest levels of the campaign organization. The way it is made depends on the quality of information available to the decision makers and how systematic their analysis is. As long ago as 1932, James A. Farley was making decisions based on analyses of probable Democratic majorities in each state.

> Acting on the principle that success can do its own succeeding without help from anyone, the Democratic National Committee merely adapted its campaign expenditures to Mr. Hurja's method. A campaign chairman, with the even-handed justice of a blinded divinity, would spill his funds equitably and inefficiently over an entire map. Armed with the Hurja prognostication Mr. Farley . . . tempered the wind to the shorn lamb, turned the hose on the dry ground, and made his nickels last. (*Fortune*, April 1935, p. 136, quoted in Herring, 1940)

In most recent campaigns, both parties have made their decisions about geographic concentration quite systematically. In 1976, Hamilton Jordan wrote a long memorandum for Jimmy Carter and Walter Mondale in which 31 pages were devoted to formulas to determine the amount of effort to be devoted to each state. The formulas reflected three criteria: size, Democratic potential, and need. Size reflected the number of electoral votes cast. There were four categories of Democratic potential, which reflected the state's likelihood of voting Democratic if worked effectively. The estimates of need were based on four pieces of information: strategic premises, survey information, whether Carter had campaigned in a primary election in the state, and the results of that primary. Finally, the entire percent-of-effort computation (based on size, Democratic potential, and need) was matched against a "value of a day's campaigning" estimate, in which, for example, Jimmy Carter was assigned 7 points and Chip Carter only 2 points to determine how often spokespersons for the ticket ought to go into a state (Schramm, 1977, pp. 239–50, 386–91).

---

[6] Seemingly forgotten in the recurring discussion about possible elimination of the Electoral College is the state's power to cast its electoral votes in some other way than by giving all of them to the candidate winning a plurality. Michigan cast its electoral votes by congressional district in 1892, and its right to do so was upheld by the Supreme Court in *Shoemaker* v. *United States* (Corwin, 1948, pp. 50, 418).

The 1976 Republican plan was quite different. It was a long document that took into account the position in which Ford found himself (far behind Carter) and the voters' perceptions of the candidates and then set forth a strategy to change those perceptions so they would be more favorable to Ford. A three-fold classification of states—"our base," "swing states," and "his base"—was included in this strategy plan. In general, the classification of states by the Republican strategy group was similar to Jordan's, except that the Republican group had a much longer list of swing states and they saw Ford's base as being much smaller than the Carter base envisioned by Jordan.

In 1980, the allocation of resources to states in the Democratic campaign was governed by a document known as the Orange Book. A regression analysis of the Democratic presidential vote from 1956 through 1976 yielded estimates of turnout, average Democratic vote, and "persuadability." Based essentially on the mean Democratic vote from 1956 through 1976, 3 states were classified as "safe," 4 as "marginal plus," 24 as "marginal," 3 as "marginal minus," and 17 as "lost."

Eleven states had their classifications shifted because of special considerations. For example, Massachusetts was shifted from safe to marginal plus because of the attractiveness of John Anderson to Bay State voters, and Georgia was shifted from marginal to safe because it was Carter's home state. No resources were to be devoted to the safe states or the lost states, and twice as many resources were to be devoted to the marginal states as to the marginal-plus or the marginal-minus states. For example, 10.8 percent of all effort was to be devoted to New York because the Empire State was on the marginal list and because it cast 41 electoral votes. Thus, Democratic targeting was a function of the likelihood of a state's voting Democratic and the number of its electoral votes.[7]

The 1980 Reagan strategy had a regional character, but it wasn't based on regional assumptions. The three assumptions were: (1) Based on survey data, whatever electoral base Jimmy Carter had assembled in 1976 no longer existed by 1980. (2) Ronald Reagan could not be presumed to have an electoral base, because he had never been a candidate in a general election. (3) Since Governor Reagan was a conservative candidate who would move toward the center in the course of the campaign, the election was likely to turn on states with large numbers of independent and moderate voters, specifically a few Great Lakes states. Not surprisingly, when strategists began to count electoral votes most likely to be cast for Reagan, they came from the West, the Pacific Coast to the Plains states, Indiana, and Virginia. This initial Reagan base added up to 162 electoral votes, which meant that there were several different ways they could get from there to the needed 270. When Texas, Florida, Iowa, and Kentucky were added, increasing the Reagan base to 213, the election could be won by carrying any two of the four Great Lakes target states: Illinois,

---

[7] Further calculations extended this reasoning down to the county and media market level.

Michigan, Ohio, and Pennsylvania. (New Jersey, Connecticut, and Mississippi were alternate targets in case three Great Lakes states eluded them.) Therefore, advertising and organizational efforts were fairly soft in the West, a little heavier in the Pacific Northwest, still heavier in Texas, Florida, Missouri, Kentucky, and Virginia, and concentrated as much as possible in the four Great Lakes target states.

Both parties faced difficulties in constructing their 1984 targeting plans. When they did their state-by-state analysis, the Democrats came up with essentially the same small base that they had in 1980. They found only six states plus the District of Columbia that could could be regarded as safe or leaning toward Mondale. Georgia, regarded as safe for Carter in 1980, was dropped from the list, and Maryland was added as leaning toward Mondale. Otherwise, the list of states was the same.[8] The real difference in Democratic estimations was in probable Republican states. In 1980, they had reckoned that only 150 electoral votes were leaning toward or were safe for Governor Reagan. Therefore, it was conceivable that Carter could win by sweeping the marginal states. But in 1984, the Democrats believed that there were 276 electoral votes safe or leaning toward President Reagan. In the face of an analysis that predicted Reagan's almost certain reelection, the Democrats' options were to try to take votes away from Reagan, either in the South or in California—or to abandon any pretense of a targeting strategy. They tried both of these but didn't seem to pursue either very consistently.

The Republicans' initial plan was drawn up in 1983 at a time when Walter Mondale was running ahead of Ronald Reagan in trial heats. Given a need to improve Reagan's standing with several demographic groups, Richard Wirthlin's 1983 plan set demographic targets within states, as well as picking out states for concentration. So far as the states themselves were concerned, the Reagan base was constructed around California, Florida, Indiana, Virginia, and 13 smaller states for 153 votes. Texas and five smaller states were seen as leaning toward Reagan, with an additional 55 electoral votes. The Republicans' difficulties evaporated in 1984 as the economy picked up and Reagan's popularity increased, but they continued with their very sophisticated targeting strategy.

While the tendency toward the systematic use of campaign resources has become much more pronounced in recent years, campaigners do not always make rational decisions. In 1960, Richard Nixon pledged to visit all 50 states; in order to do so, he devoted most of the Sunday before the election to a long flight to Alaska, a state that cast barely 1 percent of the electoral votes needed. During the final week of the 1964 campaign, Barry Goldwater visited four great metropolitan centers, but he also devoted time to the voters in Dover, Delaware; Cedar Rapids, Iowa; Cheyenne, Wyoming; and Las Vegas, Ne-

---

[8] Only the District of Columbia was thought to be safe for Carter in 1980 and safe for Mondale in 1984. This says something about the geographic shrinkage of the New Deal coalition.

vada. These were not locations where the election was going to be won or lost. Even if the campaign managers do nothing more than acquiesce to local pressures—schedule the candidate where state leaders want him to come and keep him away from areas where he is unpopular—this decision controls much of what the campaign does.

The Plane

Wherever the candidate is to go, there must be some way of moving him around, and this means "the plane." The shift to planes as the primary means of moving the candidate around was a gradual consequence of technological developments. The advent of jet aircraft meant that it was no longer possible to reject the plea of a West Coast politico for a presidential candidate's appearance on the grounds that he was campaigning in, say, Pennsylvania that day. Now it is possible to get him to the West Coast if the reason is sufficiently compelling. The development of the Boeing 727 in the 1960's made it possible to stay on the same aircraft and still get into smaller airports with shorter runways. Finally, increasingly sophisticated communications equipment (and having enough money to install it in the aircraft) meant reasonably constant communications between "the plane" and other campaign headquarters.

Campaign trains are still used but as a way of evoking nostalgia for "traditional" politics, giving the television cameramen something different to shoot, and reaching groups of small and medium-sized cities that might affect important electoral votes. Jimmy Carter took a whistlestop tour in 1976 from Newark across New Jersey and Pennsylvania toward Chicago, hoping to evoke the spirit of Harry Truman's 1948 effort, and Ronald Reagan rode a train through western Ohio in 1984, taking advantage of the opportunity to speak to audiences in smaller communities. Of course, there is still the motorcade that is used to move the candidate through suburban areas and back and forth from an airport to a rally site.

Obviously, more is involved here than just moving the candidate himself. A considerable retinue accompanies him, which sometimes complicates logistics. A plane, such as Peanut One that carried Jimmy Carter in 1976 or the Louisville Slugger used by Walter Mondale in 1984,[9] usually carries senior advisors and friends, speech writers, press secretary and aides, state dignitaries, Secret Service personnel, pool reporters, and the secretaries to help these people get their work done. The configuration of the plane must provide some privacy for the candidate, working space, an area for typewriters, mimeograph, and photocopier, and communications equipment. Since there isn't enough space aboard the candidate's plane for the traveling press, a press plane follows along.

---

[9] The most evocatively named was Barry Goldwater's 1964 aircraft, Yai Bi Kin. This is Navajo for House in the Sky.

Scheduling

Responsibility for planning campaign trips is divided among four sets of persons: the strategy committee (or some ranking decision maker), regional and state coordinators and state party leaders, the tour committee, and advance men. Basic decisions about time allocations are made at the highest levels of the campaign in the manner already discussed. Questions about where the candidate will go within the state have been talked out between regional and state coordinators and state party leaders.[10] The candidate's general schedule (3:00 P.M., press plane arrives Metropolitan Airport; 3:30 P.M., candidate plane arrives Metropolitan Airport; 3:45 P.M., candidate departs for Metro City Hotel; and so on) is worked out by a person on the tour committee.[11] Since the candidate will be making appearances in several cities in a single day, all of these details have to be combined into a master schedule. Finally, responsibility for arrangements in the community where the candidate is to appear is in the hands of an advance man.

The Advance Man

The person who advances a candidate's appearance usually gets to the city about five days to a week before the appearance. Any number of things must be done. The route between the airport and the rally site must be checked out and timed exactly in traffic conditions similar to those the candidate's motorcade will encounter. The rally site (auditorium, shopping center, or whatever) must be checked out so it will accord with the candidate's preferences and so locations for the photographers and press traveling with the candidate will be available but not interfere with the voters who ought to be present. There may be problems with the prospective audience. For example, large numbers of local politicos will want to be close to the candidate, or too small an audience may be in prospect. In these cases, the advance man must cut the number of politicos down to a manageable size and do what he can to increase the size of the crowd. If the candidate is staying overnight, hotel reservations must be made. Arrangements must be made with the local police to ensure the candidate's safety. If available, the Secret Service can be of great help with all this. They are familiar with the things that need to be done, and there is enough overlap between logistical needs and safety needs that many of the necessary arrangements fall into their province.

---

[10] This decision is beginning to move to national strategists as they develop more refined ideas about the target audience *within* the state they want to reach. There was noticeable movement in this direction in the Reagan campaign in 1980. Needless to say, state leaders are not happy about losing control of a decison they have been accustomed to making.

[11] The tour committee will typically have one person working on the presidential candidate's schedule; one on the vice presidential candidate's schedule; one handling party notables, such as ex-presidents; one handling celebrities, such as movie stars; and one or more coordinating the appearances of others working on behalf of the ticket.

The advance man normally has the final say about all of the details of the appearance. There are certain to be things that will be disputed—who will have an opportunity to shake the candidate's hand, whose car will be how close to the candidate's in the motorcade, and so on—and it is up to the advance man to settle these matters.[12]

Once the candidate shows up, the advance man is at his side and in charge of things as long as the candidate is in the city. When the candidate's plane leaves for the next city, where another advance man will have been setting things up, the advance man says good-bye and leaves for another city to make arrangements for another appearance some days hence (Hoagland, 1960; Ogden & Peterson, 1968, chap. 9).

Demographic Organization

The rest of the persons involved in campaign operations are usually organized along demographic group or regional lines. The nature of a demographic group operation is suggested by these names of units that have been organized in one campaign or another: Youth for Reagan, Viva Kennedy, Scientists and Engineers for Johnson-Humphrey, Mothers for a Moral America, Pilots for Goldwater-Miller, Nationalities Division, Civil Rights Division, Citizens—Farm and Food, Funeral Directors Committee for the Reelection of the President, Motorcyclists Committee for the Reelection of the President, Heritage Groups, Veteran Voter Groups, and National McGovern-Shriver Labor Committee. Each of these campaign units is set up to reach a certain segment of the population. One must know something more than the name of the unit, of course, to be certain that it is a functioning part of the campaign organization. It may be only a paper committee that was set up to sponsor a campaign event, as was Mothers for a Moral America, or it may be essentially a fund-raising operation in which one receives a membership card in return for the payment of dues.

Assuming that the campaign unit is more than a letterhead committee, it is likely to have certain characteristics. First, the target population must be large enough and have enough political importance for its support to be worth the expenditure of resources. Often, attention is devoted to areas where the party is weak. For example, the Republicans usually have a labor unit, whereas the Democrats (who already have a lot of support from organized labor) will often omit a labor unit in their structure.

---

[12] There are good reasons for this. The local party leaders have to work with each other after the rally, and the object of the whole campaign is to make the candidate more popular rather than less so. Consequently, if the local leaders are going to be angry with anyone, it is better that they be upset with the advance man rather than being angry with each other or with the candidate. Sometimes the advance man can avoid this altogther. If he has any experience, he can assure local leaders that his decisions are exactly in line with procedures followed in all the other campaign events being staged for the candidate.

Second, the person in charge of the effort has some knowledge of the population in question. Thus an Arts and Sciences Division once organized by the Republican National Committee was headed by an academic on leave of absence, and the executive director of the Senior Citizens for Johnson and Humphrey was on leave from the United Automobile Workers' Department of Older and Retired Workers.

Third, there needs to be some means of communicating with the target population. A not unusual pattern includes a mailing list and a newsletter. The essential job of the staff members heading these units is to explain the candidate and the positions being taken in language that their groups understand. If they are sufficiently persuasive, they may also convey the wishes of the population segment back to the campaign leaders.

Regional Organization

The alternate form of campaign organization follows geographic lines. In this form, the head of the campaign division will be assisted by regional directors. The regions used vary a little from one campaign to another but generally adhere to familiar areas, such as the Middle Atlantic states, the Middle West, or the West Coast. If resources permit, a pair of regional directors is used for each area. One remains at campaign headquarters while the other travels in the region. When this arrangement is used, the codirectors change place every 10 days or so. This means that there is a familiar voice on the headquarters telephone when the state directors call in, and someone is out in the field giving encouragement to campaign workers and gathering fresh information.

Establishing lines of communication through regional directors to state directors has the advantage of following the lines of the Electoral College, and the things the regional directors do are directly related to producing electoral votes in their areas. As already noted, once the strategy group has decided that the candidate or other spokespersons will spend time in the state, then the regional director and the state chairperson are likely to be involved in the decision as to where the appearances should take place. Which areas of the state are most likely to produce votes for the ticket without any effort? Which areas may do so but require some campaigning? What demographic groupings (located in what part of the state) are targets of state or national campaign strategies? These factors would be assessed in making a decision that the candidate ought to appear in, say, Rochester and Syracuse but not in Buffalo.

Regional directors make similar judgments about states in their areas. This allows decisions to be made about allocations of resources. In 1960, for example, national campaign manager Robert Kennedy was told that Democratic prospects did not look good in Iowa but that there was a chance for his brother to carry Illinois. His response was simple: "We'll spend our money in Illinois."

A third activity of regional directors is coordination of straightforward registration and get-out-the-vote drives. Since registration is a major factor in determining election day turnout (Kelley, Ayers & Bowen, 1967; Rosenstone & Wolfinger, 1978) and since Democrats are less likely to register than Republicans, Democratic campaigns are somewhat more prone to emphasize registration drives than are Republicans.[13]

Both parties are interested in maximizing their turnout. The election day efforts to do this were simple in the small towns of the 19th century. Each party had a poll watcher who knew the town's inhabitants. If supporters did not show up by midafternoon, someone would be sent round to remind them to come and vote. The technique is still essentially the same, though its application has been made more complex by changes in the population, and more efficient through the use of telephones and computers.

For election day activity to be effective, it must be preceded by planning and by identifying supporters, beginning with an estimate of the total vote needed to carry a state. (A new figure is necessary for each election because, with population growth, the vote that carried the state in the preceding election is likely to be inadequate.) The total vote for the state is then decomposed into county quotas, these likewise based on knowledge of party strength and the county populations. If each county meets its quota, then the state goal will be reached.

Next, the county leaders must locate the voters who will enable them to meet their quota. If there is registration by party, they will have a pretty good idea where to start; but even where registration lists are available, additional work needs to be done. Population mobility brings any number of new residents to the community, and the greater incidence of independent voting makes it necessary to find out whether each "loyal Democrat" intends in fact to vote for the Democratic candidate. This has been done traditionally by precinct workers calling on voters in their areas. If funds are available to set up phone banks, however, voters can be contacted much more speedily by bringing volunteers together in a "boiler shop," from which telephone calls are placed. The calls usually include a gentle sales pitch; but the crucial elements are to determine whether persons living in the household intend to vote, whether they need any aid in doing so (such as transportation or a babysitter), and whether they intend to support the party's candidate, are undecided, or intend to vote for the opposition.

The immediate results of the telephone work provide information on how well the candidate is running. They are aggregated and forwarded up the line to state headquarters and national headquarters. Much of this information also is fed into computers in order to provide useful lists and sets of address labels. Undecided voters are sent literature. Depending on the quality of the information elicited and the sophistication of the computer operation, voters may receive personal letters presenting arguments about the issues of concern to them. Those undecided about whether to vote receive extra calls just before the election, encouraging them to do so. Names of persons who need

---

[13] The greater tendency for Democratic voters to remain unregistered accounts for the greater Democratic interest in schemes of automatic or permanent registration.

transportation to the polls appear on special lists so this can be provided. And the names of all those likely to vote appear on lists that allow traditional election day contact to go forward.

This telephone and computer operation is simple enough to describe, but enormous amounts of effort are necessary to carry it out. During the 1972 Nixon campaign, nearly 16 million households were contacted in this way. More people were reached through this contact operation than had voted for Nixon in 1968—undoubtedly the high point of this kind of campaigning. Some $12 million were poured into this contact operation (White, 1973, pp. 322–28), and money that would allow citizen contact on this lavish a scale is not available under the campaign finance laws that went into effect in 1974.

RESEARCH

The "research" that is needed in the middle of a campaign has very little to do with academic research; its aim is not the discovery of information that may be regarded as a contribution to knowledge. There is an element of discovery in polls taken to determine voters' perceptions, but much more campaign research involves processing already available information so it can be used for electoral purposes. When one speaks of research in campaign headquarters, the usual reference is to the activities of the people who work in a research division. They are the speech writers, "issue persons," pollsters, and some individuals whose tasks are similar to those of reference librarians.

The Art of Producing Campaign Speeches

The speech given most often during a campaign is not written at all. It evolves—a pastiche of applause lines the candidate has discovered in previous months of campaigning a "theme song" made up of phrases that the candidate likes and that have demonstrated their ability to spark crowd reaction. It includes such lines as John Kennedy's "It's time to get America moving again"; George Wallace's references to "pointy-headed bureaucrats who send us guidelines telling us when we can go to sleep at night and when we can get up in the morning"; Richard Nixon's 1968 declaration that "it's time for new leadership"; Jimmy Carter's 1976 promise, "I'll never lie to you"; and Ronald Reagan's tantalizing 1984 forecast, "You ain't seen notin' yet."

Such a speech is used during the numerous brief stops when "remarks" are called for. There are too many of these stops for anything approaching an original statement to be developed for each, and neither a tired candidate nor a weary speech writer has any desire to depart from the familiar. The repetition is tedious to the candidate and to reporters who have heard the lines dozens of times, but repetition helps develop a candidate's image in the same way that endless exposure to Anacin or Tylenol commercials fix the names of these products in the minds of television viewers.

Major addresses on foreign policy, economics, welfare, civil rights, or whatever are quite different. When a candidate is making a major speech to, say, the Detroit Council on Foreign Relations or giving an address on nation-wide television, he is expected to state a position with some precision. Speeches for these occasions are carefully considered and often pass through several drafts.

Just how the candidate and the speech writers work together in such circumstances varies considerably. Theodore Sorenson drafted most of John Kennedy's speeches in 1960; those he did not write, he at least reviewed. Most speech topics were "discussed with the Senator only, and they were decided by him, in his plane or hotel and without reference to other materials, a day or two before the speech was given" (Sorenson, 1965, p. 208).

In 1968, Richard Nixon worked with a number of speech writers and set forth what he wanted in memorandums or oral instructions. For example, in late September, he distributed a memorandum asking for excerpts running a page to a page and a half. The excerpts, he said, should be

> meaty and quotable and . . . zero in primarily on the four major themes. If we scatter-gun too much we are not going to have an impact. . . . We must have at least two excerpts a week which hit some aspect of the law and order theme and one or two a week which hit some aspect of the spending theme and two or three a week which hit the foreign policy–respect for America theme. (Safire, 1975, pp. 71–72)

In a third pattern, members of the strategy group agree that certain material is called for and set a speech writer to work on it. For example, late in the 1976 campaign, Jody Powell and Greg Schneiders agreed with speech writer Patrick Anderson that for a Pittsburgh dinner, material was needed that would show Carter knew about the difficulties caused by poor leadership but was optimistic about the future. Anderson wrote a speech including a number of "I see" lines:—"I see a new spirit in America. I see a national pride restored. I see a revival of patriotism" (Schram, 1977, p. 344). A similar series of I-see lines were used in Carter's acceptance speech. For that matter, such lines had been penned by William Safire for Richard Nixon in 1968, used by Barry Goldwater in 1964, written for Franklin Roosevelt, and spoken by Robert Ingersoll when he nominated James G. Blaine for president in 1876 (Safire, 1975, p. 54).

For any major address, drafts flow back and forth between the candidate and the speech writers. This allows the candidate to continue making changes until he gets what he wants. For example, Patrick Anderson wrote for Jimmy Carter, "When I started to run for president, there were those who said that I would fail, because there was another governor who spoke for the South, a man who once stood in a schoolhouse door and cried out, segregation forever." Carter, not wishing to insult George Wallace unnecessarily, changed the reason to "there were those who said I would fail because I was from the South" (Schram, 1977, p. 180). Toward the end of the 1968 campaign, Richard Nixon wanted to make a statement concerning then President Lyndon Johnson. As drafted by Bryce Harlow, it began, "Throughout this campaign the

President has been evenhanded and straightforward with the major presidential contenders about Vietnam. I know he has been under intense pressure to contrive a fake peace." Nixon altered this to read, "Throughout this campaign I have found the President impartial and candid with the major presidential contenders about Vietnam. I know he has been subjected—for many months, beginning long before the national convention—to intense pressure to contrive what he has appropriately described as a fake peace" (Safire, 1975, p. 85). While the circumstances of a campaign hardly allow a candidate to write every word that he speaks or that is released in his name, the speech writing process certainly allows him to place his personal tone on important texts.

Insofar as the term *speech writer* suggests that a writer is in control of the process and the candidate simply reads the words, it distorts what goes on as a candidate presents his ideas to the electorate. Raymond Moley, who wrote speeches for Governor Franklin Roosevelt in 1932, described the process much more clearly. He distinguished between "the principal" who gives the addresses, "the collaborator" who has continuous access to the principal and provides him with drafts, and "the feeders" who route their ideas to the collaborator (1960). Collaborators need to have a facility with words and some political experience; more important, they should have the confidence of the principal, a knowledge of the phrasing the principal likes to use, and a willingness to set forth the ideas the principal wants to use whether they think the ideas are wise or not.

The feeders may be "issues persons" in the campaign organization proper, or they may be interested citizens who simply want to pass ideas along. Their existence does not imply that either the candidate or the speech writers are barren of ideas themselves. Rather, many ideas are needed in the course of a campaign, and a large number of people think they have ideas that are going to win the election for the candidate. The combination of a need for good ideas and a need for enough working time to develop substantive proposals so they will be helpful to the candidate leads to a unique organizational imperative. There must be some kind of screen to protect the issues staff and the speech writers from the large number of people who want to help but don't quite know how; at the same time, there must be some provision so that good ideas do get through.

New Ideas and the Triple Test

While there are likely to be many good ideas, the number of usable ones tends to be limited. This may surprise people who have not been through a presidential campaign, but any idea must pass a number of tests before it is politically useful. If a candidate takes a position that gives offense to any group in the supporting coalition, they may not work for him with continued fervor. A position that is unappealing to a target constituency will reduce the number of votes he might otherwise receive.

Furthermore, a proposal, once made, is certain to be scrutinized by both the opposition and the media. If the program is inconsistent with some previously taken position, the candidate will be asked which of the policies he intends to pursue seriously. If he chooses the earlier policy, the just-announced program will be called frivolous. If he chooses the just-announced policy, he will be accused of inconsistency. If he says he will implement both policies, opponents and reporters will say that he has not thought through the consequences of what he says. Finally, the proposal should be one that can be accomplished with the resources available to the government. It is this triple test—acceptability to coalition members and voters who are potential supporters, consistency with previously announced positions, and capability of being carried out with existing resources—that limits the number of ideas that are usable in a campaign.

In consequence, the chief qualification of a good issues person is the ability to sense which ideas pass this triple test and should therefore be brought to the attention of the candidate and the speech writers. This is likely to be someone motivated by an interest in the substance of politics and with enough previous campaign experience not to be a dogmatic advocate of any particular approach. Persons who have these skills (for example, Michael Baroody in the Republican party or Peter Edelman in the Democratic party) are apt to be well known in the upper echelons of presidential politics and almost invisible to the general public. They may, of course, become well known if appointed to relatively visible positions. This happened when Republican Rudolph Penner was chosen as head of the Congressional Budget Office and when Democrat Stuart Eizenstat became head of President Carter's Domestic Policy Staff.

In any particular campaign, there is likely to be a small in-house issues staff and a larger number of outside consultants. The head of the in-house issues staff will have worked with the candidate for some time. Outside consultants are active in many areas, and there are usually special groups dealing with the imperative policy areas of international involvement and economic management.

The Increasing Importance of Polling

The importance of polling has been increasing for some time. This is evident both in the location of the principal pollster within the campaign staff and in the sophistication of the information that is provided about the voters. Private polls for candidates, of course, are not new; but as recently as the 1960s, they were used in a rather rudimentary manner. Older politicians regarded surveys with some skepticism. Even proponents seemed fascinated by any similarity between survey results and election results. The usual pattern was to hire an outside polling firm whose head would come in occasionally during the campaign to present findings. Otherwise, liaison with the polling firm was maintained by a relatively low ranking staff member. The reliability of the data was kept high through large numbers of interviews, and the presentation of results was restricted to marginals (that is, 57 percent for Candidate A and 43 percent for Candidate B) and very simple cross-tabulations. In the 1964

Goldwater campaign, for example, three national surveys of this kind were taken. The reports were kept by an intelligent young graduate of Stanford Law School (who had no training in survey analysis), and the last scheduled survey was canceled because the surveys were bringing bad news.

This situation changed, not because of arguments about the importance of surveys but because successful politicians put great reliance on them. Ray Bliss was known to study his polls very closely, and knowledgeable analysts (especially Louis Harris among the Democrats and Walter deVries among the Republicans) spread the word about what could be done. By 1976, pollsters were principal members of the strategy groups in both parties. Robert Teeter of Market Opinion Research provided continuous information for the Republicans, and Pat Caddell did the same for the Democrats. In 1980, Richard Wirthlin of Decision/Making/Information was one of four senior decision makers on the Republican side, and Pat Caddell continued to play a similar role for the Democrats. In 1984, both Teeter and Wirthlin contributed to Republican strategy, and both Peter Hart and Caddell helped shape Democratic themes.

Not only were pollsters located where they could be much more active in charting campaign strategy, but the kind of information they provided was much more detailed. In 1968, David Derge based his analysis for the Nixon campaign on a panel study of voters in 13 states and small daily cross sections. The state-level data gave information on where campaign resources should be concentrated, and the daily information allowed him to pick up trends as they began to develop. Pat Caddell similarly had daily information that he could provide to the Carter campaign in 1976 and 1980. In 1976, he was able to tell them early on that Carter's support was soft; as it eroded during the campaign, he was able to point to particular segments of the electorate as contributing more than others to Democratic difficulties. Caddell's daily information was accurate enough in 1980 to give him the sad task of telling Carter on election eve, "Mr. President, I'm afraid it's gone."

Robert Teeter added a number of useful analyses for the Republicans in 1976. Telephone polls allowed quick answers of interest to strategists; picked audiences watched the debates, indicating their agreement with the candidates by adjusting rheostats; spatial analyses summarized information on where candidates stood with respect to each other and the voters (Parry, 1977; Schram, 1977). By 1980, Richard Wirthlin and Richard Beal had put together a Political Information System (PINS) that incorporated a great deal of polling data from various sources and allowed Reagan leaders to simulate the probable consequences of various campaign strategies.

The movement from simple cross-tabulations to multidimensional scaling (the type of spatial analysis used to produce Figures 3–2 and 3–3)[14] and simulation in little more than a decade's time is a measure of the progress

---

[14] One wonders what the reaction of the politicos would be if they had any idea of the assumptions necessary to sustain multidimensional scaling.

made in using survey information; but having knowledgeable pollsters sitting in on strategy discussions is more important in making effective use of these data.

Information Retrieval

While pollsters and other professionals are making use of survey data at the top levels of campaigns, the "reference librarians" of politics busy themselves storing information so it can be made available when needed and can be distributed throughout the campaign organization. Files are kept of statements made by one's own candidates and by opposition candidates. This allows a quick check of what has actually been said when an opponent makes a charge during the campaign. If, for example, an opponent says, "Speaking in Houston last October, the President promised to reduce unemployment to 5 percent," it is possible for the campaign committee to reply, "The President said that he hoped to reduce unemployment as quickly as possible but did not mention any specific target," and to release the exact quotation. This can be very helpful in rebutting the charge.

Another standard activity is the production of speaker's manuals and issue books. Stock speeches are written on various issues, and booklets summarize the stands being taken by both parties. These will be broken down by topic and will have facts and quotations showing the virtues of the party's stand over against the limitations of what the opposition is doing. These are arranged so that a speaker will be able to find an effective reply while listening to opposition statements.

A third headquarters project is an "answer desk" with a well-advertised telephone number. The persons who take the incoming calls are likely to be political veterans whose qualifications are similar to those working on the issues staff. They provide quick replies to what the party's stand is on energy or agriculture or whatever the caller is concerned about. All of these activities are routine. A fair amount of work is necessary, though, to prepare for these tasks and to keep the files up-to-date as the campaign develops.

PUBLIC RELATIONS

James Travis. Gerald Rafshoon. Peter Dailey. John Deardourff. Douglas Bailey. These men are typical of the publicists who carry senior responsibility in political campaigns. Travis, Rafshoon, and Dailey came from advertising. James Travis, a partner in Della Femina, Travisano & Partners, a medium-sized advertising firm in New York City, organized the "Tuesday Team" that handled the Reagan media in 1984. Gerald Rafshoon Advertising, Inc. is a general advertising firm (that is, the bulk of its income comes from nonpolitical accounts) in Atlanta. Rafshoon, whose ties with Jimmy Carter went back to the first Carter gubernatorial campaign in 1966, was in charge of public relations in both Carter presidential campaigns. Peter Dailey formed Dailey and Associates in Los Angeles in 1968 after gaining experience in some very large advertising firms. He was in charge of the Nixon media campaign in 1972, worked on space acquisition during the 1976 Ford campaign, and was again in charge of the Reagan advertising in 1980. John Deardourff and Douglas Bailey, on the other hand, have a firm that specializes in politics. Both came from a background in Republican politics (Deardourff in New York and Bailey in Massachusetts), and both learned enough about media campaigns that they set up their own campaign management firm. Deardourff and Bailey handled the Ford campaign in 1976.

Being at the center of a campaign organization is not new for publicists. Of all the things done by an electoral coalition to reach their primary audience, public relations is one of the most crucial and has been so recognized for a very long time. It emerged as a distinct occupation in the early decades of the 20th century, and political applications were not too long in coming. Charles Michelson was active in the Democratic campaign in 1932; and in 1936, Chicago advertising man Hill Blackett became the Republican's first public relations director (Kelley, 1956, chap. 1). Since that time, public relations has most commonly been directed by a combination of an in-house division and either a public relations or a campaign management firm. As television has become more important, so have the media specialists.

This is *not* to say that public relations people have taken control of campaigns. It is only one segment of a campaign, and the influence of a firm ranges from a maximum, when one of their chiefs sits on the strategy group with the other principals, to a minimum, when the agency is restricted to the technical functions of space and time acquisition. Still, the great days of *party* public relations directors probably came in the 1950s, with Jack Redding and Sam Brightman in the Democratic party and Robert Humphreys and Lou Guylay in the Republican party. With television so prominent in the 1980s, influence would inevitably flow to the Travises, Rafshoons, Daileys, Deardourffs, and Baileys who know how to work with that medium.

To keep these things in perspective, it may help to remember that almost everything but the television material usually comes from the public relations division within the campaign organization. Even in Charles Michelson's time, this was not inconsiderable. Working before electronic media began to rival newspapers, Michelson concentrated on getting stories and phrases into print. He sent statements to prominent Democrats whose names would draw public attention. He sent news items and editorial suggestions directly to newspapers. His basic assumption was that he wanted to create anti-Hoover news, a task that became much easier once the Depression began (Kelley, 1956, p. 31).

Newspaper Contact

By the 1950s, Michelson's one-person operation had evolved into what amounted to a small public relations firm within the national committee staff. This division had a number of responsibilities. First, it worked directly with the Washington-based press. This meant the distribution of press releases. These included speeches and statements of the presidential candidate, which were made available in Washington at the same time that they were released on the campaign plane, and also statements by other party leaders as well. (If one wished to attack the opposition candidate directly, such a statement might come from a recognized partisan figure, such as the national chairman. In this way, the presidential candidate could maintain a more statesmanlike manner.) Dealing with the press also meant answering media queries. This is less time consuming now that most of the major media have their political reporters traveling with the candidate, but it still involves some effort.

A second activity growing directly out of Michelson's distribution of materials is the press service directed at the weekly newspapers published around the country. Most of them operate with much tighter resources than the dailies and have no Washington contacts. They are quite willing to run material if it can be provided. Consequently, canned news articles, features, editorials, and photographs are sent out, often in mat format to make reproduction as simple as possible.

Campaign Materials

A third public relations group is concerned with art and production. Having an artist available means that pamphlets and brochures can be designed to say exactly what party leaders want them to say. Once the pamphlets are ready to go, they are turned over to a commercial printer in the Washington area. Samples are sent around the country, and anyone wanting them for distribution orders them directly from the printer. The production department also has a small offset press. Photoreproduction makes it possible to make copies of newspaper articles that appear. Obviously, it is an advantage to have favorable comments coming from neutral reporters, since their source credibility is so much higher.

The production department is also involved, with frankly partisan party publications and campaign newsletters directed to an audience of committed activists. They vary from one-page, mimeographed newsletters to slickly produced small magazines. With the rise of sustaining memberships, these party publications fit into a useful dual relation. Because supporters receive "subscriptions" when they make contributions, these publications bring in money at the same time that they provide a channel for the distribution of party propaganda.

Campaign materials—bumper stickers, campaign buttons, balloons, hats, inflatable elephants and donkeys, and all the rest—are produced commercially. The public relations division may, to be sure, suggest the wording for a bumper sticker to a friendly supplier. But for the most part, these initiatives come from those who want to make money from the campaign. The task for the public relations division is simply to catalog all these materials and send copies of the catalog out through party channels to persons who might buy them. From that point on, the transactions take place between the buyer and manufacturer (Cotter & Hennessy, 1964, pp. 129–33; Guylay, 1960).

Campaign materials, if any, prepared for the electronic media by the public relations staff at campaign headquarters are likely to be for radio. There are two reasons for this. Radio spots do not require the elaborate technical facilities needed for television. And since radio time is so much less expensive than television time, it is more feasible for local committees to sponsor radio spots. When that is done, the local sponsors can obtain tapes through the campaign headquarters.

Television

Television materials come from the advertising agency or campaign management firm that has been hired.[15] If there is an advertising section in the headquarters public relations staff, the chances are that its chief activity is liaison with the outside agency. The core of the outside agency's responsibility—that is, the task to which it attends even if it does nothing else—is the purchase of advertising space (if print media are being used) and television time. This is a technical task that a campaign headquarters is not equipped to undertake. A good advertising agency can immediately translate a desired geographic concentration to a number of spots that must be purchased in given market areas. It also knows which programs to buy in order to attract either a large audience or one that has certain characteristics. In 1976, for example, large numbers of Jimmy Carter commercials appeared on "Hee-Haw" and the "Lawrence Welk Show" because large numbers of potential Carter voters watched these programs (Lelyveld, 1976a).

The television time itself is sold by station representatives to time buyers in the ad agencies. Given that much political time is purchased late and that other advertisers are competing for the same time spots (General Motors, General Foods, and all the rest don't suspend their sales campaigns just because there is an election in the offing), it is in the interests of politicos to have the time buying done by professionals who have been dealing with the sales representatives for a long time. In other words, tell the agency what kind of audience is sought and leave in its hands the decision about how the audience will be reached.

If there is a heavy concentration on a media campaign—and in 1980, the Carter campaign spent $20.5 million and the Reagan campaign $16.8 million of the federally supplied $29.4 million on mass media advertising—the agency is going to do more than just buy time. The central task of the media campaign is to communicate the candidate's strengths to the voters. There is no single way of doing this; there are as many variations as there are advertising personnel and candidates.

In 1968, Harry Treleaven built a campaign for Nixon around two things. He

---

[15] There is another possibility besides an advertising agency or a campaign management firm. This is the creation of an ad hoc "firm" composed of professional advertising personnel who take leaves of absence from their own firms. This arrangement was used in the 1960 and 1972 Nixon campaigns and the 1980 and 1984 Reagan campaigns. In 1960, the "firm" was called Campaign Associates; in 1972, the November Group; in 1980, Campaign '80; and in 1984, the Tuesday Team.

used commercials made from montages of still photographs, with Nixon's voice on an accompanying sound track. This took advantage of Nixon's greater attractiveness on radio, where only his voice was heard. He also set up a series of studio question-and-answer sessions that allowed Nixon to answer relatively easy questions and thus exhibit his knowledge and experience (McGinniss, 1969). In 1972, the central theme of the campaign was "Reelect the President," not a bad idea since "the President" was undoubtedly more popular than "Richard M. Nixon" (Greenstein, 1974, p. 137).

In the case of Jimmy Carter in 1976, Jerry Rafshoon departed from the general belief that a short commercial was better because of a limited viewer tolerance for politics. He produced five-minute and two-minute advertisements on the assumption that Carter was still credible after one had listened to him for a while and that more time was needed to let that credibility come across to the viewer (Lelyveld, 1976a). In 1980, when the Democratic strategy called for drawing as sharp a distinction between Carter and Reagan as possible, Rafshoon's cameras focused on an empty Oval Office while an announcer asked the audience: "What kind of person should occupy the Oval Office? Should it be . . . Ronald Reagan . . . who attacks the minimum wage and calls unemployment insurance a prepaid vacation? Or should another kind of man sit here, an experienced man who knows how to be responsive to all Americans?"

Since one of the points that 1980 Republican strategists wanted to establish was that Reagan *was* qualified to be president, a frequently used Peter Dailey commercial showed film clips of Reagan as governor while an announcer boasted: "In 1966 he was elected governor of the state of California, next to the president the biggest job in the nation. What he inherited was a state of crisis. . . . Governor Reagan got things back on track." But in 1984, when President Reagan had a presidential record of his own to defend, a commercial was built around the theme, "It's Morning Again in America," featuring happy citizens hard at work. Many Republican commercials in both years featured Ronald Reagan speaking directly into the camera to take advantage of his professional ease with a spoken text and his ability to present a simple and convincing argument.

The themes that are selected to reach the voter are, of course, subject to change. October 25, 1968, and October 19, 1976, both found candidates in New York City. The importance of New York in the Electoral College makes attention to the area almost standard in the closing days of campaigns, but in these instances, candidate Nixon and candidate Carter were both recording new commercials for use in the closing days of the campaigns. Both had started far ahead of their rivals, and both had seen their margins grow smaller and smaller with the passage of time. So now they were trying for themes that would keep them ahead. The aim of the Carter spots was to reassure women voters and to shore up support in the South, two audiences whose judgments about Carter had been trending downward in 1976 (McGinniss, 1969, chap. 1; Schram, 1977, pp. 330–32; Witcover, 1977, pp. 622–23).

While the media specialists are important, it would be well to conclude this discussion with two caveats. First, such specialists cannot erase a candidate's weaknesses. They can remind voters of a candidate's strengths, but advertising could not make Richard Nixon come across as a warm and open human being, or convince reporters that Jimmy Carter was being precise on the issues, or portray Ronald Reagan as having a first-class mind. Second, advertising does not create an entire campaign. As is evident from the other parts of this chapter, public relations is only one part of a campaign. The basic decisions are made by the candidates and the strategy groups on which they rely. The media specialists may be represented in the strategy groups; if they are skillful, they may be persuasive. But theirs are not the only voices.

FINANCE

All the activity we have been discussing increases the ability of the electoral coalition to reach the voters. If a candidate can be moved at jet speed across the country, he will be able to reach more widely dispersed voters than a candidate could when campaigns moved along the rails from one town to another. If pollsters have daily telephone surveys, they can estimate public reaction with vastly greater precision than when campaign managers had to rely on such cues as crowd size and how loudly they cheered. If the candidates can reach an audience of 100 million people on television,[16] they are in simultaneous contact with more people than lived in the entire country when Woodrow Wilson was president. So a good case can be made that these developments help make the democratic process more effective. At the same time, many of the same developments have made campaigning much more expensive. Therefore, new methods of fund-raising have been necessary.

The Increasing Cost of Campaigning

For some time, the costs of presidential campaigns were relatively stable, at least when compared with changes elsewhere in American society. In 1884, the campaigns of both James G. Blaine and Grover Cleveland cost some $2.7 million. Costs went up and down in ensuing years. But as late as 1948, the costs of the Dewey and Truman campaigns together were estimated at $4.9 million. The costs of campaigning had increased some 80 percent over 64 years. By 1972, however, the costs of the Nixon and McGovern campaigns had reached $91.4 million. The institution of public funding in 1976 began a different system of finance, but the cost of presidential campaigns had gone up an astronomic 1,879 percent in the 24 years between 1948 and 1972 (Alexander, 1984a, p. 7).

What had led to this nearly 19-fold increase? Part of the cause was specific

---

[16] This is a very high figure. It is the estimated size of the audiences for the first Ford-Carter debate in 1976, the Carter-Reagan debate in 1980, the first Mondale-Reagan debate in 1984. These have been the largest audiences for any political events to date.

to 1972: the orgy of spending by the Nixon reelection campaign. They raised and spent some $61.4 million, roughly the amount used by *all* parties for *all* candidates four years earlier. But a more fundamental reason is the cost of the items we have been discussing. The campaign train used by Democrat James Cox in 1920 cost that campaign $20,000; it cost the Republicans $3.9 million to transport their candidates and battalions of surrogates and advance men in 1972. Polling was nonexistent in an earlier day; the 1968 Nixon campaign spent some $384,000 on surveys, and the Humphrey campaign put out $262,000 for theirs.

The biggest factor in the constantly increasing costs, though, has been television. In 1948, the last year of principal reliance on radio, the Republicans spent about $500,000 and the Democrats over $600,000 on that medium. In 1952, however, the parties spent about $6.1 million, split about equally between radio and television. From there the media costs went to $9.8 million, $14.2 million, $24.6 million, and $40.4 million in 1956, 1960, 1964, and 1968, respectively, with about twice as much being spent on television as on radio each year. Media costs actually dropped a bit in 1972, primarily because the Republicans put so much effort into the voter contact strategy effort described earlier (Alexander, 1972, 1976).

Professional Fund–Raising

While the amount of money needed for political campaigns is modest when compared to commercial advertising, campaign organizations need people who know how to raise substantial amounts of cash. Professional fund-raising came to national politics in 1937 in the person of Carlton G. Ketchum, a professional fund-raiser from Pittsburgh. He convinced the Republicans to undertake raising money systematically, based on a number of principles that he had found effective in raising money for private causes. First, there was to be a single fund drive each year so donors would not be subject to repeated appeals. Second, national needs were to be divided into state quotas based on such factors as population and wealth. (The needs of the states and counties where the money was being raised would be added to their national quotas at the time of their annual fund drive.) Third, the money was to be raised by a separate finance committee. This reduced the problem of contributors who wanted to be political strategists, and it placed a "fire wall" between the party and any persons who might expect an explicit quid pro quo for making a contribution. Fourth, the fund drives were to be in the hands of professionals, often hired from Ketchum, Inc., for the duration of the fund-raising effort.

Many of these principles were neglected in practice. There were emergency drives for individual candidates; many states failed to meet the quotas assigned to them. Still, the plan was adopted and, for a long time, was the basic structure within the Republican party. The system placed the Republican National Finance Committee in the same posture as a United Fund. The finance committee negotiated with the candidates and organizations about the amount of money they needed and with the states about the amount of money they were willing to raise (Heard, 1960, pp. 212–19; Ogden & Peterson, 1968, pp. 284–85).

In spite of this fundamental restructuring, a good deal of improvisation marked fund-raising in both parties during the following decades. Both parties raised money any way they could think of—fund-raising dinners, private meetings with leading party figures, personal appeals by candidates to their wealthy friends, and so on.

Until the 1960s, a number of things held true. Other things being equal, Republicans were able to raise more money than Democrats, in part because of better access to possible donors and in part because of the Ketchum system just described. One of the things that was not equal was control of the White House. The party in power could raise money with relative ease, while the party out of power had great difficulty in doing so. Neither party began a campaign with enough cash on hand. This prevented budgeting, meant that cash was often required to acquire needed services, and also meant that campaign organizations often had to pay a premium to acquire things (e.g., television time) at the last moment.

The result of all this was that both parties ran up debts to finance presidential campaigns, and both hoped they would win in order to be able to pay off the debt with the help of an incumbent president. For example, by the end of the 1960 campaign, the Democrats had a debt of $3.5 million, and the Republicans had a debt of $750,000. With the help of John Kennedy in the White House, though, the Democrats retired all but $500,000 of their debt by early 1963; the Republicans only got their originally much smaller debt down to $225,000 by early 1964 (Cotter & Hennessy, 1964, p. 174). Two developments of the 60s and 70s changed this situation: mass fund appeals and federal financing.

Mass Fund Appeals

By the 1960s, mass fund appeals had been discussed for a long time. There were some obvious advantages to the idea. If the parties could develop a mass base, they would reduce their dependence on large givers and identify a cadre of party supporters. Solicitations for small contributions had been tried on several occasions—for example, by the Republicans in the late 30s and in a Dollars for Democrats drive in the late 50s—but without producing enough revenue to effect any real change in party financing. There were problems. One was the administrative cost of processing a small contribution. After proper records had been made, the donor thanked, and so on, the parties often lost money. Another element was time. It took less time to ask one large donor than a host of small donors; and in a campaign, money was often needed in a hurry.

The first successful mass fund drive was sponsored by the Republicans in the early 60s under the stimulus of a real financial shortage. The Republican National Committee did not have enough money for its staff operation, in part because the Democrats controlled the White House. The Republican money that was available was going to the congressional committees in anticipation of the upcoming election. After some discussion, the national committee decided to solicit $10 sustaining memberships by sending appeals to names that appeared on various commercially available mailing lists.

So as not to upset any ongoing fund-raising operation, the program was first tried experimentally in three states that were not contributing anything. When the program proved successful in the test states, appeals were sent nationwide. The program brought in $700,000 in 1962 and slightly over $1 million in 1963, about two thirds of the national committee's operating funds that year. The contributors were sent a party newsletter, thus giving the party an additional publicity opportunity, and many of them provided the names of additional potential donors.

Over time, the Republican direct-mail campaign was built up to the point that it was regularly bringing in between $7 and $8 million and between 75 and 80 percent of all Republican contributions by the late 1970s. By 1984, President Reagan, unopposed for the nomination, was able to raise $16 million for this "race," $12 million of it by mail.

The origin of this successful mass fund drive is usually attributed to the appeal of Barry Goldwater to conservative Republicans in 1964, but credit should be given to William S. Warner, then executive director of the Republican National Committee, who started the program two years before the Goldwater nomination.

The first real Democratic success with a mass fund appeal was part of the 1972 McGovern campaign. George McGovern had accumulated several lists, some from South Dakota, some from his activity in opposition to the war in Vietnam, and some from various liberal appeals with which he had been associated. When the Senator decided to run, he consulted with an Alabama direct-mail expert, Morris Dees, and Dees brought in Thomas Collins from a New York City direct-mail firm. Collins wrote a seven-page letter setting forth McGovern's positions and appealing for funds. (For some reason, contributors to direct-mail campaigns are said to prefer long, detailed letters.) This was sent out at the time that McGovern announced his candidacy. The returns were quite good, and a number of subsequent appeals followed. Previous donors were contacted repeatedly; Democratic National Committee lists were used once McGovern was the party nominee; television appeals were combined with direct-mail appeals. The response to this was so substantial that special nighttime mail-opening sessions had to be used just to get the money into the bank. In consequence of these efforts, the McGovern campaign raised $3 million before he was nominated and $12 million during the general election campaign, at a total cost of $4.5 million (Alexander, 1976, pp. 299–304; Hart, 1973, pp. 42–44, 309–10).

The Democratic party was not able to build on the McGovern program during the ensuing decade. Morris Dees was recruited into the 1976 Carter campaign but reportedly was unable to match his 1972 success. And, as we saw much earlier in this chapter, the Democratic National Committee was far behind its Republican counterpart in the 1980s. The Democratic leadership recognized the importance of institutionalized fund-raising, but the Republicans had a two-decade head start.

Federal Financing

Beginning in 1976, an entirely new system of financing presidential campaigns was in place. The Federal Election Campaign Act of 1971 was amended in 1974 to provide for public financing of presidential (but not congressional) campaigns. Federal financing had long been advocated, in part to reduce the dependence of officeholders on financial supporters and in part because of the rising cost of campaigning. In the aftermath of the Watergate revelations, it was possible to get such legislation through Congress.

The law allowed $20 million plus an inflation allowance for the major presidential candidates. The national committees could also spend 2 cents per person in the voting-age population on behalf of their candidates. Taken together, these two amounts meant that each major party candidate was allowed to spend $25 million, $34 million, and $47.3 million in 1976, 1980, and 1984, respectively (Alexander, 1985). The candidates were not required to accept these funds; but if they did so, they had to promise not to accept other contributions.

This was a major change in the constraints affecting external activities. We have already seen the consequences of this for organized fund-raising in the Early Days of nomination politics and for the centralization of authority in a national campaign organization. But, how did it affect the funds available for the general election campaign and the way they were spent?

To begin with, the federal funds were not a great deal of money as national media campaigns go. One way of putting this into perspective is to compare it with the advertising budgets of commercial firms. The largest advertising budget in 1984 was $872 million, spent by Procter & Gamble. The firms with the next largest budgets in 1984 were General Motors ($763.8 million), Sears, Roebuck ($746.9 million), Beatrice Coe ($680 million), and R. J. Reynolds Industries ($678.2 million). An American presidential campaign that spent the allowable $47.3 million in 1984 would have ranked behind a hundred firms with larger advertising budgets (Endicott, 1985, p. 1).[17]

The amounts available were, in effect, expanded in 1979 by further changes in the law. Responding to criticism that the law restricted local activity, one 1979 amendment permitted state and local parties to buy buttons, bumper stickers, pamphlets, yard signs, and so forth. Another allowed state and local parties to conduct registration and get-out-the-vote drives. There were no financial limits placed on what the state and local parties could spend on these activities. The Republicans spent $15 million and the Democrats $4

---

[17] In making this comparison, remember that campaign advertising tends to be concentrated in the months before the election while commercial firms advertise throughout the year, and the federal funds provided for campaigns must cover *all* campaign expenses, not just advertising.

million on these "local" activities in 1980. Comparably reliable figures for 1984 are not available, but private estimates put GOP local spending at $10.6 million and Democratic spending at around $5 million[18] (Alexander, 1984a, 1984b, 1985).

Even with the additional state and local spending, the constraints imposed by public funding are quite real. In some respects, they have become more stringent with the passage of time. The cost of television to political candidates has gone up much more sharply than the general cost of living. Consequently, the federal funds (indexed to inflation) buy less than they did when Congress first authorized them. In 1976, the Ford strategy group foresaw the consequences of limited spending a good deal better than the Carter strategists. The latter spent a lot of money during September moving the candidate and his entourage around the country. The Ford strategists held money back for a media effort in the closing days of the campaign, and the Carter forces found they were without money to counter it. In 1980, Republican strategist Richard Beal pointed out, "We've got to target (that is, concentrate resources). There just isn't enough money to do anything else."

Campaign strategists have also found that they must make their decisions in the company of lawyers who know the provisions of the Federal Election Campaign Acts and accountants who know how much has already been spent in particular categories. Reflecting on the 1980 campaign, Democratic campaign manager Les Francis lamented: "I was meeting every morning with an accountant and a lawyer. Many of our decisions were not based on what we *ought* to do to be politically effective, but on what we *could* do within the law." And even though compliance costs are exempted from the spending limits, the professional advice to keep campaigns within the law and the effort needed to file all the reports with the Federal Election Commission add to campaign expenses. The Reagan campaign spent $1.6 million and the Mondale campaign $1 million on compliance costs in 1984.

Still another consequence of the spending limits has been the ingenuity exhibited by politicos in devising ways to get around them. The political action committees organized by those seeking presidential nominations are one example. Candidates have discovered that they can set up subsidiary committees in states, many of which have looser regulations, and allow them to spend money outside the federal limits. If national campaigns cannot accept private donations, contributors can be guided to state committees. And independent campaigns can be conducted for liberal or conservative causes that *may* aid presidential campaigns.

If candidates continue to accept federal funds and the spending limits remain the same, another long-run effect may be to force some decisions about which activities are cost effective. The 1972 Nixon voter-contact opera-

---

[18] The Republican advantage in this spending was offset by labor spending on similar activities. Organized labor spent $16.5 million in 1980, $15 million on behalf of Democrats, and $26 million in 1984, $20 million for Democrats.

tion alone cost some $12 million. The 1968 electronic media campaign conducted in Nixon's behalf cost $12.6 million. In other words, these two programs alone would exceed the present spending limits, without allowing anything for a campaign tour, polling, print advertising, headquarters salaries, or anything else. In the past, the strong tendency has been to carry on all possible campaign activities on an *implicit* assumption that whatever was done was going to increase a candidate's chances of winning. But is it really true, for example, that a candidate wins votes by campaigning in a community? Could he do better by staying home and, together with his issues staff, working out just what he wants to say? Such questions have not been closely examined, but a fixed limit on spending may provide an impetus in this direction.

SUMMARY

In this chapter, we have covered the four major types of activities that go into a presidential campaign: campaign operations, research, public relations, and finance. Much of this organizational effort goes unreported in media accounts of campaigns; but there must be some way of moving the presidential and vice presidential candidates around the country, figuring out what they are going to say and what the citizens will think of it, getting the campaign story out through the media, and obtaining funds to do all this.

While the internal structure covered in the last chapter was largely ideological, the external activities that we have examined in this chapter are largely logistical. In other words, a structure of regional and state coordination, survey research to determine voter attitudes, buying television time and producing spots, and raising money are not intrinsically liberal, moderate, or conservative. A campaign organization that could provide these services ought to be able to work for any candidate, regardless of his ideological bent.

While it is certainly true that a conservative or liberal ideologue who lacks organizational, research, communications, or fund-raising skills is next to useless around campaign headquarters, this distinction between ideological positioning and logistical services should not be pressed too far. The personal contacts through which one sets up a campaign organization are different in the two parties; the phrases that ring true in a conservative speech would not fit into a liberal appeal; the sources of funds tend to be different; and so on.

The factor that ties issues most closely to these external activities is their intent to win the support of a particular set of voters. Therefore, the appeals that are directed to them must be consistent with their issue preferences. This reminds us of the dual set of constraints that shape any campaign strategy. It must be consistent with the issue preferences of the supporting coalition and, at the same time, win the votes of the citizens to whom the campaign appeals are directed.

Part Three

Campaign Strategies

Chapter 5

The 1970s

"The president defended his economic policy in a speech in New York." Whether this was broadcast as part of a news summary, was the lead sentence in a newspaper story, or was found in the middle of a paragraph in a history book, it is typical of the events that make up a campaign. By itself, it tells us very little. The sentence is much more interesting for the questions it calls to mind. Was the president running ahead of his opponent or was he behind? If ahead, was he maintaining his lead, or was his opponent catching up? Why was the president talking about economic management instead of international involvement or civil liberties? Was he addressing a business or labor audience? Why was the president giving this speech in New York instead of Chicago or Cheyenne? With answers to these and some related questions in hand, we could give some meaning to the report. Without them, the fact that the president has given a speech on economics tells us no more than any other unexamined event.

Speeches, statements, television spots, and all the rest can be understood as part of a campaign strategy; but in order to do so, we need contextual information. First of all, we need to know about the *structural context*. What is the composition of the candidate's supporting coalition? What voters is the candidate trying to reach? What kinds of things can the candidate do and say to maintain the approval of the supporting coalition and win votes at the same time?

There is also a larger sense in which structural context can be understood. This is the structure formed by the interplay of the major strategies. Are both coalitions intent on winning the swing votes in the large industrial states, as was the case in 1976? Does the strategy of one involve a vigorous exposition of what is a minority view nationwide? This happened in 1972 and gave the other party a lot of maneuvering room in the middle ground of American politics. Are there a large number of voters unrepresented by the major parties, and is there a candidate who will try to speak to their concerns? This gave rise to important third parties in 1968 and 1980, and the presence of the third party made for much more complex politics.

Another important set of questions concerns the *temporal context*. In a narrow sense, these questions arise from the temporal pattern that we reviewed at the beginning of Chapter 3. Is the speech a trial balloon that is given during the Planning stage of the campaign? Is it a considered statement that is part of the Grand Opening? Is it a Strategic Adjustment that tries to respond to some particular problem? Or is it part of a last attempt during the Time's Up stage?

What might be called a longer-term temporal concern also leads to questions about the *historic context*. What did citizens regard as the leading problems in a given election year? How widely were looming problems, such as those implicit in baby booms or energy shortages, understood in the society? Was America involved in a war, or was there a real threat of war? Was the economy prosperous, or was inflation or unemployment or both a problem? All these considerations are important in understanding the opportunities open to campaign strategists, and you will want to keep them in mind when reading about specific campaigns.

THE 1972 CAMPAIGN

The 1972 campaign is often interpreted as a mirror image of 1964, when Lyndon Johnson decisively defeated Barry Goldwater. In important ways, this is true. In 1964, a Democratic incumbent faced a Republican challenge from the right; in 1972, a Republican incumbent faced a Democratic challenge from the left. Both challengers proposed fairly drastic policy reorientations, and both had difficulty obtaining electoral support. Both incumbents had considerable freedom of action in selecting their strategies, and both won victories of historic proportions. But some features of the 1972 campaign were quite unlike anything seen eight years earlier.

The issues were different in 1972. The nation was not confronted with serious international or economic problems in the mid-60s, but these were the major points of contention in 1972. In spite of four years of negotiations and (by 1972) a total withdrawal of American ground troops, the Vietnam War was not over. Early in the year, President Nixon traveled to China (with which diplomatic contacts had begun); in late spring, he went to Moscow to sign the first Strategic Arms Limitations Treaty. In domestic affairs, the inflation that had begun as a consequence of the Vietnam War was proving difficult to check, and wage and price controls were instituted in 1971. With controls in place, the rise in the consumer price index was held to 3.3 percent in 1972.

There were two events unique to 1972: the replacement of Democratic vice presidential candidate Thomas Eagleton and the break-in at the Democratic National Committee headquarters by five men working for the Committee to Re-elect the President. In early August, Senator Eagleton revealed that he had been hospitalized for nervous exhaustion and had received shock treatment. Senator McGovern immediately stated that he was "1,000 percent for Tom Eagleton" and had no intention of dropping him from the ticket; but within two weeks, he accepted his resignation. It never became clear what the five men were looking for at the Democratic National Committee, but we do know that they were working for the Committee to Re-elect the President and that committee officials, White House staff members, and President Nixon himself took action to prevent legal authorities from finding out what had happened. The departure of Senator Eagleton had more serious political consequences in 1972. What became known as the Watergate affair had fewer consequences that year. The cover-up kept the public in the dark until after the election, and those who distrusted Richard Nixon enough to believe that he was personally involved were likely to vote for George McGovern in any case. Ultimately, of course, the Watergate affair had far more serious consequences, culminating in Nixon's resignation from office.

George McGovern's Moral Challenge

George McGovern's bid for the presidency was reminiscent of William Jennings Bryan's campaign in 1900. Both men came from the plains, and both spoke in terms of moral certainty. McGovern's views about the influence of business in the Nixon administration could be seen as a latter-day instance of Bryan's "Democracy against Plutocracy," and his attacks on Nixon's Vietnam policies showed the same fervor as Bryan's complaints about American imperialism. This analogy shouldn't be pressed too far. America in the 1970s was very different from the turn-of-the-century country just emerging as a world power. Still, the Bryan comparison sheds some light on the questions McGovern was trying to raise and on his political difficulties in doing so.

McGovern's Left-Center Plan and Organizational Difficulties

The organizational stage of the McGovern campaign would have been difficult in the best of circumstances. His nomination coalition was built around the most liberal groups in the Democratic party: the antiwar movement and those favoring much expanded social programs and further busing. The idea behind this was a left-centrist strategy: to co-opt the left as a base for a nomination drive but to keep the organization open to centrist politicians so that McGovern could appeal to a normal Democratic spectrum in the general election. The Democratic left was brought in all right, but many of their views and personnel were unacceptable to veterans of past Democratic campaigns.

One standard way of handling this situation is to work through those with good ties to both the successful nomination coalition and party groups that are not part of this winning coalition. Lawrence O'Brien and Senator Eagleton might have been very effective in this task. O'Brien had reassumed the chairmanship of the Democratic National Committee a couple of years earlier because he was the one person acceptable to all the leading Democrats, and Eagleton was a Roman Catholic with good ties to urban politicians and organized labor. But their organizational talents were not to be used. O'Brien was unhappy about the way the campaign was structured, and Eagleton was forced to resign as the vice presidential candidate.

The Eagleton affair was costly to Senator McGovern's standing with the public. McGovern's swift move from "1,000 percent support" for Eagleton to willingness to accept his resignation raised troublesome questions about his competence. But to appreciate the temporal impact of the affair, one must remember that it came smack in the middle of what should have been the Organization phase of the campaign. In place of contributions and appointments, there were statements from Democratic leaders and the mass media, many to the effect that Senator Eagleton should leave the ticket. Contributors who had pledged large amounts to get the campaign started let McGovern leaders know the money might not be forthcoming. Regional directors and state leaders reported no activity going on in the field. The reaction of the McGovern core group to all this was that Eagleton must go. There might be costs to dropping him from the ticket, but the campaign could not get under way with him.

August, the extra month normally available to the out party because of the earlier convention, was largely devoted to repair efforts of one kind and another. First came the selection of Sargent Shriver to replace Senator Eagleton. Some prominent Democrats were not interested in running with McGovern, but Shriver accepted eagerly, and his selection was ratified at a meeting of the Democratic National Committee. Organizational difficulties continued, notably over the management and budget for an urgent get-out-the-vote drive, but a campaign staff (regional and state coordinators) came into being, and some activity began throughout the country.

Senator McGovern did make two or three campaign trips during August to keep his name in the headlines. The most important of these was a speech to the New York Society of Security Analysts on August 29. During the primaries, the Senator had proposed giving $1,000 a month to every American and had rather casually attached a cost figure of $21 in additional taxation for persons earning $20,000 or more. Now, after some weeks of staff analysis, McGovern was ready to present a more carefully thought out proposal (Hart, 1973, p. 279; White, 1973, pp. 126–28). In his New York speech, he called for a $10 billion cut in defense spending over each of the next three years and a "fair-share tax reform" that would bring in an additional $22 billion by various changes in the tax laws. These funds would be used for two programs: $15 billion to local school systems, and a "National Income Insurance Program" consisting of public service jobs, expansion of social security, and "approximately $4,000 in cash and food stamps for a family of four with no other income who are unable to work."

Multiple Plans and Unappealing Positions

There did not appear to be an agreed-upon plan for the McGovern coalition by the time of the Grand Opening. Rather, there were a number of plans. None of these lasted long, and portions of each appeared to conflict with other plans that were presumably in effect. For example, George McGovern told Theodore White he thought he would carry California and New York, and the geographic concentration of the campaign would be on Illinois, Michigan, Ohio, Pennsylvania, and New Jersey (White, 1973, p. 168). But the McGovern coalition was responsible for expelling Chicago's Mayor Richard Daley from the Democratic convention, and in spite of a personal appeal, Mayor Daley stated that each member of his organization was free to make his own judgment about supporting the McGovern-Shriver ticket. Labor would also be important in winning this band of states, but McGovern had only about half the labor support assembled for most Democrats, and AFL-CIO President George Meany announced that he was neutral between Nixon and McGovern.

Then there was the matter of the positions McGovern was taking. In international involvement, George McGovern wanted an immediate cessation of Vietnam hostilities as well as a rather deep cut in defense spending. His New York economic speech called for higher taxes and further spending. Social benefits programs included income maintenance, more school aid, and national health insurance. On civil liberties, the Senator supported busing, favored control of hand guns, and said that crime was related to economic and racial discrimination. These liberal positions were quite consistent with the internal structure of the McGovern coalition, but they caused external trouble with the voters George McGovern was trying to reach. Pennsylvania steelworkers, for example, saw McGovern's position on the Vietnam War as the equivalent of surrender and felt that he wanted to give welfare recipients more than they were making in take-home pay (Sperling, 1972).

The lack of an overall campaign plan was possibly the least of McGovern's difficulties. The McGovern coalition was short on many of the essentials of a successful campaign: a smoothly working organization, external support, and positions that would attract large numbers of voters.

In part because of a lack of resources, in part to take advantage of the speed of jet travel, and in part because of a hope that the Senator could arouse American voters, the McGovern campaign scheduled appearances in two to four different media markets each day. On September 6, for example, he was in San Diego, Dallas, and Houston. On September 12, he campaigned in Chicago, Cleveland, and Detroit. The idea was to generate local stories in addition to those filed by the traveling press for the national media. The underlying theme of these stories, regardless of the policy area being discussed, was one of opposition to the Nixon administration.

A controversy was taking place within the McGovern coalition leadership over how this opposition should be conveyed: with a negative accent on

Nixon and the Republicans or using more positive material. A key factor in this dispute was the Senator's own sense of moral fervor. He didn't need a plan to tell him that Richard Nixon and all of his works were evil. And as September wore on, he became more and more negative.[1] Speaking in the inner-city Hill district of Pittsburgh, for example, he explicitly blamed poverty conditions on the war in Vietnam:

> As much as any village bombed into rubble, the Hill district is a victim of the war in Vietnam—the longest, the cruelest, and the stupidest war in American history. Why aren't there any better schools here? Because your money has been used to blow up schools in Vietnam. Why aren't there more clinics to protect your health? Because your money has been used to bomb the life out of innocent civilians in Indochina. Every bomb that is dropped and every bullet that is fired in Southeast Asia has an echo that is heard in the Hill district. We have paid for the devastation of another land with the devastation, not just of our conscience, but of our own country.

Such language portrayed the depth of Senator McGovern's feelings, but it was not adding much support to his coalition. Nor were the efforts of the campaigners working in his behalf. The polls, public and private, continued to show President Nixon far in the lead. This disheartening situation produced anxiety among the coalition leaders. As campaign director Gary Hart put it:

> There was nothing tangible, nothing concrete, nothing to show movement and progress. At the headquarters, the staff and volunteers grasped at straws for encouragement, cheering each appearance of one of the candidates on the evening news, savoring each favorable editorial or report of new administrative malfeasance, longing for some proof that victory lay ahead. (Hart, 1973, pp. 299–300)

A Strategic Turn to a More Positive Approach

The manifest lack of progress dictated a Strategic Adjustment. Senator McGovern decided to make a series of nationally televised addresses during October and reduced the number of negative references in his own public statements. The first televised speech on October 10 dealt with McGovern's plan to end the Vietnam War by withdrawing all American forces within 90 days.

> When all is said and done, our purpose in Vietnam now comes down to this— our policymakers want to save face and they want to save the Saigon regime of General Thieu. Now, that is a fundamental difference between President Nixon and me. . . . It is a choice between four more years of war; or four years of peace. . . . On the night when the last American soldier from Vietnam has

---

[1] This conclusion about McGovern's negativism and those to follow about a positive or negative tone to the 1972 campaign or policy areas being emphasized are based on a content analysis of the McGovern and Nixon speeches.

landed in San Francisco, there will be a new birth of confidence and hope for all of us.

The Senator's second speech on October 20 dealt with economic management, the policy area to which he devoted the most attention during the fall campaign. McGovern criticized Nixon administration policies concerning interest, employment, wage and price controls, and taxes, linking all of these to the administration's economic philosophy.

> Every single time this administration has faced an important economic choice, they have picked a policy that was right for the few and wrong for you. . . . This election is more than a contest between George McGovern and Richard Nixon. It is a fundamental struggle between the little people of America and the big rich of America, between the average working man or woman and a powerful elite. . . . I want to be the kind of president who will see to it that America is good to every one of her people. I want us to claim that promise of Isaiah, "The people shall be righteous and they shall inherit the land."

These October efforts did produce some financial results. An appeal for funds at the end of the Vietnam speech brought in more than a million dollars, and by the end of the month, so much money was coming in that there was difficulty in opening the mail. This was a happy contrast to the desperate lack of financial resources in August, but there was still no evidence that American voters were changing their minds.

A Final Bitterness

By the time of the third speech, on October 25, a good deal of negativism was creeping back into Senator McGovern's rhetoric. The theme for this speech was corruption in the Nixon administration. Favors extended to campaign contributors, Watergate, and extensions of executive power were all discussed.

> The men who have collected millions in secret money, who have passed out special favors, who have ordered political sabotage, who have invaded our offices in the dead of night—all these men work for Mr. Nixon. Most of them he hired himself. And their power comes from him alone. They act on his behalf, and they accept his orders.

This speech, a direct attack on Nixon's integrity, was symptomatic of McGovern's mood as the campaign moved into the Time's Up stage. It was now clear that he was not going to win, and the Senator became increasingly bitter in his public comments. In late October, statements from both Hanoi and Washington indicated the probability of success in peace negotiations. Senator McGovern's reaction was to say that "when Dr. Kissinger came out and said peace is at hand, he was misleading the American people. He knew what he said was false." McGovern told questioners in Los Angeles that Nixon had "conducted an evil administration. . . . I think exploiting of racial fears is an evil practice. . . . I think the aerial bombardment of Southeast

Asia by Richard Nixon is the most evil thing ever done by any American president." And in Chicago, on the Saturday night before the election, George McGovern said:

> It's all right for the people to be fooled once as they were in 1968. If they do it again, if they let this man lead them down the false hope of peace once again in 1972, then the people have nobody to blame but themselves. . . . I'm going to give you one more warning. If Mr. Nixon is reelected on Tuesday, we may very well have four more years of war in Southeast Asia. Our prisoners will sit in their cells for another four years. Don't let this man trick you into believing that he stands for peace, when he's a man who makes war.

It was almost as though Senator McGovern was angry with the voters for refusing to listen to him. Whether or no, he was in the same position as Senator Goldwater on election eve in 1964. He had tried to raise some fundamental questions, and he knew that this would not lead to electoral success.

Reelect the President: Nixon 1972

A Positive, Ethnic, Centrist Approach

"I ask everyone listening to me tonight—Democrats, Republicans, and independents—to join our new majority; not on the basis of the party label you wear on your lapel but what you believe in you hearts." This appeal for a new majority was an important part of Richard Nixon's nomination acceptance speech in 1972. Internally, the Nixon coalition was composed of groups supporting American involvement overseas and a strong defense posture, conservative economics, few new social programs, increased police authority, and opposition to busing. The "new majority" Nixon sought referred to his coalition's need for additional external support. Many moves had been made by his administration to win support from three traditional Democratic groupings: Roman Catholics, labor, and Southerners. The nomination of a Democrat unpopular with these constituencies gave Nixon a chance to capitalize on the moves he had already made. This was the major focus of the 1972 Republican campaign.

Perhaps the most important move to gain Catholic support was Nixon's consistent championship of aid to parochial schools. He urged this on a number of occasions, such as in a 1971 speech to the Knights of Columbus. Nixon also made known his opposition to abortion in a letter to Terence Cardinal Cooke of New York. During the election campaign, an unusual amount of effort went into heritage (that is, white ethnic) groups, and three of the ethnic groups selected for inclusion in a massive mailing campaign conducted that year were Irish, Polish, and Italian. Among other things, the President visited an immigration museum at the Statue of Liberty; stopped his motorcade in Wilkes-Barre, Pennsylvania, in order to pose with members of an Italian wedding party that happened to be emerging from a church as he drove by; turned up at an Italian-American celebration in Maryland, explaining that his daughter Julie couldn't make it and he was substituting for her; and spoke at a Columbus Day dinner. In that speech, he said;

> When we honor [labor leader] Peter Fosco, we see [an important attribute] quite clearly, and that is, putting it quite bluntly, hard work. Italian-Americans came to this country by the hundreds of thousands, and then by the millions. They came here not asking for something, only asking for the opportunity to work. They have worked and they have built. There is a second feature which is represented by this head table tonight. Those of Italian background bring with them a very deep religious faith.

This prose was typical of the 1972 Nixon campaign in two respects. First, Nixon spoke positively of the virtues of whatever group he was addressing. Second, his constant references to the importance of hard work were an integral part of his appeal to blue-collar voters.

Relations between organized labor and the Nixon administration had been cool and were to become so again. But in 1972, there was a tactical truce that presented an unusual opportunity for the Republicans to get labor votes. Labor was by no means pro-Nixon. Rather, McGovern positions reduced the amount of labor support that would normally flow to a Democratic candidate.[2] As one labor leader put it, "Most of our members get the creeps when they think about Nixon, but McGovern worries them." The AFL–CIO was neutral, and the Nixon administration worked hard to take advantage of this posture. A well-advertised golf game was played by Richard Nixon and AFL–CIO president George Meany, and a plank supporting Section 14–B of the Taft-Hartley Act (permitting state right-to-work laws that were anathema to organized labor) was dropped from the Republican platform. Secretary of Labor James Hodgson addressed the Steelworkers, who did not endorse either candidate, but canceled a speech before the Machinists, who endorsed McGovern.

In his Labor Day speech, which had been reviewed with AFL–CIO leaders before delivery (Safire, 1975, p. 595), President Nixon drew a contrast between the work ethic and the welfare ethic. "Above all," he argued, "the work ethic puts responsibility in the hands of the individual, in the belief that self-reliance and the willingness to work makes a person a better human being. . . . (whereas) the welfare ethic destroys character and leads to a vicious cycle of dependency." Richard Nixon cited hard work over and over again during the campaign. He believed that it was responsible for his own success, and it was a natural link with the labor vote he hoped to win.

Southern support for a Republican presidential candidate was not unusual. Herbert Hoover carried five states in the "Solid South" as long ago as 1928, and Republicans had been making real efforts to increase their strength there since the 1950s. Still, southern voters were another large group of Democrats who disliked George McGovern and to whom the center-right policies of the

---

[2] Twenty individual unions endorsed McGovern; only the Teamsters endorsed Nixon.

Nixon administration were acceptable. Some seven former Democratic governors and scores of lesser Democratic officials in the South endorsed Richard Nixon rather than George McGovern. When President Nixon visited John Connally's Texas ranch in September, he was welcomed by some 200 Democrats, mostly southern, whom Connally had recruited to the Democrats for Nixon organization he headed. And when Nixon campaigned in Atlanta, he argued that Southerners were not racist, any more than Michiganders were racist, because they opposed busing. "It simply means . . . parents in Georgia and parents all over the country want better education for their children, and that better education is going to come in the schools that are close to home and not clear across town." He went on to assert that issues that were important in the South—peace, jobs, safety, local control—were the same issues that were important all over the country.

A Triumphal March for the Incumbent

There were few temporal effects in the 1972 Nixon campaign. All the appeals to give added external support to his coalition—those to Roman Catholics, labor, and the South—were in place by the Grand Opening, and the campaign went well enough that there was no need for either Strategic or Tactical Adjustments. Nixon used the traditional techniques of the incumbent: the ability to schedule headline-making events when his opponent was trying to make news, conferences with foreign leaders, a fiscal policy designed to stimulate the economy at election time, and visibly being president while surrogates spoke around the country in his name.

Nixon resurrected one technique he had begun in his 1968 campaign: using radio for several more-thoughtful addresses. One devoted to his philosophy picked up the theme of a new majority and contained a good exposition of moderate conservative beliefs.

> The new American majority believes that each person should have more of the say in how he lives his own life . . . in taking care of those persons who cannot take care of themselves . . . in taking whatever action is needed to hold down the cost of living . . . and in a national defense second to none. . . . These are not the beliefs of a selfish people. On the contrary, they are the beliefs of a generous and self-reliant people, a people of intellect and character, whose values deserve respect in every segment of our population.

Richard Nixon's greatest asset in 1972, however, was not a capacity to give an articulate presentation of his political philosophy. It was the success of his foreign policy. He had made trips to Beijing and Moscow earlier in the year; and the announcement of a breakthrough in the Vietnam peace negotiations (being conducted in France between Henry Kissinger and Le Duc Tho) more or less coincided with the Time's Up phase, when the President began campaigning full time. Throughout the campaign, he devoted much more attention to international involvement than to any other policy area and concluded his campaign in Ontario, California, on election eve with further references to his foreign policy record and his hopes for a "Generation of Peace."

Finally we have had a breakthrough in the [Vietnam peace] negotiations and I can tell you today that the significant point of that breakthrough is [that] the three principles that I laid down on May 8 . . . have been agreed to. . . . The trip to Beijing . . . has great meaning . . . to [the] younger generation. . . . Imagine how dangerous the world would be if one fourth of all the people in the world who live in the People's Republic of China, 10, 15 years from now had gathered enormous nuclear capability and had no communication with the United States. . . . We cannot allow that danger. . . . The trip to Moscow had a similar purpose. Imagine what we would leave to the younger generation had we . . . gone down the road to an inevitable confrontation and a nuclear explosion that would have destroyed civilization as we know it.

In common with many winning campaigns, the 1972 Nixon campaign went too smoothly. There was electoral success based on appeals to Democrats alienated by the McGovern candidacy and on a foreign policy record that was appreciated by many voters. But as all too soon became apparent, there were also political sabotage, vast overspending, and a cover-up involving the President himself. This was tragic for Nixon and his hopes for future accomplishment. In 1960, he had shown a high order of statesmanship on at least two occasions: in forbidding any discussion of his opponent's religion and in refusing to bring on a constitutional crisis by challenging the very close election results. Had a hint of these values been reflected in the actions of Richard Nixon and his appointees, he would have been able to govern on the basis of the record majority he won and to lead the nation in its bicentennial in 1976.

THE 1976 CAMPAIGN

The 1976 campaign was normal, and it was anything but normal. For the first time since 1960, most Democrats were in the Democratic coalition, and most Republicans were in the Republican coalition. But the Democratic coalition was organized in support of a one-term governor from the Deep South, and the Republican coalition was led by a former congressman from Grand Rapids who was the first unelected president in American history. Neither candidate could count on full support from *all* his nominal partisans, and therein lay the interesting strategic challenges of the 1976 campaign.

Gerald Ford began his short administration with the reassuring statement that "our long national nightmare is over." But his initial popularity dropped sharply after he pardoned Richard Nixon, and by fall 1974, America was in a deep recession. The unemployment rate was 8.4 percent in 1975, and inflation (led by sharp increases in the costs of food, fuel, housing, and medical care) was worse than ever. By 1976, a 1972 dollar was worth only 73 cents.[3] Against this background of Watergate and economic problems, questions of which

---

[3] As of 1976, this was the worst four-year record on inflation since World War II. The 1976–80 record was to be even worse. A 1976 dollar was worth only 69 cents in 1980, but 1976 voters had no way of foreseeing that.

candidate could be trusted and who could manage the economy loomed large in 1976.

An Outsider Leads the Majority Party

In midsummer, there were certainly some favorable omens for the Carter coalition. Internally, the coalition was expanded in the classic manner by the selection of a vice presidential candidate, Walter Mondale, who was highly respected by liberals. Externally, the Gallup Poll showed Jimmy Carter running ahead of Gerald Ford by a remarkable 62 to 29 percent margin.

But to those who looked a bit more closely, there were signs of possible trouble. The campaign organization made minimal use of the Democratic talent now available to Carter. Walter Mondale and his ranking aide, Richard Moe, were admitted to the strategy group, but that was the only expansion. Campaign headquarters were kept in Atlanta, and staff responsibilities remained essentially what they had been. Following a 1960 Kennedy pattern, Carter designees from out of state were put in charge of each state's presidential campaign. And while the external support available for Carter was widespread, it was very soft. Jimmy Carter might be the majority party's nominee, but many Democrats and independents were unenthusiastic about him.

A Southern-Based Strategy

Planning for the campaign, summarized in two memorandums written by campaign director Hamilton Jordan in June and August, did not assume that the early support would hold up. Quite the opposite. "We will probably not know until mid-October if the election is going to be close or if there is potential for a big victory." Therefore, Jordan asserted, the Carter coalition must "always maintain a high degree of flexibility in the allocation of our resources and the objectives of strategy." But the main key to the Carter strategy was an assumption that had not been possible to make since 1944: a sweep of the southern and border states. The South is the largest of the four sections of the country, and when Jordan added the District of Columbia, Massachusetts, Minnesota, and Wisconsin to this base, there was a total of 199 electoral votes. This would not be enough to win; additional electoral votes would have to come from eight large industrial states, such as New York and Pennsylvania, and these critical states were scheduled for more intensive campaign efforts. If the 199-vote base held, though, the additional necessary votes could be obtained by winning any of several combinations of states. Therefore, Jordan claimed, "the only way we can lose in November is to have this base fragmented" (Schram, 1977, pp. 239–50; Witcover, 1977, chap. 35).

The Jordan plan was quite specific about where the campaign was to be waged but not about how it was to be done. The plan was silent about the issues that were to be used to appeal to voters in large industrial states while retaining support in the essential southern base. Indeed, it was not until nearly time for the Grand Opening that Carter himself asked his strategy group, "What are our themes going to be?" The absence of a clear answer to this question was to hobble the Carter campaign throughout the fall.

A Downhill Slide

The implicit statement made by the Grand Opening was that the Roosevelt coalition had been reassembled. The formal opening took place at FDR's "Little White House" in Warm Springs, Georgia, with two Roosevelt sons present and the late President's favorite black accordionist playing "Happy Days Are Here Again." This was followed by a couple of other regional stops, presumably sufficient to reinforce regional pride, and then the Carter entourage moved north, where the additional electoral votes had to be won. In the following days, Governor Carter met voters at a New York subway stop and at a suburban rally in Columbus, Ohio, put on a "Polish Hill" T-shirt in Pittsburgh, addressed the AFL–CIO convention in Dearborn, Michigan, took part in a torchlight parade in Chicago, and rode across Pennsylvania on a campaign train in emulation of Harry Truman's whistle-stop campaign of 1948.

A lot of little things seemed to go wrong as Carter sought support from blue-collar, ethnic voters. There was difficulty in dealing with questions about abortion, a fluff in which he said that he would shift the tax burden to those over the median income, and publicity about an interview in *Playboy* in which he admitted lust in his heart and made some adverse comments about Lyndon Johnson. The difficulty with Carter's Grand Opening, though, was not little things going wrong. It was a lack of big things going right. On the one hand, he identified with liberal Democratic predecessors and invoked their names whenever possible. But he was also making conservative statements, such as, "Whenever there's a choice between government performing a function and the private sector performing a function, I believe in the private sector," and undecided voters did not know what to make of the contrast.

On September 23, the campaign was punctuated by the first of a series of televised debates. If any advantage was to be gained, it would likely come in the first debate "because of the large audience, and the mild 'openness' encouraged in the uncommitted by the debate format." The advantage went to President Ford, in part because of the candidates' performances but much more because of the postdebate media focus on the question of who won (Sears, 1979; Sears & Chaffee, 1979). By this point, the race between Carter and Ford outside the South was even.

Tactical Adjustments

At this juncture, there was a Tactical Adjustment: Jimmy Carter became much more negative in his comments about Gerald Ford. A number of explanations were given for this—that Carter was frustrated by the difficulty of running against an incumbent, that Carter hoped to go for the kill, and so on. Whatever the reason, President Ford was now likened to a car with four flat tires. His vetoes were said to be designed to keep people out of work. "Gerald Ford," Carter charged in Cleveland, "has hidden himself from the public even more than Richard Nixon at the depths of Watergate." After the President's second debate gaffe, when he denied Soviet domination of Eastern Europe, Carter continued this attack, calling Ford's comment "a disgrace to the country." This gambit did not work. By mid-October, Harris showed Carter with a 4 percent lead nationwide, Gallup showed a 6 percent lead, and Pat Caddell's state-by-state polls for Carter showed a decline "in the West, in the border states, and even in the South" (Schram, 1977, p. 329).

Bad news, of course, increases tension among campaign leaders. When Elizabeth Drew was interviewing at this time, she found that the Carter leaders, "for all their confident talk, seemed tense and skittish. . . . It is clear that a decision has been made among Carter's top aides in Atlanta that he must cut out the strident tone that his campaign has taken on recently" (1977, p. 471). Another Tactical Adjustment was in order.

This time, a decision was made to spend money on media in the South to protect the essential base and to prepare new television ads for voters elsewhere, especially women, who preferred Carter on issues but thought Ford a lesser risk in the White House. An announcer on a commercial made for the South claimed that "the South is being readmitted to the Union on November 2"; and in a commercial aimed at wavering Northerners, Carter stated that mismanagement affected the quality of lives. These ads were taped on October 19. Efforts were also made to present a reassuring Carter during the third debate (in place of the aggressive Carter of the second debate); but essentially, the last Tactical Adjustment of the campaign had been made (Schram, 1977, pp. 329–36; Witcover, 1977, pp. 622–23).

Hang On and Hope

The principal activity of the Time's Up phase could be described as "hang on and hope." Hope that the southern base would hold. Hope that enough wavering voters would eventually come down on Carter's side. Because a large proportion of the available federal funds had been spent earlier in the campaign, there were no more resources to be committed. The Carter strategy could operate only at the margins. The candidate's time was devoted to crucial states: New York, New Jersey, Pennsylvania, Ohio, Illinois, Texas (to protect the southern base), and California. Appeals were made to Democrats to turn out on election day. The local Democratic parties could provide some help here (although 1976 spending limits meant that the presidential campaign could not encourage them by providing "walking-around money"), and the AFL–CIO could provide more substantial assistance. Political director Al Barkan pledged to have 100,000 workers on telephones and in the streets to turn out the labor vote. And finally, Governor Carter seemed to be reaching for the moderate vote when he modified liberal pledges already made by stating that a tax cut was a possibility in a Carter administration. Still, the principal ingredient of the Time's Up stage was hope. The final polls showed a virtual tie.

The Ford Reelection Fight

A Bold Plan to Obtain External Support

Three plans were written for the Ford campaign. There was a long basic document (120 pages plus appendixes) written by several planners under the direction of White House Chief of Staff Richard Cheney. There were plans emerging from the polls conducted by Robert Teeter. And there was a media plan developed by Doug Bailey and John Deardourff. What was unusual about these plans was the extent to which they coincided, the directness with which they dealt with Gerald Ford's weaknesses, and the degree to which they dealt with the external need to reach the voters rather than the internal need to hold the supporting coalition together. These unusual aspects could be traced to the professional backgrounds of the planners.

The one major violation of the plans was the selection of Robert Dole as the vice presidential nominee. The campaign plan had called for a nominee "who is perceived as an independent, or at least as a moderate Republican, without strong party identification [and with]. . . a strong image of freshness and non-Washington establishment." These were not Robert Dole's characteristics. His selection served an internal need to satisfy conservative groups that had supported Ronald Reagan's drive for the nomination.

The campaign plans dealt with the voters' perception of the candidates as individuals, their perception of issue stands, geographic concentration, timing, and the use of available funds. Discussion of the candidates as individuals stressed differences between their actual strengths and weaknesses and public perceptions of them. Ford was perceived as an honest and decent person, but there were questions as to whether he was intelligent enough to be president and decisive enough as a leader. Carter had the advantage of supporting traditional American values and being a member of the majority party, but he lacked a record of accomplishment and was vague on issues. The implication of this was a campaign that would lay to rest questions about President Ford's intelligence and leadership capacity and would attack Governor Carter's inexperience and wavering stand on issues.

The plans dealing with issues grew out of the first use in a presidential campaign of multidimensional scaling (the type of spatial analysis used to produce Figures 3–1 and 3–2). A two-dimensional solution was used. The horizontal dimension represented partisanship and economic management, and the vertical dimension reflected a social issue (specifically, defense spending and civil liberties questions about lifestyle). Not surprisingly, Carter was slightly to the left and Ford slightly to the right on the partisan-economic dimension. But to Robert Teeter's considerable astonishment, Jimmy Carter was seen as relatively conservative and Gerald Ford as relatively liberal on the social question. This implied a need for an attack on Governor Carter's positions to try to alter the advantageous posture he enjoyed and for a campaign that would stress Gerald Ford's support of traditional positions on the social issue.

The audience to whom the campaign should be directed was described in some detail. The Electoral College was divided into "our base" (83 votes, principally from the Plains states and the Mountain states), "his base" (87 votes, principally from the South), and the balance of 368 votes designated as "swing states," including most of the large industrial states. How did the Ford strategists hope to carry these states, considering that Carter was far ahead in the polls in midsummer when these were drawn? The report pointed to a specific swing constituency:

> The target constituency in the suburbs for the president is the upper blue-collar and white-collar workers, often from a family that has risen in mobility in the last generation. . . . The upwardly mobile Catholics are a group becoming more independent and conservative, and they represent the key to victory in the northern industrial states where they are from 25% to 48% of the voters. (Schram, 1977, p. 263)

So far as timing was concerned, the President was told to hold off campaigning as long as possible. He should stay in the White House, appear "presidential," and husband resources for a final blitz. The financial recommendations carried the same message. Of the $21.8 million, only $500,000 was allocated for presidential travel, compared to $800,000 for polling. The largest allocation was $10 million for a media campaign. The plan said that perceptions of both Ford and Carter had to be altered. "In order to win, we must persuade over 15% (or about 10 million people) to change their opinions. *This will require very aggressive—media oriented efforts.*" Finally, another $2.8 million was to be set aside as a reserve to be used as necessary in the final days of the campaign.

This was a bold, intelligent plan that gave President Ford some chance of catching up with his rival.[4] As already noted, it was unusual in the amount of attention it paid to the external needs of the Ford coalition and in the bluntness with which it addressed Ford's own liabilities. Gerald Ford had spent a decade as Republican leader in Congress, as vice president, and as president; the report told him that he was not seen as an effective leader. Ford had spent as many as 200 days a year on the road and loved to campaign; the document stated flatly that he was a terrible campaigner. The President's reaction was that it was pretty strong stuff. But after thinking about it overnight, he told

---

[4] The one bit of bad advice contained in the plan was that Carter, a native of the Deep South (which had *never* seen one of its citizens elected to the White House), would be vulnerable in the South.

his strategy group to go ahead (Naughton, 1976; Parry, 1977; Schram, 1977, pp. 251–71; Witcover, 1977, chap. 36).

A Quiet Opening

Since the plans developed by the strategists were in effect during the Grand Opening, there was little visible campaigning on the President's part. During September, he held cabinet meetings, signed bills passed by Congress, talked about tax reform while strolling around the Rose Garden, and said that he was dismayed about Hanoi's failure to do more about American servicemen missing in action in the Vietnam War. Not forgetting who his primary audience was, Ford also met with six Roman Catholic bishops to discuss abortion and posed for pictures with Polish-Americans. When he did go to the University of Michigan for a campaign speech and newsmen asked press secretary Ron Nessen if this was the formal beginning of the campaign, Nessen replied that this was the first campaign speech since the last one. All this made Ford look presidential, husbanded resources, and kept the focus of attention on Jimmy Carter, about whom many voters were undecided. Combined with Ford's success in the first debate, this strategy turned a wide Carter margin into a very tight race by the end of September.

Gerald Ford took one brief campaign swing through the Deep South after the first debate, then headed back to Washington to prepare for the second. Since this was to deal with foreign affairs, the Ford strategy group was optimistic and arranged a campaign trip through southern California, Texas, and Oklahoma to capitalize on what it expected to be Ford's continued success. It was in the course of the second debate, though, that Ford made a gaffe about the autonomy of Eastern European governments.[5] Further, it took some time for Ford to concede that he had made a mistake. The beginning of a Tactical Adjustment came the following afternoon in a hastily called news conference. But it was not until five days later, after a meeting with ethnic leaders, that Ford said unequivocally, "I made a mistake." The original statement was not all that unusual a form of verbal reversal; but it was given considerable coverage by the media after the debate, and it concerned precisely the constituency that was the focus of the Ford strategy. "The Poles hadn't made up their minds," said Andrew Greeley, "but they have now and there's nothing Ford can do to change it" (Apple, 1976). This judgment was later confirmed in a study of ethnic voters. Eighty percent heard of this comment, and those who did were very likely to cite it as a reason for their vote (Sears & Chaffee, 1979).

A Final Media Blitz

Mid-October was not the best of times for the Ford campaign. Agriculture Secretary Earl Butz was forced to resign because of a widely reported racial

---

[5] In answering a question about relations with the Soviet Union, President Ford said, "There is no Soviet domination of Eastern Europe, and there never will be under a Ford administration."

slur, and there were some charges about Ford's personal and political finances. But soon it was late October, and the resources that had been carefully set aside for the Time's Up phase could be used.

A new series of commercials prepared by the Deardourff-Bailey firm was
widely used during the closing days of the campaign. One raised questions
about Governor Carter's ability through the use of films of Atlanta residents
saying they did not want Carter to become president. Others portrayed Ford
as a man who inspired confidence. In one, an announcer praised Ford's quiet
style of leadership, and the President pointed out that, "we've certainly created in the Ford administration a nonimperial presidency." Still another
sketched warm relationships within the Ford family. Michael Ford, a divinity
student, spoke of his father as very devout; Susan and Jack Ford had kind
things to say about their father; Susan Ford was shown hugging her father
from the back. "Sometimes," the announcer said, "a man's family can say a
lot about a man." Together, the Deardourff-Bailey commercials presented
Ford rather than Carter as the man to be trusted by wavering voters
(Lelyveld, 1976b).

Another element of the television strategy was a series of conversations
between President Ford, Edith Green (an Oregon Democrat Ford had known
when both were in the House of Representatives), and sportscaster Joe Garagiola, whose political preferences were unknown but whose sports background was in keeping with the Jocks-for-Jerry tone of the campaign and
whose visible Italian-Americanism was perfect. Garagiola proved to be an
effective interlocutor for the President. For example, he asked about the difference between the Nixon and Ford administrations, allowing Ford to reply,
"Joe, there's one very, very fundamental difference. Under President Ford,
there's not an imperial White House, which means there's no pomp, there's
no ceremony, there's no dictatorial authority."

A final element to the Time's Up drive was intensive personal campaigning
by the President himself, quite unlike the September seclusion. Generally, he
spoke for a strong policy in international involvement and moderate conservatism in economic management. "Give me your mandate," he implored. "I
stand on your side, for limited government, for fiscal responsibility, for rising
prosperity, for lower taxes, for military strength, and for peace in the world."

What Mr. Ford said was perhaps less important than where he said it and
to whom he said it. His trip included some stops in middle-sized states
thought to be close (Virginia, the Carolinas, Missouri, Oregon, and Washington), but the bulk of his time was devoted to California, Illinois, Ohio, Pennsylvania, New Jersey, and New York. In Columbus, Ohio, and Syracuse,
New York, he appeared not only with football coaches Woody Hayes and Ben
Schwartzwalder but also with Frank Lausche (a former five-time governor of
Ohio who had come out of the "nationality" politics of Cleveland), with
Cardinal Krol in Philadelphia, and with Cardinal Cooke in New York.

Ford was reaching as best he could for those last few needed votes, and he
poured all his energy into it. By the time he reached Grand Rapids on election

eve, his voice was gone, and his wife Betty had to read his concession statement the day after the election. The Carter coalition prevailed, but Gerald Ford and his strategy group had the satisfaction of knowing that their plan almost led to a come-from-far-behind victory.

SUMMARY

The 1972 and 1976 campaigns both involved a Republican incumbent who followed moderate conservative policies and a Democratic challenger. But there were enormous differences between the two. In 1972, the challenge came from the left side of the Democratic party. Senator McGovern proposed policies that were very different than those being followed by the Nixon administration. Since McGovern's positions made it difficult for him to compete for the moderate vote, President Nixon had a good deal of freedom in deciding on his strategy. The President was far ahead of his challenger at the beginning of the campaign and remained so throughout. The passage of time, therefore, brought a sense of triumph to the incumbent and a sense of hopelessness to the challenger.

In 1976, on the other hand, both parties were fighting for the political center. The incumbent emphasized restraint in spending but held out the possibility of social programs in some areas. The challenger emphasized social justice but held out the possibility of a tax cut. In other words, center-right versus center-left. Jimmy Carter had a substantial lead over Gerald Ford after the two conventions but saw the lead fade away as the election drew closer. President Ford had a well-planned campaign and came from far behind to near-victory. Both had well-grounded hopes for victory as the votes were being counted, but Governor Carter emerged with a narrow victory.

Chapter 6

The 1980 Campaign

The economic issues that troubled Americans during the 1970s continued to dominate their thinking in 1980. The inflation rate got worse in every year of the Carter administration. The consumer price index rose 6.5 percent in 1977, 7.6 percent in 1978, 11.5 percent in 1979, and 13.5 percent in 1980. Other worries about loss of jobs showed up in an increasing number of people who, even in the face of uncontrolled inflation, thought unemployment was more important. On the foreign scene, no war loomed on the horizon; but the continuing plight of the diplomats held hostage in Tehran seemed to symbolize American incapacity overseas. All of these together contributed to a public perception of Jimmy Carter as a good man but an incompetent president.

Many voters were no more taken with Ronald Reagan. On Friday, April 18, an article appeared on the front page of the *New York Times*. "To half the American public," the lead sentence said, "President Carter and Ronald Reagan . . . represent an unsatisfactory choice for president, [according to] the latest *New York Times*/CBS News Poll." Even more opposition was to be found in certain groups of voters. Sixty percent of eastern liberals, western liberals, and college graduates wanted a choice other than Carter and Reagan, as did 56 percent of the 18- to 29-year-olds and 54 percent of independent voters.

Obviously, there were voters who regarded Ronald Reagan and Jimmy Carter as eminently satisfactory candidates. Governor Reagan was passionately supported by the conservative Republicans he had led for over a decade, and President Carter had the respectful support of Democrats who thought he had done his best with difficult problems. As time passed and Reagan and Carter became their parties' nominees, the number of their supporters grew, and 92 percent of the voters ended up casting ballots for one of the major party candidates. Even so, the extent of dissatisfaction with Reagan and Carter said something about the strategic opportunities that were open to the major contenders in 1980.

This discontent also indicated an unusual opportunity for a third-party candidate. On April 24, having concluded that he could not win the Republican nomination and that he had something he wanted to say, John Anderson announced his "National Unity" campaign.

The presence of a relatively strong third candidate alters the opportunities open to campaign strategists. It introduces into general election politics a little of the structure-of-competition problem that is part of multi-candidate nomination politics. A third candidate has an importance in campaign strategy that is greater than the number of votes he ultimately receives. In two-candidate campaigns, a strategist for Candidate A must think of things that will attract voters to Candidate A rather than Candidate B without offending members of Candidate A's supporting coalition. In three-candidate campaigns, a strategist for Candidate A must think of things that will attract voters to Candidate A rather than Candidate B without offending members of Candidate A's supporting coalition *and* without losing voters to Candidate C. Therefore, the strategic opportunities for Candidate A are reduced.

Just whose opportunities are, in fact, reduced in a given campaign depends on the interplay between the three strategies—in 1980, on the interplay between the Reagan strategy, the Carter strategy, and the Anderson strategy.

JOHN ANDERSON'S SOLITARY QUEST

The nature of the appeal John Anderson could make was shaped by characteristics of the constituency he had attracted. As is typical of third-party candidates, Anderson had an appeal to young voters and to independents. But beyond that, his constituency was disproportionately affluent, well educated, and professional. While his backers represented a growing segment of American society, it was far too small to elect a president by itself. Furthermore, Anderson's constituency was dispersed geographically. Unlike Strom Thurmond in 1948 or George Wallace in 1968, he did not have a regional base to which he could add and which would contribute some electoral votes even if his national campaign did not prosper. With Anderson support spread across campuses and suburbs in several parts of the country, he could affect outcomes in individual states by taking votes from Carter or Reagan but was not likely to get electoral votes unless his national standing rose impressively.

In part because of his moderate constituency and in part because of the positions he had been taking for a long time, John Anderson was positioned between Jimmy Carter and Ronald Reagan on most issues. This meant that

Anderson was going to have to fight both candidates for the votes of the political center.

The Problem of Remaining Visible

A third-party candidate has a few advantages and a lot of disadvantages. Not bound by past positions, he has tactical mobility and an ability to present new ideas. But without support from an existing party, he lacks an experienced campaign organization, the capacity to locate voters and get them to the polls, and the financial support the federal government makes available to the major party candidates. Moreover, the record of history is that third-party candidates lose votes to major party candidates as the election approaches.

This last consideration was perhaps Anderson's most important challenge. A Louis Harris poll taken in May showed candidate standings of Reagan 39 percent, Carter 33 percent, and Anderson 23 percent. But when respondents were asked who they would vote for if Anderson had a real chance to win, the trial heat changed to Reagan 35 percent, Carter 31 percent, and Anderson 29 percent. If Anderson remained a credible candidate, he could challenge both Reagan and Carter. If voters became skeptical, he faced an erosion of support.

As John Anderson undertook his independent candidacy, there were four small groups and one large "group" in his nascent coalition. First of all, there were members of his congressional staff. Second, there were persons who had been active in the Ripon Society, a liberal Republican organization. Staff member Michael MacLeod had been executive director, and he recruited others, including Clifford Brown (who was to become research director). After Anderson's strong showing in the Massachusetts primary, a third group became involved, veterans of Congressman Morris Udall's 1976 presidential campaign. This group provided contacts with Democratic politicians. Fourth, when Anderson launched his National Unity campaign, they were joined by some experienced campaigners, of whom the most important were David Garth and Tom Matthews. Garth was a well-known campaign consultant whose ties with the New York-based media community enabled him to give credibility to the thought that Anderson could win; Matthews was a direct-mail expert who had worked for a number of liberal causes. The large "group" was made up of inexperienced but enthusiastic volunteers. Their only common element was that they were attracted to John Anderson. Some of them came to play prominent roles as they gradually gained political experience.

During the summer of 1980, the candidate himself was kept in the news while serious organization and planning work went forward. During the Republican National Convention, Congressman Anderson went off to visit Israel, Egypt, Germany, France, and Britain. His meetings with foreign leaders were not very substantive, and in his efforts to court Jewish support, he came close to endorsement of many Israeli foreign policy goals. At the end of July, Anderson had a meeting with Senator Edward Kennedy. Not much happened in the meeting. Speaking to the press later, Kennedy said that his nomination could "eliminate the need" for a third-party candidacy, and Anderson said he *might* not run if the Democrats did not nominate Carter. These events generated some publicity, but were hardly political triumphs.

Throughout the summer, the principal organizational effort was to get Anderson's name on the ballot. The regional and state organizations were heavily involved in this because many states required large numbers of signatures (e.g., over 100,000 in California) to qualify a candidate for a ballot position. The ballot effort also required substantial litigation. In addition to the suits necessary to get on the ballot in some states, the Democratic National Committee set aside $225,000 for litigation to keep Anderson *off* the ballot in states, such as Massachusetts, where they thought that Anderson would be popular enough to draw votes away from Carter. Milton Ragovin's legal work on Anderson's behalf was remarkably successful although quite expensive. He won every suit he filed, getting the laws of five states declared unconstitutional and persuading a federal district judge to overrule the Georgia Supreme Court. John Anderson's name appeared on the ballot in all 50 states but at a cost of $2 million for organization and legal services, a substantial drain on the lean Anderson treasury.[1]

The other major requirement for legitimacy was finding a vice presidential candidate. The ideal vice presidential candidate was easy to describe: a well-known Democrat from a major state such as New York or California with a reputation for independence, a lot of voter appeal, and policy views similar to Congressman Anderson's. Such qualifications would have added votes to the National Unity ticket. The problem, of course, was that most prominent Democrats who had even some of these qualifications were not anxious to risk their political careers by running on a minor ticket. But with the help of Udall veterans, Patrick J. Lucey was persuaded to accept the vice presidential designation. If Lucey was not the strongest possible candidate, he was at least plausible. He was active in the John F. Kennedy campaign in 1960 as Wisconsin Democratic state chairman, was elected to two terms as governor of Wisconsin, served briefly as ambassador to Mexico, and then worked for the nomination of Edward Kennedy after a falling out with President Carter. So, with the announcement on August 25 that Lucey would run, the Anderson coalition could feel that they had made reasonable progress in remaining in the public eye while getting on the ballot.

A Third-Party Strategy

There were several elements to the Anderson strategy: the relative strength of the major candidates, geographic concentration, demographic concentration, and issues. A common consideration linking all of these was the Anderson coalition's lack of resources. Without strength themselves, they had to rely on the jujitsu method of anticipating an opponent's moves so that the opponent's weight and motion can be turned against him. This, of course, was

---

[1] The total expenditures of the Anderson general election campaign were $14.4 million.

risky business. The assumptions about Reagan's and Carter's strategies had to be correct, Anderson's feints had to be made at just the right time, and there had to be *at least some* resources just to make the needed moves in this underdog strategy.

John Anderson's ultimate goal was to become the second candidate, so that voters would think of Reagan versus Anderson or Carter versus Anderson rather than Reagan versus Carter with Anderson being considered only in case the first two were unsatisfactory. (Theodore Roosevelt, who ran second to Woodrow Wilson as the Bull Moose candidate in 1912, was the only third-party candidate able to accomplish this in recent history.) In thinking about this, Anderson strategists reckoned that Reagan had a solid conservative base that guaranteed him about 30 percent, no matter what. Carter, they felt, had no solid support except from blacks. This meant that Reagan was going to be the strongest man in a three-candidate race. Therefore, they had little hope of getting ahead of Reagan in the polls by taking moderate-conservative positions, but they could perhaps get ahead of Carter by taking moderate-liberal positions. They recognized that they had to fight Carter first in order to get the voters to eventually think of Reagan and Anderson as the alternatives. Carter was the immediate tactical opponent. If all went well, Reagan would be the ultimate strategic opponent.

It was assumed that Carter would try to build on a southern base by adding frequently Democratic industrial states in the Northeast. Reagan, however, was seen as stronger than Carter in the South. The Anderson strategists felt that President Carter could carry Georgia and Arkansas but that Governor Reagan could take the rest. Therefore, the most rational Reagan strategy was to concentrate on the South, to win by adding Indiana, Kentucky, Tennessee, and several southern states to his western base, to pay attention to Ohio and Illinois as insurance states, and not to bother with the upper Midwest or the Northeast.

The Anderson geographic targets were based on these assumptions about what Carter and Reagan were likely to do and on survey results. A Louis Harris poll, again asking respondents how they would vote if they thought Anderson could win, found Anderson leads in Massachusetts, New York, New Jersey, Pennsylvania, Ohio, Illinois, and California. These states, which cast 216 electoral votes, were Anderson's prime targets.[2] This implied Carter as the principal opponent in New York, New Jersey, and Pennsylvania; Reagan as the principal opponent only in California (where they thought Carter was too weak to make much of a race); and a three-candidate contest only in Ohio and Illinois. This was a second reason why Carter was seen as

---

[2] Anderson's secondary targets were Connecticut, Rhode Island, Vermont, and Maine in New England; Delaware and Maryland; Wisconsin, Minnesota, Iowa, and South Dakota in the upper Midwest; Colorado; Hawaii; and Oregon and Washington in the Pacific Northwest. These secondary target states cast an additional 91 electoral votes in 1980, giving Anderson 307 electoral votes if he won *all* the primary and secondary target states.

Anderson's tactical opponent. There were simply more states where they thought they would be in a contest with Carter.[3]

Strategically, the most likely Anderson voters were upper-middle-class professionals. The problem was how to expand the Anderson coalition beyond the "brie and chablis" set to include more of Middle America. If Anderson was to become a genuine contender, he needed to gain the support of blue-collar voters, blacks, and Hispanics *without* losing the support that was coming from suburbs and campuses.

The National Unity issue positions were chosen with an eye to attracting these additional voters. There were very strong urban and civil rights emphases. An urban reinvestment trust fund was to be established to rebuild streets, bridges, sidewalks, sewers, and other deteriorating facilities, and neighborhood development was to be emphasized. John Anderson had a strong civil rights record, including support for open housing, and this was also stressed. The repair of infrastructure and emphasis on civil liberties were both compatible with fiscal conservatism; in this way, the Anderson coalition hoped to attract Middle American support without losing votes from the suburbs. For this to work, of course, Middle America had to be paying attention.

A Month of Auspicious Developments

Electoral campaigns usually do not open with a crisis, but third-party activities often depart from the customary. The immediate cause of the crisis was financial. The ballot access campaign, while successful, had been very costly. Money was flowing from national headquarters to the field. Now, short of funds, the Anderson campaign had to decide between continuing to sustain the field operation and putting on a media campaign. The August 28 decision was to ask the state organizations to raise money, to spend no more than absolutely necessary on travel, and to concentrate whatever funds were available on media. At the same time, media advisor David Garth was put in full control of the campaign. (His first decision was to cancel a $225,000 whistle-stop tour from Illinois to Pennsylvania.) Garth's appointment led to the departure of the senior Udall veterans, who had been building bridges to the Democratic party, and Char Sadalak, who had been an important leader of the field organization. This shake-up did not help with the shortage of resources, but it settled how the scarce resources were to be used.

On Labor Day weekend, the Anderson-Lucey campaign released their platform. The positions were reflections of the stands that Congressman Anderson had been taking for some time and were useful in reaching the voters they hoped to attract. The contents could be summarized as liberal in international involvement (reflecting what had been bipartisan foreign policy in

---

[3] Another implication of this strategy was that the Anderson tacticians recognized there were whole regions of the country—the South and the intermountain West—where they could do nothing to affect the outcome.

former years), conservative in economic management, moderate in social benefits, liberal in civil liberties, and liberal in natural resources. The natural resources provisions, designed to attract environmentalists, represented the only real shift from recent Anderson positions.

The platform was touted as longer and more meaningful than "normal" party platforms. These claims were exaggerated. It was, however, more coherent, having been spared the bargaining that is part of a convention. It had been written by the research division under John Anderson's active, personal direction and also reflected a number of suggestions made by Patrick Lucey. Another unusual feature was the promise to release a detailed budget analysis of the cost of the platform if implemented.[4] *Washington Post* reporter David S. Broder wrote that the Anderson platform "may be the most valuable collection of innovative policy ideas so far assembled for the 1980s."

The month of September was hopeful for the Anderson campaign. The first auspicious development was a ruling from the Federal Election Commission that the National Unity campaign would be eligible for federal funds if Anderson received at least 5 percent of the total vote. The basis for this was the conclusion that the Anderson effort was the functional equivalent of a political party. This ruling brought hope of an end to the financial drought; Anderson leaders planned to seek $10 million in bank loans. Such loans could be used for a media campaign and could be repaid when federal moneys became available.

The following weekend, the policy committee of the Liberal party in New York State recommended that the party endorse John Anderson. This was important for both symbolic and practical reasons. Symbolically, it gave Anderson an endorsement that had gone to Democratic candidates during the Liberal party's 36-year history, thus strengthening Anderson's claim to nonpartisan support. Practically, the endorsement guaranteed Anderson a party line (and thus a number of votes) in New York and strengthened his hand against Jimmy Carter in the Empire State.

Still another happy development came with the League of Women Voters' decision that John Anderson—slightly above the league's 15 percent criterion in some polls and slightly below in others—should be invited to take part in the presidential debates the league was sponsoring. This brought different reactions from the two major parties. Reagan strategists were willing to take part in a debate that included Anderson, but Carter strategists were not. Carter leaders, simultaneously trying to convince banks they should *not* give Anderson any loans, reasoned that they just could not afford to give the Anderson candidacy the credibility that would come with an appearance against the President. Therefore a Reagan-Anderson debate was scheduled in Baltimore for Sunday, September 21.

Congressman Anderson, by now aiming more and more of his salvos at President Carter, broke off his campaigning on the preceding Wednesday

---

[4] This was released on October 13.

morning and returned to Washington to rest and prepare for the debate, which showed two able candidates who differed on almost every single issue. Both showed their strengths very well. Anderson was the more impressive intellectually and perhaps better able to state facts. Reagan was more relaxed. Viewers could see him as a plausible president, one who did not seem likely to start a nuclear war as soon as he was sworn in. The difference was in the stakes of the debate for the two. For Reagan, a major party nominee with ample resources, the debate was one of a series of campaign events. For Anderson, as a *New York Times* headline put it, the future was a single hour. And after the debate was over, the spotlight of attention began to dim.

Fading Hopes

The immediate postdebate polls suggested that both Anderson and Reagan did about equally well. The Harris results showed that Anderson did a little better; the Gallup results showed Reagan with an edge. But John Anderson was not able to capitalize on his hour in the sun to improve his standing against the two major party candidates, and more serious difficulties became apparent in the postdebate campaigning. Gambling as they had to that their candidate would do well in the debate, Anderson leaders organized major appearances for the day after the debate, and an augmented press corps went along to see how he would do. Things went well at a noon-hour rally in Chicago, where Anderson enjoyed attacking Carter for his refusal to debate, but not that evening in Philadelphia. Appearing in a 3,500-seat auditorium, he faced a painfully small crowd of about 500. The headline in the *Philadelphia Inquirer* was "Empty Hall Swallows Anderson Momentum," and David Broder pointed out that Anderson lacked just the kind of support that a political party can provide for its candidate.

By the end of the week, a number of political observers had concluded that the Anderson campaign was likely to meet the fate of most third-party efforts. Writing in the *Washington Star*, Jack Germond and Jules Witcover asserted: "With some exceptions, Anderson's leading supporters and advisors. . . now see the rest of the campaign as a case of playing out their hand against essentially hopeless odds." This was challenged in a letter to the *Star* signed by Anderson's 10 senior advisors. But while the political judgment of the media experts could be argued, the effects of their editorial judgment could not. John Anderson was all but invisible on the television network newscasts on Tuesday, Wednesday, Thursday, and Friday of the week after the Baltimore debate. And on September 30, a *Washington Post* story on Anderson was relegated to page 6.

The news judgment that cost John Anderson television time and removed him from front pages was the more harmful because the Anderson forces still lacked the resources to afford a media campaign. Anderson leaders were not able to borrow money. In part, the problem was White House opposition, but it was also the risky nature of the loans from the banks' perspective. Anderson's collateral was to be found in public opinion polls. His standing was well above the required 5 percent at the time the loans were being sought, but the Anderson coalition could not *guarantee* the banks that Anderson's standing would not drop below 5 percent by election day.[5]

Consequently, the Anderson forces tried another tactic. On September 29, they mailed letters to previous Anderson donors asking that they make small loans to the Anderson campaign to be paid back when federal funds became available. Almost $1 million was raised this way by mid-October. This was far short of the $10 million that was originally sought from banks but enough to permit a *very* modest media campaign.

These adverse developments did not spell the end of the campaign. Anderson support was declining, but it did not disappear. Anderson voters continued to be found among young people, among the better educated, among professionals, on campuses, and in suburbs. If the Anderson coalition was not able to expand to include blue-collar workers, there were also supporters who were staying with him. And the candidate himself continued his own efforts. When he was good, as he often was in campus appearances, he could engender excitement about himself and the ideas about which he spoke. But on other occasions, he sounded strident, stubborn, and had a tendency to preach to his audiences. These not-so-good appearances happened too frequently. The truth was that John Anderson was by now very tired. Lacking resources for a media campaign that would amplify his own voice, he had been carrying much of the campaign himself for a long time, and weariness often reduced his effectiveness as a campaigner.

The Anderson strategy was in many ways the most interesting of those adopted by the three candidates. Even if the resources to implement it were not available, it was recognized from the outset as a long shot. And to the extent that resources were available, the plan remained in effect from the Grand Opening throughout much of the campaign. Decisions about Congressman Anderson's schedule and the limited media campaign were made in accordance with it. This meant that for much of the campaign, the Anderson coalition *was* trying to win.

It was not until Time's Up that the strategy was altered. In the last week of the campaign, Anderson's schedule was changed. A final swing through the Midwest was canceled, and John Anderson went instead to New England and California, his two strongest areas. In this Time's Up effort, it was thought that the larger crowds likelier to appear in friendly territory would look better on television. When he did return to his own alma mater on the night before the election, John Anderson could say: "Whatever the outcome, our goal has been to wake up America and to bring a new sense of hope in the future of our country. You give me heart to believe that in the hearts of young Americans we have succeeded." But for most of the campaign, he was trying to win the election as well.

---

[5] The effort to obtain bank loans was not given up until October 15.

KEEPING THE WOLF FROM THE DOOR: CARTER 1980

Organization and Planning

By 1980, the political novices who had managed the 1976 campaign had the advantage of four years of experience. This could be seen in some of their plans. But they also bore the scars of a number of political defeats. Their precarious situation was summarized in pollster Pat Caddell's reflections: "Simply stated. . . our strategy was. . . trying to keep the wolf from the door. . . . I often had the terrible feeling we were like the German army being sent to Moscow to take it without winter uniforms."

The leadership of the 1980 coalition consisted of a core group that was augmented from time to time. The four central decision makers were Hamilton Jordan, who came from the White House to take charge of the campaign in June, presidential press secretary Jody Powell, media specialist Gerald Rafshoon, and Pat Caddell. Jordan, Powell, and Rafshoon had worked with each other since the days of Carter's gubernatorial campaigns; Caddell had worked with them since 1976. Robert Strauss, who bore the title of chairman, provided liaison with the media, potential donors, and Democrats outside the Carter coalition. Others were brought into campaign decision making from time to time, depending on the question that arose.

There were three layers to the Carter strategy in 1980. The most fundamental layer was a strategy memorandum written for President Carter by Hamilton Jordan as soon as he moved from the White House to the campaign staff. The second layer was the Orange Book, a geographic analysis that indicated where the electoral votes would have to be sought. It was used, especially early in the campaign, to guide decisions about field budget, travel, and phone banks. The third layer was a series of memorandums written by Pat Caddell on the basis of surveys. (The first of these went to President Carter on June 25, the same day as the Jordan memorandum.) The poll information kept the strategy current during the campaign and was used to make decisions about scheduling and whether or not to take part in presidential debates.[6] None of these three analyses suggested that it would be easy to reelect Jimmy Carter.

The Jordan memorandum began by placing the blame for the difficult political situation not on any failures of the preceding four years but rather on

---

[6] A number of these documents were published after the campaign was over, as was the case in 1976. Their availability gives the analyst a chance to see what recommendations are being made during the campaign. A short portion of the Jordan memorandum appears in his book, *Crisis*, on pages 305–9. Two memorandums written by Pat Caddell and five written by Richard Wirthlin for Governor Reagan appear in the appendix of *Portrait of an Election*, by Elizabeth Drew. A very informative discussion between Pat Caddell and Richard Wirthlin appears in the December 1980–January 1981 issue of *Public Opinion*, published by the American Enterprise Institute. And an article by Richard Wirthlin, Vincent Breglio, and Richard Beal in the February–March 1981 issue of *Public Opinion* presents the strategy that the Reagan coalition was following during the last month of the campaign.

"Kennedy's sustained and exaggerated attacks on your record." The central strategic message of Jordan's analysis was:

> You will not be elected President unless we succeed partially in dispelling the notion that it doesn't matter who the President is, unless we convince the American people that this is a critical election in the life of our country and that there are real and substantial differences between you and Ronald Reagan. (Jordan, 1982, p. 308)

Unless voters were convinced that it made a real difference whether Carter or Reagan was elected, Jordan predicted a number of adverse consequences: the Democratic coalition would not come together, minority voters would not turn out, liberals would defect, and the Anderson candidacy would flourish. Hence, drawing a sharp distinction between Carter and Reagan became the cornerstone supporting the entire Carter strategy.

The Orange Book was based on an analysis of election data from 1956 through 1976. These elections were chosen because they included three Republican and three Democratic victories, and because going back to 1956 would begin the time series with a normal-turnout election rather than the high-turnout election of 1960. The analysis proper was focused on three political concerns: turnout, performance, and persuadability. The measure of probable 1980 turnout was a projection of the regression line for each state from 1956 through 1976. Democratic performance was measured by the mean Democratic vote over this time period, and persuadability was measured by the standard deviation of this mean.

In practice, Democratic performance was the basic consideration in determining targeting. After inspecting the mean Democratic vote and making certain "commonsense" adjustments, all states were classified as safe, marginal, or lost. The marginal states were subclassified into marginal plus, marginal, and marginal minus. Considerations of turnout and persuadability, converted into estimates of the amount of effort required to produce electoral votes, were raised only after the basic decision about the likelihood of a state voting Democratic had been made.

The grim prospect facing a Democratic candidate[7] can be seen by adding up the electoral votes that could be regarded as safe, marginal, and lost. Only two states, Georgia and West Virginia, and the District of Columbia were regarded as safe. Four more states—Massachusetts, Rhode Island, Minnesota, and Hawaii—were classified as marginal plus. Twenty-four more

---

[7] Remember that this calculation was based on the average Democratic vote and did not reflect any additional liabilities Jimmy Carter might have had because of his personal unpopularity in 1980. Taking this series of elections, however, did produce a slight Republican bias. There were three close elections (1960, 1968, and 1976), one Democratic landslide (1964), and two Republican landslides (1956 and 1972). Consequently, in an even election, a Democratic candidate should have done slightly better than these estimates.

states—including all the rest of the South, the Middle Atlantic states, and the Great Lakes states except Indiana—were seen as marginal. The safe states cast 21 electoral votes, and the marginal-plus states cast 32 more. This meant that for the Democrats to win, they would have to get 217 (65 percent) of the 335 electoral votes being cast by the marginal states. Consequently, the targeting committee recommended concentrating all resources on the marginal states, spending proportionately to the size of each state's electoral vote and spending half as much on the 5 marginal-plus states and the 3 marginal-minus states as on the 24 marginal states. So the Democrats began their campaign devoting the greatest amount of their resources to New York, Pennsylvania, Texas, Illinois, and Ohio—the marginal states casting the largest electoral votes—and intending to spend nothing on the 3 safe states or the 17 lost states.

If the Carter coalition was to carry enough of the states needed for victory, the first order of business had to be assembling a strong Democratic coalition. This meant Roman Catholics, labor union members, Jews, and blacks—all members of a normal Democratic coalition. Running against Ronald Reagan, it also meant women.

The coalition also planned to appeal to suburban voters. When Carter ran against Ford in 1976, Ford had more appeal in the suburbs, but Jimmy Carter was able to compensate for that by an unusual (for a Democrat) appeal to small-town residents in some areas such as central Pennsylvania and southern Ohio. Facing someone with Ronald Reagan's small-town appeal, Jimmy Carter could not duplicate his 1976 feat, but his strategists hoped that he could compensate by getting votes in the suburbs, where Reagan might be less attractive. The problem with this strategy, of course, was that John Anderson also was attractive to suburban voters.

In past campaigns, as Pat Caddell pointed out in his first memorandum on election strategy, Jimmy Carter had been positioned in the political center with an ability to move right or left as the situation required. In 1980, he saw two problems with this.

> First, Carter is in jeopardy of losing the center to Reagan. Surveys already indicate that Reagan is placed by the electorate as closer to them on general issues than Carter. Second, in a general election sense Anderson is assaulting much of Carter's liberal base whose normal certainty would allow Carter to move right toward Reagan. These factors are further complicated by the fact that Carter, to win, must hold the more conservative South and the more liberal blue collar Northeast. An all out move to secure one area could lead to the alienation of the other. (Drew, 1981, p. 402)

All of this led to a general strategy of emphasizing the differences (especially on foreign policy) between President Carter and Governor Reagan together with specific appeals to the groups they hoped to entice to the Carter coalition. The general contrast the Democrats wanted to stress was a choice between two different visions of the American future.[8]

The central Democratic themes were set forth in the convention speeches of Senator Kennedy and Vice President Mondale. When Kennedy pointed out that the Republican nominee, had said; "Unemployment insurance is a pre-paid vacation plan for freeloaders," and when Mondale said that Ronald Reagan had advocated sending troops to Angola, Rhodesia, Panama, Ecuador, North Korea, Pakistan, Cyprus, and the Middle East but the American people want a president "who's demonstrated he knows how to keep the peace," they were emphasizing the choice Carter strategists wanted the voters to think about.

There were no distinctive issues emphasized to attract Roman Catholic voters. "With Catholics," as a campaign leader put it, "it's a matter of working the community. Going out and campaigning through their areas." However, there were issues that were stressed for each of the other groups. Close ties had existed between labor leaders and Democratic leaders for some time, and there was cooperation in 1980. In appealing to labor, Carter supporters underscored the Reagan and Anderson records. Old Reagan quotes were resurrected. In May 1976, commenting on Carter's support for the Humphrey-Hawkins bill, Governor Reagan had said, "If ever there was a design for fascism, that's it. Fascism was really the basis for the New Deal." In John Anderson's case, the Carterites went back to his voting record. They pointed to an AFL–CIO COPE statement that Anderson voted "right" only 52 times during his career and "wrong" 136 times. Anderson's antilabor votes included Section 14b of the Taft-Hartley Act, common situs picketing, minimum wage, and the Davis-Bacon Act, all issues of great concern to labor leaders.

Blacks were reminded of Jimmy Carter's judicial appointments and of the budget commitments the Carter administration had made to support civil rights activities. An ad was run in black newspapers reading: "Jimmy Carter has named 37 black judges. Cracked down on job bias. And created 1 million jobs. That's why the Republicans are out to beat him." To appeal to Jews, considerable emphasis was given to the peace issue. Jewish fears about weakening the separation between church and state were appealed to by pointing to Ronald Reagan's support of school prayer and John Anderson's Christianity amendment.[9] And women were reminded of Ronald Reagan's opposition to abortion, to the Equal Rights Amendment, and to equal opportunity in

---

[8] The Carter core group wanted above all to avoid making the election a referendum on the Carter administration. There were some Carter aides, especially those involved in policy formation, who wanted to explain the accomplishments of the Carter administration. Surveys, however, suggested that if the election turned on what the Carter administration had done, Carter would lose. Carter strategists felt that the two-month election campaign was too short a time to alter perceptions that had taken four years to form.

[9] Early in his congressional career, Anderson had proposed adding "This Nation devoutly recognized the authority and law of Jesus Christ, Savior and Ruler of nations, through whom are bestowed the blessing of Almighty God" to the Constitution.

general. None of these specific appeals conflicted with the general theme that Carter and Reagan had different visions of the future of America, but the emphasis given them facilitated coalition building.

A Double Offensive

When Jimmy Carter began his public campaigning, he was faced with the need for a double offensive. He had to draw the distinction between himself and Ronald Reagan to portray the different futures the Democrats wanted voters to contemplate, and he had to show that he was the *real* liberal in order to prevent John Anderson from taking Carter votes in industrial states. The Carter offensive against Reagan had to be highly visible, but the anti-Anderson effort had to be less visible so Anderson's candidacy would not be given credibility.

The television ads that began running the first week of September were subtle rather than strident. The emphasis was on the complexity of the presidency. The pictures showed President Carter working in the Oval Office, conferring with foreign leaders, or taking part in the "town meetings" that he had held in various communities. The announcer read messages such as "Today, the chief of state is an international figure," "The office has a powerful effect on the United States and upon the whole world," and "The responsibility never ends." There were positive references about Jimmy Carter, not negative references to Ronald Reagan. It was left to the viewer to make a comparison between the two men and consider who was better suited for the presidency.

President Carter began his own campaigning on Labor Day in Tuscumbia, Alabama, to shore up his southern support. The President did make reference to the two-futures theme. But he was joined on the platform by southern Democratic leaders and told the crowd: "You people here have the same background, the same families, the same upbringing that I have. . . . I've come back to the part of this nation that will always be my home to ask you to join me once again." His schedule thereafter paid attention to states classified as marginal in the Orange Book. The next day, he went to Harry Truman's hometown, Independence, Missouri, and on Wednesday, he campaigned through ethnic neighborhoods in Philadelphia. The next week, Carter went to Perth Amboy, New Jersey, for the opening of a new steel plant, and the third week of September, he took a two-day swing through Texas, Georgia, South Carolina, and Ohio.

Some of the things that the President said on the hustings, however, went beyond the campaign plans. In his basic campaign memorandum, Hamilton Jordan reminded Mr. Carter:

> You were at times strident and personal in your attacks on President Ford. Because Ford was widely perceived as being a "good man" rhetoric directed at Ford that seemed personal and harsh hurt us. I believe that we will find ourselves in a similar posture in the fall campaign when anything that smacks of a personal attack on Reagan will be counterproductive. (Jordan, 1982, p. 309)

But in a town meeting in Independence, Missouri, President Carter charged that Governor Reagan would break off a tradition of arms control negotiations that went back to President Eisenhower. "I consider this," the President continued, "one of the most serious threats to the safety and the peace of our nation and of the world that is being dramatized in this 1980 election." And speaking in Martin Luther King, Sr.'s church in Atlanta, Jimmy Carter told the audience, "You've seen in this campaign the stirrings of hate and the rebirth of code words like 'state's rights' in a speech in Mississippi, in a campaign reference to the Ku Klux Klan relating to the South."

Charges that Governor Reagan was a threat to world peace and that Reagan had introduced hatred and racism into the campaign were hardly in keeping with the advice to avoid personal attacks on the Governor. Jimmy Carter was not completely responsible for this. The Democratic plan called for Vice President Mondale to carry the brunt of the attack on Governor Reagan. The media, however, failed to carry Mondale's attacks. But Carter, attacking Reagan's position on nuclear arms negotiations on September 2, did not wait to see what would happen before making charges himself. And in an editorial entitled "Running Mean," the Washington Post said that the racial attack "fits into Jimmy Carter's miserable record of personally savaging political opponents (Hubert Humphrey, Edward Kennedy) whenever the going got rough."

The Carter coalition's offensive against John Anderson wasn't attracting nearly as much attention, but it was being pursued seriously because of the Anderson threat to the Carter strategy. They didn't think that John Anderson could win, but they did think he was a threat in nine key industrial states. Carter leaders also discovered, to their horror, that the Anderson strategy of trying to add to his campus-suburban base was making some headway. There was an Anderson vote among young working people, among young blacks, among Jews. Therefore, while public statements were made about falling Anderson support, specific appeals were made to each of these audiences.

The anti-Anderson appeal to young labor was essentially that already referred to: Anderson had voted against many labor positions while a member of the Republican leadership in Congress. Therefore, labor voters should not be taken in by his 1980 rhetoric. The anti-Anderson argument to blacks took two forms. The more prominent argument was that while Anderson had an "adequate civil rights record,"[10] the real issues in 1980 were economic. Anderson was an economic conservative, and Anderson would end up electing the even worse Ronald Reagan by drawing votes away from Jimmy Carter. The sub-rosa anti-Anderson move was a distortion of Anderson's civil rights record that was played on local radio stations. When Anderson supporters complained in Detroit, the tape was pulled—and moved to Chicago. From Chicago, it was moved to Seattle.

---

[10] In fact, Congressman John Anderson had voted consistently for civil rights legislation in the early 1960s while State Senator Jimmy Carter had been silent on this issue.

A centerpiece in the appeal to Jewish voters, and to liberal voters more generally, was a pamphlet entitled "Will the Real John Anderson Please Stand Up?" This asked whether John Anderson should be judged by his progressive campaign rhetoric of 1980 or by his 19 years in the Republican congressional mainstream. The answer, with references to issues particularly important to groups sought for the Carter coalition, was that Anderson was fundamentally a conservative.

Perhaps the most salient Anderson question in September was whether President Carter should take part in a debate after the League of Women Voters invited both Governor Reagan and Congressman Anderson. Campaign director Les Francis described this decision:

> It occupied a good deal of discussion at several meetings. . . . Essentially it came down to the fact that a large number of people were moving in the direction of Anderson at the time, at least more potential Carter voters than potential Reagan voters. So we felt that being involved in the debate would enhance Mr. Anderson's credibility as a candidate and make it harder to get those people back. (Moore, 1981, pp. 201–2)

Francis went on to say that this was the toughest political call he'd seen anyone have to make; but once the decision was made, they all felt comfortable with it.

From Debate to Debate

Since President Carter did not participate in the Baltimore debate, there was nothing the Carter camp could do to control the outcome. All they had was hope that Anderson and Reagan would not do well. This turned out to be a reasonable bet about Anderson. As we have seen, Anderson did well in the debate itself, but the media stopped taking him seriously shortly thereafter. The Carter coalition added to Anderson's troubles by making a small Strategic Adjustment. They began to emphasize the "Anderson is a spoiler" argument. Until this time, the Anderson candidacy had been publicly ignored by the Carter field organization. Now they were instructed to argue that a vote for John Anderson was a vote for Ronald Reagan.

The Carter forces were not so lucky with Ronald Reagan. The former California Governor emerged from the Baltimore debate as a plausible presidential candidate. This was costly because of temporal assumptions that had been built into the Democratic strategy. Since late-summer polls showed that President Carter was behind Governor Reagan, September was intended to be a catch-up month. The Carter strategists wanted to get to a situation by early October where the two candidates were about even and where doubts about Reagan's competence had been raised that they hoped would be decisive in the end. Pat Caddell's polls showed that they were successful in moving in this direction until the debate, but then Reagan pulled ahead again. By staying out of the Baltimore debate, the Carter coalition avoided giving credibility to the Anderson candidacy, but that cost them time in their strategy against Reagan.

At this point, some Strategic and Tactical Adjustments were made. The Strategic Adjustment was to give greater emphasis to the war-and-peace issue. This was an issue where polls showed that Carter was making some progress at Reagan's expense, and it was an issue that was persuading women to vote for Carter rather than Reagan. Some new television commercials emphasized this. One (an imitation of a very successful Ford ad of 1976 in which Georgia residents said they did not intend to vote for Governor Carter) had California residents expressing their concerns about whether Governor Reagan would shoot from the hip if he were elected president.

Second, President Carter continued to make harsh public criticisms of Governor Reagan. Why was this a Tactical Adjustment if Carter had already been doing so? The difference was that Carter strategists had now decided that questions *must* be raised about Reagan to catch up in the polls and that the only way they could get coverage was to have the President make the charges himself. In California the night after the debate, Jimmy Carter said that American voters faced a choice between peace and war in November. At a fundraiser in Washington, he suggested that a Reagan victory would mean "the alienation of black from white, Christian from Jew, rich from poor, and North from South." In Chicago on October 6, the President said, "If . . . you just want to push people around and show the macho of the United States, that is an excellent way to lead our country toward war."

For this stridency the President was paying a price in many media comments about the "meanness" issue. According to the evidence of the Caddell polls, the meanness issue was not having much impact on the general public. Nonetheless, Hamilton Jordan decided on another Tactical Adjustment: Jimmy Carter would apologize. On an already scheduled interview with Barbara Walters, the President said: "Some of the issues are just burning with fervor in my mind and in my heart and I have to sometimes speak extemporaneously and I have gotten carried away on a couple of occasions. . . . I'll try. . . to be sure that we do not have a lowering of the tone of the campaign." The following day, attacks on Reagan came not from the President but from Secretary of Defense Harold Brown and Labor Secretary Ray Marshall, as intended. But two days later, Carter said in Florida that Reagan "would not be a good president or a good man to trust with the affairs of this nation," and the meanness issue was revived.

A more hopeful change took place in mid-October, when Senator Kennedy began to make appearances for President Carter. Carter had an urgent need for Kennedy's support to bring liberal Democrats back to the fold, and Kennedy had an interest in demonstrating his support of the Democratic candidate. Kennedy taped some television commercials endorsing Carter. During the week of October 13, Kennedy and Carter appeared together in Massachusetts (where Anderson was still showing a lot of strength), New Jersey, and Washington, D.C. The Senator made trips by himself to other areas where he was popular: Detroit, Wisconsin, and the Chicano area of Texas.

Poll information was a little more encouraging in mid-October. In the second wave of a panel study directed by Pat Caddell, interviewers discovered that 95 percent of the respondents who supported either Reagan or Carter prior to the Baltimore debate were still in favor of the same candidate. President Carter apparently had begun to catch up again after Governor Reagan's postdebate surge. In the public polls, Gallup, Harris, and NBC/ Associated Press all continued to show Reagan leads; but in their October 16– 20 survey, CBS News/*New York Times* found a very small Carter lead. This did not lead to wild optimism, but it did hold open the possibility of a Carter victory.

The Cleveland Debate and the End

On October 17, the equilibrium in the campaign was upset by a Reagan decision. Governor Reagan agreed to meet President Carter in a one-on-one debate. Although Reagan had been insisting that John Anderson be included in any debate, Reagan leaders had taken care not to close the door absolutely, and previous positions taken by the Carter coalition left them with no alternative but to debate. Within the Carter core group, having a debate was strongly opposed by Pat Caddell. Richard Wirthlin took a similar position in the Reagan core group. Both pollsters saw debates as high-risk events; and since this debate was scheduled for October 28, a bare week before the election, there would be almost no time to recover from any major error. Caddell was more worried than Wirthlin because Carter was running behind.

Pat Caddell wrote a 29-page memorandum placing the coming debate in a strategic context. It contained a great deal of information, too much to be easily digested, but it did make three vital points. First, he pointed out the risk to Jimmy Carter. "We can think of our debate as a football game with each team having only one chance to move the ball and score. However, we get the ball on our five-yard line. Reagan starts with the ball on *our* 40 yard line" (Drew, 1981, p. 412). Therefore, Caddell went on, only "excellent precision, bold strategies, and high-risk plays" were likely to lead to real Carter success. Second, there were two target groups: college-educated voters and women. College-educated voters were more likely than others to support Anderson, and they were less likely to support Reagan than previous Republican candidates. Women were supporting Carter in much greater numbers than men. Third, issues were classified from those that showed a large Carter edge and should therefore be emphasized to those that showed a large Reagan edge and were therefore likely to be dangerous. Among the issues helping Carter were war and peace, the Equal Rights Amendment, and social issues. Issues where the polls showed a Reagan edge[11] included inflation and unemployment (Drew, 1981, pp. 431–32).

---

[11] Discussing advantage alone simplifies what Caddell said. He considered both salience and partisan advantage.

The debate drew an enormous audience. According to the Nielson organization, 58.9 percent of all television homes watched the debate. President Carter did many of the things that were vital to his strategy. He suggested several times that issues were more complex than Governor Reagan seemed to think (an important point in appealing to the college-educated target group) and discussed their differences on the Equal Rights Amendment and social issues. But in discussing arms control, he referred to a discussion with his 13-year-old daughter Amy in which "she said she thought nuclear weaponry and control of nuclear arms (were) the most important issues," thus trivializing the war-and-peace issue that had been one of his few real advantages. And in his closing statement, Governor Reagan suggested a series of questions for voters to think about: "Are you better off than you were four years ago? Is it easier for you to go and buy things in the stores than it was four years ago? Is there more or less unemployment in the country than there was four years ago?" By asking these questions, Ronald Reagan put the focus of attention on inflation and unemployment, two issues of enormous benefit to him.

The postdebate surveys were mixed, but CBS reported that 44 percent thought that Reagan won the debate compared to 36 percent who thought that Carter won. The Associated Press found that both candidates gained 6 percent additional support, but they had been showing Mr. Reagan ahead, and an equal gain implied victory for the Republican. Louis Harris said that the election was now Reagan's to lose, and Gerald Rafshoon said, "The wolf was no longer at the door. He was inside, running through the house" (White, 1982, p. 405).

For the balance of the week, President Carter campaigned through critical states. The day after the debate, he went to Pittsburgh, Rochester, Newark, and Philadelphia. On Thursday, he began in Philadelphia, went to New York City for a big noontime garment district rally, and then ended up in South Carolina. The next two days were devoted to more southern and border states: Mississippi, Florida, Texas, Tennessee, and Missouri. He continued to stress issues that were strategically important, often using statements made during the debate. "Every American," the President told a Pittsburgh town meeting, "ought to stop and think what will happen to this world if we have no control over nuclear weapons between ourselves and the Soviet Union." "Governor Reagan may not have known" the country had a racial problem when he was young, Carter told a black congregation in Newark, "but to millions and millions of Americans. . . it was not simply a problem, but a lifelong disaster." And in Texas on Saturday, he repeated once again, "In four years as President, I've learned a great deal."

The President's campaigning was halted early Sunday morning to return to the White House. The Iranian Parliament had stated four conditions for the release of the diplomats being held hostage in Tehran, and Mr. Carter had to see the exact translation, as well as confer with his foreign policy advisors, to know how to reply. A statement was agreed on and released, and the President departed on Monday morning for one last, long day of campaigning.[12] It was after midnight in Seattle when the phone call from Washington brought the bad news to the President. "Mr. President," said Pat Caddell, "I'm afraid that it's gone." Caddell had now seen the final day's survey data. The conclusion that he shared with fellow senior strategists Jordan, Rafshoon, and Powell—and now the President—was that Jimmy Carter was going to lose by 8 to 10 percentage points (Jordan, 1982, pp. 367–68).

RONALD REAGAN'S CONSERVATIVE CRUSADE

An Early Comprehensive Plan

In one sense, the 1980 Reagan strategy was set forth earlier than in any preceding campaign. In another, it was not. The reason for this seeming contradiction was the nature of the campaign plan. Written, approved, and adopted before the Fourth of July, it filled two large loose-leaf notebooks. This document, however, was more of a statement of how strategists Richard Wirthlin and Richard Beal conceptualized the electorate than it was a series of operational steps. The basic plan, for example, contained a list called "Conditions of Victory." It did not, however, state how these conditions were to be achieved. The specific steps to do this were provided in a series of memorandums written throughout the campaign on the basis of the latest survey information. The campaign plan in effect at any time was the June document as updated by the latest memorandums.[13]

There were originally some 21 conditions of victory. The number was gradually reduced as succeeding memorandums were written. Two things were happening to shorten the list. One was that some of the conditions were coming to be seen as more important. Keeping them on a shorter list was a way of accenting them. The other was that certain conditions had been satisfied and could therefore be removed. By early October, there were seven conditions of victory being focused upon; by the end of the campaign, there were only five.

The list of target states was also being updated constantly. The original Reagan base consisted of the West plus Indiana and Virginia. If Texas, Florida, Kentucky, and Iowa were added, the number of electoral votes rose to 213. The original battleground states were therefore seen as four industrialized states around the Great Lakes: Illinois, Ohio, Pennsylvania, and Michi-

---

[12] The fatigue of the Time's Up phase was particularly evident to those who had been involved since the beginning of nomination politics. During the last week, campaign director Les Francis said: "Of course, we had a vigorous contest for the nomination. But then there's the length of the contest itself. There's a lot of wear and tear on the campaign staff. There are a lot of people around here who are just god-damned tired. They are just holding on now. There is similar wear and tear on the candidate." In the face of such exhaustion, it is not surprising that there are occasional fluffs and mistakes. The surprise is that they do not occur more often.

[13] Several of these memorandums have been published. The basic document, kept locked in a safe at campaign headquarters, has not.

gan. Allocations of the candidate's time, media placement, and organizational effort were all heaviest in the battleground states. As time went on, it appeared that this list of states that Governor Reagan might hope to carry was too modest. In September, Wisconsin, Connecticut, New Jersey, and Louisiana became possible Reagan targets.

The greatest change took place in October, by which time substantial cracks were appearing in Carter's southern base. Tennessee, North Carolina, Mississippi, Alabama, South Carolina, and Arkansas all were added as battleground states. There were resource considerations in these southern additions. The Reagan strategists believed that they could hold their western base by spending 15 percent of their resources, principally on the Pacific Coast states. If they could force the Carter coalition to spend as much as 30 percent of its resources defending its southern base, the Reagan coalition would have more of a competitive advantage in the large industrial states that both were contesting.

Finally, at the end of October, it even seemed possible to carry New York. As this list of target states was expanding, the dimensions of the Reagan Electoral College victory were increasing. The number of electoral votes for Reagan if they held their base and carried *all* of their target states increased from 302 at the end of June to 367 by the end of September to 472 at the end of October.

A closely related objective had to do with target populations. In general, Governor Reagan had to pick up support from moderates. The Wirthlin polls showed that he had a majority of conservative votes in June, but only a quarter of the moderates intended to cast Reagan ballots. While it was heartening to know that Reagan was supported by his fellow conservatives, there just weren't enough of them to elect him, so gains with moderates were essential. There were three demographic targets: Roman Catholics, labor, and senior citizens. Each of these was a group where Richard Wirthlin felt Reagan had shown some special appeal. More importantly, each of these groups was large enough to affect the outcome in some target states.

The labor vote was concentrated in Pennsylvania, Ohio, Illinois, and Michigan. The Roman Catholic vote was less concentrated. Substantial numbers were to be found in New England and New York, which weren't geographic targets, but also in New Jersey, Pennsylvania, Ohio, Illinois, Louisiana, and Texas, which were. The senior citizen efforts were carried on primarily in Florida, with some attention to southern California. Thus the demographic and geographic strategies were coordinated with one another.

The section of the campaign plan dealing with issues began with a review of a summer 1979 survey of the values and aspirations of the American people. Decision/Making/Information (the name of the Wirthlin firm) found that the public was fundamentally optimistic. They further reported that the issue agenda had been quite stable for the preceding two years. Inflation was the most important issue. Selection of an issue as important, however, was not related to vote intent. The link to vote intent came through the question of leadership. Since the public tended to have a "can do" point of view, it followed that the country could accomplish more with better leaders. Leadership, therefore, had to be stressed along with economics. It was not enough to talk about inflation; the message had to be that Ronald Reagan could do something about inflation because he was an effective leader.[14]

Still another section of the campaign plan laid out the expected Carter attack strategy. The attack could be expected to say that the Governor was dumb, dangerous, and deceitful: dumb in that he was over his head in government, dangerous because he was a right-wing, knee-jerk reactionary, and deceitful on the grounds that he was exaggerating his claims of accomplishment as governor of California. The Reagan campaign plan then made some suggestions for dealing with this anticipated Carter attack strategy. The Republican National Convention, for example, should be used to inoculate the public against these anticipated charges by having other speakers portray Reagan as conservative but reasonable and as one who *had* accomplished some things as governor of California.

Perhaps most important for an understanding of the Reagan strategy, the plan divided the campaign into three periods, each with a different objective. The first phase, from the end of the Democratic convention until shortly after Labor Day, was called "Deal to Strength." It was to be used to solidify the geographic and ideological base that Reagan had established. The Reagan people did not want to spend many resources on this base, but they wanted to make sure that it was solid (especially California's 45 electoral votes) so they could proceed.

The second temporal period, from about the second week of September until October 20, was to be used to deepen public perceptions of Governor Reagan and to broaden his political base. However much he was respected by conservative Republicans, there weren't enough of them to elect him president. Therefore, a number of things had to be done to establish the Governor as strong, competent, and caring and to go after the independent vote.

The third period, from October 20 until November 4, was seen as the period in which the election would be won. Resources—money, candidate time, and professional time—should be husbanded for use then. How these resources should be used could not be anticipated far in advance, but they should be kept ready to motivate the Reagan vote to turn out on election day. In brief, first solidify the Reagan vote, then broaden it, then turn it out.

The Four Blunders and the Death of Focused Impact

One of the problems of a challenger is how to get his stories carried by the news media. An incumbent president can make news in a number of ways: by signing a piece of legislation, by appointing a government official, by

---

[14] See Edwards (1983) for a similar finding that the public's perception of the skill of the president in managing the economy, not the economic record per se, is related to the president's approval rating.

conferring with a foreign leader, and so on. He can be sure that each of these things will be duly recorded by the news media. The idea of focused impact was to give a challenger a similar capacity. By selecting a chosen theme and by speaking only about that topic for a given period of time, the challenger could ensure that the media would report *something* about this subject. Further, if several stories succeeded one another, the person who was paying casual attention (i.e., the average voter) would get an impression that the candidate was dealing with the subject.

The subject selected for the first focused impact was foreign affairs, and Ambassador Bush's trip to China was to be part of it. Foreign affairs was selected because the strategists saw this as Carter's issue rather than Reagan's. The Camp David agreement between Israel and Egypt had been the high point of the Carter administration and one that the President could be expected to stress. The economy was Reagan's issue. Therefore, the strategists wanted to do something with foreign affairs but to do it early. Then they could come back to it later in the campaign if they chose. Since George Bush had been permanent representative in China, he could go there on a fact-finding mission. The posture would not be one of announcing plans for a Reagan administration but of talking with the Chinese leaders to gain their views and then returning to report to Governor Reagan.

The planned sequence was to begin with a press conference at the time of Ambassador Bush's departure. While Bush was in China, Reagan would give two defense speeches to conservative audiences. The speech to the Veterans of Foreign Wars (VFW) was to emphasize peace, and the address to the American Legion would focus on strength. When George Bush returned for the debriefing, there would be another press conference at which he would do most of the talking. This would build up Bush a bit and demonstrate the competence of a Reagan-Bush administration to handle foreign affairs.

What did happen was this. At the departure press conference, Governor Reagan said that he would favor an "official government relationship" with Taiwan. This would be illegal according to the Taiwan Relations Act, and the Governor's statement produced headlines that guaranteed a chilly reception for Ambassador Bush in Beijing. In his "Peace through Strength" speech to the VFW in Chicago two days later, Governor Reagan brought up the subject of Vietnam, adding "It is time that we recognized that ours, in truth, was a noble cause." There were many who did not consider Vietnam to have been a noble cause, of course, and this reference produced more headlines and cartoons. Nothing unplanned took place at the American Legion speech on Wednesday; but on Friday, August 22, in Dallas to speak to fundamentalist Christians, Reagan was asked at a press conference for his views on creationism. "I think that recent discoveries down through the years have pointed [to] great flaws in" the theory of evolution, he replied, suggesting that creationism might be taught as an alternative. At the press conference after Ambassador Bush's return, a nine-page statement was issued stating that Reagan would continue the unofficial relationship with Taiwan. This was consistent with existing American law and what Bush had been saying in China but produced headlines such as "Reagan Abandons Taiwan Office Plan." This succession of stories certainly produced a focused impact but hardly the one the Reagan strategists had in mind.

The second focused impact was to deal with the pocketbook. Pocketbook issues, inflation and unemployment, were seen as highly salient and favorable to Reagan. The first event was to be a short speech to the Ohio Teamsters' Conference in Cleveland on August 27. When Governor Reagan arrived in Ohio, he was urged by Governor James A. Rhodes to use strong and specific language in speaking about jobs. In response, a reference in Reagan's speech to a U.S. "recession" was changed to a "severe depression." Alan Greenspan, who was not consulted about this change although he was traveling with Reagan as an economic advisor, said this was not the word he would have chosen.[15] Reagan countered by adding some lines to his Labor Day speech, "A recession is when a neighbor loses his job. A depression is when you lose yours. Recovery is when Jimmy Carter loses his." But the same papers that carried this Reagan speech added that he had departed from his economics text at the Michigan State Fair later the same day to say, "I'm happy to be here where you're dealing at first hand with [economics] . . . and [President Carter's] opening his campaign down in the city that gave birth to and is the parent body of the Ku Klux Klan." In fact, Tuscumbia, Alabama, was not the city where the Klan was founded, and President Carter had been sharply critical of the organization.[16]

At campaign headquarters, these Reagan comments—that Vietnam was a noble cause, that creationism should be taught as an alternative to evolution, that the country was in a depression rather than a recession, and the reference to the Ku Klux Klan—were known as the Four Blunders. None was very helpful to the campaign, to put it most gently, but it was the sequence of events in connection with George Bush's China trip that had the most pronounced strategic consequences. The idea of focused impact had been to have a high concentration on a single topic, but what was in fact being communicated was the wreckage resulting from the gaffes. With nothing else scheduled, there was nothing to which the campaigners could shift to divert attention from the embarrassing statements. Consequently, by the middle of September, there was a Strategic Adjustment in which the whole idea of focused impact was dropped.

The coalition leadership had evolved into two groups: the headquarters

---

[15] The common distinction between recessions and depressions is that depressions are of much longer duration and have much more widespread unemployment. During the recession of 1957–58, the unemployment rate was 7.5 percent; in the recession of 1973–75, it reached 9.0 percent. In the depression year of 1932, in contrast, the unemployment rate was 25 percent. In July 1980, unemployment stood at 7.8 percent.

[16] Mr. Carter departed from his text, saying: "As the first man from the Deep South in 140 years to be president of this nation, I say these people in white sheets do not understand our region and what it's been through. They do not understand what our country stands for."

group in Arlington, Virginia, and the tour group that traveled with Reagan on the plane, LeaderShip '80. During the period of the Four Blunders, it became painfully evident that the tour group needed someone who had a good sense of the political impact of issues and who was close enough to Governor Reagan to speak with authority.

The person recruited to play this role was Stuart Spencer, the California campaign consultant who had managed Ronald Reagan's gubernatorial campaigns and played such an important role in the 1976 Ford campaign. Three days after the Ku Klux Klan blunder, Stuart Spencer was on the plane. The addition of Spencer began to remove some of the rough edges from the tour. While other members of the tour group had been close to Reagan for some time, none had been through a national campaign before, and they had a hard time distinguishing between tactics appropriate for primary campaigns (where they had a lot of experience) and tactics appropriate to a general election campaign.

Eventually, the tour leaders settled into a pattern of two planning meetings every evening. The first dealt with logistics for the following day: the timing of events, the motorcade routes, and so on. Mike Deaver (tour chief of staff) presided over this meeting. Then came a strategy meeting whose agenda varied all the way from major questions such as whether the Governor should take part in debates to smaller questions such as how a particular statement ought to be phrased. This meeting was jointly run by Deaver and Spencer. As would be expected, there were misunderstandings between the headquarters group and the tour group, but one important link between the two existed between Stu Spencer and Richard Wirthlin. Spencer, a believer in data, was in daily contact with Wirthlin, and this helped the two groups to coordinate their efforts.

Broadening the Reagan Appeal

The Reagan campaign plan called for a shift in mid-September. Two things needed to be done. Public perceptions of the Governor needed to be given greater depth, and he needed much greater appeal to voters in the middle of the political spectrum. The Wirthlin survey data showed that, while Governor Reagan had widespread name recognition, most Americans knew only three things about him: his name, that he had been a movie star, and that he was a conservative. This information level was too low for citizens to feel comfortable in voting for him and insufficient to establish the Governor as a credible spokesman.

The strategists had found out very early that Reagan's record as Governor of California was a useful vehicle to establish him as a credible public figure. Media specialist Peter Dailey prepared a series of commercials of varying length presenting Reagan as governor of California. In one, the announcer boasted:

> In 1966 he was elected governor of the state of California, next to president the biggest job in the nation. What he inherited was a state of crisis. . . . Working

with teams of volunteers from all sectors, Governor Reagan got things back on track. His commonsense style and strong, creative leadership won him a second term in 1970. Governor Reagan was the greatest tax reformer in the state's history.

These commercials began running quite early, and their use peaked during this second phase of the campaign. Political buffs who already knew Reagan had been governor wondered why they had to watch him being sworn in over and over, but the idea was to get the less attentive, average citizen to begin to think of Reagan as a man with executive experience and a good record in California.

Another opportunity to present Ronald Reagan as a credible political leader came with the Reagan-Anderson debate on September 21. Richard Wirthlin was a key player in setting the strategy for the debate, but the preparations for the debate were put in the hands of a separate group headed by James A. Baker, who had managed the Ford campaign in 1976 and the Bush primary campaign in 1980.[17] The essential goal was to reassure the country that here was a man who was competent and who knew what he was talking about. Consequently, much of the preparation consisted of putting questions to Reagan, who would give his answer, after which Stockman would give the Anderson answer. Reagan intentionally went into the debate without any notes to demonstrate that he could think on his feet. The other major point to the debate strategy was that the Reagan leaders did not want Anderson to disappear as a factor in the election. They wanted to make sure that they "won" the debate, but they had no interest in harming Anderson too much in the process.

There were some interesting arguments about who was being hurt more by Anderson's candidacy. The core of the Anderson vote was made up of independent Republicans. Reduced to this core, most of the votes would come from Reagan. However, all three camps thought that Anderson was taking more votes from Carter in the East but was competing with both Reagan and Carter in the Great Lakes states of Illinois and Ohio. If Reagan hoped for only a minimum Electoral College victory, he should have tried to eliminate Anderson to ensure a victory in Illinois and Ohio. On the other hand, if he was optimistic about his electoral vote count, Reagan should have tried to keep Anderson alive in order to carry some of the "bonus" states in the East. Whatever the arguments, the Carter strategists were desperately anxious to

---

[17] The Reagan leadership was anxious to use Baker's talents, and Baker wanted something that could be segmented off and would be his responsibility. When the decision to give Baker authority over the debate was made, Baker recruited the people he wanted to work on it. David Gergen was in charge of putting together briefing books, and Bill Carruthers was in charge of some of the television aspects. Gergen thought that David Stockman, a Michigan congressman who had once been an assistant to John Anderson, would be a good impersonator for Anderson in the debate preparation. Three of the four—Baker, Gergen, and Stockman—ended up in senior positions in the Reagan White House. Presumably Reagan's satisfaction with the debate preparation had something to do with this.

eliminate Anderson, and the Reagan strategists wanted to keep him as a factor in the election.

So Reagan was following a "pass through" strategy: go through Anderson to get at Carter. And even when allusions were being made to Carter, the references should not be too strident—in part because Carter wasn't there and in part because the campaign had been so negative that the Reagan strategists wanted to offer some reassurance. Governor Reagan did appear to be relaxed and sufficiently competent, and the postdebate polls showed small increases in the proportions of voters intending to vote for him. More important, the debate aided in the major objective of this phase of the campaign: to deepen the voters' understanding of Ronald Reagan.

In order to give Governor Reagan more appeal to voters in the middle of the political spectrum, steps were taken to erase any image he might have as a doctrinaire conservative. The "move toward the middle" was accomplished not by changing any of the Governor's basic public policy but by making some changes on a few specific issues, which suggested in turn that Reagan was willing to change his mind on occasion.

Social security is a case in point. In 1964, Reagan endorsed making social security voluntary; in 1976, he suggested investing social security funds "in the industrial might of America." But in 1980, surveys implied that if there was any hint that social security would be eliminated, then the whole senior citizen vote was gone. Hence, Reagan began talking about reform of social security rather than any attack on the system itself. Campaigning in St. Petersburg, Florida, for example, he said that the provision under which benefits are reduced by earnings over $5,000 should be eliminated and thus came out on the positive side of social security.

Similar shifts on other matters led to press comments such as "the Republican candidate appears to have modified his views on such potentially costly issues as federal aid to New York City, bailouts like Chrysler's, occupational health policy, and labor policy." President Carter attacked some of the Reagan proposals; but the more the media pointed to policy changes and the more Carter attacked, the better the Reagan strategists liked it. Inconsistency in policy suggested flexibility, and their goal was to present Governor Reagan as a flexible leader rather than a rigid conservative.

While this middle phase of the campaign was accomplishing its objectives of increasing the information level about Reagan and modifying his positions on enough issues to make him more attractive to moderate voters, there was pressure within the Reagan coalition for a Strategic Adjustment, for three reasons. First of all, the campaigning was rather boring. After focused impact was abandoned, the campaign went first to stump speeches and then to podium speeches with "local inserts." The podium speeches were short speeches, about four or five pages, that were standard Reagan prose. The local inserts were references to topics of special interest to the areas where Governor Reagan was campaigning that might provide a news line. In Miami, Florida, for example, Reagan attacked Fidel Castro; in El Paso, Texas, he said that Carter had "broken a solemn promise" to the governors of Louisiana, Oklahoma, and Texas to work for deregulation of natural gas prices; in Roman Catholic areas of Pennsylvania and New Jersey, he endorsed the idea of tuition tax credits. All this was rather pedestrian. It reduced the danger of gaffes,[18] but it also meant that the candidate's voice was muted. It seemed as though little was happening in the campaign.

A second problem was that the strategy of moderating Reagan stands on selected issues was directed to the external need of communicating with independent voters rather than the internal need of keeping conservative groups already in the Reagan coalition happy. Peter Dailey reflected about this:

> There were tremendous pressures for change, and it was because of a fundamental difference in dimension of the '76 and the '80 campaigns, versus 1972. It was interesting to me to have been in both campaigns to see that change. In 1972, in going after the 10–15 percent of the undecided independents and Democrats, the strategy and the tactics to reach them happened to be the same strategy and tactics to reinforce your own core vote. So every time you ran an ad that was directed at them, your own people said, "That's terrific." In 1980 the strategy to reach the undecided 10 or 12 percent—which we absolutely had to have or we would have had a marvelous Goldwater campaign and all gone home losers—did not necessarily reinforce your core old-line Reagan votes. So, the campaign moved along; the core group, particularly the old-line people and the workers, became more and more incensed. (Moore, 1981, pp. 211–12)

True believers, unaware of the campaign plan, suspected that the relatively moderate statements reflected the influence of Stuart Spencer, Bill Timmons, and James Baker, all of whom had worked for Ford in 1976.

Perhaps the most worrisome factor was the information in the Wirthlin polls during early October. The Reagan vote was remaining fairly constant in the 39–42 percent range. But the Carter vote was climbing from 33 to 35 to 37 to 39 percent. Then on October 11, the data showed a narrow Carter lead. Within the Reagan campaign, the survey data showing a Reagan lead had been trusted all along. But some campaigners feared the same thing that the Democrats were counting on: that as the election drew close, many of the undecided would make up their minds to vote for the President simply because he was the trusted incumbent. The gain in the Carter vote made it look as though this was about to happen.

In spite of a good deal of pressure—including some from Governor Reagan, who was becoming anxious to go after President Carter more aggressively—the campaign plan was not abandoned. For one thing, the plan called

---

[18] It did not eliminate them. In Steubenville, Ohio, Reagan said that the eruption of Mount St. Helens had released more sulphur dioxide than 10 years of automobile driving, and he defended a previous statement about trees being a source of air pollution. When he arrived on a college campus a couple of days later, someone had put a sign on a tree saying "Chop Me Down before I Kill Again."

for a shift on October 20 anyway. For another, Richard Wirthlin and Richard Beal were quite confident that Reagan would win the electoral vote. In one of the true innovations of 1980, they created an elaborate political information system (PINS).

PINS contained two ways to estimate the probable electoral vote. The simpler was an "electoral scoreboard" that calculated the electoral vote as a function of selected variables—for example, that a candidate had x percent of the Roman Catholic vote or y percent of the rural vote. The more elaborate was a simulation that first eliminated the undecided vote and then provided a series of questions so that the analyst could state the assumptions he wished to make, such as the proportion of the vote Anderson was expected to keep. The simulation also took into consideration the analyst's expectations about trend. The simulation then calculated the changes that would take place between that date and the election and produced electoral counts for each assumption the analyst made. On the basis of their PINS analyses, Wirthlin and Beal knew that Carter was not close in the electoral vote, however well he might be doing in nationwide trial heats.

The mounting criticism did, however, lead to two decisions important enough to be taken as Strategic Adjustments. The polls, both public and private, were showing what has come to be called a gender gap. Women were about 10 percent less likely to vote for Reagan than men. Related to this was fear that Reagan might lead the nation into war, as well as the fact that the Governor was the only major candidate to oppose the Equal Rights Amendment in 1980. So at a news conference on October 14, Governor Reagan declared, "It is time for a woman to sit among our highest jurists," and pledged to name a woman to "one of the first Supreme Court vacancies in my administration."

The more important decision was to accept a two-person debate with President Carter. This decision was one that found important members of the tour group—Stuart Spencer, Mike Deaver, and Lyn Nofziger—opposing two key headquarters decision makers, Bill Timmons and Richard Wirthlin. While everybody agreed that Reagan would do well in a debate against Carter (especially after seeing the two of them together at the Alfred E. Smith Memorial Dinner in New York), the leaders of the tour group had a stronger sense of the campaign having gone flat and being in need of something to give it additional movement. Timmons' opposition was based on his knowledge that the campaign plan had set aside abundant resources for use in the closing days of the campaign and his belief in the relative strength of the field organization he had built. Wirthlin, while he also thought a debate unnecessary, was most concerned about the timing. Another person close to this discussion explained the timing consideration, speaking privately on October 1:

> Everyone agrees that he's got to debate by the 20th or so. He can't debate much later than that because you need those last 14 days to go around and touch your significant bases. Also, it's much higher risk. If you make a mistake, it's too late.

> If you make a mistake and you've still got 14 days or so, you've got a chance to turn it around.

Governor Reagan made the debate decision himself. After listening to the arguments on both sides, he concluded that if he wanted to succeed Jimmy Carter in the White House, he ought to be willing to debate him face to face.

One final point on the debate decision. On October 17, the pollsters began their daily tracking. They used a three-day moving average with a total of 1,500 respondents, adding 500 new ones each day and dropping 500 after they had been contacted for three days. When the debate decision was made, the Wirthlin data showed Reagan leading Carter 43 percent to 37 percent, and the most likely outcome from their PINS electoral projections was 310 votes for Reagan, 40 more than necessary. The Reagan coalition was heading into the final phase of the campaign in a strong position and with resources set aside.

Motivating a Reagan Vote

The third phase of the Reagan campaign was the least completely described in the campaign plan. The plan said that resources—money, professional time, candidate time—should be allocated so that they would have the highest impact. It also said that the election would be won between October 20 and November 4. But it did not say how these resources should be allocated or how the election would be won.

When the last phase of the campaign began, most of the Reagan base looked safe, but most of the Carter base was being contested. The final list of battleground states *excluded* Virginia, Indiana, and all of the West except the three Pacific Coast states. The campaign focused on the seven largest states, the Middle Atlantic region, and all of the South except Georgia. And at least $7 million had been set aside for media directed to these battleground states.

While the goals of the long middle phase had been to give depth to Governor Reagan and to make him more appealing to moderate voters, the goal of this phase was to motivate voters to turn out on election day. This could be done best, the strategists felt, by attacking President Carter. The television mix had heretofore been about 80 percent positive ads about Ronald Reagan and 20 percent negative ads about Jimmy Carter. In the attack phase, this was shifted to 60 percent positive and 40 percent negative and then to a 50–50 mix as election day neared. The negative ads were not too harsh. One showed Ronald Reagan standing in a meat market behind two shopping carts. One was filled with the quantity of meat, milk, and bread that $60 would buy in 1976; the other contained the smaller amount that $60 would buy in 1980. Governor Reagan concluded his statement by saying: "If you are better off today than you were four years ago, vote for Jimmy Carter." Another spot used graphics to make the point that while Carter had been in office, food prices had increased 35 percent, automobile prices 31 percent, and clothing prices 20 percent. Simply reminding viewers of the record was sufficient when inflation was the dominant issue and the voters were already conscious of President Carter's record in office.

The ads were only one part of the television campaign. Another was programs designed for use in parts of battleground states where votes were urgently being sought. Sometimes these were "citizens' press conferences" where residents were given a chance to ask questions. Another type was called "TV Wrap-Up," 15-minute programs in which the candidate said, in essence, "I've been campaigning in this area, and here are my views on some of the issues people have asked me about." A third element was a series of nationally broadcast speeches by Mr. Reagan. Little was new in these speeches, certainly no concrete information about just what Reagan would do as president. But together they adhered to the 50–50 mix of projecting a combination of compassion, care, and strength about himself while attacking President Carter.

In the strategists' view, the campaign was now at the stage where the candidate was the only useful asset. In was not that the television campaign was not having an effect or that the field organization would not be conducting a get-out-the-vote drive on election day. Rather, it was sufficiently late in the campaign so that everything had to be in place—the media time purchased, the phone banks active, and so on—or there wouldn't be time to get them in place. Therefore, the candidate's time and words were the only maneuverable resource left to implement strategy.

The most important event in Ronald Reagan's last week was the debate with Jimmy Carter in Cleveland. The preparations for the debate were in the hands of the same group headed by James Baker that had worked with Governor Reagan prior to the debate with John Anderson. They seem to have been equally effective.

Two points were made by Mr. Reagan during the debate that were particularly compelling. When President Carter attacked Reagan's record on medicare, the Governor shook his head and said, "There you go again," reminding those who had been following the campaign of the many Carter attacks on Reagan and drawing an effective contrast between the humorless President and his challenger. And in his summation, Ronald Reagan drew attention to the central economic issue by asking the series of questions beginning "Are you better off than you were four years ago?" Some knowledgeable observers claimed that Governor Reagan won the election by asking that question. It certainly helped. But as we know from the Reagan strategy, the conclusion of the debate was just the most visible occasion on which Governor Reagan made this point. He was repeating it again and again during this attack phase of the campaign.

The favorable survey results after the debate brought a Time's Up feeling of impending triumph to the Reagan entourage. But the locations visited by Governor Reagan pointed out areas of continuing concern to the strategists. These were chosen through the use of the PINS simulations and in consultation with Bill Timmons' field organization. The day after the debate, Reagan was in Dallas, Fort Worth, and Houston, Texas. On Thursday, he went to Texarkana, New Orleans, and on to New Jersey and Pennsylvania. Friday and Saturday were spent in Illinois, Wisconsin, and Michigan. Sunday morning, Governor Reagan went to church in Columbus, Ohio, then went to Marietta and took a swing through the southern part of the Buckeye State, ending up in Dayton. The Monday before the election, he appeared in Peoria, Illinois, flew on to Portland, Oregon, and ended up in San Diego. The Reagans were returning to California to vote, of course, but the political meaning of the travel schedule was that the strategists wanted to make sure of Texas, thought they had chances to carry Arkansas, Louisiana, Wisconsin, Michigan, and Oregon, and were worried about softness in the Reagan vote around Philadelphia and in southwestern Ohio and central Illinois.

The Reagan speeches on this last swing were in keeping with the attack theme. In New Orleans, he said that "in place of competence, [Carter] has given us ineptitude." In Des Plaines, Illinois, Reagan said Carter was "like the guy who can name you 50 parts of a car—he just can't drive it or fix it." In Dayton, he accused President Carter of mismanagement of the economy. And on his last day of campaigning, he continued to ask, "Are you happier today than when Mr. Carter became president of the United States?"

The mood aboard LeaderShip '80 as the plane headed west on the last campaign swing was variously described as "exhilarated" and "exhausted but happy." It certainly must have been pleasant for Ronald Reagan to know that the conservative crusade he had been leading for years was going to culminate in his own election as president. But the feeling of intellectual elation belonged to the strategists who had written the campaign plan six months earlier. When their final simulation was run at Reagan headquarters on October 31, the vote estimation was Reagan 50.0 percent, Carter 40.5 percent, and Anderson 9.3 percent. The actual election result on November 4 was Reagan 50.8 percent, Carter 41.0 percent, and Anderson 6.6 percent.

SUMMARY

The strategic competition in 1980 was interesting. Each of the candidacies was flawed, yet each had a plausible strategy. John Anderson was handicapped by the traditional bugbears of third-party candidates: the lack of organized support and the absence of resources. Jimmy Carter could be held responsible for runaway inflation, and his approval rating had fallen to 21 percent in the summer of 1980. Ronald Reagan's name was widely known, but little else was known about him and he was vulnerable to being portrayed as a doctrinaire right-winger.

John Anderson did well enough through September to be accepted as a participant in presidential debates. He did well in the debate, too. But he was so resource poor that he had to do better than "well" and vanished as a central figure soon thereafter. Jimmy Carter had problems through the summer and early fall, but by October it looked as though he *might* catch up if he did everything right in his late-October debate with Governor Reagan. When he did not, his candidacy was doomed. Ronald Reagan was fortunate enough to make his most serious mistakes early. Thereafter, his strategists broadened and deepened the Reagan image so that he was well positioned to challenge President Carter by asking voters, "Are you better off than you were four years ago?"

Chapter 7

The 1984 Campaign

Incumbent Ronald Reagan began his campaign for reelection in very favorable circumstances. In the preceding half-century, only three presidents had been defeated when they had run for a second term—Herbert Hoover, Gerald Ford, and Jimmy Carter—and all three were handicapped by adverse economic developments. Hoover, of course, was charged with responsibility for the depression of the 1930s; Gerald Ford had been in office during the recession of 1974–75; Jimmy Carter's administration had been flawed by runaway inflation. In 1984, in contrast, the voters had more money in their pockets. The real disposable income per capita increased 5.8 percent. The only recent presidential election year with an economic record close to that was 1964,[1] when incumbent Lyndon Johnson had been reelected in a landslide.

Ronald Reagan also entered the election as the head of a united Republican party. He was the first incumbent since Dwight Eisenhower who did not have to face primary opposition within his own party. Walter Mondale, on the other hand, could not count on the support of those who had voted for his primary opponents. Furthermore, he was identified with traditional Democratic social welfare and civil rights positions. However popular these positions may have been elsewhere, they were quite unpopular in the South.

Steven J. Rosenstone (1983) has developed a model to forecast presidential

---

[1] The 1964 increase in real disposable income per capita was 5.6 percent. The average annual increase for 1952–1980 was 2.24 percent. (Fortunately for Reagan, he did not have to run for reelection in 1982, when the unemployment rate reached 10.7 percent.)

elections. When he entered the above factors—a prosperous economy, an incumbent candidate, and the challenger's positions on welfare and civil rights issues—into his model in July, his prediction was remarkably close to the November outcome. He forecast that the Democrats would obtain 41.1 percent of the vote and carry only three states and the District of Columbia (1985, p. 26).[2] This forecast, based on factors already in place, provides a context for understanding the 1984 strategies. The Mondale coalition faced a desperate search for some means of diverting attention from the popular incumbent and prosperous economy. All the Reagan coalition needed to do to win was to avoid serious errors, although the favorable conditions also gave them a chance to increase Republican strength.

PEACE ABROAD AND TRADITIONAL DEMOCRATIC THEMES AT HOME

Early Difficulties

It was no secret that Walter Mondale began his campaign a long way behind. There were at least three campaign plans written, one by Mike Ford (an erstwhile Kennedy supporter who for a time was "political director" of the Mondale campaign), one by pollster Peter Hart, and one by Pat Caddell (Goldman & Fuller, 1985, pp. 408–11, 418–26).

The common theme was that a lot of ground had to be made up; hence, something dramatic was needed. Unless something is done, wrote Ford, "we will get no more than our 'base state' electoral vote (50)." "We have a lot of ground to make up in a very short time," reported Hart. "If the 1984 vote decision follows the normal pattern" warned Caddell, "then Ronald Reagan will be assured of a decisive, perhaps even historic victory."

Ford argued in a June memorandum that the Mondale campaign needed more vision and that Mondale should try "a pass which catches all defense by surprise" rather than always running with the ball. Hart urged Mondale to reach inside his soul to attain "the intensity you had when you were fighting back from political extinction this spring." In a more detailed September memorandum, Hart urged that three issues be emphasized: the war-and-peace issue, the idea "that we are robbing tomorrow to pay for today," and fairness—"fair trade, fair taxes, fairness for our senior citizens." Pat Caddell likened Reagan's leadership and personality strengths to the Maginot line and recommended an indirect strategy that would circumvent these strengths much as the Germans had gone around the French defensive fortifications in 1940.[3] He urged that the election be made "a referendum on the national

---

[2] The Democrats got 40.8 percent of the national vote and carried Minnesota and the District of Columbia. The two states that Rosenstone's model forecast incorrectly were Rhode Island and Massachusetts, where Mondale got 48 percent and 49 percent, respectively.

[3] Caddell writes with such passion and at such length that it is hard to find short quotes that illustrate his suggestions.

character and values" in order "to seize the future issue." Clearly, in the case of younger voters, Caddell concluded:

> The Democratic party has been sending the wrong message. What I fear is that the signals have been that party is anti-change, anti-growth, anti-participation, and primarily concerned with restoring the New Deal agenda and the primacy of the New Deal coalition members. . . . The party has been busy trying to put Humpty Dumpty back together again.

However clear these proposals were about the need to do something dramatic, they did not have much impact on the initial shape of the Mondale campaign. In part, this was because while they were read by members of the core group—John Reilly, James Johnson, Mike Berman, and Mondale himself—these memorandums did not come from them. And in part, it was because Mondale leaders spent much of August reacting to events rather than shaping them.

Many candidates who begin a long way behind—(Goldwater in 1964, Humphrey in 1968, McGovern in 1972) have trouble assembling the coalition normally available to their party's candidates. Mondale was no exception to this. The principal difficulties lay with the ideologically most distant groups: the Southerners on Mondale's right and the blacks on Mondale's left. Walter Mondale made a number of campaign forays into the South during August, but they seemed to do little good. Claiborne Darden, an Atlanta-based pollster who specializes in the South, found Reagan leading Mondale by 60 to 34 percent. And Mr. Mondale was forced to cancel a stop at Macon, Georgia, after Senator Sam Nunn said he planned to be with his family at the time, Lieutenant Governor Zell Miller announced he had "to talk with a bunch of poultry folks up in Gainesville," and Governor Joe Frank Harris and state chairman Bert Lance were unavailable. Clearly, Mondale positions were unappealing to many Southern voters, and the treatment of Bert Lance at the convention still rankled within the party.

Jesse Jackson, dissatisfied with the recognition his followers had received, announced that he might not support Mondale unless the Democratic candidate committed himself to a very expensive federal jobs and training program for the hard-core unemployed. Such a program was urgently needed by young blacks faced with a critical unemployment problem, but commitment to such a program would have made it impossible for Mondale to honor his budget cutting promise or to reach undecided white voters. Moreover, even Mayor Andrew Young of Atlanta, who had been booed by other blacks at the convention for his support of Mondale, said that Mondale was surrounded by "smart-assed white boys" who wouldn't listen to anyone. Faced with dissension from this major Democratic grouping, a unity meeting between Mondale and major black leaders was scheduled in St. Paul for the last week in August. Jackson supporters spent much of the day telling Mondale he had to support the jobs program. Eventually, Mondale allies prevailed, and Jackson called for a unanimous endorsement of the ticket. The endorsement was welcome, but it had not come easily.

The most visible interruption of the Organization and Planning stage arose from the financial affairs of Geraldine Ferraro's husband, John Zacarro. On July 24, Ferraro had announced that she would disclose "my tax returns and my husband's tax returns for the past several years." But when a question was asked about it at the end of a news conference on August 12, she replied, "I have to say that I requested my husband to do that, and my husband feels quite frankly that his business interests would be affected. The reaction was, 'Gerry, I am not going to tell you how to run the country. Don't tell me how to run my business.' So at this point, it's no. If you're married to an Italian man, you know what it's like."

This statement was a shock to the Mondale leadership. They had allowed themselves only 48 hours to go over the Ferraro-Zacarro finances prior to her selection, were not aware of any difficulty, and had *not* been advised before the news conference of Mr. Zacarro's refusal to release the information. Eventually, Zacarro agreed to release the information, and once accountants and lawyers had enough time to sort out ill-kept records, the financial statements were made public. When the facts were released, there were a couple of questionable items: $53,000 owed in back taxes and $175,000 that John Zacarro had borrowed from an estate for which he was a court-appointed conservator.

In terms of political impact, this was small potatoes. Voters' choices were going to be guided by their reactions to Ronald Reagan and Walter Mondale and by the candidates' positions on the issues, not by their opinions about the business affairs of John Zacarro or Barbara Bush. But two things had happened. One was that all the publicity about Geraldine Ferraro as the daughter of an immigrant seamstress was now balanced by headlines declaring the Zacarros were millionaires. The other was that time had been lost. This affair was not nearly as disruptive as the revelations that led to Senator Thomas Eagleton's departure from the McGovern ticket in 1972, but it had come at the same phase of the campaign. Because of the attention to the business affairs of P. Zacarro & Company, August passed with relatively little planning about how the campaign was to be run.

Mondale's Initial Emphases

As we've already seen, Walter Mondale and Geraldine Ferraro spent some time in August campaigning in the South. At the end of the month, Mondale leaders shifted resources in order to make a major effort in California. Both of these actions occasioned some wonder. Ronald Reagan was very strong in the South, and California, of course, was the President's home state.

Mondale leaders were not willing to concede either the South or California. In their planning, they listed only Alabama and Virginia as safe for Reagan in the South, and they included California as leaning to Reagan. Mondale leaders had not taken leave of their senses. Their problem was an extraordinarily difficult exercise in Electoral College arithmetic. Their plans listed only the District of Columbia, Hawaii, and Minnesota as safe for Mondale and only

Maryland, Massachusetts, Rhode Island, and West Virginia as leaning to Mondale. If Mondale carried *all* of these base states, he would receive only 50 electoral votes. On the other hand, their analyses showed states (all in the South or West except for Indiana) with 276 electoral votes as safe or leaning to Reagan (Taylor, 1984).[4] Even if they made the unusually optimistic assumption that they would carry *all* of their base states and *all* of the swing states, they would still lose the election. They did not think it would be easy to beat Reagan in the South or in California. Rather, they simply had to break some of Reagan's base away from him or lose the election.[5]

The first issue to be developed, religion, was a reply to positions taken by the Republicans. The religious right had played a prominent part at the Republican National Convention. A letter over the signature of Senator Paul Laxalt had gone to 45,000 ministers read, "As leaders under God's authority, we cannot afford to resign ourselves to idle neutrality in an election that will confirm or silence the president who has worked so diligently on your behalf." President Reagan had told a Dallas prayer breakfast that anyone opposing a constitutional amendment banning abortion was intolerant.

Speaking to B'nai B'rith, Mr. Mondale joked that "most Americans would be surprised to learn that God is a Republican." Continuing more seriously, he said:

> I believe in an America where government is not permitted to dictate the religious life of our people; where religion is a private matter between individuals and their God, between families and their churches and synagogues, with no room for politicians in between. I do not for one moment claim a partisan monopoly on the beliefs I've just outlined. They are the common heritage of all Americans: Protestants; Catholics, and Jews; Democrats and Republicans—everyone.

This should have had some impact on young, well-educated voters, who tend to be conservative on economics but liberal on social questions. It also may have complicated Mr. Mondale's geographic problem. After the exchange, pollster Louis Harris reported that it had helped Mondale in the Northeast but increased Reagan's already large lead in the South.

Other issues accented during the Mondale Grand Opening showed the imprint of Peter Hart's polling to identify themes Walter Mondale could use to advantage. One was the fairness issue. "I see an America," Mondale repeatedly declared, "that's kind and caring." Speaking in Iowa in mid-September, he attacked Reagan: "He wanted to cut $80 billion out of Social Security, just rip it apart. He got rid of student assistance for the youngsters of widows going on to college. He's proud of that." And following Pat Caddell's urging

---

[4] To make matters worse, Reagan was leading in the large swing states of New York, New Jersey, Pennsylvania, Ohio, and Illinois.

[5] The difficulty of this Electoral College problem led some, including campaign chairman James Johnson, to ignore geographic considerations and assert that the campaign was being planned demographically.

that debate be joined over fundamental American values, the former Vice President asked: "Doesn't it bother us that in this country of so much abundance, where food is one of the miracles of our country, that somehow we can't help a child who needs enough to eat a lunch? What kind of people are we?"

The war-and-peace issue was another on which Mondale thought Reagan vulnerable. Speaking to the American Legion, he said that Reagan was "the first president since Hoover not to have met with the Soviets" and promised that he would call on the Russian leadership to arrange such a meeting on his first day in office. Mondale's charges that Reagan was careless about foreign policy were given some credibility by events. On September 17, Mondale said that "the swamp of policy confusion led to the deaths of nearly 300 Marines in Lebanon." Just three days later, there was another bombing in Lebanon, this time of the American embassy. President Reagan, explaining delays in security arrangements at the embassy, said, "Anyone that's ever had their kitchen done over knows it never gets done as soon as you wish it would," and Mr. Mondale countered, "That's the problem right there."

The centerpiece of the Mondale Grand Opening strategy, however, was his plan to reduce the deficit by a claimed $263 billion by 1989. He called for $85 billion in new taxes (none on those earning under $25,000 and a surtax on those earning over $70,000) dedicated exclusively to deficit reduction. The rate of increase in defense spending would be cut $25 billion. (Note that this is different from a cut in defense spending.) Key domestic programs (principally education) would be increased by $30 billion, while $39 billion would be saved in other domestic programs, largely through improved management. Seventeen billion dollars would be gained with an assumed 3.5 percent growth rate, and $51 billion would be saved because of smaller interest payments on a smaller national debt.

Especially as compared to the liberalism of the 1960s, this was a moderate approach. But there were problems with it as a centerpiece of strategy. First, challenging President Reagan to present his budget plan so the two could be debated was reminiscent of Barry Goldwater in 1964. Goldwater presented some conservative programs, assuming that President Johnson would then present some liberal programs, which in turn would lead to a principled debate between the two. Lyndon Johnson, however, had no intention of having a principled debate with Barry Goldwater. Neither did Ronald Reagan intend to be drawn into a debate over the budget with Walter Mondale. Second, the national debt lacked political sex appeal. As Republican strategist John Sears put it, "I've been trying to make an issue of deficit spending for years. I wish them luck." And finally, there was an audible silence from other Democratic candidates. They had been distancing themselves from Mondale anyhow and had no wish to link their campaigns to a call for higher taxes.

A Strategic Adjustment and the First Debate

Of much less consequence than the strategic problems but of great frustration to candidate Mondale were a number of difficulties encountered on the road.

For example, the campaign began with both Mondale and Ferraro taking part on a Labor Day parade in New York City.[6] It was scheduled at 9:30 A.M., and the crowds were very sparse. At other times, poor advance work put the candidate in embarrassing circumstances. At still other times, the loud-speakers seemed to have been hooked up by Republicans; often they just didn't work.

The scheduling difficulties could be summarized in a stop in Tupelo, Mississippi, on September 12 and 13. Mondale spent 23 hours there, most of it in a motel. When he did appear, he spoke on abortion and school prayer, issues on which his views had little appeal to Mississippi voters. In fact, the candidate had summoned James Johnson and Mike Berman to Tupelo for a meeting. He made it clear that he was tired of poor scheduling and did not want any further events that were for photographic purposes only. Faithful aide Mike Berman, whose assignment always seemed to shift with the latest crisis, was now put in charge of scheduling and advance, and the logistics began to improve a little.

About the same time, pressure was building for a Strategic Adjustment. Veteran political observer Richard Scammon noted, "The problem always in this situation is when a guy is running behind, everybody assumes he's doing something wrong. I doubt that Mondale is doing anything wrong." Active Democratic politicos, however, did not share these views. "I don't think they have any game plan" and "We're going to work for our local candidates" were much more common comments. Democratic congressional leaders were worried about what might happen to their majority if Reagan did beat Mondale by 20 points. Senior Mondale strategists were also concerned, in part because they were hearing these messages from worried Democrats, in part because they could not detect any movement in the polls themselves.

The Strategic Adjustment was based largely on Pat Caddell's earlier memorandum on the importance of focusing on the future. The hope was to reassemble the normal Democratic majority by reattracting blue-collar voters who were tempted to vote for Reagan and by appealing to the young, urban professionals who had supported Hart in the spring. The principal change was that the deficit-tax proposal, unveiled with so much attention, quietly disappeared from view. The discussion of religion was personalized in attacks of Jerry Falwell rather than the abstractions of church-state relations. "This election," Mondale would say, "is not about Republicans sending hecklers to my rallies. It is about Jerry Falwell picking justices for the Supreme Court." The other two themes from the Grand Opening strategy, fairness and foreign policy, remained in place (Weinraub, 1984b).

This revised strategy was in effect by late September. For example, in a September 25 speech at George Washington University, Mondale attacked Reagan's recent foreign policy statements. "For four years, they failed to reach a single arms control agreement with the Soviets. They proposed to

---

[6] The event had not been part of their original schedule but was added at the request of AFL–CIO president Lane Kirkland.

extend the arms race into the heavens. But now, six weeks before the election, they talk of arms control." In Pittsburgh the following day, Mondale declared, "There is a difference between the two political parties. Both platforms were prepared by Jerrys, ours under the leadership of Geraldine Ferraro and theirs by Jerry Falwell."

As September turned into October, Mondale strategists were giving a great deal of attention to preparations for the debates with President Reagan. The Strategic Adjustment of September had led to fewer negative comments about Mr. Mondale, but there had been almost no movement in the polls. A *New York Times*/CBS poll in mid-September had shown Reagan with a 54 to 33 percent lead; one taken at the very beginning of October showed an almost identical 54 to 31 percent lead. So the stakes were very high. Unless Walter Mondale was able to do well in the debates, most participants would feel that the election was as good as over.

There were two sources of advice. Mondale spent eight full days prior to the debate practicing with a group headed by labor lawyer Lewis Kaden. Columbia University president Michael Sovern played the role of Ronald Reagan. Kaden urged Mondale to emphasize his fairness and his concern with the future and, while granting Reagan's optimism and good intentions, to suggest that the President was out of touch. In another long memorandum, Pat Caddell urged Mondale not to debate issue by issue, as Reagan's coaches would expect, but to surprise Reagan by redefining the issues and to physically dominate the television screen by pivoting at some point and taking a step toward Reagan to convey the idea that he was pressing him (Goldman & Fuller, 1985, pp. 430–34).

Mr. Mondale did press the President during the Louisville debate. Early in the debate, he said, "I'm reminded a little bit of what Will Rogers once said about Hoover. He said, 'It's not what he doesn't know that bothers me; it's what he knows for sure that just ain't so.' The fact of it is, the president's budget sought to cut social security by 25 percent. It's not an opinion; it's a fact." Somewhat later, Ronald Reagan used his 1980 debate line, "There you go again." Walter Mondale pivoted toward him and, with the television camera showing them looking at each other, used well-prepared lines:

> Remember the last time you said that? You said it when President Carter said you were going to cut Medicare, and you said, "Oh no, there you go again, Mr. President." And what did you do right after the election? You went right out and tried to cut $20 billion out of Medicare. And so when you say, "There you go again," people remember this.

At the end of the program, Mondale broke the adversarial format by saying:

> I'm going to give the president some credit. I think the president has done some things to raise the sense of spirit and morale, good feeling, in this country. And I think he's entitled to credit for that. What I think we need, however, is not just that but to move forward not just congratulating ourselves, but challenging ourselves to get on with the business of dealing with America's problems.

This was not a flawless performance, but it was a good one—and the President's performance was inferior.

An Infusion of Hope

Surveys of audience reaction brought the first good news to the Mondale coalition since the euphoria of Geraldine Ferraro's selection. There had been a huge audience. The Gallup Poll estimated that 84 percent of registered voters watched all or some of it. A *USA Today* poll reported that 39 percent thought that Mondale had won while 34 percent thought that Reagan had won. *Newsweek* gave Mondale a 54 to 35 percent margin.

The postdebate effect, captured in two *New York Times* surveys, was even more important. The first survey, taken on Sunday night, found that 43 percent thought that Mondale had won while only 34 percent thought that Reagan had won. But when a second survey was taken on Tuesday, the Mondale margin had grown to a whopping 66 to 17 percent. As with previous debates (especially when there is a consensus "winner"), the effects of multiple news reports that one debater has defeated another, as well as hearing the same thing repeated in personal conversation, were much stronger than the effects of listening to the debate itself.

Suddenly the campaign had heart. The Mondale campaign plane was rechristened "The Louisville Slugger," and an upsurge of confidence was felt within the Democratic party. When it had looked as though Mondale was certain to lose, other Democrats put distance between themselves and the candidate. After the Louisville debate, they were more willing to be identified with him. For example, when Ohio Governor Richard Celeste was told in late September that Walter Mondale was speaking to a steelworker's union, he commented that he knew of six other events that would be better for Mondale than that. But when Mondale campaigned through the state after the debate, Celeste presented him with a Louisville Slugger bat to symbolize his triumph over the president. Also, Democrats began making financial contributions. A good many checks arrived dated October 8 (the day after the debate), often with messages scrawled about Mondale having done a good job in the debate.

The Mondale victory in the first debate increased the attention given to a vice presidential debate scheduled between George Bush and Geraldine Ferraro on Thursday, October 11. Here the results were more equivocal. The overall poll results showed Bush the winner, but two things took the edge off the result. First, reaction was strongly related to sex. For example, while a *USA Today* poll found that Bush was the *overall* winner by a 48 to 29 percent margin, the same survey reported that when men were asked which candidate had done better, 59 percent picked Bush while only 18 percent chose Ferraro. Among women, however, the results were a virtual tie: 39 percent for Bush to 38 percent for Ferraro. Second, at one point during the debate, the question of terrorism came up. George Bush said, "Let me help you." Geraldine Ferraro replied, "I almost resent your patronizing attitude. You [don't] have to teach me about foreign policy." That exchange, with

Geraldine Ferraro fighting back, was the part of the debate most frequently used on news programs the next day.

During the period just before the second debate, Walter Mondale's use of the war-and-peace issue became very effective. In his speeches, he continued to attack Reagan's approach.

> If there's an arms agreement, oppose it. If there's a dangerous weapon, buy it. If the Pentagon wants a blank check, sign it. If there's a crucial fact, don't learn it. If there's a diplomatic problem, militarize it. If there's a regional conflict, Americanize it.

Effective media ads about war and peace reinforced Mondale's attack. For example, to the accompaniment of computer sounds, television viewers heard: "Ronald Reagan is determined to put killer weapons in space. The Soviets will have to match us, and the arms race will rage out of control. Orbiting, aiming, waiting." At this point, a telephone rang. "With response time to fire so short, there'll be no time to wake a president. Computers will take control." Then, with music: "On November 6th you can take control. No weapons in space by either side. Draw the line at the heavens, with Mondale."

And the news of the period focused on foreign policy, underscoring war-and-peace themes in ways that campaign strategists cannot count upon but which can be very effective. There were reports that the State Department had been warned that the American Embassy was going to be attacked (as it was on September 20). The Central Intelligence Agency had produced a booklet giving Nicaraguan rebels instructions on such topics as assassination. A plane crash in El Salvador killed four Americans, all CIA employees. Mr. Mondale called attention to these events by demanding that President Reagan fire CIA director William J. Casey.

It would seem that Walter Mondale was heading into the second debate in Kansas City in good shape. He had done better than Ronald Reagan in the first debate; he was now being taken seriously as a candidate; the second debate was to focus on foreign policy. His debate team, now including foreign policy advisor David Aaron, sent him a memo advising that Mondale "state a coherent foreign policy strategy, consisting of three themes: A. You would keep America strong. B. You would use that strength to keep the peace and control nuclear arms. C. You would use that strength to stand up for American values" (Goldman & Fuller, 1985, p. 438).

With all that Walter Mondale had accomplished, though, there was one thing missing. Going into the Kansas City debate, the *New York Times* poll still showed Walter Mondale trailing Ronald Reagan 50 percent to 37 percent. Hence, Mondale's debate team advised him to "raise the stakes by proving that . . . Reagan cannot grasp critical details, is out of touch, is not in command, and doesn't understand the world." In a separate memorandum, Pat Caddell argued that a victory on foreign policy would not be enough. Writing in capitals, he asserted:

FROM THE OUTSET WE MUST RECOGNIZE THAT OUR ELECTORAL POSI-
TION REQUIRES NOT JUST A DECISIVE VICTORY BUT A KNOCKOUT. . . .
THE MONDALE STRATEGIC IMPERATIVE MUST BE TO IGNITE THE AGE
CONCERN TO A SALIENT FIRESTORM.

In order to demonstrate Reagan's age and incapacity, Caddell urged the
use of such lines as, "Mr. President, I don't think you understand," "Mr.
President, I think you are confused," and "Mr. President, you've got the facts
mixed up" (Goldman & Fuller, 1985, pp. 438–443). In other words, Walter
Mondale had to do even better in the second debate than he had in the first.
That was a tall order indeed.

There was foreign policy debate aplenty in Kansas City. Speaking of the
CIA manual distributed to Nicaraguan rebels, Mondale asked, "How can this
happen? How can something this serious occur in an administration and have
the president of the United States, in a situation like this, say he didn't know?
A president must know these things." Concerning Lebanon, Mondale complained, "We had to leave in humiliation." And there was an extended exchange between the candidates about the strategic defense initiative (SDI, or
Star Wars) proposal. But the central question of Mr. Reagan's age was put
directly to the president by a panelist, and he disposed of it with a joke.

If it had been a contest between equals, David Broder wrote, the Democrats would have had every reason to be jubilant. "By almost any kind of
detached and rational analysis, Mondale won the debate. He was more precise, more coherent, and for the most part, more competent-sounding than
the incumbent" (1984c). But it was not a contest between equals. Mr. Mondale came into the debate an underdog and did not achieve the absolute
mastery (or witness the unquestionable ineptitude on Mr. Reagan's part) that
would have been necessary to change that.

A Liberal Finale

USA Today published a poll that showed President Reagan the winner by 45 to
26 percent, but all the other surveys were a lot closer. The *New York Times*/CBS
survey found that 41 percent thought President Reagan had done better,
compared to 38 percent who picked Mondale, and Gallup gave President
Reagan a 43 to 40 percent edge. Since the Reagan edge in many of the polls
was within sampling error, the second debate was for practical purposes a
dead heat. The Mondale campaign needed a good deal more than that. Therefore, the outcome led to another Strategic Adjustment.

The day after the debate, President Reagan opened up an even larger lead
in Peter Hart's survey. In view of the size of the Reagan lead and with the
campaign now entering the Time's Up stage, Hart could see only two possible
strategies. One was a high-risk direct frontal assault on President Reagan.
This would suggest that, whatever his accomplishments in the past, he was
losing touch as he got older and that his reelection would be dangerous. The
risk, of course, was that President Reagan was popular with the electorate so

that strategy might do more harm than good. The other possibility was to concentrate on the most-Democratic states. Although this would reduce the possibility of an Electoral College victory, it might help other Democratic candidates.[7] "In our last ten days," Hart wrote, "we want to send a message that maximizes our potential in an uphill battle and allows us to help the entire Democratic cause. Win or lose, it's a campaign that will have the ring of truth" (Goldman & Fuller, 1985, pp. 344–45).

Campaign chairman James Johnson, reacting to this and other ill tidings, thought Walter Mondale should be formally advised. He met the traveling party in Milwaukee and told Mondale the bad news. Walter Mondale was perfectly familiar with the adverse surveys;[8] but he also knew about the crowd reactions he was now getting. He countered with that. "Those aren't loser's crowds," he told Johnson.

A formal decision for a last-minute Strategic Adjustment was not taken. But for practical purposes—where Mondale campaigned, what he said, and how he said it—it was. During the last two weeks of the campaign, Walter Mondale campaigned in three areas. He spent time in the Northeast: Massachusetts, New York, New Jersey, and Pennsylvania. He campaigned on the West Coast: California, Oregon, and Washington. And he crisscrossed the Middle West: Michigan, Ohio, Illinois, Missouri, Iowa, Wisconsin, and his own Minnesota. His attention to the South was confined to brief stops in Kentucky and Texas. In one sense, this pattern was not at all unusual. Mondale's travels took him into the seven states casting the largest electoral votes, and this is where presidential campaigns usually end up. But looking at the locations within those states—big cities, hard-hit farm areas, depressed industrial areas—it is clear that Walter Mondale was ending his campaign in the Democratic heartland. Moreover, the concentration of Mondale's personal energies was reinforced by the location of Geraldine Ferraro's campaigning and the concentration of the Democratic media campaign.

The Mondale messages during this Time's Up phase were vintage Democratic appeals. In Iowa, he recalled that his first campaign had been in 1948 and that he had ridden on Harry Truman's train even though he had been too young to vote. Rural America had been crucial to Truman's victory then, and he asked his audience to weigh their vote carefully in 1984. "I ask you to use these days now, think it through, see what you see, ask who you trust, and then . . . walk into the polling booth and take control of your government once again." In Seattle, he drew a distinction between Reagan foreign policy and what he, Mondale, proposed to do. "I will not only strengthen the Marine Corps; I will strengthen the Peace Corps. I want the world to know

---

[7] This strategy is not unknown for a coalition that is a long way behind. In the Time's Up phase of the 1964 campaign, Barry Goldwater ended up fighting for support in the Deep South. During the preceding weeks, these southern electoral votes had been taken for granted.

[8] In a postelection press conference, Mondale said that he "thought we had a chance" after the first debate but that his "chances of winning probably disappeared" after the second.

America at its finest, through our young students, our teachers and engineers, our doctors and poets." And he recalled his past accomplishments for a union audience north of Detroit:

> I've traveled across this state hundreds of times over the years. Every time Michigan has asked for help, I've said yes. Every time the workers of this state have needed help, I've been there. When your kids needed an education, I helped. When you needed trade adjustment assistance, I've been there. I love this state. We're fellow Midwesterners. Give me this chance to be your president.

While making these appeals, Walter Mondale appeared to be relaxed and comfortable. His speaking was as effective as it had been at any time during the year, and the crowd responses were genuine. Mr. Mondale was certainly aware of the adverse news from survey after survey and the consequent probability that he was closing out his public career. But he did so with themes familiar from many years of campaigning, and the cheers that rang in his ears gave assurance that many voters agreed with him on war and peace and on fundamental questions of fairness.

Election night brought final confirmation that the issues raised by Mondale had not been enough to counter the attractiveness of Reagan and prosperity. Even so, Walter Mondale could look back to his victory in the first debate as an effort that held the Democratic coalition together. Moreover, he could remember the close of the campaign as a period when he presented an unapologetic Democratic appeal—and did so with unflagging good spirit.

MORNING IN AMERICA: REAGAN'S REELECTION

Plans and Plans

The twinkle in his eye was the same. The grin was just as confident. His optimism was as firmly fixed as ever. But there were differences too. In 1980, Ronald Reagan was the challenger. In 1984, he was the president with a record to defend.

On parts of the record, he was vulnerable to attack. Foreign policy concerns included Central America, the Middle East, and the possibility that his hawkishness would increase the chances of war. At home, there was the cluster of issues the Democrats summed up as fairness. But the incumbent could focus on the economy. As Herbert Stein explained it:

> Most four-year presidential terms contain a recession and a recovery. If the recession comes in the fourth year of the term, as it did in 1960 and 1980, that is bad for the incumbent or his party. If the recovery comes in the fourth year, as it did in 1956, 1964 or 1972, that is good for the reelection of the incumbent. There have been exceptions—such as 1968 and 1976. But 1984 was no exception. The recovery of 1984 endowed Reagan economics with the sweet smell of success. (Stein, 1985, p. 381)

In addition to the favorable economic climate, Ronald Reagan himself was popular with the American voters. So, in 1984, Reagan was a popular incumbent running on a record that was easy to defend.

In further contrast to the 1980 Reagan campaign, 1984 was marked by a surfeit of strategies. In 1980, the campaign generally followed the single plan developed by Richard Wirthlin and Richard Beal.[9] In 1984, there were several plans developed for Reagan's reelection campaign. All these strategies aimed at the President's reelection but seemed motivated by different visions of what would come after the election. Lee Atwater, principal deputy to campaign chairman Ed Rollins, envisioned a southern-western fortress that could be developed for Reagan. Much of this had been in place in 1972 and 1980 and could provide a base for the election of future conservative presidents. Richard Darman, the principal assistant to White House Chief-of-Staff James Baker, seemed concerned with putting the President on a footing that would make governing easier in a second term. The plans of Richard Wirthlin and Stuart Spencer were more instrumental, focusing more on the reelection of Ronald Reagan in 1984 than on any postelection developments. It might be that the strategists, sensing a Reagan victory in the offing, were contending with each other to claim some share of the credit. In any case, no one plan controlled the campaign, but there was enough overlap between them that each strategist could claim his plan was in effect.

Of the several strategies, Richard Wirthlin's was the first to be written, was the longest, and carried the personal approval of President Reagan. His 150-page campaign action plan was written in the summer of 1983. He met with President Reagan on September 23, 1983, and went over the plan with him. Mr. Reagan made a few changes and then gave it his blessing.

The plan was detailed and precise. It called for developing a winning coalition in 1984 that would garner 52 percent of the vote. This target might seem modest in view of the 59 percent that President Reagan would ultimately receive, but 1983 data showed a different picture than the summer '84 polls that pointed to a Reagan victory. In the summer of 1983, Mr. Reagan's approval rating was hovering in the mid-40 percent range, and the Wirthlin data showed Reagan with only 47 percent of the vote in a prospective race against Mondale. Consequently, the strategic problem was how to add 5 percent to the Reagan vote.

Wirthlin's plan laid out demographic targets, electoral vote targets, and discussed themes to be developed in the campaign. First, demographic goals were specified. For example, the 52 percent was decomposed by sex, with 25 percent to be contributed by women and 27 percent by men. Given Reagan's standing with these two categories, this implied improving his female support by 5 percent and his male support by 4. Similar calculations were made for eight other demographic categories.

---

[9] A sad note. Richard Beal, by 1984 a member of the National Security Council staff, did not live to see President Reagan's second term. He died in the fall of 1984.

It was easier to see where electoral votes were coming from. The Reagan base consisted of California, Florida, Indiana, Virginia, and 13 smaller states (of which all but New Hampshire were in the West) for a total of 153 electoral votes. Texas and five smaller states were seen as leaning to Reagan for an additional 55 votes. The Mondale base, on the other hand, was restricted to Michigan, Massachusetts, Minnesota, West Virginia, and the District of Columbia for only 86 votes. Pennsylvania, Ohio, Hawaii, and half a dozen southern and border states were listed as leaning to Mondale for 89 more. Hence, President Reagan was coming into the race with a probable 208 electoral votes. He could get to the needed 270 in many different ways. Walter Mondale, on the other hand, needed to carry almost all of the swing states to be a danger to Reagan in the Electoral College.

It was apparent, Wirthlin wrote, that the reelection of any incumbent is based on his record of performance as that record is perceived by the American people. The question was how that record was to be presented. Wirthlin recommended three themes: leadership, effectiveness, and the future.

The first two themes were combined into an emphasis on effective leadership. This focused on the President himself rather than on any specific issue. Roughly speaking, the electorate could be divided into thirds: those who liked the President and his policies; those who liked the President and disliked his policies; and those who disliked the President. If those in the middle category focused on the leader rather than on his less popular policies, this would create a Reagan majority (Light & Lake, 1985, p. 92).

The theme of the future was more interesting. Wirthlin argued that the record of the administration must be the anvil against which the future is forged. Even if the record is popular, the people must feel good about the future, must feel that pleasant things are going to happen. The resulting sense of the future—that growth will continue, that there are open possibilities—was seen as particularly important in appealing to younger voters.[10]

Lee Atwater's memorandum, "Building an Electoral Fortress in 1984," written later in the fall of 1983, focused just on regions and Electoral College arithmetic.[11] He began by noting what many observers have pointed out: that the West has been solidly Republican since 1968. If the South, with 155 electoral votes, was added to the West, with its 107 electoral votes, the "fortress" would be so strong that the election of a Republican would be certain.[12] Atwater, a South Carolinian himself, argued that this was a Reagan opportu-

---

[10] As the Democratic nomination race developed, Wirthlin was concerned with Gary Hart's effective use of future-oriented themes. He saw the possibility that Hart, if nominated, might preempt some of the things that the Reagan campaign was planning to do.

[11] Richard Wirthlin's campaign action plan has not been published, but excerpts from the other plans have (Goldman & Fuller, 1985, Appendix).

[12] The real difference between Wirthlin's and Atwater's analyses of the Reagan base was that the former was more variegated. Proceeding on a state-by-state basis, Wirthlin included Virginia (which had voted Republican seven of the last eight elections) and Florida (which had done so in six elections) in the Reagan base. But Georgia and North Carolina, both of which had gone Democratic in five of these elections, were listed as leaning to Mondale.

nity more than a Republican opportunity because it followed from Reagan's own conservatism.

What was important about the Atwater memorandum was its focus on realignment. Ronald Reagan's appeal to Southerners could be used to construct a Republican asset in future elections. For that reason, Republicans should "openly welcome disgruntled Southern Democrats into the Reagan-Bush/Republican fold. . . . The Sunbelt coalition—Ronald Reagan's legacy to the party—can become the Republican base for decades to come" (Germond & Witcover, 1985, p. 91; Goldman & Fuller, 1985, pp. 385–86).

Richard Darman's memorandum was not written until June 1984, by which time the situation was much clearer. He urged that Mondale should be painted as weak, an extension of Jimmy Carter. Ronald Reagan, however, should be presented as "the personification of all that's right with, or heroized by America. Leave Mondale in a position where an attack on Reagan is tantamount to an attack on America's idealized sense of itself—where a vote against Reagan is, in some subliminal sense, a vote against a mythic 'AMERICA'" (Goldman & Fuller, 1985, p. 413).

Finally, there were two memorandums written by Stuart Spencer in August 1984. The first gave some initial impressions; the second set forth a campaign plan. These can be taken as consensus documents, because the first was written after consultation with Richard Wirthlin and Bob Teeter and because of the no-nonsense, this-is-what-needs-to-be-done tone of both. Spencer's campaign plan called for dominating the campaign so as to deprive Mondale of the opportunity to establish his agenda. While parts of the memorandums dealt with attacks to be expected from Mondale (fairness, social security, worry about war and peace, and so forth), the central portion set forth general campaign themes.

> We need to establish the over-arching themes required in a national election. It is relatively clear what we will say to a variety of groups, but we have not determined the overall theme we want delivered to the electorate as a whole.
> . . . The umbrella theme will be leadership. The president has fundamentally changed the direction of the country, particularly the economy, in a manner that has produced good results, and will continue to do so. . . . The future vision that the president establishes should include challenges, but reaffirm our faith in the country's ability to progress and meet those challenges.[13] (Goldman & Fuller, 1985, p. 416)

By the time that all of these memorandums had been written, the identity of the central players in the Reagan camp was clear: James Baker first, then Stu Spencer and Bob Teeter.[14] The identity of other decision makers de-

---

[13] Note the overlap between the Wirthlin plan and the Spencer plan in the references to leadership and the future as central campaign themes.

[14] It is interesting and ironic that three men who had played such important roles in defeating Ronald Reagan in his bid for the 1976 Republican nomination ended up running his 1984 reelection campaign.

pended on the topic, but it is not inaccurate to think of a White House group and a campaign group.[15]

Major decisions were made at meetings held in Jim Baker's office once or twice a week, with participants from the White House group and from the campaign group. The campaign group also held meetings every morning at 7:30. The last phone calls in the daily tracking polls were finished at 1:30 A.M. on the West Coast. Two hours later (6:30 A.M. eastern time), the results were phoned to Richard Wirthlin, and he took them to the 7:30 meeting of the campaign group.

By Labor Day, the news was very good. The only states causing any concern at this point were West Virginia and Hawaii. This simplified the geographic focus of the campaign enormously. Reagan had the West and the South. This meant that if Reagan could pick off Ohio or Michigan or Pennsylvania or New York, the election was won. And with the Sun Belt "fortress" secure, the Republicans could lavish resources—media, the President's time, and so on—on these target states.

A Confident Beginning

The Grand Opening had three parts: President Reagan's own appearances, the media campaign, and an anti-Mondale campaign.[16] Mr. Reagan unveiled his own campaign lines in two Labor Day rallies in California. He could not speak directly about effective leadership, but he did talk about the economy: that inflation had been reduced from 12.4 to 4.1 percent; that 6 million jobs had been created in the past 20 months, more jobs each month during the preceding year than all the countries of Western Europe had created during the preceding 19 years; that from the Jersey shore to San Francisco Bay, economic expansion was carrying America forward.

Much more of Mr. Reagan's speech picked up the theme of the future. It was summarized in the "You ain't seen nothin' yet" phrase that Ronald Reagan was to repeat over and over during the campaign.

> As far as I'm concerned, that's America's message to the world. We've got everything before us. . . . That's our message this year. We'll carry it across America. You ain't seen nothin' yet. . . . Our work isn't done. The future is waiting to be seized, great frontiers in science, in technology, in space waiting to be discovered and pushed back. We can do it because, as we saw with our great

---

[15] Margaret Tutwiler, who had been Jim Baker's executive assistant, served as liaison between the two groups.

[16] This is a much simplified version of a quite complex Republican strategy. In addition to the national campaign plan and the regional campaign plans, individual campaign plans were developed for 20 states. There were also special plans developed for a number of demographic groupings, such as young voters, blue-collar voters, Roman Catholics, and white Southerners.

The early Reagan references to politics and morality being inseparable were probably part of a special appeal aimed at fundamentalists. When enough had been said, the President moved back to the traditional constitutional posture that there is a "wall of separation" between church and state.

Olympic athletes, when America goes for the gold, nothing is going to hold her back. . . .

We're going to build a peace that won't fail, if we don't fail. . . . We're going to leave, and proudly leave, sturdy and indestructible values so that in the 21st century our shield shall be their shield.

President Reagan not only portrayed himself and the Republicans as the party of the future, so important in appealing to younger voters, but he also cast the Democrats as the party of the past. "I hate to say this, but the age factor may well play a part in this election. Their ideas are just too old." And although motivating changes in party identification was not an explicit theme of the campaign plans—as leadership, effectiveness, and the future were—the President certainly urged Democrats to switch.

To all those Democrats, and I hope there are many here, who have been loyal to the party of F.D.R. and Harry Truman and J.F.K., people who believe in protecting the interests of working people, who are not ashamed or afraid of America's standing in the world—we say to you: join us. Come walk with us down that new path of hope and opportunity.

Having switched parties himself, the President was in an advantageous position to urge others to do so.

I was a Democrat most of my adult life. I didn't leave my party, and we're not suggesting that you leave yours. I am telling you that what I felt was that the leadership of the Democratic party had left me and millions of patriotic Democrats in this country who believed in freedom.

These elements—a growing economy, confidence in dealing with the future, and an appeal to Democrats to switch parties—were all elements in "The Speech" that Ronald Reagan delivered again and again throughout the fall. During September, Mr. Reagan spoke to an outdoor rally at the National Shrine of Our Lady of Czestochowa, a Polish-American shrine in Doylestown, Pennsylvania, and at the dedication of the Santa Maria Towers, a senior citizen housing project in Buffalo built with the support of the federal government and local Roman Catholic and Italian groups. He also delivered versions of The Speech to a group of steelworkers in Canton, Ohio, and a group of union carpenters in Grand Rapids, Michigan. These were not the only places that the President spoke, of course, but on these and many other occasions, he spoke to traditional Democratic audiences.

Part of the television campaign came from Ronald Reagan's own appearances. His professional acting skills in delivering lines and sensing how his audience would react were part of this, but only part. His public appearances were structured so that they could be "commercials" when excerpts appeared on television news. Banks of loudspeakers were brought in so his voice would carry. Professional lighting contractors were hired to make sure that his face would not be lost in shadows. And on most occasions, the background was painted in cerulean blue, a shade close to sky blue, against which Ronald Reagan's facial coloring looked particularly good. The payments to local contractors were costly—but cheap if they allowed President Reagan to look better when appearing on millions of television screens across the country.

There were also occasions when a Reagan campaign stop would be arranged not for any serious discussion of issues but because it provided a good visual background. On September 13, for example, Mr. Reagan appeared on stage at the Grand Ole Opry in Nashville, Tennessee, to join the celebration of country singer Roy Acuff's 81st birthday. He paid tribute to Roy Acuff, Davy Crockett, Andrew Jackson, and other Tennessee heroes; joined in singing "God Bless the U.S.A."; and made liberal use of country music references. For example, he claimed that "the other side's promises are a little like Minnie Pearl's hats. They both have big price tags hanging from them." Hardly deep, but effective in reaching a mass audience.

Still other parts of the television campaign came from the Tuesday Team, an ad hoc "firm" of well-known media specialists that had been assembled to handle Reagan's television. Republican polling had found that many people did feel that things were getting better in America, and the television ads in the Grand Opening phase were designed to reinforce these feelings. In one, with appropriate pictures and music, the announcer said:

> This is America, spring of '84. Just four years ago people were saying that its problems were too big and too difficult to be handled by any one president. Yet today, housing is coming back, hope for the future is coming back, and isn't it interesting that no one anywhere is saying that the job of president is too big for one person. President Reagan. He's doing what he was elected to do.

Another Tuesday Team effort picked up the theme that independents and Democrats were going to vote for Reagan. This contained film clips of "typical citizens" giving reasons why they intended to vote Republican. One said, "I'm a registered Democrat, and I'm voting for Reagan because I can see what he's done in the past four years." Another added, "I like Ronald Reagan because I believe he's turned the nation around and he's got things back on the track again." A third stated, "Most of the people when I go on jobs say they're Democrats but they're voting for Reagan this year." And this ad, as most of the Reagan spots, closed with the slogan that combined the themes of leadership and effectiveness: "Leadership That's Working."

The negative campaign against Mondale focused on his deficit reduction plan, the centerpiece of his Grand Opening Strategy. This was dealt with in the first instance by one of the classic techniques available to an incumbent president. Mr. Mondale announced his plan with some fanfare on Monday, September 10. A story about it appeared in the *Columbus Citizen-Journal* of September 11 under the headline "Mondale Betting All on Deficit Issue." The story, however, was carried on page 3. The first page had another headline, "Soviet, Reagan Agree to Meet." Foreign Minister Andrei Gromyko had agreed to a meeting with the President when in the United States for the opening of the United Nations. President Reagan simply had covered an important story by releasing a more important story the same day.

The Republicans also focused their reply and, hence, public attention on one aspect of the deficit reduction plan: that taxes would be increased. Speaking in upstate New York on September 12, President Reagan said: "We're not going to let them enact their tax plan, not on your life. . . . The main difference between us and the other side is, we see an America where every day is the Fourth of July, and they see an America where every day is April 15th." The principal Reagan position on the deficit thus became *opposition* to Mondale's tax proposal. A Tuesday Team television spot emphasized this same point. The announcer's voice said:

> Here's the difference in the two ways of dealing with the nation's economy. With Reaganomics, you cut taxes. With Mondalenomics, you raise taxes. Reaganomics, you cut deficits through growth and less government spending. Mondalenomics, you raise taxes. With Reaganomics, you create incentives that move us all forward. With Mondalenomics, you raise taxes. They both work. The difference is that Reaganomics works for you. Mondalenomics works against you.

The coupling of "Mondale" and "raise taxes" was carried on in many ways by Republican spokespersons throughout the campaign.

The Debate Interlude

As September came to a close, Republican strategists saw no need to modify their plans in any important way and did not do so. Two events, though, provided opportunities to deal with foreign policy.

The first was a speech President Reagan delivered to the U.N. General Assembly on September 24. The address was quite conciliatory in tone. Reagan quoted Mohandas Gandhi's appeal for a "tenfold trust and a thousandfold affection" among peoples and said, "We are not ideologically rigid. We do have principles, and we will stand by them, but we also seek the friendship and good will of all." The speech raised questions as to whether this was serious foreign policy or simply part of the election campaign. It was probably a little of both. The State Department had urged a friendlier approach to the Soviet Union more than a year before, but that policy was put on hold after a Korean jetliner was shot down by a Russian aircraft in September 1983. The policy of seeking a constructive approach to the USSR was resumed early in 1984, and this speech was part of it. At the same time, the Reagan address was good politics, as it alleviated fears about hostilities between the United States and the Soviet Union. Mr. Reagan's White House meeting with Foreign Minister Gromyko two days later had the same effect, as well as providing some insulation against the Democratic charge that Ronald Reagan was the only American president since FDR who had not met with Russian leaders.[17]

---

[17] There had been talk about arranging a summit meeting sometime during Reagan's first term, but this was virtually impossible because of the poor health of three successive Soviet leaders.

The practice sessions for the Louisville debate with Walter Mondale were not much different from the rehearsals four years earlier; David Stockman once again played the role of Reagan's opponent. But for whatever reason, Mr. Reagan was not up for the first debate. He had been advised to stay away from questions about social security whenever possible, but he went back to the topic repeatedly. The President's closing statement, normally something at which he excels, went quite badly. It began with some question over whether he had time for a last rebuttal statement. After discussing this with moderator Barbara Walters, he said, "I'm all confused now." Then, as if to prove his point, he included passages such as:

> Now, maybe I'm expected to ask [the same closing question as in 1980] again. I'm not going to because I think all of you, or not everyone, those people that have—are in those pockets of poverty and haven't caught up, they couldn't answer the question the way I would want them to.

On the matter of defense spending, he argued:

> Yes, we have an increase in the defense budget. But back then we had planes that couldn't fly for lack of spare parts or pilots. We had navy vessels that couldn't leave harbor because of lack of crew or, again, lack of spare parts. Today we're well on our way to a 600-ship navy. We have 543 at present. We have—our military, the morale is high. I think people should understand that two thirds of the defense budget pays for pay and salary—or pay and pension. And then when you add to that food and wardrobe and all the other things and you only have a small portion going for weapons.

These rambling words were hardly models of clear logic or persuasive rhetoric.

President Reagan's poor performance had several immediate consequences. First, there was some scapegoating, led by a very angry Mrs. Reagan.[18] Second, the debate changed the tone of the discussion among the campaign managers. As one participant recalled it: "The first debate got everyone's attention. I remember that was the first time that we were [really] in a race. Up to that point you couldn't find anyone who thought the Republicans were going to lose.[19] Third, Reagan's incoherence (at least in contrast to his usual polished performance) raised the age issue for the 73-year-old President. A good many commentators began to ask if Mr. Reagan was slipping and whether he was still up to the demanding job of the presidency. All this was enough to justify two Tactical Adjustments.

---

[18] She did not wish to hear that Ronald Reagan himself was responsible. Nor, for that matter, would it have been very helpful to say so at a time when the campaign managers wanted to build Mr. Reagan's confidence for the second debate only two weeks hence.

[19] One of the most interesting revelations in a postcampaign discussion with Peter Hart and Richard Wirthlin is that both campaigns were getting essentially the same information about the voters' reactions. In Hart's words, "Wirthlin and I compared notes after the election, as any two baseball managers would. From September 1st through November 4th, our figures never varied from each other by more than 2 percent, so our candidates were getting the same numbers" (Hart & Wirthlin, 1985, p. 59).

The first was a response to the age issue itself. Dr. Daniel Ruge, Mr. Reagan's physician, said that the President's health was "excellent." Ruge released data from a May physical examination of the President at Bethesda Naval Hospital. In his statement, Ruge quoted Dr. W. W. Karney, the internist who had supervised the springtime physical, as saying that Mr. Reagan was "a mentally alert, robust man who appears younger than his stated age." Jim Baker offered the opinion that the age issue would not be any more use to Reagan opponents than it had been in 1976 or 1980. "It just won't wash," Baker continued. "If you work with him on a daily basis and see how vigorous he is, you know that the statement that he is too old to be president just isn't the case." The real Republican response to the age issue, of course, would be an abler Reagan performance in the second debate. But until that took place, all the strategists could do was wait in uneasy expectation.[20]

The other Tactical Adjustment concerned foreign policy. It came about because Mondale's campaigning (questioning, for example, whether Reagan understood that submarine missiles could not be recalled), his media ("The arms race is out of control. On November 6th, you can take control."), and news stories (the CIA manual about subversion in Central America) combined into what Richard Wirthlin called "Mondale's last and most serious challenge to the President" (Hart & Wirthlin, 1985, p. 11). Part of the Tactical Adjustment consisted of statements by Reagan and others. In South Carolina on October 14, Reagan charged that "my opponent had one of the weakest records in the United States Congress for supporting a strong national defense." In Illinois the next day, he claimed that before he came to office the United States had been "unilaterally disarmed." A couple of days later, Melvin Laird and Donald Rumsfeld, defense secretaries in the Nixon and Ford administrations, joined in the attack on Mondale's defense votes in the Senate.

The media portion of the Tactical Adjustment on foreign policy was built around the theme of "being prepared for peace"—a shift from "peace through strength," which had been used in 1980. The most effective part of this was the "bear in the woods" spot. As the camera followed a bear moving through the woods, the announcer said: "There's a bear in the woods. For some people, the bear is easy to see. Others don't see it at all. Some people say the bear is tame. Others say it is vicious and dangerous. Since no one can be sure who's right, isn't it smart to be as strong as the bear?" At this point, the bear stopped and looked up. The camera then moved back enough to show a hunter with a gun over his shoulder, and the announcer concluded, "If there is a bear." The closing words on the television screen were "President Reagan. Prepared for Peace." Filmed in lush Oregon woods in May, this

---

[20] A plan for a Strategic Adjustment to be used if Reagan should be defeated in the second debate was drafted by Lee Atwater. Essentially, it called for every possible Republican spokesperson to make every possible charge against Mondale (Goldman & Fuller, 1985, pp. 434–38).

was sufficiently soft so the viewer would not be threatened. At the same time, its appeal for strength in the face of uncertainty was remarkably effective.

The Kansas City debate began with serious questions posed concerning American actions in Central America, the circumstances justifying the commitment of American troops, and how to cope with terrorism. Then panel member Henry Trewitt was called on for his first question:

> Mr. President, I want to raise an issue that I think has been lurking out there for two or three weeks, and cast it specifically in national security terms. You already are the oldest president in history, and some of your staff say you were tired after your most recent encounter with Mr. Mondale. I recall, yes, that President Kennedy, who had to go for days on end with very little sleep during the Cuban Missile Crisis. Is there any doubt in your mind that you would be able to function in such circumstances?

Mr. Reagan was ready for that question:

> Not at all, Mr. Trewitt, and I want you to know that also I will not make age an issue of this campaign. I am not going to exploit for political purposes my opponent's youth and inexperience.

There was more, much more, to this debate. Walter Mondale sought repeatedly to demonstrate that Ronald Reagan did not have command of the facts that a commander-in-chief needed to know. Important differences in the Mondale and Reagan approaches to foreign policy became evident. President Reagan once again rambled during his close, taking time for a story about a trip down the Pacific Coast Highway, so that moderator Edwin Newman had to cut him off. But in disposing of the age question with a quip, Mr. Reagan had shown the voters that he was the president they had come to know, and that was enough to restore the race to the status quo ante. Since President Reagan had come into the first debate with a commanding lead—and there were now a bare two weeks until the election—the question was no longer *whether* he would win but *how* he would win.

A Pleasant Close

When Reagan strategists discussed how he should campaign during the Time's Up phase, one of the more interesting suggestions came from Richard Darman. He urged that the campaign adopt a more positive tone (which seemingly was done) and that the President go on an "American Victory Tour" visiting historic American sites (which was not done). Darman's reasoning reflected his concern with how President Reagan was going to govern during his second term. "There is a major risk of presidential support eroding in a second term—compounded by our need to get a difficult legislative program through in '85. With this in view we need to get the president's popularity—and his claim to a national 'mandate' to the highest possible level by the time of the State of the Union" (Goldman & Fuller, 1985, p. 450).

In purely electoral terms, no change was needed in the Republican themes of leadership, effectiveness, and the future. There had been some advances in the simulation capacity that had been developed in 1980. One of these incorporated 30 different issues and a dozen image elements and showed what would happen with different campaign emphases. This allowed Richard Wirthlin to investigate the effects of proposed campaign foci. What would happen, for example, if the campaign focused on foreign policy? His results confirmed the appeal of leadership, effectiveness, and the future as campaign themes. So this was a case in which the strategists stayed with selected themes, not simply because they had decided upon them at some earlier point but because they had positive information that the combination was the best available.

The closing media spots exuded good feelings and confidence about the future. After an appropriate musical opening, candidate Reagan addressed televiewers:

> This campaign's nearly over now. The noisy excitement and sharp debate draw to a close, until that moment arrives which belongs only to you. But there's been something special for me this year. In this autumn season with its colors and crisp air hinting of family holidays, I see America coming together again. I've seen it in the eyes of thousands of young people who've come to our rallies. There's more than the sparkle of youth on their faces. . . . Tomorrow is theirs, one in which they deserve to do anything, be anything, and fly as high as their talents will take them. . . . How can anyone doubt that our best days are yet to come?

The reference to thousands of young people who've come to our rallies was something more than a scriptwriter's imagination. President Reagan spoke often on campuses. For example, he came to Ohio State for a noontime rally on October 24. A three-city-block line of neatly dressed students was waiting for admission to the basketball arena by 10:30 in the morning. President Reagan did not break any new ground in his remarks, but the speech, scheduled for less than 15 minutes, lasted over half an hour. The students were enthusiastic, and Mr. Reagan played the responsive audience for all it was worth.

Ronald Reagan had campaigned frequently in Ohio, Michigan, Pennsylvania, and New York throughout the fall, and he stopped in three of these states once more during his last campaign swing. There were 10 states altogether on this trip; he appeared in a few states where the margins still were a little close, before heading home to California for final appearances before voting. He began at City Hall in Boston, then flew to Rochester, New York, and on to a Detroit suburb. On Saturday, he visited medium-sized states in the Mississippi valley: Arkansas, Iowa, and Wisconsin. Farm income was not good, and Reagan support—especially in the upper Mississippi valley—was comparatively low. On Sunday, Air Force One headed for an airport news conference in Rochester, Minnesota, a sign that the campaign was going so well that strategists thought it possible that Mr. Reagan might even carry Mondale's home state. With this hastily added stop out of the way, Mr. Reagan proceeded to already scheduled speeches at Gateway Arch in St. Louis and in a Chicago suburb. The day before the election, President Reagan concluded his tour with big rallies at the state capitol in Sacramento and at a shopping mall in San Diego.

Richard Wirthlin's final estimate, expressed both privately to President Reagan and publicly to reporters, was that only Minnesota was still Walter Mondale's and even Minnesota was within reach. His final tracking poll on the night before the election was 57 percent for Reagan to 37 percent for Mondale.[21]

The strategic challenge facing Ronald Reagan in 1984 had not been great. All he had to do was to avoid serious mistakes in order to become the first president in a dozen years to gain reelection. His strategists did a bit better than that. They used the opportunity of 1984 to maximize the Reagan vote and increase Republican strength.

SUMMARY OF THE CAMPAIGN

Walter Mondale, beginning his campaign far behind the incumbent, chose to emphasize his own deficit reduction plan, to attack the bellicosity of administration foreign policy, and to question the fairness of administration social programs. When the tax increase portion of his deficit reduction plan proved vulnerable, it was dropped in a first Strategic Adjustment. Mondale did well in the first debate, and his subsequent success attacking foreign policy breathed life into his campaign. When Reagan's lead was confirmed after the second debate, a second Strategic Adjustment emphasized an unapologetic liberal appeal to Democratic strongholds.

The Reagan campaign was built around leadership, the prosperous economy, and the future. These themes were emphasized in President Reagan's own appearances and through the media, and they carried the campaign well enough that they did not need to be altered. After Mr. Reagan appeared to stumble in the first debate, one Tactical Adjustment denied that the President had any incapacity due to age, and another responded to Mondale's foreign policy charges by arguing that the country had to be prepared for peace. When confidence was renewed by Reagan's relative success in the second debate, he was able to wind up with his favorite theme, "You ain't seen nothin' yet," without ever telling the voters what they were going to see.

CONSTRAINTS

As we have seen, the selection of a presidential campaign strategy is subject to very real constraints. A candidate is not free to express all of his inner

---

[21] With election results of 59 percent to 41 percent and correct predictions in all 50 states, Richard Wirthlin once again had confirmation of the accuracy of his survey estimates.

yearnings. A strategy group is not free to come up with any approach it thinks might win votes. Instead, there are *internal constraints, external constraints,* and *temporal constraints.*

Internal Constraints

The internal constraints arise from the attitudes of the groups that are members of the coalition. As we saw in Chapter 3, there was a substantial correlation between the attitudes of the Nixon and McGovern coalitions and the positions emphasized by these candidates. In a similar way, one could argue that all of the strategies surveyed in this section of the book were acceptable to members of the supporting coalitions. Thus we saw Gerald Ford favoring moderately conservative economic policies, Jimmy Carter and Walter Mondale supporting a number of social programs favored by Democratic groups, John Anderson proposing only those programs that could be fit into the federal budget, and Ronald Reagan calling for a reduction in government spending and activities.

But what is more important—at least to understand internal constraints—is what was *not* done. George McGovern could have moderated his spring-time appeals, and Ronald Reagan could have done more in 1980 than just suggest an open mind on such issues as social security and federal aid to New York City. This would have made it easier to reach middle-of-the-road voters but would have disappointed the young militants supporting McGovern and cost Reagan the support of conservative ideologues. Or Senator McGovern could have proposed more radical redistributions of wealth, and Governor Reagan could have confined his campaign to the more conservative parts of the country. Either strategy would have made it more difficult for them to retain support from moderate members of their own coalitions.

Elizabeth Drew pointed out that both President Ford and Governor Carter were committed to expensive programs in 1976. Shortly after the Republican convention, Ford called for further progress in housing, health, recreation, and education; Carter was pledged to support job programs, health insurance, child care, federalization of welfare, housing, aid to cities, and aid to education (1977, p. 438). Both Ford and Carter could have consistently argued that to accomplish the goals to which their parties were pledged, some increase in taxes would be necessary. But to assert this would offend the economic conservatives to be found in both the Ford and Carter coalitions. President Ford could certainly have found a vice presidential candidate who would have had greater appeal than Robert Dole to independent voters in large industrial states, but selection of a more moderate running mate would have put off Reagan supporters.

Ronald Reagan logically could have said either that we needed to rebuild our defenses and we must have the taxes to do it *or* that the American economy needed the stimulus of a tax cut and therefore we must defer a substantial increase in military expenditures. But many conservatives (including Reagan himself) wanted both a big tax cut *and* a big arms buildup. And

Walter Mondale could have accepted black demands for an expensive jobs and training program to aid the hard-core unemployed, but the spending required would not have been popular with Democratic moderates and conservatives.

Doubtless you can think of other plausible campaign strategies consistent with some campaign goal or a fair reading of public policy. The central point, though, is that none of the strategies mentioned in this list was used. Each was avoided because it would have given offense to some group in the candidate's supporting coalition.

External Constraints

External constraints result from some inadequacy in the structure needed to obtain citizen support, from the need to reach some particular set of voters, or from lack of freedom to maneuver because of the positions taken by an opposing coalition.

The most common defects with respect to campaign operations, research, or public relations result from inexperience. Unless an incumbent president has been renominated, an electoral coalition is based on the preceding nomination coalition. Especially in the out party, key decision makers may be taking part in their first general election campaign for the presidency. This was true, for example, of John Mitchell in the 1968 Nixon campaign, Gary Hart in the 1972 McGovern campaign, Hamilton Jordan and Jody Powell in the 1976 Carter effort, and Edwin Meese and Michael Deaver in the 1980 Reagan campaign. There are usually some persons around with experience, but there have been campaigns (Carter's in 1976, for example) run almost entirely by novices. Newspaper articles are written about the "political geniuses" who are managing the campaign, but the simple fact is that some are in a situation they do not understand. Frequently, they will try to repeat tactics to which they attribute their success in nomination politics, and these tactics are often inappropriate.

Financial inadequacies have hobbled campaigns in two ways. Prior to federal funding, it was a simple lack of cash for candidates thought to be running behind. This was a very serious problem for the Humphrey campaign in 1968. It also caused great difficulties for the Anderson campaign in 1980, even though this was a special case of the third party, for which federal funds were not made available *during* the campaign. Since federal funds have been made available to the major parties, the funding limit has brought the need for much more careful planning for the use of available but finite resources. Such planning gave the Ford coalition a real strategic advantage in the closing days of the 1976 campaign.

The need—real or perceived—to reach certain sets of voters often excludes certain campaign gambits. For example, in 1972, President Nixon could have attacked the Democratic party quite directly by telling voters: "For years, we've been telling you that the Democrats were controlled by radicals, and you wouldn't listen. Now you have proof! They've nominated George

McGovern!" Such an attack could have had a long-term payoff by weakening identification with the Democratic party, but it would also have hampered Nixon's 1972 efforts to get Democrats to cast Nixon votes. Similarly, Ronald Reagan could have castigated the entire Democratic party for liberal stands taken by Walter Mondale in 1984. Instead, Mr. Reagan, speaking as a former Democrat, distinguished between the Democratic party and Democratic leadership and invited Democrats to join him if they felt abandoned by Democratic leaders.

The activities of the rival coalition (or coalitions) create an external constraint similar to that resulting from the structure of competition in nomination politics. A candidate frequently lacks maneuvering room because of positions already taken by a rival or because of positions the candidate has already taken in response to a rival's gambit. For example, when Jimmy Carter spoke about a tax cut in a last-minute appeal to voters who were worried about the cost of living, he was moving into a position that Gerald Ford had already occupied with a highly advertised tax cut plan. In 1980, when Ronald Reagan had relatively little (for a Republican) appeal to well-educated suburban voters and Jimmy Carter hoped to pick up some of this support, Carter found that he had to contend with the suburban appeal of John Anderson. In 1984, Reagan strategists were worried about the possibility of a Hart nomination, because they thought he might preempt "the future," a campaign theme they wanted to use in the fall.

A further difficulty, of course, is that internal and external constraints often have different consequences. Few of the groups with the 1972 Nixon coalition would have been offended by an attack on Democrats, but this was not done because of external constraints. The 1976 Ford coalition would certainly have been strengthened externally by the selection of a moderate vice presidential candidate, but this was not done because of internal constraints.[22] The problem with the unapologetic liberal stands that Walter Mondale took during the Time's Up phase of the 1984 campaign is that they were more responsive to internal needs—that is, these stands had more appeal to groups already within the Mondale coalition than to undecided voters. The central goal of any campaign is to discover a strategy that is acceptable in view of both internal and external constraints.

Temporal Constraints

The temporal constraints have already been discussed rather explicitly, so there is little need to do more than summarize them here. An electoral coalition has relatively little time for organization and planning. Plans adopted

---

[22] In recent campaigns, professional campaign managers have tended to pay less attention to internal constraints in order to design a strategy that is better suited to the external need to attract certain sets of voters. There was an unusual external emphasis to the Ford strategy in 1976 and to the Reagan strategy in 1980.

and launched during the Grand Opening are difficult to modify. It takes time to learn that a strategy is inappropriate and still more time to hit on a politically viable alternative. Hence, one seldom sees more than one or two Strategic Adjustments, even though it may be apparent to outside observers that a strategy is unsuccessful.

Temporal constraints are more apparent, of course, during the Time's Up stage. Both candidates are likely to be bone tired by this point; but both know that one will soon begin the slow transition from titular leader of the party to the "where are they now" category, while the other will soon experience the exhilarations and the frustrations of the White House.

Part Four

The Citizen in Presidential Elections

Chapter 8

The Structure of Citizen Knowledge

The difference is dramatic. Throughout the campaign, thousands of persons are engaged in the joint enterprise of trying to persuade the electorate to support one party or the other. On election day, the solitary citizen is alone in the voting booth. To be sure, the outcome of the election is the result of decisions made by millions of voters across the country, but each citizen has to make an individual choice.

To this point, the acting unit has been the coalition-in-institution. In order to analyze this acting unit in electoral politics, we considered the individuals aggregated into groups that made up the internal structure of the coalition, examined the institutionally patterned activities that constituted the external structure, and observed these as campaigns moved through the four stages of the temporal pattern. Now our acting unit becomes the individual.

The link between campaign strategy and citizen response is information. Broadly speaking, the aim of the entire campaign is to transmit information to the electorate. The citizen's response is similarly based on knowledge. If very little is known, the citizen may not bother to vote. If the bulk of what is known favors one party, the citizen is likely to vote for that party's candidate. If the citizen is aware of information favoring both sides, there must be some means of resolving this conflict. It follows that to analyze this individual activity, *the internal structure is the citizen's cognitive structure,* specifically what that citizen knows about politics.[1]

There are several elements to cognitive structure. Perhaps the most basic is *information level,* how much the citizen knows. Whatever information a citizen possesses is organized into *attitudes,* valenced cognitions about political objects. The valence (a person's feelings about the object being cognized) may be positive, negative, or neutral. In other words, there are some political objects (a candidate, a political party, Congress, a particular economic policy, and so on) about which the citizen has positive, negative, or neutral views.

Since attitudes may be positive, negative, or neutral, one is led to theories of *cognitive consistency.* For example, if a person was a Democrat and had positive views about the Democratic candidate, liked the record of the last Democratic president, favored high levels of government spending, and thought welfare programs should be maintained, we would say that the person's views were consistent when judged against a partisan criterion. If, on the other hand, a Democrat preferred the Republican candidate and the Democratic party's position on issues, we would say there was an attitude conflict.

Not all attitude objects are of equal importance. At one time, whether the candidates seem trustworthy may get the most attention; at another, foreign policy may be dominant. Politics itself may be quite visible in one person's cognitive landscape and remote from the concerns of another who is more interested in art. These variations in the relative prominence of attitude objects are referred to as *salience* and *centrality.* If the situation calls attention to the attitude object (for example, if some dramatic foreign development leads to greater news coverage), we say that object (international involvement) is more salient. If the attitude object is of more enduring concern, as with a person who is more interested in politics than art or business affairs, we say that politics is central to this person. If an attitude object is more salient or central or both, then attitudes about that topic will be more important in the citizen's cognitive structure.

For the citizen, the *external structure consists of the informational environment and the citizen's opportunities for political participation.* The notion of an informational environment is that an individual is surrounded at all times by a number of information sources. These include television, radio, magazines, books, and all of the things that a citizen can see or listen to. When the citizen is in contact with these sources, whether sitting at home reading a newspaper or walking into a campaign rally, information is absorbed from them. The citizen's opportunities for participation range from such effortless

---

[1] There are, of course, other internal structures that could be used for individual-level analysis. *Personality* is often used, as is *motivation.* In common with cognitive structure, these cannot be directly observed but must be inferred from other evidence. Cognitive structure is the concept that is more appropriate for analysis of this subject matter.

things as simply taking in information or voting all the way to quite demanding activities, such as making a financial contribution or actually campaigning on behalf of a candidate. The citizen may choose whether or not to take part in any of these activities. The decisions about whether or not to vote and the choice of presidential candidate are of prime concern as far as the election outcome is concerned.

Internal and external structure are intimately dependent on one another. As Daniel Levinson puts it:

> An essential feature of human life is the *interpenetration* of self and world. Each is inside the other. Our thinking about one must take account of the other. The interpenetration of self and world has been beautifully portrayed by Arthur Miller: . . . Society is inside of man and man is inside society. . . . The fish is in the water and the water is in the fish. (1977, p. 47)

This is clearly true for individual political activity. The citizen's cognitive structure is the result of all the information that has been absorbed and organized, whether from a forgotten civics book read 30 years earlier or a television newscast heard that very day. The citizen's attitudes, in turn, are linked to votes and other forms of political participation. To the extent that the citizen cares about politics and is involved in it, further information is acquired, and so the cycle continues. Thus the question as to *why* a citizen takes a particular action depends on internal and external structure—on both the citizen's attitudes and on the opportunities for learning and participation.

There are also temporal patterns on the individual level. A citizen's attitudes or behavior or both may remain stable or fluctuate. The resulting *temporal patterns may be observed within a campaign, between elections, or over one's lifetime.* In general, a person who is concerned about politics and who strongly identifies with one political party is more likely to exhibit stable attitudes and stable behavior. A person with little political information and little interest may show quite irregular behavior—not bothering to vote in many instances and swinging unpredictably between the parties when casting a ballot. Also, speaking generally, the longer the time period, the greater the likelihood of a change in attitudes or a variation in behavior. In this part of the book, we shall be concerned with all these matters as they affect a citizen's response to campaign strategies.

In this chapter, we first ask how much citizens know—what the distribution of information is across the electorate. Then we turn to the content of political information in the mass media—the relationship between the information in the media and the citizen's political knowledge, and the degree to which that knowledge depends on the citizen's involvement with the informational environment. We conclude with a look at the temporal patterns within a single campaign. Chapter 9 will deal with the relationships between citizen attitudes and presidential choice. Chapter 10 will look at party identification, cognitive consistency, and the stability of attitudes between elections.

HOW MUCH DO CITIZENS KNOW ABOUT
PRESIDENTIAL POLITICS?

At 6:25 P.M. on Monday, September 27, 1976, an interviewer from the Center for Political Studies at the University of Michigan began questioning a 34-year-old airline ramp attendant who lived on Long Island. After some initial items, the interviewer came to a series of questions that the Center for Political Studies has used in every election survey since 1952.[2]

Interviewer: Now, back to national politics, I'd like to ask what you think are the good and bad points about both parties. Is there anything in particular that you like about the Democratic party?

Respondent: They will spend more domestically than out of the country.

Interviewer: Is there anything in particular that you don't like about the Democratic party?

Respondent: No.

Interviewer: Is there anything in particular that you like about the Republican party?

Respondent: Ford's firm stand in Korea, and getting people out of Lebanon.

Interviewer: Is there anything in particular that you don't like about the Republican party?

Respondent: Lack of domestic spending.

Interviewer: Now I'd like to ask you about the good and bad points of the two major candidates for president. Is there anything in particular about Mr. Carter that might make you want to vote for him?

Respondent: Just a change.

Interviewer: Is there anything in particular about Mr. Carter that might make you want to vote against him?

Respondent: No.

Interviewer: Is there anything in particular about Mr. Ford that might make you want to vote for him?

Respondent: I like his foreign policy.

Interviewer: Is there anything in particular about Mr. Ford that might make you want to vote against him?

Respondent: Cutting domestic spending.

This voter was close to the middle of several social and political spectra. He was in his mid-30s, was a high school graduate, regarded himself as average middle class, and was an independent. He liked Republican foreign policy and Democratic domestic spending. As a Roman Catholic who lived in New York, he was also the type of voter regarded as crucial in both the Ford and Carter campaign strategies. Balanced between the attractions of Republican foreign policy and Democratic domestic policy, he resolved his own dilemma with the belief that it was time for a change. He decided during the Demo-

---

[2] Answers to these questions from 1984 interviews are not available, but as Figure 11–1 shows, the information level exhibited in these responses has been stable over time.

cratic convention to vote for Jimmy Carter and did so in November. What is most important to our present purpose, though, is the amount of information the airline ramp attendant showed in his responses. He was as close to the average level of information as it was possible to be.

However typical this airline employee may have been, it is hazardous to rest an analysis on any single case. We can develop a better sense of information levels by seeing how several citizens answered this series of questions. Let's begin with a woman from Philadelphia. She was 30 years old, single, and a free-lance photographer who was working as an artist. Politically, she was an independent; and she had a good deal to say about the parties and candidates.[3]

Interviewer: Like about the Democratic party?

Respondent: I think in general that the Democrats have more interest in the average person. The social reform and work with the underprivileged is stronger.

Interviewer: Anything else?

Respondent: Their economic policies are usually different than the Republicans; there is usually larger government spending and more concern about unemployment.

Interviewer: Dislike about the Democratic party?

Respondent: I don't like the close identification with the labor movement—an inordinate amount of influence.

Interviewer: Anything else?

Respondent: There is corruption in all the parties, especially at the local level.

Interviewer: Like about the Republican party?

Respondent: To me financially, the usual tax shelters and financial policies are better due to my income.

Interviewer: Anything else?

Respondent: At times there is not a great deal of difference. The liberal part of the Republican party is much more applicable to me. I don't like to see the two-party system die.

Interviewer: Dislike about the Republican party?

Respondent: I don't like the increased military spending. The ultraconservative factions. The often large influence by the very powerful large companies.

Interviewer: Anything else?

Respondent: That's all.

Interviewer: Like about Carter?

Respondent: He seems very sincere; that's possibly cosmetically done. I prefer his stands on abortion, and I admire him for standing up for that—not being snowed under by the Catholic Church.

Interviewer: Dislike about Carter?

Respondent: The main thing is not knowing enough about him. I think he's naive in international affairs.

---

[3] Since the full wording of the basic question sequence was given for the ramp attendant, an abbreviated form will be used for the photographer and subsequent examples.

Interviewer: Anything else?

Respondent: At times the whole southern mafia type of feeling upsets me. I'm also concerned about how his tax changes would affect my bracket.

Interviewer: Like about Ford?

Respondent: "Old Jer's too dumb to be crooked." That's facetious. I think he's very honest.

Interviewer: Anything else?

Respondent: He's certainly had enough practice so the country won't have to sit around and wait another one and a half years to figure out what's going on the way Carter will, I'm afraid.

Interviewer: Dislike about Ford?

Respondent: His increased military spending. His stand on abortion.

Interviewer: Anything else?

Respondent: That's all I can think of right now. Lackluster. Neither of them are terribly attractive.

In comparison with other respondents, this photographer was quite articulate—enough so that it would be risky to assert which of her many attitudes was most important in her voting decision. She delayed making her choice until mid-October and then concluded that she would vote for "Old Jer."

An interviewer in St. Louis talked with a 67-year-old woman who was born in central Europe and lived there until World War I. Her husband had been a tool-and-die maker until his retirement. She impressed the interviewer with her warmth and expansiveness.

Interviewer: Like about the Democratic party?

Respondent: They are more progressive; do more for the workers. They believe in the unions. Of course, the Teamsters are overdoing it. They are for socialized medicine to curb doctors' abuses; they charge too much.

Interviewer: Anything else?

Respondent: More for the people. I'd like to see Mondale for president and Carter VP. It's not true they're warmongers. It's not true they're big spenders. The Republicans are big spenders too. The Democrats gave us social security and medicare. It's not like we paid for it.

Interviewer: Dislike about the Democratic party?

Respondent: A few old fogies I don't care for: Hays, Wilbur Mills. I wish they would vote some old fogies out and vote some new, young ones in.

Interviewer: Like about the Republican party?

Respondent: There are some good progressive ones: Javits, Brooke, Percy.

Interviewer: Dislike about the Republican party?

Respondent: Too conservative. They should help the cities, not give money to foreign countries. That nutty Kissinger; they depend too much on him.

Interviewer: Anything else?

Respondent: Why do we have to have a foreign-born secretary of state? Of course, I'm foreign born.

Interviewer: Like about Carter?

Respondent: He promises to do something about unemployment and inflation. Government should do something about unemployment—teach a trade rather than pass out food stamps and welfare. He promises to pass socialized medicine; cut out bureaucrats, expensive do-nothing bureaucrats in Washington. He says he never told a lie. He shouldn't have interviewed *Playboy*. Carter's and Ford's stands are the same on abortion. He's not connected with the Washington Establishment. He'll work with Congress.

Interviewer: Dislike about Carter?

Respondent: No.

Interviewer: Like about Ford?

Respondent: No.

Interviewer: Dislike about Ford?

Respondent: I don't like his vetoes, his pardon of Nixon, so many things. He's a do-nothing president. He's for unemployment to curb the inflation. Always against progressiveness.

Interviewer: Anything else?

Respondent: He was the biggest hawk in Congress. Now he's talking about peace. He's picking on Carter on the Yugoslav issue; that means he would send troops to Yugoslavia. We're from Yugoslavia. Why should we support one communist regime against another? That makes no sense. We were there five years ago. No freedom. Americans are good politicians but bad statesmen. Europeans outwit us all the time.

In contrast with the balanced comments of the airline ramp attendant and the photographer, almost everything this woman said favored the Democrats. Not surprisingly, she had decided during the primaries to vote for Jimmy Carter.

Our next example is a 40-year-old housewife who lived in a frame house in Bellingham, Washington. A staunch Lutheran, she had been in the middle of a conversation about church affairs when the interviewer arrived.

Interviewer: Like about the Democratic party?

Respondent: One thing that has been good: tax loopholes are going to have to be checked a lot more, they are saying.

Interviewer: Dislike about the Democratic party?

Respondent: I feel that their platform at the convention just wanted to do too much, and it worries me. Too expensive.

Interviewer: Like about the Republican party?

Respondent: The fact that they didn't want to do quite as much. They didn't want to get quite as many new projects going.

Interviewer: Anything else?

Respondent: They feel that private enterprise should be encouraged more to solve the problems of inflation. It's a matter of degree with the two parties. They are not as much for price control either. Things would have to be pretty bad before I'd go for price controls. Republicans wouldn't be as hasty as Democrats on this.

Interviewer: Dislike about the Republican party?

Respondent: No.

Interviewer: Like about Carter?

Respondent: Certainly a personable guy. He seems so very human. The fact that he's a Christian—not that Ford isn't. He seems to be very honest.

Interviewer: Dislike about Carter?

Respondent: I think he hasn't had anywhere near the experience that President Ford has had. And he seems to want to start a lot of programs that would cost a lot of money.

Interviewer: Like about Ford?

Respondent: I think his experience above all. He was in Congress before. He has had to deal with national and international issues, and his record has been good.

Interviewer: Dislike about Ford?

Respondent: I wasn't happy about his having Dole. That's about all.

Things that she liked about the Republicans came as easily to the mind of this middle-class Westerner as attractive aspects of the Democratic party came to the St. Louis immigrant. Both could list things they liked about the opposition, but both made their own voting decisions very early. The St. Louis resident voted for Carter; the Washingtonian voted for Ford.

A 32-year-old Arkansan had grown up in a family of 10 children. She now had two of her own and juggled a busy schedule so as to care for them and work as a counselor in a Little Rock high school.

Interviewer: Like about the Democratic party?

Respondent: As a party, concern with the small person. The average person tends to see them as a party with strength.

Interviewer: Anything else?

Respondent: No. I'm not much for following politicians.

Interviewer: Dislike about the Democratic party?

Respondent: Even though it seems they're working for the poor excluded urban groups and ethnic groups, I still think they have a lot of work to be done on involvement on the part of women.

Interviewer: Like about the Republican party?

Respondent: No.

Interviewer: Dislike about the Republican party?

Respondent: Favoritism toward big business. It shows up in the way they like to run government.

Interviewer: Anything else?

Respondent: Just their feeling that money is power.

Interviewer: Like about Carter?

Respondent: He hasn't been president before. Therefore he hasn't had a chance to make errors. I'll give him a chance.

Interviewer: Anything else?

Respondent: Basic cut of honesty.

Interviewer: Dislike about Carter?

Respondent: I'm skeptical as most blacks about his being a southern white. I know that's prejudiced, but I just can't help it.

Interviewer: Like about Ford?

Respondent: I think his experience gives him the potential to do . . . a good job if he'd use his experience.

Interviewer: Anything else?

Respondent: That's his only asset.

Interviewer: Dislike about Ford?

Respondent: He's a Richard Nixon appointee.

Interviewer: Anything else?

Respondent: I could go on and scream about failure to act on positive social legislation and his general unconcern for the working class.

In spite of her generally pro-Democratic attitudes, her skepticism about Carter and positive view of President Ford's experience were enough to delay her decision until election day. Then she voted for Carter.

Then there was a high school graduate in Findlay, Ohio. He spent his working hours making pull tabs for the tops of beer cans.

Interviewer: Like about the Democratic party?

Respondent: No.

Interviewer: Dislike about the Democratic party?

Respondent: Just somewhat of the talk I've heard about Carter's opinions.

Interviewer: What did you hear?

Respondent: How he won't let the money get back to the people.

Interviewer: What money?

Respondent: The government money.

Interviewer: Anything else?

Respondent: No.

Interviewer: Like about the Republican party?

Respondent: I like what Ford has already done in office. Nothing in particular.

Interviewer: Dislike about the Republican party?

Respondent: No.

Interviewer: Like about Carter?

Respondent: When I first saw him on TV and such, he gave me the impression of a real go-getter—one who wanted to do everything.

Interviewer: Dislike about Carter?

Respondent: Just the talk I've heard.

Interviewer: What?

Respondent: All about taking money from people, the programs, cutting the budget.

Interviewer: Like about Ford?

Respondent: His past experience. And I think he shows his power more than Carter.

Interviewer: Dislike about Ford?

Respondent: No.

There is no way to know from the interview what this Findlay worker had heard about Jimmy Carter's spending plans, but he was disturbed about it. In any case, he was pro-Ford because of his positive, if amorphous, attitude about Ford's experience. He had decided to vote for President Ford before either convention.

Finally, there was a white-haired, 72-year-old lady who lived with her daughter's family in a small frame house outside Richmond, Virginia. Her education had stopped with the 10th grade, and her knowledge of politics was meager.

Interviewer: Like about the Democratic party?
Respondent: No.
Interviewer: Dislike about the Democratic party?
Respondent: They're different from the Republicans.
Interviewer: Like about the Republican party?
Respondent: No.
Interviewer: Dislike about the Republican party?
Respondent: No.
Interviewer: Like about Carter?
Respondent: No.
Interviewer: Dislike about Carter?
Respondent: No.
Interviewer: Like about Ford?
Respondent: No.
Interviewer: Dislike about Ford?
Respondent: No.

How this woman might have decided between the candidates, knowing only that there was some kind of difference between the parties makes for interesting speculation but nothing more. Along with many other uninformed persons, she didn't vote.

With seven examples, we are in a little better position to understand citizens' perceptions than when we had only one.[4] We have the views of two Easterners, two Midwesterners, two Southerners, and one Westerner. In a very close election, three respondents reported voting for Carter, three for Ford, and one did not vote. We certainly saw some common attitudes: that the Democratic party takes more interest in the underprivileged, that Republican fiscal policies are more advantageous for the middle class, admiration for Jimmy Carter's sincerity, and trust of Gerald Ford's experience. But what these seven interviews best illustrate are the various information levels among the electorate. The Long Island airline ramp attendant had an average

---

[4] This subsample of seven respondents also illustrates why it is risky to generalize on the basis of a small number of cases. For instance, our seven respondents included no one in their 20s or their 50s, no one from any of the Sun Belt states, and only two men.

FIGURE 8–1
Distribution of Information Levels, 1976

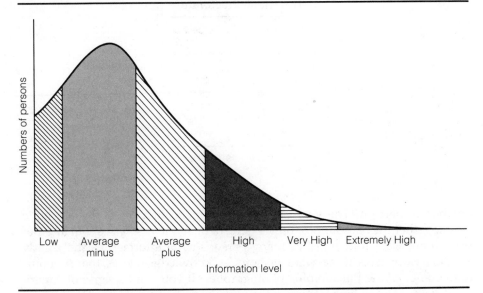

The distribution figure shows "Numbers of persons" on the vertical axis and "Information level" on the horizontal axis, with categories labeled: Low, Average minus, Average plus, High, Very High, Extremely High.

level of information, and the succeeding half-dozen examples illustrated—in decreasing order—the various levels of knowledge about politics.

The distribution of information across the electorate is stable over time. Figure 8–1 portrays the information levels these 1976 examples typify. The free-lance photographer from Philadelphia is in the *extremely high category*.[5] The Yugoslav immigrant living in St. Louis comes from the *very high* category. The housewife from Bellingham, Washington, displayed *high* knowledge. The school counselor in Little Rock was closer to typical and is in the middle of the *average plus* category. The ramp attendant from Long Island falls right between the *average plus* and the *average minus* ranges. The worker from the Findlay, Ohio, beer-can factory knows a little less than most American citizens and thus represents the *average minus* category. The elderly lady living outside Richmond, Virginia, showed a *low* level of information.[6]

The proportion of citizens falling into each of the information categories is shown in Table 8–1. Fully two thirds of all citizens are in either the average-minus or average-plus categories. The low and high categories account for

---

[5] While the language that follows will be varied to avoid six identically worded sentences, each of the examples comes from the middle of the range that it typifies. For a discussion of how the information-level categories were constructed, see Appendix A–8.1.

[6] There are three high categories and only one low category, because the names were chosen to indicate the category's distance from the mean. Since the mean information level itself is close to zero, there is room for only the average-minus and low categories between the mean and zero points.

TABLE 8–1

**Distribution of Information
Levels within Electorate**

Information Level	Percent of Electorate
Low	17.5%
Average minus	41.2
Average plus	25.5
High	11.7
Very high	3.2
Extremely high	0.9

Data source: 1976 Election
Study, Center for Political Studies.

another 29 percent. The very high and extremely high categories are quite rare; together they account for only 4 percent of all the responses. Put another way, there were four times as many persons as uninformed as the elderly Virginia woman as there were persons as knowledgeable as the St. Louis immigrant *and* the Philadelphia photographer. If you want a sense of Americans' political knowledge, think of the Ohio beer-can worker, the Long Island airline ramp attendant, and the Little Rock high school counselor. Two out of three Americans know this much about politics.

This finding—that *most* people know relatively little about politics—is one of the most familiar in public opinion research. But why should this be? Should we be alarmed by this? That depends on the theory one brings to bear.

If we accept a crude theory of democracy holding that every citizen should be fully informed in order to cast an intelligent vote, then the number of less knowledgeable citizens is upsetting. But as Walter Lippmann pointed out long ago, such a theory makes impossible demands on the average citizen. Imagine a man who is resolved to be fully informed. His day begins by listening to National Public Radio's "Morning Report" for an hour and a half, followed by watching NBC's "Today." After breakfast, he settles down to read both his hometown paper and the *New York Times* in their entirety. In late morning, he leaves for a luncheon to be followed by a speech on foreign policy and lingers afterward for conversations about local politics. Home by midafternoon, he plunges into the latest *U.S. News and World Report*, finishing barely in time for an hour and a half of National Public Radio's "All Things Considered." While eating supper, he watches Dan Rather on the "CBS Evening News" and then sits down to read a new book on the Middle East. A little weary after all this, he drifts off to sleep but not, of course, before watching the late evening television news and ABC's "Nightline." Among other things, our dutiful citizen does not have time to go shopping, play softball with his children, pursue any interests he might have in, say, Rembrandt or hard rock, or earn a living.

Alternatively, our theory holds that a state of events can be explained partly by internal structure and partly by external structure. In this instance, the level of information should be explained by how central politics is to a given citizen and how rich the informational environment is. We ought to expect variation from one citizen to another in the importance (and hence, centrality) of politics.

While politics is remote from the lives of many citizens,[7] there are some who are quite interested. In percentage terms, the proportions seem small. Only 4 percent fall into the very high and extremely high information categories. But with an adult population of 175 million, this translates to over 7 million citizens in these highest information categories. This is certainly a large enough cadre to provide leadership to our political dialogue. So, we need to ask about the informational environment. Is it rich enough to sustain those who are quite interested in politics as well as those whose political concerns are no more than average? And how do citizens' interactions with the informational environment affect their information levels? It is to these questions that we now turn.

SOURCES OF INFORMATION ABOUT POLITICS

Contact with Electronic and Print Sources

Most citizens acquire their information about politics through the mass media. Table 8–2 presents information about the extent of use of the mass media and about each medium's impact on information level. Television is the most widely used, as has been the case for some time. Eighty-nine percent report using television as a news source, in contrast to 72 percent who say they read newspapers and slightly less than half who report reading magazines. When one looks at the association between use of a news source and information level, however, the ordering is reversed.[8] Television, which is readily available even to those in the low information category, has the least impact on information level. Newspapers and especially magazines, used by fewer persons and requiring more effort, have a much stronger association with a respondent's level of information.

Why should print media have greater impact than television on what people know about politics? One possible explanation is that people are making different uses of the media. It might be that people are being entertained by watching soap operas, sports, and miniseries on television, while they are reading articles about politics in newspapers and magazines. This is a plausible explanation, but it can be rejected. When the comparison is limited to the

---

[7] For the less interested, less informed citizens, the crucial question is whether the strategies followed by the contending coalitions provide a choice they can make on the basis of their limited information.

[8] For an explanation of how we know two variables, in this case a news source and information level, are associated with each other, see the box on pp. 253–254.

TABLE 8–2
Information Level by Medium Used

		Information Level					
Medium	Low	Average Minus	Average Plus	High	Very High	Extremely High	Total
Magazines							
Not used......	78.6%	59.5%	42.3%	23.8%	17.3%	13.3%	51.8%
Used.........	21.4	40.5	57.7	76.2	82.7	86.7	48.2
Kendall's Tau–c = .39							
Newspapers							
Not used......	44.3	33.0	21.8	10.3	14.5	11.1	28.3
Used.........	55.7	67.0	78.2	89.7	85.5	88.9	71.7
Kendall's Tau–c = .23							
Television							
Not used......	27.4	11.7	4.8	4.3	2.9	0	11.2
Used.........	72.6	88.3	95.2	95.7	97.1	100.0	88.8
Kendall's Tau–c = .16							

Data source: 1976 Election Study, Center for Political Studies.

TABLE 8–3
Information Level by Use of Specific Sources

		Information Level					
Medium Use	Low	Average Minus	Average Plus	High	Very High	Extremely High	Total
Newspapers to read about national politics							
Never...........	35.4%	16.8%	6.7%	2.7%	0%	0%	14.8%
Rarely...........	32.9	24.9	12.6	7.7	6.9	0	20.0
Sometimes.......	27.4	42.1	40.0	28.6	36.4	33.3	37.2
Frequently	4.3	16.1	40.7	60.9	56.6	66.7	28.0
Kendall's Tau–c = .40							
Television to watch evening network news							
Never...........	15.2	9.6	6.7	4.8	10.4	11.1	9.2
Rarely...........	19.1	12.9	12.0	13.7	9.2	8.9	13.6
Sometimes.......	28.4	24.3	22.1	18.8	18.5	28.9	23.6
Frequently	37.2	53.2	59.2	62.7	61.8	51.1	53.6
Kendall's Tau–c = .12							

Data source: 1976 Election Study, Center for Political Studies.

prime information sources in both print and electronic media, the print advantage emerges even more strongly. Table 8–3 presents data on the relation between information level and the frequency with which persons read newspaper articles about national politics and watch the evening news shows on television. Again, nearly twice as many persons say they frequently watch network news as report frequently reading about national politics. But watching television news has relatively little impact on one's political knowledge, while reading about national politics has a substantial impact. Why so?

Bivariate Correlation = Association between Two Things

Bivariate correlation may be understood simply as an association between two things that take on different values. The prefix *bi* means two, and a variable is any mathematical term other than a constant. The fundamental idea in correlation is association as opposed to independence. Hence, bivariate correlation just means association between two variables.

The underlying ideas go back some time. The central notion of constant conjunction came from the 18th-century Scottish philosopher, David Hume. John Stuart Mill, the 19th-century British philosopher, extended this idea in his Method of Concomitant Variation. Essentially, if an increase in Variable A tends to produce an increase in Variable B, it may be taken as evidence that the two are associated.

In the accompanying table, information is associated with reading newspapers, but information level is independent of the hypothetical variable. There are two ways to see this. The first is to inspect the pattern of the cell entries (in this case, column percentages) and compare these to the characteristics of the total sample.

Let's take the newspaper example first. Of those in the low information column, only 55.7 percent read newspapers as compared to 71.7 percent in the total sample. This percentage increases to 67.0 in the average-minus column. By

		Information Level					
	Low	Average Minus	Average Plus	High	Very High	Extremely High	Total
Newspapers read?							
No	44.3%	33.0%	21.8%	10.3%	14.5%	11.1%	28.3%
Yes	55.7	67.0	78.2	89.7	85.5	88.9	71.7
Kendall's Tau–c = .23							
Hypothetical variable							
Present	56.1	59.9	59.1	58.0	62.1	60.9	58.9
Absent	43.9	40.1	40.9	42.0	37.9	39.1	41.1
Kendall's Tau–c = 0							

the time we get to the average-plus column, more people are reading newspapers (78.2 percent) than is the case in the total sample. In the high column, 89.7 percent read newspapers as compared to 71.7 percent overall. The percentage drops back just slightly in the very high column, but then comes back up in the extremely high column. As you move across all six magnitudes in the information-level scale, the percentage of those reading newspapers increases from 55.7 to 88.9, as compared to 71.7 for the total sample. The opposite is true for those who do not read newspapers. Therefore, you conclude that there is an association between reading newspapers and having a higher information level.

If you read across the rows for the hypothetical variable and compare the entries with the figures for the total sample, you see that the percentages in both rows are virtually the same as those for the total sample. Since it doesn't make any difference which column a given case falls into, we say that information level is independent of the hypothetical variable.

The second way to tell whether there is an association is to look at the summary measure of association (in this case, Kendall's Tau–*c*) printed beneath each of the tables. It is called a summary measure because it summarizes the strength of the correlation—you can see at a glance that .23 is greater than 0 in the example—but it doesn't tell you anything else. A value of 0 means that the two variables are totally independent of each other. A value of 1.0 (almost never seen with real-world political data) means there is complete association between the variables. Generally, you judge the strength of the association by seeing how far away it is from 0. You show that two variables are associated by showing that they are *not* independent of each other.

Different measures of correlation are used, depending on the nature of the data. For instance, Kendall's Tau–*c* was used in this example, but Pearson's *r* was used in Chapter 3. There are differences between various measures, but the fundamental idea is covariation.

Measures of correlation are often used to infer cause and effect. Before one concludes that there is causation, though, one must show both a statistical association and a logical reason for the relationship between the variables. There may be accidental statistical association. For example, the divorce rate in Manhattan might increase at the same time as wheat production in Kansas. Clearly, Kansas wheat does not cause Manhattan divorces. In the instance of newspaper reading, however, it is plausible to assume that one picks up information from reading newspapers. Since there is also a statistical association, we may say that we have shown cause and effect in this particular sense.

Television

The first reason why television conveys relatively little information is that there is simply less news on television. The evening network news shows last half an hour, but the average time per show actually devoted to news in one week was 21 minutes, 17 seconds.[9] Between 15 and 25 stories were carried on

---

[9] The data in this paragraph come from an analysis of the evening news shows from Monday, September 14, 1981, through Friday, September 18, 1981. No week is "typical," but there is no

each show; between 4 and 10 were on all three networks, and another half dozen were on two of them. Lead stories typically lasted a little over two minutes, and quick references later in the show might be as brief as 10 seconds. Only 10 stories in the week lasted longer than three minutes, and only 1 of these (on CBS) was a lead news story. The rest of the longer stories were features or analyses late in the newscasts. CBS, with the smallest number of stories and the most news time, had the longest average story. ABC, with a combination of longer analyses and brief references and the least total news time, had the shortest average story. These differences, however, were small variations within a similar news format. During the week, CBS presented 90 stories averaging 1 minute, 16 seconds; NBC, 94 stories averaging 1 minute, 10 seconds; ABC, 98 stories averaging 1 minute, 1 second.[10] With little more than a minute to devote to each story, the standard network format of the 1980s is essentially a headline service. It scarcely goes beyond the topics on the front page of a newspaper, and even these front-page items are covered in very abbreviated form.

Another consideration is the kind of news on which television chooses to focus. In an exhaustive study of all network newscasts between July 10 and election day, 1972, Richard Hofstetter (1976) distinguished between "political bias" (a tendency to favor one candidate or the other) and "structural bias" (a tendency to use a particular kind of story thought to be more appropriate for television). There was very little political bias but a lot of structural bias. The producers of television news had a preference for pictures over explanation. The consequences of this were pointed out by two other students of television news, Thomas Patterson and Robert McClure.

> One dimension of the election fits perfectly the networks' demand for good pictures. It is the "horse race" aspect of the run for the White House. For a presidential election is surely a super contest with all of the elements that are associated with spectacular sports events: huge crowds, rabid followers, dramatic do-or-die battles, winners and losers. It is this part of the election that the networks emphasize." (1976, pp. 40–41)

Their analyses showed that horse-race topics dominated political television in both 1972 and 1976. In 1976, 60 percent of television coverage was devoted to horse-race topics, 28 percent to substantive topics, and 12 percent fell into a miscellaneous category (Patterson, 1978, p. 184).

---

reason to think this September week was atypical. For similar findings from an analysis of network news coverage during the week of March 7–11, 1977, see Levin (1977). I should like to thank James Barnes for the 1981 data.

[10] There are certainly other possible uses of time. PBS's "MacNeil-Lehrer NewsHour" begins each program with a news summary and then follows with newsmaker interviews and focus segments, typically covering three or four stories each evening. NPR's "All Things Considered" has headlines at the beginning of each half hour, then follows with extended coverage of just a few stories. When she said farewell as host of "All Things Considered" on September 8, 1986, Susan Stamberg said that "All Things Considered" had attempted nothing less than redefining news reporting. Both "All Things Considered" and the "MacNeil-Lehrer NewsHour" have succeeded brilliantly in showing what can be done with alternative formats.

Comparison of Television and Newspaper Coverage

Doris Graber (1976; 1980) studied television and newspaper coverage during the 1968, 1972, and 1976 presidential campaigns. During the last 30 days of each campaign, she obtained and analyzed 20 newspapers published in various parts of the country. For 1972, a similar content analysis was done of videotapes of the network newscasts; for 1968 and 1976, story logs (which contain the same information in more abbreviated form) were analyzed.

The first cut in her coding procedure separated issue coverage from discussion of the qualities of the presidential candidates. For the press, in 1968, the ratio of issues to personal qualities was 44 to 56, devoting greater attention to the candidates but still more or less in balance. In 1972, however, she found that press attention to issues had slipped and was about the same as that for television. The ratio of issues to qualities was 39 to 61. Both newspapers and television were carrying about three issue stories for every five dealing with the candidates.

The issue coverage was further analyzed into five categories. Three of these were roughly the same as the issue areas we have been discussing. The fourth dealt with what might be called general politics: the institutions of government, the incumbent's and the challenger's policies, ethics, opinion polls, and so on. The last dealt with campaign stories. The proportions of television and newspaper coverage in each of these five categories are shown in Table 8–4.

Professor Graber's research supports several generalizations. First, relatively little journalistic attention is being paid to the policy areas. Since 36 percent and 37 percent of all 1972 press and television coverage, respectively, went to issues, the figures in Table 8–4 mean that only 7.5 percent of all press coverage and only 4.9 percent of all television coverage were devoted to international involvement in 1972. Second, the bulk of television coverage has gone to campaign topics. (Graber's estimate of 57 percent of 1976 coverage going to campaign topics is remarkably similar to the McClure-Patterson estimate of 60 percent devoted to horse-race coverage that year.) Third, perhaps most surprising in view of the different capacities of the two media, newspapers have devoted less and less attention to the three policy areas. In a study of *New York Times* coverage of the 1980 campaign, Graber found that the proportion of their space devoted to campaign stories stayed about the same as in 1976; but the proportion devoted to general politics increased, and the space given to foreign policy and economics declined from 1976. The amount of space devoted to the three policy areas by the *New York Times* was less than a third of the space being devoted to them by newspapers a dozen years earlier (1982a, p. 4).

The televised debates between Gerald Ford and Jimmy Carter in 1976 (and presumably the Reagan-Anderson, Reagan-Carter, and Reagan-Mondale debates) provided an important exception to the media tendency to avoid issues. The first 1976 debate stressed economics, the second foreign policy, and

TABLE 8–4

Issue Coverage in Television and Newspapers

Coverage, by Medium	1968	1972	1976
Television			
International involvement	11.5%	13.1%	15.8%
Economic management	3.2	6.1	8.8
Social benefits and civil liberties	4.6	4.6	5.9
General politics	23.9	17.0	12.2
Campaign	56.9	59.2	57.2
Newspapers			
International involvement	26.3%	20.9%	16.9%
Economic management	16.4	12.4	11.9
Social benefits and civil liberties	13.9	7.5	6.4
General politics	23.7	23.7	20.0
Campaign	19.6	35.4	44.9

Source: Doris Graber, *The Mass Media and Politics* (Washington, D.C.: Congressional Quarterly Press, 1980).

the third a mix of issues. The postdebate coverage did not maintain this focus. Instead, more attention was paid to the familiar questions of personality, performance, and who the media felt had "won" the debate.[11] Even so, issue coverage was estimated at 37 percent for both television and newspapers, a figure substantially higher than that for normal campaign content (Sears & Chaffee, 1978).

Print Media

If television has the advantage of vivid pictures, writers have the advantage of being able to discuss topics at sufficient length to convey detailed information. Many of them—especially the best—worry about what to write. Thus David Broder, the *Washington Post*'s thoughtful political analyst; asked:

> Where do the candidates come from? What motivates them to want to be president? . . . When they have a decision to make, do they pull in a big group of people or go with whatever seems to be the consensus or do they go off by themselves and meditate on what they should do? . . . Are they really open for questioning, or do they go into a debate or a press conference to defend their own views? (Barber, 1978, p. 134)

Theodore White, "The Making of the President" series author, has been called by James David Barber "our age's most influential artist of pointillistic journalism: microscopic fact-dots blended by the mind's eye to compose a

---

[11] The media concentration on the identity of the "winners" had a stronger effect on citizens' judgments about who did better than did the debates themselves. The longer the time between the debate itself and a survey about the "winner," the greater the proportion of respondents who named the media-identified "winner" as the candidate who did better.

meaningful conglomerate." All wordsmiths do not compose their phrases with the skill of a Theodore White, but newspapers, magazines, and books do provide more "microscopic fact-dots" than the electronic media. This is reflected in the stronger relationship between information level and the use of print media.

Another reason for the greater impact of print is the degree of attention it requires. Television is regularly reported to be the most used medium, but what does "watching television" mean? In one careful study of network newscasts, viewers filled out diaries indicating whether they gave the program full attention or partial attention or whether they were out of the room. During the two-week period of the study, 59 percent of adult Americans did not give full attention to a single evening network program, and only 14 percent gave full attention to more than four newscasts.[12] In contrast, 73 percent reported reading two or more newspapers over any two *days* in the same two-week period (Stevenson, 1978, p. 12, Tables 1–3).

Robert Stevenson related this difference between wide apparent use of television and rather casual actual use to the contrasting skills required by television and print media.

> Television, of course, is ideally suited for . . . passive surveillance. It requires (or allows) no personal selection of content like a newspaper does, no active cognitive processing of content as reading does, and no imagination to create in the mind a picture of the event. For people who lack the mental skills to read a newspaper or magazine efficiently or the physical acuity to read easily or the interest to profit from selective reading, television is a psychologically gratifying experience. (Stevenson, 1978, p. 21)

Doris Graber echoes this as a result of her comparison of newspapers and television. "The reader who finds press coverage confusing as well as depressing can . . . turn to television for a simpler, clearer, and more encouraging image of the unfolding electoral scene" (Graber, 1976, p. 302).

Thus the content of newspapers and televison, and the cognitive processes engaged by the print and electronic media, provide explanations for the greater impact of print media. The print sources contain somewhat more stories about complex topics and have sufficient space to develop more in the way of analysis. Therefore, readers must make use of more involved cognitive processes to comprehend information from the print media.

COGNITIVE INTERACTION WITH THE INFORMATIONAL ENVIRONMENT

If the content of the informational environment provides one reason why individuals know as much as they do, a second is to be found in the extent of

---

[12] Those who most frequently watched the network newscasts tended to be over 60 and to have grade school educations. (There *is* a reason for all those false teeth, laxative, and sedative commercials you see while watching network newscasts.)

cognitive interaction with that environment. A person's cognitive structure is intimately related to the informational environment in at least two ways.

First, an individual continuously monitors the environment to pick up cues: Attention is directed to particular parts of the environment by a perceptual schema (the aspect of cognitive structure that guides one's perception and makes it more likely that some things will be noticed and others neglected) (Neisser, 1976). Because of this continual monitoring, the informational environment provides a medium that supports a cognitive structure as a person interacts with it, much as the air supports an aircraft as it moves through that medium. If the environment is rich in information, the person has the opportunity to acquire as many facts as can be absorbed.

The ability to absorb information is the second way in which cognitive structure and informational environment are interrelated. The more developed one's cognitive structure, the easier it is to understand new information as it is acquired. Any incoming cue is related to an existing cognitive category that provides contextual information to interpret the cue. Only then does the cue take on meaning for the individual. As a consequence, cognitive structure accentuates (or retards) one's ability to extract information from one's environment. *Not only will a person with a well-developed cognitive structure be more likely to pick up information, but that person will be better able to understand the meaning of the newly acquired information.*

Table 8–5 shows the relation between information level and three measures of the extent to which one is engaged in the informational environment. The more education people have, the more likely they are to have the cognitive skills to pick up cues from the environment. The greater the frequency with which individuals follow public affairs, the more likely they are to monitor campaign information. And the more interested people are in a specific campaign, the more likely they are to follow it.

We can see from Table 8–5 that the two factors that directly measure a tendency to be involved with the informational environment, following public affairs and interest in the presidential campaign, have stronger relationships with information level than does education. Therefore, we can infer that each of these three factors serves as an indicator of a generalized tendency to monitor the informational environment and that the more closely citizens follow politics, the more likely that they will be among the better informed.[13]

Now we have two explanations of why some citizens are well informed and some are poorly informed. The first has to do with how much information a given news source contains and the types of cognitive processes that are activated by use of that news source. The second has to do with how intensively the citizen monitors whatever news sources are available. Which of these is the stronger explanation?

This is a little difficult to answer. To some degree, the processes operate jointly. One's knowledge is increased both by an information-rich environ-

---

[13] Table 11–2 shows that these factors have had similar effects over time.

TABLE 8–5
Information Level by Involvement with Information Environment

		Information Level					
	Low	Aver-age Minus	Aver-age Plus	High	Very High	Extremely High	Total
Education							
Grade school.	27.6%	19.6%	11.9%	6.7%	7.6%	5.9%	17.0%
Some high school	20.4	17.5	12.2	7.3	0	5.9	14.8
High school graduate . . .	41.5	39.0	34.8	28.6	13.5	9.8	36.1
Some college	6.0	15.1	20.4	22.1	28.1	37.3	16.3
College graduate	4.5	8.9	20.6	35.3	50.8	41.2	15.8
Kendall's Tau–*c* = .28							
Frequency with which respondent follows public affairs							
Hardly at all.	32.3	13.3	4.0	1.2	2.3	4.4	12.0
Only now and then	30.8	23.2	11.1	6.8	5.2	0	18.4
Some of the time.	27.2	34.6	33.9	24.7	28.3	17.8	31.6
Most of the time.	9.7	28.9	50.9	67.3	64.2	77.8	38.0
Kendall's Tau–*c* = .37							
Respondent's interest in political campaign							
Not much interested	52.6	21.5	8.5	6.4	7.7	0	21.2
Somewhat interested. . . .	39.1	49.7	40.4	29.6	30.1	23.5	42.3
Very much interested . . .	8.3	28.8	51.1	64.0	62.3	76.5	36.5
Kendall's Tau–*c* = .40							

Data source: 1976 Election Study, Center for Political Studies.

ment *and* by more closely monitoring whatever information is available. A further complication is that at least one news source, television, seems to transmit information best to those least able to pay attention. Still, there are a couple of clues. For one thing, the relationships between information level and being engaged in the informational environment are generally stronger than those for use of specific news sources. For another, when one controls the relationship between information level and reliance on a good news source for whether or not the respondent is paying attention, the relation drops sharply.[14] The opposite does not occur. Therefore, how closely a citizen monitors the informational environment appears to be more important than how rich a given information source is.

---

[14] For example, the relation for the total sample between information level and reading about politics in newspapers (Tau-*c*) is .40. For those who said they were not much interested in the campaign, this relation drops to .19; for those who said they hardly ever followed public affairs, this same relation drops to .10. No matter how good the news source, if people don't pay attention, they aren't going to pick up that much information.

TIME AND POLITICAL KNOWLEDGE

Internal structure—at least, the amount of information arrayed within a cognitive pattern—is dependent on external structure. Are citizen's cognitions also subject to temporal effects? The answer is yes but under some special circumstances.

The first is some dramatic event in the campaign itself. For example, when Senator Thomas Eagleton was dropped as the Democratic vice presidential candidate in 1972, this made some difference in how presidential candidate George McGovern was perceived. The special circumstances in this case were obvious. Not only was the resignation of a vice presidential candidate unprecedented but since the event took place so early in the campaign, a good many persons still did not know much about Senator McGovern. For these reasons, Eagleton's resignation and the context in which it occurred created a vivid first impression.

Another instance of dramatic events that altered cognitive content comes from 1964. During October of that contest between Lyndon Johnson and Barry Goldwater, certain domestic issues (law and order, alleged corruption, social security, unemployment) were gaining in salience (prominence) while references to war and peace were declining. The increasingly salient domestic issues were being discussed by the candidates, and there hadn't been much consequential foreign news for a while. Then, within 48 hours, Nikita Khrushchev was deposed as premier of the Soviet Union, the Labour party won an unexpected election victory in Great Britain, and China exploded an atomic device. This caused foreign affairs to gain in salience at the expense of domestic campaign topics.

The dramatic events led to an explosion of information on a topic (foreign developments bearing on the chances of war and peace) that was important to voters and about which they knew relatively little. Ordinarily, citizens would have a fair amount of information about topics important to them and would not care about other matters. Both these circumstances tend to inhibit communication. In this instance, new information about a consequential matter suddenly became available. Therefore, international affairs became more salient to many voters.

A less dramatic example is an event or set of events that provides information inconsistent with previously held beliefs. For instance, Ronald Reagan's performance in the first debate with Walter Mondale in 1984 was inconsistent with a widely held perception that the President was confident and self-assured. This caused some doubt until his joke about age in the second debate provided evidence consistent with the existing favorable view of President Reagan.

Perhaps the most important temporal effect takes place over the course of the campaign. For the electorate as a whole, there is no relationship between time and citizens' information level. Well-informed citizens are likely to be as knowledgeable in early September as they are on the day before election, and uninformed persons are not likely to be knowledgeable at any particular time. There is one category of citizens, however, whose information level does tend to increase as the campaign progresses. These are persons who have attended high school, who say they are somewhat interested in the campaign, and who follow public affairs some of the time—persons, in other words, who fall into the *middle* of the scales related to monitoring the informational environment.

If one looks at those who have attended college, who say they are very much interested in the campaign, and who follow public affairs most of the time, there is no relation between time and information level. This grouping is constantly monitoring the informational environment, is likely to have picked up a good many cues before the campaign began, and hence is unlikely to learn much new information during the campaign. Nor is there any relation between time and information level for those who didn't go beyond grade school, who say they are not much interested in the campaign, and who follow public affairs only now and then if they do so at all. Politics is so remote from their lives that campaigners face insurmountable communication thresholds in trying to reach them. But a temporal effect can be found for those who are average in their receptivity to political communications, who are neither avid followers of politics nor among those who ignore public affairs altogether. For those who fall into the middle of all three scales, there is at least a moderate relationship ($r = .19$) between the passage of time in the campaign and information level.[15]

It would be a mistake to regard this temporal effect as either strong or negligible. The essential change is that as the campaign progresses, there are fewer persons with a low information level and more with an average-plus information level. This does not mean that a great deal of information is being communicated; rather, the campaign is more than a hollow ritual. When we reviewed the stages of a campaign in Chapter 3, we saw that proposals to shorten presidential campaigns did not take into account the planning and organization necessary to conduct a campaign on a subcontinental scale. To this we can now add that if campaigns were to end a month earlier, there would be a larger number of uninformed citizens and they would likely be less at ease with the electoral choice they are asked to make.

SUMMARY

In this chapter, we have seen that internal cognitive structure is dependent on external informational environment. Most citizens know relatively little about politics, but there are some who are quite well informed.

---

[15] It was necessary to isolate those in the middle of all three scales in order to find this relationship. The correlations between time and information level for those in the middle categories of the individual scales were all significant but lower. For those who attended high school but did not go on to college, $r = .05$. For those who said they were somewhat interested in the campaign, $r = .06$. For those who said they followed public affairs some of the time, $r = .10$. There were no significant correlations for those on the high or low ends of any of the three scales.

The well informed are more likely to use print sources, which contain more information to begin with and require more involved cognitive processes for comprehension. The well informed are also likely to be those who monitor the informational environment most closely because of their education or their interest in politics. The degree to which one is engaged in the informational environment is a stronger explanation of information level than the use of print sources.

Finally, time does matter. Neither the very interested nor the quite uninterested learn much as a campaign progresses; but citizens with middling involvement tend to increase their understanding.

Chapter 9

Presidential Choice

In this chapter, we deal directly with the citizen's use of knowledge to choose between presidential candidates. Whereas the last chapter dealt with how much the citizen knew about politics, our concern now shifts to how this information is organized into attitudes about various political objects and to the relation of these attitudes to voting choice. There are many areas of life in which attitudes are weak predictors of action, but voting is not one of them. Especially when there are well-developed attitudes, one can predict with considerable confidence how citizens will vote. Consequently, if you understand attitudes, you will be able to understand the citizen response to campaign strategies.

SALIENCE, PARTISAN VALENCE, AND IMPORTANCE

Three attitudinal properties are especially helpful in understanding voting. The first of these is *salience*, the prominence of an attitudinal object. The more publicized a topic, the more likely that it will be salient for the citizen. The more salient it is, the more likely the citizen is to have an attitude about it. For example, an American would have been much more likely to have an attitude about Southeast Asia during the Vietnam War, when the media were filled with information about it, than in the 1980s, when the topic is much less salient.

The second relevant attitudinal property is *valence*. One's feelings about an attitudinal object may be positive, neutral, or negative. For example, a citizen may have a very positive attitude about one candidate and a slightly negative attitude about another or a positive attitude about a candidate's trustworthiness and a negative attitude about the same candidate's intelligence. Individuals react positively or negatively to a candidate according to the valence of each one's attitudes about that candidate. (Remember that the ability of chemical ions to combine depends on the valence of each ion. When used with attitudes, valence also suggests a tendency to react positively or negatively.)

In the case of vote choice, we are not concerned with positive or negative attitudes per se but with how these attitudes about specific political objects sum to form a *partisan valence*. If one person had positive attitudes about the Republican candidate and negative attitudes about the Democratic candidate, we would say that this person's attitudes were pro-Republican. If another had negative attitudes about the Republican candidate's views on international involvement and positive attitudes about the Democratic candidate's views on economic management, we would say that these attitudes were pro-Democratic. If a third person had positive attitudes about the Republican candidate's personality and positive attitudes about the Democratic candidate's stands on issues, we would say that this partisan valence was mixed.

Finally, we are interested in *importance*. Strictly speaking, this is not an attitudinal property but the link between the citizen's attitude and the vote that is cast. An attitude that is salient and quite favorable to one party is usually important, although not always. Voters may base their decisions on other attitudes, or they may believe that a given issue is not one over which a president will have much influence. In either situation, the attitude would not be important in vote choice.

We want to separate these three properties because salience, partisan valence, and importance may vary independent of each other. As we shall see, attitudes about economic management were salient in 1980 and 1984 as were general attitudes about candidates and issues in 1976, but neither party enjoyed anything more than the barest advantage in these categories. Attitudes about persons in the parties (other than the candidates) were decidedly pro-Republican in 1984 and decidedly pro-Democratic in 1976 but were not salient in either campaign. Attitudes about the public records of the candidates were important in 1976 and 1980, although they were not too salient and only slightly favored Gerald Ford and Ronald Reagan. Attitudes about agricultural policy have never been salient in modern times, have strongly favored the Democrats in every election except 1968 and 1980, and have been important only to the small proportion of voters engaged in farming. So when someone says that a given attitude is consequential in an election, we must ask whether it is consequential because it is salient, because it favors one party rather than the other, because it is related to the voting decision, or some combination of the three.[1]

The same responses that we used to analyze information level in Chapter 8 provide data to analyze these attitudinal properties. The responses are classified by the category of attitude object, at first the broad categories—candidates, parties, and issues—then more detailed categories that allow more specific analysis. The salience of a category of attitude objects is measured by the proportion of all comments falling into the category. The larger the proportion of comments, the more salient the category. Partisan valence is measured by the proportion of comments in the category favorable to the Democrats. The proportion of comments in the category favoring the Republicans is, of course, the complement of the pro-Democratic percentage, so the single figure tells us which party has how much of an advantage. The higher the figure, the better things are for the Democrats; the lower the figure, the better things are for the Republicans. The importance of the category in the voting decision is measured by maximum likelihood estimates obtained through probit analysis. (See box.) The probit model gives us a very powerful explanation of presidential choice. Between 85 and 90 percent of the individual cases are correctly predicted in the solution for each election year.

Maximum Likelihood Estimate = Best Guess

A literal reduction of the phrase "maximum likelihood estimate" is "best guess." For our purposes in this chapter, it is the best guess about the importance of an attitude in determining a citizen's vote. The details of the maximum likelihood estimate (MLE) are a little technical, but three ideas are all that are necessary to understand the meaning.

First, in common with all statistics derived from surveys, MLE is an *estimate*. When you read of a survey that finds, for instance, that 40 percent intend to vote for George Bush if Richard Gephardt is his opponent, this 40 percent figure rests on a "confidence limit," say ±3 percent, and a "level of significance," usually 19 chances out of 20. Therefore, the full meaning of "40 percent" is: "We estimate that in 19 chances out of 20, the proportion of all population members intending to vote for Reagan will fall between 37 percent and 43 percent." In a similar way, the figure given for the MLE is the best statistical guess about the relative importance of the attitude in determining the vote. The higher the MLE, the more important the attitude.

---

[1] A number of well-known explanations of voting are based on summary measures of the effects of attitude components. Frequently, these summary measures are obtained by multiplying a measure of partisan valence by a measure of importance (Stokes, Campbell & Miller, 1958; Comparative State Election Project, 1973). These provide good explanations of the effects of attitudes on vote choice, because choice can be affected if one party has a decided advantage, if the attitude is strongly related to choice, or if both conditions are present. But one cannot tell whether partisan valence or importance is causing the summary measure to go up or down.

The second basic idea is that this is a *multivariate* procedure. The bivariate correlation explained in the box in the preceding chapter was an association between two variables, presumably one cause and one effect. A multivariate study permits analysis of multiple variables at the same time. Controls are exercised over other possible causes. For example, we can look at how attitudes about candidates, parties, and issues affect voting. The multivariate analysis allows us to isolate the effect of candidate attitudes while controlling for the effects of party and issue attitudes, to isolate the effect of party attitudes while controlling for the effects of candidate and issue attitudes, and to isolate the effect of issue attitudes while controlling for the effects of candidate and party attitudes.

The third basic idea is that probit analysis, from which the MLEs are derived, is a *curvilinear* rather than a linear procedure. This just means that the data points are assumed to fit a curve rather than a straight line. Linear regression, the form of multivariate analysis most commonly used in political science, assumes that the data points will lie on a straight line. Using linear regression and probit analysis, identical solutions were calculated with 1976, 1980, and 1984 data. With 1976 data, the linear regression explained 47 percent of the variance in vote; the probit analysis explained 73 percent of the variance in vote. With 1980 data, the linear regression explained 51 percent of the variance; the probit analysis explained 80 percent of the variance. With 1984 data, the linear regression explained 57 percent of the variance; the probit analysis explained 84 percent of the variance. Since the probit predictions were half again more powerful than those obtained from the linear regressions, the curvilinear assumption is clearly more appropriate for voting data.

The MLEs reported in this chapter are standardized. (This is why the MLE columns are headed MLE*.) For additional discussion and the method used to standardize the probit estimates, see Appendix A–9.1.

CANDIDATES, PARTIES, AND ISSUES

As a first broad approximation, let's look at the pattern formed by the mean figures for attitudes about candidates, parties, and issues. These data are presented in Figure 9–1. The ordering of the three categories is the same for both salience and importance. Issues come first, then candidates, and then— a long way back—come parties. Partisan valence is rather different. The strongest partisan advantage over time goes to the Republicans because of the relative attractiveness of their candidates. Issues, on the other hand, tend to help the Democrats; and the Democrats derive a slight advantage from the less important attitudes about parties.

Figure 9–2 presents the data for these three broad categories over time. There is, to be sure, election-to-election variation. The most pronounced variation is to be found in partisan valence. Democrats had advantages in all three attitude categories in 1964, and the Republicans did in 1968 (when analysis is confined to Nixon and Humphrey voters) and 1972. (It would be remarkable if

FIGURE 9–1

Broad Attitudes and Presidential Choice, Mean Figures 1952–1984

Category		Salience percent total	Partisan valence percent pro-D	Importance MLE*
Candidates		38.3	43.2	1.60
Parties		12.3	51.9	.71
Issues		49.4	53.4	2.16

Explanation of figure: *Salience* is measured by the proportion of the total comments dealing with the attitude object. It is indicated by the total length of the bar. The longer the bar, the more salient the category. *Partisan valence* is measured by the proportion of comments favorable to the Democrats. The farther the bar is to the left, the more favorable to the Democrats. The farther to the right, the more favorable to the Republicans. *Importance*, the relation of the attitude category to vote choice, is measured by a standardized maximum likelihood estimate. (See box on pp. 266–267.) This is indicated in the figure by shade. If a bar is black, the attitude category is very important. If a bar is dark gray, the attitude category is important. If a bar is light gray, the attitude category is somewhat important. If a bar is hollow, the attitude category is not significantly related to vote choice.

Data source: 1952 through 1984 Election Studies, Survey Research Center/Center for Political Studies.

we did not find something of this kind, since there was a Democratic land-slide in 1964 and a Republican landslide in 1972.)

There is also some variation in the salience and importance of the attitude categories. For example, attitudes about candidates were least important in 1952[2] and most important in 1976. But the general pattern is sufficiently stable that individual elections can be explained on the basis of how they depart from the normal pattern, rather than discovering a new pattern in each election. It appears that the interests of the electorate set some bounds for election-to-election variation. Fluctuation takes place between these bounds.

There have been two changes in this general pattern since the 1950s. The clearest is a decline in both salience and importance of attitudes about the parties. These attitudes have never been as salient as those about candidates and issues. But they have declined from even this low plateau, and they have been less consequential in recent elections than when Dwight Eisenhower defeated Adlai Stevenson. There was also a noticeable increase in the importance of attitudes about issues in 1980 and in the salience and importance of these attitudes in 1984. It's still too early to know whether this latter development marks a long-term change or is simply due to unusual features of these two elections.

By far the most noteworthy finding in this analysis is the relative impor-

---

[2] This finding is itself worth noting. The 1952 election is usually dismissed as a deviating election, resulting in large part from General Eisenhower's considerable personal popularity. The probit analysis indicates that attitudes about issues and parties were both more important that year.

FIGURE 9–2   Broad Attitudes and Presidential Choice

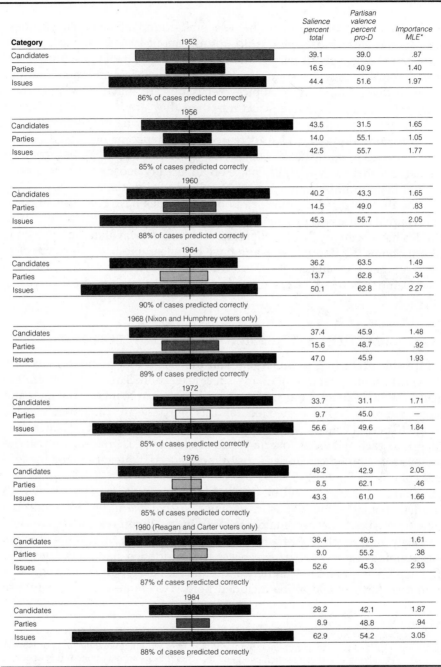

Category		Salience percent total	Partisan valence percent pro-D	Importance MLE*
1952				
Candidates		39.1	39.0	.87
Parties		16.5	40.9	1.40
Issues		44.4	51.6	1.97
86% of cases predicted correctly				
1956				
Candidates		43.5	31.5	1.65
Parties		14.0	55.1	1.05
Issues		42.5	55.7	1.77
85% of cases predicted correctly				
1960				
Candidates		40.2	43.3	1.65
Parties		14.5	49.0	.83
Issues		45.3	55.7	2.05
88% of cases predicted correctly				
1964				
Candidates		36.2	63.5	1.49
Parties		13.7	62.8	.34
Issues		50.1	62.8	2.27
90% of cases predicted correctly				
1968 (Nixon and Humphrey voters only)				
Candidates		37.4	45.9	1.48
Parties		15.6	48.7	.92
Issues		47.0	45.9	1.93
89% of cases predicted correctly				
1972				
Candidates		33.7	31.1	1.71
Parties		9.7	45.0	—
Issues		56.6	49.6	1.84
85% of cases predicted correctly				
1976				
Candidates		48.2	42.9	2.05
Parties		8.5	62.1	.46
Issues		43.3	61.0	1.66
85% of cases predicted correctly				
1980 (Reagan and Carter voters only)				
Candidates		38.4	49.5	1.61
Parties		9.0	55.2	.38
Issues		52.6	45.3	2.93
87% of cases predicted correctly				
1984				
Candidates		28.2	42.1	1.87
Parties		8.9	48.8	.94
Issues		62.9	54.2	3.05
88% of cases predicted correctly				

— denotes insignificant figure.

Explanation of figure: *Salience* is measured by the proportion of the total comments dealing with the attitude object. It is indicated by the total length of the bar. The longer the bar, the more salient the category. *Partisan valence* is measured by the proportion of comments favorable to the Democrats. The farther the bar is to the left, the more favorable to the Democrats. The farther to the right, the more favorable to the Republicans. *Importance,* the relation of the attitude category to vote choice, is measured by a standardized maximum likelihood estimate. (See box on pp. 266–267.) This is indicated in the figure by shade. If a bar is black, the attitude category is very important. If a bar is dark gray, the attitude category is important. If a bar is light gray, the attitude category is somewhat important. If a bar is hollow, the attitude category is not significantly related to vote choice.

Data source: 1952 through 1984 Election Studies, Survey Research Center/Center for Political Studies.

tance of issues.[3] This is remarkable on several grounds. First of all, the questions (quoted early in Chapter 8) do not ask about issues; they ask for the respondents' views about parties and candidates. But the largest part of the answers concern issues. Second, the mass media give less attention to issues than they do to "horse-race" topics. Yet issues are much more important within the citizens' cognitive structures than they are in the informational environment from which citizens pick up their cues. Later in this chapter, we shall note conditions that give increased prominence or decreased prominence to issues in particular elections. These are consequential, but it is vital to remember this variation takes place on an already substantial base. Issues have not been unimportant in *any* election included in the analysis.

Of the three broad categories, candidate attitudes have been salient, usually favorable to the Republicans, and very important in voting choices. Party attitudes have been much less salient, have sometimes favored the Democrats and sometimes the Republicans, and have been less important in recent elections than they were in the 1950s. Issue attitudes have been salient, favorable to the Democrats in six of the nine elections, and very important in voting choices.

REACTION AND CHOICE IN SPECIFIC ELECTIONS

Useful as the preceding sections' generalizations are, they do not take us very far toward the understanding of any specific election. The categories are too broad to allow us to trace much of the linkage between coalition strategies and citizen response. What is needed for this purpose are categories specific enough to permit concrete statements yet inclusive enough so that statements falling into each will occur over a series of elections. Therefore, we will decompose the 3 broad categories into 16 more specific categories (see the left-hand column in Figure 9–3).

Candidate references will be divided into seven classes. Two deal with attitudes about the candidates' experience. *Record and incumbency* concerns perceptions about the candidates' records in public offices they have held previously and, much more frequently, comments about an incumbent when he is running for reelection. *Experience* is a shortened name for nonpublic office experience; military experience, diplomatic background, campaign ability, and so forth would all be included here. Two more categories are also

---

[3] The salience of issues reflects some coding decisions. References to liberal or conservative policies are regarded as issue comments. Similarly, a person who mentions business or labor is assumed to be talking about economic management; when blacks are mentioned, it is assumed that the reference is to civil liberties; when farmers are mentioned, agriculture. The six-component solution devised by Donald Stokes assigns references to liberal or conservative postures to "parties as managers of government," and all references to groups to a separate "group-related" component. When choosing between candidates, parties, and issues and in view of the vocabulary a respondent might be expected to use, I think it is appropriate to code the references to liberalism, conservatism, or groups as issue references.

office related. *Management* deals with executive capacity: how the candidate would be likely to run the government if elected, as well as more general references to leadership. *Intelligence* is given a broad enough definition to include comments about the candidate's education and practical capacity as well as wisdom as such. The other specific categories relate more to judgments about the individual than about executive ability as such. *Trust* touches upon confidence, honesty, and any specific comments bearing on the candidate's integrity. *Personality* includes any comments about image and mannerisms, such as warmth, aloofness, and dignity. The *general* category includes three classes of comments: those that are too general to be assigned to one of the specific categories ("He's a good man," or "I like him"), statements on such topics as the candidate's age or wealth or family that did not occur often enough to justify the creation of separate, specific categories, and comments that occur relatively frequently in a single election (for instance, references to Mondale's having selected a woman to run for vice president in 1984) but are absent in other elections.

The relatively infrequent party comments were divided into two classes. Attitudes about *people in the party* concern all party members other than the presidential candidates: incumbent presidents not running for reelection, prominent senators and governors, party workers, and so on. All other party comments were categorized as *party affect*. These included trust of one party or the other, references to party factions, and the importance of achieving or preventing a party victory.

There were seven categories of issue attitudes. Four dealt with the same policy areas we considered in Chapter 3 in connection with the issue groups that made up the electoral coalitions: *international involvement, economic management, social benefits,*and *civil liberties*. Two more are minor policy areas. *Natural resources* may be thought of as a special case of economic management in which regulatory policy is used in the areas of the environment and energy. *Agriculture* policy has been a special case of social benefits in which the beneficiaries were the farmers, although this may be changing as farmers become a smaller proportion of the labor force and food costs rise. As with the candidate comments, there was a *general* issue category composed of comments too broad to fit into any specific class. These included references to the policy stands of the parties, liberalism or conservatism, and comments about "domestic policy" without any indication as to which domestic policy was meant.(For further information, see Appendix A–9.2)

Decomposition of the three broad categories into sixteen relatively specific categories permits a number of things. The essential difference is that we are trading the simple generalizations derived from the three-component solution for a more detailed understanding that can be obtained by inspecting the more specific categories. The detailed solution will not support statements that candidate attitudes usually favor Republicans or that issue attitudes favor the Democrats more often than not. Instead, we see that some candidate attributes favor the Democrats in some elections while others favor the Republicans and that certain issues have usually favored the Democrats while others have usually favored the Republicans.

The average pattern formed by these 16 categories over the series of elections from 1952 through 1984 is shown in Figure 9–3. Looking first at the candidate attitudes, the general attitudes are most salient and most important of all, perhaps reflecting the generally low level of information among the voters.[4] Views about the candidates' personalities are the next most salient but rank third in importance. Trust in the candidates is somewhat less salient than personality but slightly more important in voting choice. Attitudes concerning record and experience are just a little less important. Of the two, nonoffice experience is generally more salient, but record in office is both more visible and more important when an incumbent president is running for reelection. Management capacity, likewise related to performance in office, is also more salient when a president is seeking reelection. The least salient and least important candidate attribute is intelligence. This finding—that intelligence is the last thing Americans consider in voting for the most demanding office in the Western world—is one of the most dismaying in all of political science.[5]

The display in Figure 9–3 has the candidate attitudes at the far left side, reflecting only salience and importance. There is simply too much variation from one election to the next for mean partisan valence figures to have any meaning. The Reagan-Mondale comparison in 1984, for example, engendered quite different attitudes than did, say, the Ford-Carter or Nixon-Humphrey comparisons. It is, however, meaningful to speak of an average partisan advantage with regard to the specific party and issue attitudes.

The salience and importance of party affect have been declining over time; but when compared to the candidate categories, the average figures still show it to have been more visible and more important than all but the general candidate comments. Attitudes about other party leaders have not been nearly as salient and are much less important. The Democrats have had a slight advantage in party affect, and Republican party leaders have been slightly more attractive.

Among the policy attitudes, economics and general attitudes take turns as the most salient and important. In elections such as 1980 and 1984, when economic circumstances loom large, general issue comments are both less frequent and less important in vote determination. If inflation or unemployment or similar problems are less serious, then there are many more general comments. The mean figures—with economics the most salient and second

---

[4] There is a strong association between salience and importance if one looks at the mean figures for the whole series of elections. The association is much weaker in particular elections. In individual elections, there appears to be much more chance for an issue to be salient but not important, and vice versa.

[5] A ray of hope appeared in 1984. Intelligence was still sixth most important out of the seven candidate attitudes, but consideration of the potential president's mind was more important than personality.

FIGURE 9–3
Specific Attitudes and Presidential Choice, Mean Figures 1952–1984

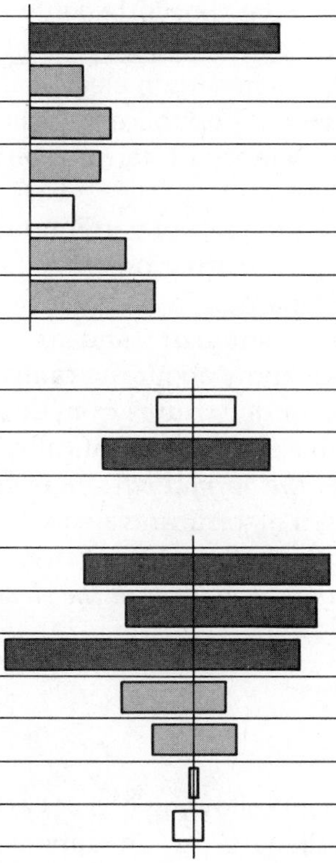

Category Candidates		Salience percent total	Partisan valence percent pro-D	Importance MLE*
General		13.2		.76
Record and incumbency		2.9		.42
Experience		4.3		.36
Management		3.8		.29
Intelligence		2.3		.18
Trust		5.1		.49
Personality		6.6		.43
Parties				
People in party		4.1	46.3	.25
Party affect		8.2	54.3	.75
Issues				
General		12.9	45.6	.96
International involvement		10.0	34.3	.69
Economic management		15.6	61.7	.95
Social benefits		5.4	70.0	.35
Civil liberties		4.3	52.3	.39
Natural resources		.3	75.9	.06
Agriculture		1.5	65.4	.16

Explanation of figure: *Salience* is measured by the proportion of the total comments dealing with the attitude object. It is indicated by the total length of the bar. The longer the bar, the more salient the category. *Partisan valence* is measured by the proportion of comments favorable to the Democrats. The farther the bar is to the left, the more favorable to the Democrats. The farther to the right, the more favorable to the Republicans. *No partisan valence is reported for the candidate categories. There is so much variation between candidate pairs that mean figures have no significance. Importance,* the relation of the attitude category to vote choice, is measured by a standardized maximum likelihood estimate. (See box on pp. 266–267.) It is indicated by the shade of the bar. The darker the bar, the more important the category. The bar is hollow to denote nonsignificance if the category was not significant in the majority of elections.

Data source: 1952 through 1984 Election Studies, Survey Research Center/Center for Political Studies.

in importance and general comments second in visibility but the most important—result from this oscillation. Economic attitudes have typically given a strong edge to the Democrats, but the general issue attitudes have been favorable to the winning party in every one of the nine elections. Seemingly, groups of persons with stable interests exist in each of the specific policy areas, so that the *subtraction of the specific comments from all issue references results in a general issue category that is a very sensitive indicator of partisan advantage in any particular election.*

Of the attitudes regarding the other policy areas, international involvement has been quite salient and usually rather important. It is also the one policy attitude that normally gives the Republicans a substantial advantage. Attitudes about social benefits and civil liberties come next and are about half as salient as international involvement. Social benefits has usually been of some importance and has provided a substantial advantage to the Democrats. Civil liberties has been of importance in certain elections, sometimes benefiting the Democrats and sometimes the Republicans. Agriculture and natural resources normally have a strong Democratic valence, but neither policy area has been salient or important.

These mean figures, especially the measures of importance, do not have any particular statistical standing, but they do provide a baseline against which specific elections can be compared. They enable us to see something of the citizens' reactions to campaign strategies and to know what attitudes determine their choices.[6] Since we know about the campaign strategies from Chapters 5, 6, and 7, we can look for departures from the normal pattern that correspond to the campaign emphases. More specifically, we want to look for citizen *reaction* in *departures from the normal pattern in salience and partisan valence* (and in the absolute pattern of partisan valence in candidate attitudes where no baseline exists). Then we shall explain *choice* in terms of the *absolute pattern of importance and partisan valence in the election in question.* We begin with the election of 1972.[7]

1972: Unusual Candidate Postures

Reaction

1972 was a year when an incumbent following policies at variance with those he had long espoused was challenged by an opponent calling for even sharper departures from established policies. Richard Nixon, long known as an opponent of communism and government regulation of the economy, traveled to Beijing and Moscow in pursuit of his hope for a "Generation of Peace," and wage and price controls were in place in an attempt to deal with an intractable inflation. George McGovern was calling for a reduction of American involvement overseas, especially in Vietnam, and another quan-

---

[6] We can only see *something* of the citizens' reactions because of the limits of what can be discerned from a single cross-sectional survey of the national electorate. To understand the impact of a campaign in detail, one would need longitudinal data to see what changes took place in voters' attitudes as the campaign progressed, and studies that focus on the particular sets of voters (southern independents, Roman Catholics from industrial states, and so forth) to whom that campaign was being directed.

[7] The detailed solutions for the elections from 1952 through 1968 are given in an endnote at the close of this chapter.

tum increase in the level of government spending and social benefit programs. This confrontation produced a high level of comments on issues, particularly in the three relevant policy areas: international involvement, economic management, and social benefits. If one adds civil liberties, on which there was also substantial disagreement between the candidates and which was a little more salient than usual, there were as many comments on these four policy areas as there were in all the candidate and party categories put together.

Even if the candidates had ignored it, economics might well have been salient because of unarrested inflation. Senator McGovern did not. He spoke more about economics than any other policy area, calling for more spending and portraying himself as being on the side of the average person in contrast to powerful, elite interests said to have the ear of Richard Nixon. President Nixon took a conservative posture, campaigning against big spenders in the Democratic Congress. The consequence of all this was that economic management was 10 percent more favorable to the Democrats than it usually was.

Both candidates also devoted a good deal of attention to international questions. Richard Nixon constantly referred to his international travels; the SALT treaty was signed in White House ceremonies during October; the "peace is at hand" announcement came shortly before the election. George McGovern stressed his public plan for peace in Vietnam. The result was that international involvement was more salient than in any other election and had its normal (pro-Republican) partisan valence.

The most decided shift away from normal partisan valence was in social benefits. Senator McGovern announced his intention to increase school funding, expand social security, provide public service jobs, and give a person unable to work approximately $1,000 a month in cash and food stamps. Mr. Nixon contrasted a work ethic built on self-reliance with a welfare ethic that he claimed destroyed character. As you can see by comparing Figures 9–3 and 9–4, attitudes on social benefits shifted 22 percent away from normal and actually produced a slight Republican advantage.

The most prominent civil liberties question in 1972 concerned the use of busing to achieve school integration. Senator McGovern said that he had fought all his political life for integration and would not change regardless of political cost. Nixon opposed busing on the ground that parents wanted better education for their children and this meant neighborhood schools. In this policy area, too, there was a marked shift in partisan valence, producing another Republican advantage. At the same time, a parallel shift was taking place with respect to general issue attitudes. These were a little less salient than usual but also favored the GOP.

Candidate attitudes were less salient, with two exceptions. One was management, which reflected a public belief that Richard Nixon was better able to cope with the presidency than George McGovern. The other was trust—and while all the other candidate attitudes favored Richard Nixon by rather sub-

FIGURE 9–4
Specific Attitudes and 1972 Vote

Category Candidates		Salience percent total	Partisan valence percent pro-D	Importance MLE*
General		10.9	32.4	.75
Record and incumbency		2.7	5.5	.58
Experience		1.9	22.0	—
Management		4.5	22.1	.28
Intelligence		2.0	11.1	.37
Trust		6.9	60.6	.85
Personality		4.6	20.2	.62
Parties				
People in party		2.9	39.0	—
Party affect		7.1	47.2	—
Issues				
General		12.3	36.2	.94
International involvement		15.2	32.8	.61
Economic management		18.4	75.0	.80
Social benefits		6.2	47.7	.35
Civil liberties		4.2	38.8	.44
Natural resources		.1	71.4	—
Agriculture		.3	66.7	—

86% of cases predicted correctly

— denotes insignificant figure.
Explanation of figure: *Salience* is measured by the proportion of the total comments dealing with the attitude object. It is indicated by the total length of the bar. The longer the bar, the more salient the category. *Partisan valence* is measured by the proportion of comments favorable to the Democrats. The farther the bar is to the left, the more favorable to the Democrats. The farther to the right, the more favorable to the Republicans. *Importance,* the relation of the attitude category to vote choice, is measured by a standardized maximum likelihood estimate. (See box on pp. 266–267.) This is indicated in the figure by shade. If a bar is black, the attitude category is very important. If a bar is dark gray, the attitude category is important. If a bar is light gray, the attitude category is somewhat important. If a bar is hollow, the attitude category is not significantly related to vote choice.
Data source: 1972 Election Study, Center for Political Studies.

stantial margins, the voters trusted George McGovern.[8] All the time that the Senator spent reminding the electorate that the "men who . . . have passed out special favors, who have ordered political sabotage . . . work for Mr. Nixon" yielded a real Democratic advantage.

Choice

Senator McGovern was twice as well off in the attitude-vote relationship as Senator Goldwater had been eight years earlier. Whereas the Arizona Senator had only the single attitude of trust (which was only somewhat important), the South Dakota Senator enjoyed a partisan advantage on two attitudes, economic management and trust, both of which were important in the voting decisions of 1972. The trouble with that, of course, was that being twice as well off as Senator Goldwater still spelled political defeat.

All the other attitudes predisposed the voters to support the incumbent president. General attitudes on issues, general attitudes about the candidates, attitudes about the candidates' personalities, Nixon's record in office, and international involvement were all important, and all had Republican valence. Attitudes about the candidates' intelligence, management capacity, social benefits, and civil liberties were all somewhat important, and all of these also favored Richard Nixon. President Nixon's 60.7 percent of the vote came close to President Johnson's 61.0 percent eight years earlier. The fortunes of politics allowed both these veteran politicians to return to the White House with substantial margins.

1976: An Outsider Barely Wins

Reaction

A principal assumption of Jimmy Carter's strategy was that 1976 would be a year when candidates were more important than issues. "There aren't many people, including me, who really understand all the issues," claimed campaign manager Hamilton Jordan. "They're so damned complex that the average fellow out there is looking beyond them to what sort of person the candidate is" (Wooten, 1976). The reaction to the campaign strategies shows this assumption was only partly correct. Comparison of Figures 9–3 and 9–5 indicates that some candidate attitudes were unusually salient in 1976. But Carter's quick rise to prominence would have been followed by an even speedier decline if it had not been for economic issues.

The data in Figure 9–5 suggest that Gerald Ford's strategy was much more successful. There were three candidate attitudes that were unusually sali-

---

[8] The same thing was true of Lyndon Johnson and Barry Goldwater in 1964. Johnson did better in every candidate category besides trust, but Goldwater was trusted. That Johnson was distrusted in 1964 and Nixon was distrusted in 1972 were probably important preludes to the later public reaction to Watergate.

ent—management capacity, record in office, and trust—and there were Ford advantages in all these areas. Recall that Ford spent most of September in the White House looking presidential, that Carter responded with a personal attack on Ford, that Ford commercials at the end of the campaign featured Georgians questioning the quality of Carter's gubernatorial record, and that other commercials praised Ford's quiet style of leadership. It is therefore significant that there was a decided Republican edge in management, a reasonably strong edge for Ford in trust, and at least a slight Ford advantage when record in office was mentioned. (Nearly a quarter of all comments about Ford's record in office concerned his pardon of former President Nixon. If it had not been for this, the public perception of Ford's record would have been very favorable.) And while the other candidate attitudes were no more salient than usual, they *all* favored Gerald Ford. 1976 was the only election year when this has happened. Since the campaign lasted only two months and Ford had been in the White House for two years, it is likely that the campaign effect was primarily one of reinforcement; but it should not be regarded as less successful for that reason.

The issue attitudes were clearly dominated by economic concerns. In common with most Democratic candidates, Governor Carter pledged to continue a number of expensive programs, although he did admit the possibility of a tax cut in the last week of the campaign. In common with most Republican candidates, President Ford was critical of government spending. He made a tax cut a central feature of his campaign. But more important than the stands being taken by either candidate, the nation had just passed through a relatively short but rather deep recession. Evaluations of President Ford were very much affected by whether the respondent had suffered any personal hardship because of the recession and by the respondent's evaluation of government economic performance (Miller & Miller, 1977). The voter reaction to all this was that economic management was even more salient and more pro-Democratic than usual.

The partisan valence in international involvement was not quite as Republican as usual. Ford was handicapped by the relative international tranquillity. Even though Ford's edge was less than that enjoyed by Eisenhower or Nixon, there was a decided Republican advantage in this policy area. But with no visible threat to peace in 1976, international involvement was much less salient.

Choice

The reasons for presidential votes were spread in 1976 as never before. Virtually every attitude category was significantly related to presidential choice. Only natural resources missed and that by the barest of margins.[9] With so

---

[9] To be considered statistically significant, a maximum likelihood estimate must be twice its standard error. The MLE for natural resources was 1.98 times its standard error.

FIGURE 9–5
Specific Attitudes and 1976 Vote

Category Candidates		Salience percent total	Partisan valence percent pro-D	Importance MLE*
General		13.1	49.8	.68
Record and incumbency		5.7	48.1	.73
Experience		4.7	28.9	.44
Management		6.7	29.6	.64
Intelligence		2.0	48.4	.27
Trust		8.3	40.8	.80
Personality		7.6	48.0	.47
Parties				
People in party		3.8	69.6	.25
Party affect		4.7	56.0	.39
Issues				
General		12.8	50.3	.48
International involvement		5.0	38.4	.31
Economic management		17.2	74.9	1.10
Social benefits		4.4	69.1	.23
Civil liberties		2.8	45.3	.28
Natural resources		.5	83.5	—
Agriculture		.5	81.4	.25

85% of cases predicted correctly

— denotes insignificant figure.
Explanation of figure: *Salience* is measured by the proportion of the total comments dealing with the attitude object. It is indicated by the total length of the bar. The longer the bar, the more salient the category. *Partisan valence* is measured by the proportion of comments favorable to the Democrats. The farther the bar is to the left, the more favorable to the Democrats. The farther to the right, the more favorable to the Republicans. *Importance*, the relation of the attitude category to vote choice, is measured by a standardized maximum likelihood estimate. (See box on pp. 266–267.) This is indicated in the figure by shade. If a bar is black, the attitude category is very important. If a bar is dark gray, the attitude category is important. If a bar is light gray, the attitude category is somewhat important. If a bar is hollow, the attitude category is not significantly related to vote choice.
Data source: 1976 Election Study, Center for Political Studies.

many attitudes involved, one cannot say that any single attitude provided the key to the election. What can be said is that economic management was the only very important attitude category, and the lopsided Democratic margin in this policy area probably sustained Jimmy Carter in the face of a well-executed Republican strategy.

There were four important attitudes: trust, record in office, management capacity, and general attitudes. All dealt with the candidates; and by varying margins, all favored Gerald Ford. The remaining 10 attitudes were only somewhat important, and they were split 5 to 5. Ford was helped by views on personality, experience, and intelligence and by the policy areas of international involvement and civil liberties. Carter was aided by both party categories, general issue attitudes, social benefits, and agriculture.

The dominant impression is that Carter was elected because of economic circumstances and in spite of his being less favorably perceived as a person. This may also explain the collapse of President Carter's popularity in office. No other president has been elected without some personal characteristics that were favorably perceived by the electorate. When the Carter administration was unable to cope with inflation, the major problem responsible for his election, there was nothing else to sustain the President's reputation.

1980: "Are You Better Off Than You Were Four Years Ago?"

Reaction

Voters' attitudes in the fall of 1980 seem to have been affected by four considerations: the economic havoc caused by the rampant inflation of the preceding four years, the wide difference between the policies being advocated by the major party candidates, the unpopularity of both of these candidates, and the Democratic and Republican campaigns. These are listed in descending order of importance. Consequently, the campaign effects that are easiest to detect are those that took advantage of the more important considerations.[10]

Some traces of the Carter effort to draw a sharp distinction between the two candidates as individuals can be seen in the comments about both. When all candidate comments are considered, there were in fact more negative than positive comments about Governor Reagan. The ratio was 46 percent positive to 54 percent negative. (President Carter had just a few more positive than negative comments, 51 percent to 49 percent. By way of comparison, President Ford enjoyed a 62 to 38 percent ratio four years earlier.) But when these comments are considered in any detail, the Carter campaign seems less successful. The four candidate categories in Figure 9–6 that show a Carter advantage—general comments, experience, intelligence, and trust—were all less salient than usual. Furthermore, the largest proportion of negative comments about Governor Reagan (22 percent) dealt with his age, and the next largest (another 12 percent) concerned Reagan's own campaign speeches. To be sure, the Carter campaign called attention to what Ronald Reagan was saying, but these liabilities were not created by the Carter campaign.

The candidate categories that were more salient than usual were record in office and management capacity. Comments about the candidates' records

---

[10] This analysis is restricted to the two major party candidates. A separate note on the Anderson vote appears at the end.

just barely favored Reagan because there were fewer negative references to the Governor's record. There was a decisive Republican advantage in comments about management capacity because of the many negative comments about the job that President Carter had done and the quality of his staff. The public perceptions of Carter as a manager resulted more from his four years in office than from the campaign, but a goal of the Reagan campaign had been to reinforce the image of "Carter as an ineffective and error-prone leader."

1980 was another year with a large proportion of comments about issues. Furthermore, there were more references in the specific policy areas[11] (except agriculture) and relatively few comments in the vague general category. The one policy area that was both more salient and more Democratic than usual was civil liberties. The reason for this was the number of negative references to Governor Reagan's stand on the Equal Rights Amendment.[12] Since the Democratic campaign was making special efforts to reach women, they could claim some credit here.

The major impact of the Reagan strategy (and of four years of inflation) can be seen in economic management. This policy area continued the very high salience of 1972 and 1976, and for the first time in the entire time series, economic attitudes gave an advantage to the Republicans. A Reagan strategy document had said: "We must not break any new ground. . . . The thrust of our speeches must be directed toward: inflation, jobs, economic growth." The success of this can be seen in a 14.5 percent shift in a Republican direction. Inflation was the great cause of this, although the voters also had an adverse impression of Jimmy Carter's ability to manage the economy.

International involvement was about as Republican as usual but much more salient, so that the normal Republican advantage weighed more heavily in the electoral scale. This was due not to the Reagan campaign but to the American diplomats being held hostage in Iran. More than 40 percent of the comments about President Carter and foreign affairs dealt with the hostages. If it had not been for this, the Carter efforts to raise the war-and-peace issue would have produced an 11 percent shift in a Democratic direction. Social benefits was slightly more salient and slightly less Democratic than usual but still a Democratic advantage.

Choice

The election of 1980 was determined by issues. As Figure 9–2 shows, the maximum likelihood estimate of the importance of issues in that election was

---

[11] The glacial speed of the increase in public interest in natural resources is interesting. After the OPEC oil embargo of 1973–74 and major congressional interest in rival energy plans, comments about this policy area increased to the "height" of 0.5 percent of all comments in 1976. After the passage of two Carter energy bills, a rapid increase in gasoline costs, and lines at gas stations, public concern reached a new "peak" of 0.8 percent in 1980.

[12] There were also a number of references to Reagan's stand on abortion, but this didn't produce any partisan advantage, as there was virtually the same number of positive and negative references.

FIGURE 9-6
Specific Attitudes and 1980 Vote (Carter and Reagan voters only)

Category	Salience percent total	Partisan valence percent pro-D	Importance MLE*
Candidates			
General	11.9	60.2	.65
Record and incumbency	6.4	49.5	.71
Experience	1.4	63.3	—
Management	6.8	25.7	.57
Intelligence	2.2	62.0	—
Trust	4.4	57.8	.31
Personality	5.4	40.2	.57
Parties			
People in party	2.4	56.8	—
Party affect	6.6	54.6	.39
Issues			
General	7.7	35.9	.75
International involvement	14.0	34.2	1.30
Economic management	19.0	48.7	1.33
Social benefits	5.5	63.0	.63
Civil liberties	5.2	57.4	.81
Natural resources	.8	47.6	—
Agriculture	.2	40.9	—

87% of cases predicted correctly

— denotes insignificant figure.

Explanation of figure: *Salience* is measured by the proportion of the total comments dealing with the attitude object. It is indicated by the total length of the bar. The longer the bar, the more salient the category. *Partisan valence* is measured by the proportion of comments favorable to the Democrats. The farther the bar is to the left, the more favorable to the Democrats. The farther to the right, the more favorable to the Republicans. *Importance*, the relation of the attitude category to vote choice, is measured by a standardized maximum likelihood estimate. (See box on pp. 266–267.) This is indicated in the figure by shade. If a bar is black, the attitude category is very important. If a bar is dark gray, the attitude category is important. If a bar is light gray, the attitude category is somewhat important. If a bar is hollow, the attitude category is not significantly related to vote choice.

Data source: 1980 Election Study, Center for Political Studies.

substantially higher than in any other election except 1984. Among issues, the two imperative policy areas—economic management and international involvement—were both very important in voting decisions, and both had a Republican valence. Since we know that inflation and Iran were causing the greatest concern in these policy areas, it would not be too much to say that the election turned on dismay over the performance of the Carter administration in these two areas.[13]

Figure 9–6 shows that the important attitudes were more evenly split. There were three that had a Republican valence: the weathervane general issues category, management capacity (where Reagan had an enormous advantage), and personality. The public records of the two candidates were important but so slightly Republican as to be essentially a standoff. The Democratic advantages came in general comments on the candidates and in the issue areas of social benefits and civil liberties.

Only two attitudes were somewhat important. These were party affect and trust. Jimmy Carter had worked hard to whip up the former and had earned the latter, but neither was very consequential in vote choice.

Of all of the attitudes that were significantly related to vote choice in 1980, five were pro-Republican, five were pro-Democratic, and one fundamentally a tie. This does not seem to suggest a landslide, but the 1980 vote was only half a landslide. In view of the negative comments about Reagan himself, the loss of votes to the Democrats on social benefits and civil liberties, and the 51 percent of the vote Reagan received, one could not say that there was a positive landslide for Ronald Reagan or for conservative ideology. But given the strength of the adverse judgments about the Carter administration's handling of economics and foreign policy and given the 59 percent of the vote that went to Carter's opponents, one could say that there was a negative landslide against the Carter administration.

The Special Problems of a Third Candidate: Anderson

Lacking the resources to carry on a campaign of the same magnitude as the major party candidates, John Anderson had to make just the right moves at just the right time. But to carry out even this long-shot strategy, Anderson needed *some* resources and *some* attention from the media, and these vital ingredients were lacking. It is therefore not surprising that Anderson was less visible during the election than either of his major rivals. While almost all respondents knew something about President Carter and Governor Reagan by April, only half claimed to know about Congressman Anderson by June, and only three quarters did so during the fall (Markus, 1982).

The magnitude of the problems facing a minor party candidate can be seen in questions that enable us to ascertain which candidate's position each voter preferred on specific issues.[14] Ninety-six percent of the voters who preferred Reagan's position on whether inflation or unemployment was more impor-

---

[13] This would appear to be another demonstration of the power of retrospective voting, choices based on citizens' evaluations of the quality of governance during the last term in office. For a splendid analysis of this important topic, see Fiorina (1981).

[14] These questions ask the respondents to state their preferred position on a seven-point scale concerning, say, defense spending, and also to state where they would locate the candidates along the same scale. These data permit us to say which candidate is located closest to each respondent and, therefore, whose position is preferred.

tant voted for him; 76 percent of those in closest agreement with Carter voted for him; only 43 percent of those who preferred Anderson's position on this issue voted for him. Across four such issues—inflation versus unemployment, defense spending, cutting social services, and whether women should play an equal role in society—Ronald Reagan received an average of 86.5 percent of the votes, Jimmy Carter an average of 69.4 percent, and John Anderson an average of only 35.6 percent of the votes of citizens *preferring* the candidate's positions. Since these questions measure the effect of single issues, the difference between Reagan and Carter shows the effect of other attitudes being more favorable to Reagan. But the difference between the major party candidates and Anderson shows the weakness of a third-party candidacy in the United States.

1984: A Popular Incumbent with Unpopular Policies

Reaction

The 1984 election turned on issues, above all. Sixty-three percent of all comments concerned issues, compared with an average of 49 percent since 1952. Fortunately for Ronald Reagan, though, there was more to the election than issues. The President fared very well when the voters compared him to Walter Mondale, and it was his further good fortune to be contrasted with Jimmy Carter in 1984 as well as in 1980.

All but one of the candidate and party attitudes were less salient than usual. (This can be seen by comparing the data in Figure 9–7 with those in Figure 9–3.) The sole exception was management—and this was less salient than it had been in either 1976 or 1980.

Four of the candidate and party attitudes—personality, record and incumbency, people in the party (other than the candidates), and intelligence—had valence scores showing one side or the other with a decided advantage. None of these were as salient as usual, but the skewed reactions of the electorate gave these attitudes some real impact. Personality gave Reagan a marked advantage. Since many of the positive comments were to the effect that Reagan was strong, decisive, and a leader, while many of the negative comments complained that Mondale was weak, indecisive, and not a leader, this clearly reflected the Republican emphasis on "Leadership That's Working."

President Reagan had an even greater advantage in comments about his record in office.[15] In large part, this reflected a simple feeling that the administration had done a good job in office. The Republican campaign, of course, had done all it could to stress the positive aspects of the Reagan record. To a lesser degree, views about the record in office reflected negative comments

---

[15] The Reagan-Mondale pairing on record and incumbency produced a partisan valence of 19.6. This seems (and was) a substantial advantage, but it ranks only fourth in the time series beginning in 1952. The Nixon-McGovern, Johnson-Goldwater, and Eisenhower-Stevenson pairings all produced greater advantages for the incumbents in comments about their records.

about Walter Mondale's record in office with the Carter administration. Mr. Mondale's bid for office in his own right was also hobbled by attitudes about people in the Democratic party. Here again, Jimmy Carter was responsible. Thus the memory of the Carter administration was still sufficiently strong and sufficiently adverse to be a real handicap to former Vice President Mondale.

Walter Mondale did have an advantage in comments about intelligence. Relatively few voters commented about this, but those who did were likely to make positive comments about Mondale and negative remarks about Reagan. Mr. Mondale was seen as intelligent, innovative, and having an understanding of the nation's problems, while there were complaints that Mr. Reagan lacked this understanding.[16] All the other candidate attitudes favored President Reagan. Considering what was happening with the issue attitudes, it was a good thing for his reelection that his personal appeal with the voters was so strong.

The success of the Mondale campaign can be seen in the issue attitudes. The Mondale campaign, you will recall, was characterized by a search for issues to take attention away from Reagan's personal popularity and the warm glow of economic prosperity. Figure 9–7 shows just how well they succeeded. All four important issue areas—international involvement, economic management, social benefits, and civil liberties—were more salient than usual; all four had shifted in a Democratic direction since 1980; and all except economic management were more Democratic than usual. The wide geographic basis of the Reagan victory obscured just how much Walter Mondale did to produce pro-Democratic issue attitudes in 1984.

For the first time since 1964, there was actually a Democratic advantage in attitudes about international affairs. Mondale's references to Reagan's recklessness, Democratic ads that effectively played on fears about war, and news stories about events in Lebanon and in Central America combined to produce an 18-point shift in a Democratic direction. While voters favored Reagan's emphasis on a strong military posture, they were plainly worried about the danger of war.

Mondale's use of the fairness issue against Reagan also appears to have struck home. Social benefits was much more salient than usual and even more lopsidedly Democratic than normal. Mondale's pleas that "I want a caring America" were particularly effective in convincing voters that he was concerned about poorer Americans and the Reagan administration was not. Similarly, Mondale positions on civil liberties led to Democratic pluses. These attitudes were nearly twice as salient as normal and more favorable to the Democrats than they had been since the 1960s. The electorate responded positively to Mondale's stress on equality and support of ERA and reacted negatively to Reagan's early comments on religion.

---

[16] The selection of a woman to run for vice president produced a substantial reaction. This can't be seen in Figure 9–7 because these comments are included in the general candidate category. When isolated, they produce a 2 to 1 advantage for Mondale.

There were two issue attitudes that produced a Republican edge. Economic management—by far the most salient category, with 23 percent of *all* comments—was 12 points more Republican than usual. This reflected both the prosperity of 1984, for which the Republicans were proud to take credit, and Republican success in focusing public attention on the tax increase portion of the Mondale deficit reduction plan. By themselves, these would have produced a big Republican edge. But Ronald Reagan was also seen as too close to big business and opposed to reforms, while Walter Mondale was given credit for being more in favor of the average person. By themselves, these attitudes would have been a big help to the Democrats. The pro-Republican and pro-Democratic attitudes virtually canceled each other and together produced a slight Republican advantage.

A more important campaign advantage came in the symbolic area of general attitudes. These were much less salient but gave greater buoyancy to the Republicans because the valence score was so much more in favor of the GOP. As already noted, this general attitude category is a sensitive indicator of which party is ahead in a given year, and the 1984 Republican valence advantage was the largest in the whole time series. This reflected the voters' sympathies for conservatism and decreased government activity.[17] But even with the benefits from general and economic attitudes, Ronald Reagan needed the candidate attitudes to win.

Choice

Two general points should be made about presidential choice in 1984. First, virtually the whole array of attitudes was related to vote choice. The maximum likelihood estimates for the broad attitudes reported in Figure 9–2 show that issues (by a narrow margin over 1980) were more strongly related to vote than in any other election, candidate attitudes had their second-strongest association with vote choice, and attitudes about parties were more important in determining vote choice than at any time since the 1950s. Of the 16 specific attitudes, only those about natural resources and agriculture were not significantly related to presidential vote.

Second, 1984 saw a historic reversal in the two most important issue attitudes. International involvement, which traditionally had favored the Republicans, shifted into a Democratic advantage. (The Democrats would have made real inroads into this Republican issue edge in 1980 if it had not been for the hostages held in Iran.) Economic management, which traditionally had favored the Democrats, helped the Republicans as it had in 1980. Neither party got much electoral profit out of their new issues. The valence scores were so close to 50 percent (52.7 for international involvement and 49.6 for economic management) that these issues had relatively little net impact. The "effects" came more from the absence of the traditional party vote-getters.

---

[17] This was not the first time that Americans expressed their support for the general idea of conservatism while, at the same time, preferring specific liberal programs.

FIGURE 9–7
Specific Attitudes and 1984 Vote

Category / Candidates		Salience percent total	Partisan valence percent pro-D	Importance MLE*
Candidates				
General		10.1	45.4	1.20
Record and incumbency		2.5	19.8	.47
Experience		.6	40.7	.34
Management		5.2	48.8	.48
Intelligence		2.0	64.0	.32
Trust		3.1	47.1	.55
Personality		4.6	26.7	.28
Parties				
People in party		3.3	32.3	.46
Party affect		5.6	58.7	.79
Issues				
General		8.5	33.8	.78
International involvement		12.6	52.7	.95
Economic management		23.0	49.6	1.93
Social benefits		9.4	76.8	.61
Civil liberties		8.3	60.5	.57
Natural resources		.7	94.5	—
Agriculture		.4	67.9	—

90% of cases predicted correctly

— denotes insignificant figure.
Explanation of figure: *Salience* is measured by the proportion of the total comments dealing with the attitude object. It is indicated by the total length of the bar. The longer the bar, the more salient the category. *Partisan valence* is measured by the proportion of comments favorable to the Democrats. The farther the bar is to the left, the more favorable to the Democrats. The farther to the right, the more favorable to the Republicans. *Importance*, the relation of the attitude category to vote choice, is measured by a standardized maximum likelihood estimate. (See box on pp. 266–267.) This is indicated in the figure by shade. If a bar is black, the attitude category is very important. If a bar is dark gray, the attitude category is important. If a bar is light gray, the attitude category is somewhat important. If a bar is hollow, the attitude category is not significantly related to vote choice.
Data source: 1984 Election Study, Center for Political Studies.

The absence of a big Republican advantage on foreign policy and the lack of a big Democratic advantage on economics allowed other attitudes to come into play.

The maximum likelihood estimates showed that in determining 1984 votes, two attitudes were very important: economic management and general attitudes about the candidates. Economics had by far the highest MLE in this whole time series and thus was extraordinarily important in determining individual votes. But as just noted, its valence was so close to the neutral 50 percent mark that it didn't help the Republicans too much overall. No such qualification is needed about the general candidate attitudes. These were very important; more people favored Reagan and voted accordingly for his reelection.

Half a dozen attitudes were important in determining 1984 vote choice, and four of these favored the Democrats. International involvement, important as it was, did not produce too many Democratic votes because its valence was so close to the neutral point. Social benefits, though less closely tied to vote choice, shifted more votes than any other single attitude. The question of fairness and the popularity of many government programs provided an enormous Democratic advantage. Civil liberties also produced a good many Democratic votes, although the lower MLE and valence score indicate fewer Democratic benefits than those resulting from welfare questions. Finally, the Democrats gained votes from attitudes about party affect. As the majority party, they are usually aided by these attitudes, and they got a little more help than usual in 1984.

The two important attitudes that led to Reagan votes were trust and general issue attitudes. Both Reagan and Mondale were trusted but Reagan slightly more so, so this attitude produced some Republican votes. The general attitudes about conservatism and liberalism, however, were so favorable to the incumbent that they led to a great many Republican votes. They were not strong enough to cancel the Democratic advantage on social benefits, but they were a significant pro-Republican force.

Five of the six somewhat important attitudes (shown in light grey in Figure 9–7) favored the Republicans. Attitudes about the candidates' intelligence were associated with Democratic votes, but all the rest helped the GOP. When MLE and valence are both considered, the most substantial help came from attitudes about record in office and party members other than the candidates. Reagan could thank his own record in office for some of this, but he also owed thanks to the continued unpopularity of Jimmy Carter. The Republicans got a little help from attitudes about management and the candidates' nonoffice experience. Attitudes about the candidates' personalities were the least influential of any specific attitudes in 1984,[18] but Reagan's advantage over Mondale was so great in this category that a number of Republican votes can be traced to this comparison.

To recapitulate, Walter Mondale won the "issue" election in 1984, gaining votes from three of the five significant issues. Ronald Reagan, however, won when all attitudes were considered, taking both of the very important atti-

---

[18] Stated more exactly, they had the lowest MLE of any attitude significantly related to vote choice. Agriculture and natural resources were still less important, but they were not significant in this 1984 vote solution.

tudes, two of the six important attitudes, and five of the six somewhat important attitudes. His "issue" mandate could be questioned, but there was no
doubt about the extent of his overall support.

SUMMARY

By asking how the citizen's political knowledge was organized into attitudes,
we have been able to see the relation between what was known and the
citizen's choice of presidential candidates. Considering the broad categories
of candidates, parties, and issues, issues and candidates are much more important. Issues have typically helped the Democrats, and candidates have
helped the Republicans. Attitudes about parties have not been as consequential, even less so in recent decades.

By decomposing the three broad categories into sixteen specific categories,
we lost the easy generalizations about issues and candidates helping one
party or the other. But at the same time, we could see more. Some of the most
interesting findings concern candidates. Many citizens are able to discriminate among various candidate attributes. Even in the face of the victorious
campaigns that led to the Johnson and Nixon landslides in 1964 and 1972,
voters continued to distrust these presidents while regarding them as more
qualified in all other respects. Similarly, Reagan was preferred to Mondale in
1984 in every respect except intelligence. As a consequence of this ability to
discriminate, rarely do all of the candidate attitudes favor one side or the
other. The only case was in 1976. Given a Ford-Carter comparison, all the
candidate attitudes were in a pro-Republican direction.[19]

The most noteworthy variation over time has been in trust. It was salient in
1952, disappeared from the forefront of our national consciousness during the
Eisenhower years, returned as a more urgent concern with Johnson and
Nixon, and then declined in concern after Ford and Carter had been in the
White House. Management capacity has also become more salient in the last
four elections, an encouraging development that means more attention is
being paid to a candidate's ability to serve as chief executive.

The variation we have seen in the role of issues is significant because it
casts some light on the conditions under which issue voting is more likely to
occur. Generally speaking, there are three theories about issue voting. One
holds that issues become important when candidates take positions distinctive enough to give the voters real issue choices. For example, Norman Nie,
Sidney Verba and John Petrocik argue:

> By the fifties [New Deal] issues had faded. The times were prosperous and the
> candidates in 1952 and 1956 were not perceived as polarized on the issues. Nor
> were there other issues to take their place. The result was that citizens did not
> take coherent issue positions, nor did they vote on the basis of issues. . . . In

---

[19] The same point applies to issue attitudes as well. The only instance when all the issue
attitudes favored one party (the Democrats) was in 1964.

the 1960s we see a reemergence of issues. They become more coherent, and they become more closely tied to the vote than in the Eisenhower years. (1976, pp. 192–193)

A second theory holds that issue voting is more likely to take place when there is an incumbent president running for reelection, because the voters are better informed. The record compiled by an administration in office for four years provides evidence that is both readily available and credible. The authors of *The American Voter* argue along these lines in discussing the impact of economic management in Eisenhower's first term.

Not until economic prosperity had been experienced with a Republican in the White House did the party make any substantial headway against [the] theme [that Republicans could not be trusted to deal with the economy]. The point is not that economic prosperity during Eisenhower's first term was any better evidence for the Republican case than what had been cited by Messrs. Landon, Willkie and Dewey (witness the events of Eisenhower's second term). The point is rather that the evidence was visible enough that it could enter the awareness of the mass electorate and have a broad impact on perceptions of the parties. (Campbell et al., 1960, p. 61)

A variant on this is the idea of retrospective voting—that while citizens may have difficulty judging claims about what will be done, it is relatively easy to judge what has been done. After all, Morris Fiorina points out, citizens

have one comparatively hard bit of data: they know what life has been like during the incumbent's administration. They need *not* know the precise economic or foreign policies of the incumbent administration in order to see or feel the *results* of those policies. And is it not reasonable to base voting decisions on results as well as intentions? (1981, p. 5)

The third type of theory is temporal. Here the effect of issues is said to increase (or decrease) with the passage of years, with issue voting becoming more (or less) important in later elections. Time stands as a surrogate for some other factor. It is not the passage of time itself that is the cause of increased issue voting but the presence of some condition in the later elections that was absent in the earlier elections. A frequently offered temporal explanation rests on education. As the extent of education has increased over time, voters are said to be able to comprehend the issues more easily and are therefore likelier to cast issue-motivated votes.

With data on nine elections since 1952, we are in a position to test these three theories. By pooling the judgments of 37 scholars, Steven J. Rosenstone has developed robust measures of the candidates' issue positions.[20] The maximum likelihood estimates from the probit analyses give us measures of the

[20] He did this in order to operationalize the election forecasting model discussed at the beginning of Chapter 7. I should like to thank Professor Rosenstone for his willingness to share these data and especially for his patient coaching on interpretation of regressions with a limited number of data points.

importance of issue voting in each election. And of course, we know whether an incumbent was running for reelection and the year in which the election took place.

The data are displayed in Figure 9–8. This shows the issue distances calculated from the Rosenstone data, the maximum likelihood estimates for all issue references, the maximum likelihood estimates for specific-issue references (more about these in a moment), whether an incumbent was running for reelection, and the year. Figure 9–8 is a semilogarithmic graph. This means that if two lines are parallel (as they are for issue distance and the MLEs for all issues between 1952 and 1956), the rates of change are the same.[21] In turn, this indicates that one can account for all of the variation in issue voting by the change in issue distance.

As you can see, the lines for issue distance and all issue voting go in the same general direction all across the graph. Only between 1968 and 1972 do the two lines go in different directions. Here is a major result. Greater distance between candidates does lead to increased issue voting. These data are different than those used by Nie et al. for particular years. The level of all issue voting in 1964 is not much higher than it was in 1952; and in 1968 and 1972, it was lower than it had been in 1952. However, their general argument that greater issue distance increases issue voting is strongly supported.

Another interesting possiblity is that there are two kinds of issue voting. Figure 9–8 shows both all issue voting (the issue MLEs from Figure 9–2) and specific-issue voting (weighted averages of the MLEs for the specific policy areas in the detailed analyses). What are the differences between the two? In all likelihood, the attitudes categorized in the specific policy areas are better informed. A respondent must mention something about economic policy or some economic group (business, labor, etc.) to have a response coded under economic management. Similarly, one must mention agriculture or farmers to have an attitude placed in the agriculture category. These coding rules mean that a respondent is likely to know something.

In addition to these references, the broader category also contains general responses—references to liberalism and conservatism, and all responses that are too vague to be put in any specific category. These general responses form a large category, 13 percent of *all* responses *by themselves*. This category has proven to be a sensitive indicator, its partisan valence having favored the winner in every one of the nine elections. The implication is that it reflects short-term forces. This suggests two kinds of issue attitudes: specific attitudes that are sufficiently well informed to refer to particular policy areas, and vague general attitudes that shift with short-term forces.

Now notice what happens to the two issue lines in Figure 9–8. The line for

---

[21] The rates of change for specific-issue voting and issue distance between 1952 and 1956 are different. One *cannot* tell this by the fact that the line for specific-issue voting is farther away from the line for issue distance than the line for all issue voting. One knows this because the two lines are *not* parallel.

FIGURE 9–8
Comparison of Issue Distance with All Issue Voting and Specific-Issue Voting

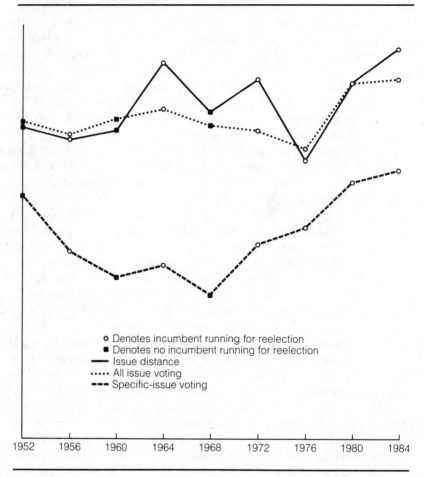

o Denotes incumbent running for reelection
■ Denotes no incumbent running for reelection
— Issue distance
····· All issue voting
--- Specific-issue voting

1952   1956   1960   1964   1968   1972   1976   1980   1984

all issue references (that includes the vague general references) does follow the line for issue distance. However, the line for specific-issue references does not follow it as closely. It hits its second lowest level in 1960 and reaches its nadir in 1968, two of the three elections in which incumbents were not running for reelection.

Another hint that incumbency may play a role in specific-issue voting comes from counting the number of policy areas significantly related to vote choice in each election. In five of the six elections with an incumbent candidate, four specific-issue categories (usually international, economics, social benefits, and civil liberties) have been significantly related to vote; in 1976, five issue categories were significant. Without an incumbent candidate, only two issue areas were significant in 1952 and 1960 and only one was in 1968.

When these theories were tested by multivariate analysis, however, issue distance proved to be much the strongest explanation. Greater issue distance between competing candidates was significantly related to all issue voting. Issue distance was not quite as strongly related to specific-issue voting, but it did have an important effect. A search for separate effects of incumbency was generally unavailing. And of the three possible causes, time was the weakest. When controlled for issue and incumbency, it did not show any independent impact at all.[22]

There are, of course, still more questions that grow out of the findings in this chapter. If citizens can discriminate between different facets of politics so that some attitudes favor Republicans and other attitudes favor Democrats, how do they resolve the attitude conflicts that result? And if attitudes are related to vote choice in a given election but are not as important in the following election, what does this imply about the stability of attitudes from one election to the next? These are among the questions we shall explore in Chapter 10.

ENDNOTE

The table on the following page gives detailed solutions for 1952, 1956, 1960, 1964, and 1968 elections.

---

[22] For further information about this multivariate analysis, see Appendix A–9.3.

Detailed Solutions for 1952, 1956, 1960, 1964, and 1968 Elections

Category	1952			1956		
	Salience Percent Total	Partisan Valence Percent Pro-D	Importance MLE*	Salience Percent Total	Partisan Valence Percent Pro-D	Importance MLE*
Candidates						
General	11.1%	35.3%	0.26	19.6%	33.2%	0.44
Record and incumbency	1.0	86.3	—	3.5	13.1	0.38
Experence	9.1	61.1	0.29	3.7	36.6	0.40
Management	2.2	21.3	0.29	2.1	41.5	0.44
Intelligence	1.9	58.5	—	2.6	65.9	—
Trust	8.7	21.8	0.63	5.9	18.8	—
Personality	5.1	26.7	0.26	6.2	28.3	0.51
Parties						
People in party	5.9	33.6	—	5.2	55.6	0.29
Party affect	10.7	45.0	1.36	8.8	54.8	1.10
Issues						
General	8.3	45.8	0.77	10.0	45.7	0.71
International involvement	8.8	20.1	0.76	8.8	16.9	0.58
Economic management	22.8	62.5	1.25	13.1	74.1	0.71
Social benefits	1.8	80.9	—	5.0	83.5	0.51
Civil liberties	1.4	40.7	—	2.0	46.2	—
National resources	0.2	82.1	—	0.4	67.4	—
Agriculture	1.1	80.1	0.34	3.1	79.7	0.47
	87% predicted right			86% predicted right		

1960			1964			1968		
Salience Percent Total	Partisan Valence Percent Pro-D	Importance MLE*	Salience Percent Total	Partisan Valence Percent Pro-D	Importance MLE*	Salience Percent Total	Partisan Valence Percent Pro-D	Importance MLE*
17.3%	41.7%	0.82	10.6%	66.5%	.86	13.8%	43.3%	.64
0.9	35.3	0.22	2.3	93.1	—	1.7	61.6	.49
9.1	30.9	1.02	6.3	76.4	—	3.0	39.8	.33
1.8	34.6	0.24	2.7	64.7	—	2.6	34.0	—
3.6	63.0	0.26	1.6	75.5	—	2.2	50.0	—
1.4	46.5	—	2.1	18.2	.38	4.3	52.1	.39
6.0	58.2	—	10.4	52.9	.53	9.9	48.2	.44
4.9	39.4	—	3.0	49.0	—	5.4	40.9	.44
9.6	53.9	0.76	10.7	66.7	1.12	10.2	52.8	.76
19.2	64.3	1.38	17.6	54.5	1.59	19.7	44.4	1.23
9.4	32.3	0.80	8.0	54.4	.65	8.4	27.2	—
10.9	56.1	0.32	7.5	59.5	.55	9.4	55.0	.61
1.5	53.4	—	10.5	88.7	.38	4.0	67.6	—
2.2	64.6	—	5.5	67.3	.64	5.1	50.1	—
0.2	76.2	—	.2	77.3	—	—	—	—
1.9	70.8	—	.7	64.9	—	0.5	35.7	—
88% predicted right			90% predicted right			88% predicted right		

— denotes insignificant figure. Data source: 1952 through 1968 Election Studies, Survey Research Center.

Chapter 10

Party Identification

Since 1952, scores of interviewers have asked thousands of respondents: "Generally speaking, do you think of yourself as a Republican, a Democrat, an independent, or what?" If the respondent says Republican, the next question is: "Would you call yourself a strong Republican or a not very strong Republican?" If the respondent says Democrat, the same follow-up question is asked with respect to the Democratic party. If the answer to the first question is independent, then the respondent is asked: "Do you think of yourself as closer to the Republican or Democratic party?"

Party identification, the concept measured by these questions, is thought of as having a *strength component* and a *direction component*. Each individual is categorized on the strength component according to the answers to the follow-up questions. The respondent who says strong to the partisan follow-up question is treated as a Strong Partisan. If the answer is not very strong, then the respondent is called a Weak Partisan. Anyone who answers the independent follow-up question by saying that they are closer to one party rather than the other, is regarded as an Independent Partisan or Leaner. Only after asserting independence twice is the respondent called an Independent. The direction component is simply Republican versus Democrat.

When the strength component and the direction component are combined, the result is a seven-magnitude scale: Strong Democrat, Weak Democrat, Independent Democrat, Independent, Independent Republican, Weak Republican, Strong Republican. An eighth category, Apolitical, is often added, not as a magnitude that belongs at any point on the party identification scale but as a category to include those few persons who are so uninformed and uninterested in politics that the questions are meaningless.

The basic idea is that each individual has an attachment to or repulsion from a political party. Persons attracted to the Republican party are not supposed to be attracted to the Democratic party, and vice versa. As the formal statement in *The American Voter* put it, party identification is "the individual's affective orientation to an important group-object in the environment . . . . The political party serves as the group toward which the individual may develop an identification, positive or negative, of some degree of intensity" (Campbell, Converse, Miller & Stokes, 1960, pp. 121–22). Party identification is the individual's standing decision to support one party or another.

It is important to note that the party identification question invokes two types of attitude objects. The first is the self in the part of the question that asks "Do you think of yourself . . . ?" The second set of attitude objects is comprised of Republicans, Democrats, and independents in the subsequent phrases of the questions. What this implies is that the respondent is in fact being asked: What is your self-perception? What are your perceptions of Republicans, Democrats, and independents? And given your self-perception and your perception of each of these political groups, how do you relate to them? Since an individual's self-image is likely to be both relatively stable and relatively central in the individual's cognitive structure and since an individual will be on the receiving end of a constant stream of cues about Republicans, Democrats, and independents, this more complex understanding of the question has important implications for the measurement of party identification. This is a point to which we shall want to return.

Aggregate Stability

Until 1964, the distribution of party identification was remarkably stable. As you can see from the data in Table 10–1, the proportion of Democrats (Strong plus Weak) varied between 44 and 47 percent, and the proportion of Republicans varied between 27 and 29 percent. This much variation can be accounted for by sampling error alone. The Democratic advantage of roughly 7 to 4 seemed relatively fixed. A similar point can be made about the strength component alone. The proportions of Strong Partisans (disregarding whether they were Democrats or Republicans) were 35 percent, 36 percent, and 35 percent in 1952, 1956, and 1960, respectively.

The proportion of Strong Republicans dropped in 1964, and the proportion of Strong Democrats dropped soon thereafter. In recent elections, the Strong Partisans have been a smaller component of the electorate. The proportions in 1976, 1980, and 1984 were 24, 27, and 29 percent, respectively.

Another way of looking at this change is the increase in the number of Independents. If one looks only at the Independents (those in the middle category), the proportion of citizens not identifying with either political party rose from 5 percent in 1952 to 13 percent in 1980. If Leaners are included along

TABLE 10–1
Distribution of Party Identification by Year

Category	1952	1956	1960	1964	1968	1972	1976	1980	1984
Strong Democrat	22%	21%	21%	26%	20%	15%	15%	18%	17%
Weak Democrat	25	23	25	25	25	25	25	23	20
Independent									
Democrat	10	7	8	9	10	11	12	11	11
Independent.	5	9	8	8	11	13	14	13	11
Independent									
Republican.	7	8	7	6	9	11	10	10	12
Weak Republican	14	14	13	13	14	13	14	14	15
Strong Republican. . . .	13	15	14	11	10	10	9	9	12
Apolitical	4	3	4	2	1	2	1	2	2

Data source: 1952 through 1984 Election Studies, Survey Research Center/Center for Political Studies.

with Independents, then the increase is from 22 percent of the electorate in 1952 to 34 percent in 1984. Either way, the greater number of Independents and the smaller number of Strong Partisans open the possibility of much wider swings from one election to the next.

A good deal has been written to the effect that the smaller number of persons identifying with the parties spells party weakness, if not the demise of the party system itself. Consequently, it is worth paying some attention to the evidence of stability in Table 10–1. While there are fewer Strong Partisans now than during the 1950s, the Democrats have remained the majority party. The extent of their advantage has varied somewhat from one election to the next. Republicans were best off in 1984; the Democrats were in 1964. If one calculates the ratio of all Strong, Weak, and Independent Democrats to all Strong, Weak, and Independent Republicans, the figures are 1.67, 1.37, 1.58, 2.0, 1.61, 1.50, 1.57, 1.57, and 1.23 for the presidential election years from 1952 through 1984. The ratios for 1956 (1.37), 1964 (2.0), and 1984 (1.23) stand out from the others in this series. Otherwise, the partisan balance has been remarkably stable.

Most of the change in the distribution of party identification took place between 1962 and 1972 and again in 1984. There are two sources of change that deserve comment: the growth in the number of independents and the increase in Republican identifiers in 1984. Let's take them one at a time.

Kent Jennings, Richard Niemi, and Gregory Markus have shown that the increase in independents is due to the entry of a new generation of voters. Their data come from a 17-year study of two generations. The voters-to-be were first interviewed as high school seniors in 1965. They were reinterviewed as 25 year olds in 1973 and as 34 year olds in 1982. At the same time, their parents (whose mean ages were 46, 54, and 63 in 1965, 1973, and 1982, respectively) were also interviewed. These scholars found that the party identifications of *both* generations were becoming more stable with the passage of time.[1] But they also reported that the younger generation was stabilizing at a much higher level of independence than the older generation. In 1982, 44 percent of the younger generation thought of themselves as independents as compared to only 27 percent of their parents (Jennings & Markus, 1984, pp. 1004–5; Jennings & Niemi, 1981). It is the addition of these younger voters to the electorate (and the deaths of still older voters, who were more likely to be partisans) that has produced the more independent electorate.

We must be especially cautious in commenting on the increase in Republican identifiers in 1984. Here, there are two possible explanations. One is that the 1984 shift was a response to short-term pro-Republican forces. The data in Table 10–1 show that there were more Republican identifiers during the 1956 Eisenhower landslide and more Democratic identifiers during the 1964 Johnson landslide. But these data also show that the ratio of Democrats to Republicans went right back to its customary value in 1960 and 1968. The same thing *may* happen in 1988; we simply do not know yet.

The second explanation gives more hope to the GOP. It happens that the pro-Republican changes were concentrated among two groups: Southerners and young voters. This combination of geography and generation suggests that the Republicans may look forward to better times. Southerners have been voting Republican for president for some time. If southern conservatives now think of themselves as Republicans, this could benefit the GOP in the Electoral College. And if the young voters' Republicanism turns out to be more than a temporary reaction to the contrast between Carter and Reagan, this could help the GOP well into the future. But again, we must reserve judgment about this. We know that changes took place in 1984 (Allsop, forthcoming; Allsop & Weisberg, 1986; Shanks & Miller, 1985; Weisberg, 1985). We do not yet know how lasting the changes will be.

Association with Presidential Choice

Another striking fact about party identification has been the strong association between that attitude and presidential choice. The authors of *The Voter Decides* and *The American Voter* were very careful to avoid saying that party identification caused citizens to vote one way or the other; there were other attitudes involved. (Other authors were not always as meticulous about this point.) Clear, however, was a strong bivariate correlation between party identification and vote choice. If you could know only one thing about each voter and had to predict the voter's presidential choice on the basis of this fact, party identification would be the best information to have.

---

[1] Specifically, Jennings and Markus reported that the Kendall's Tau-*b* correlations were .40 between 1965 and 1973, and .57 between 1973 and 1982 for the younger generation; .67 between 1965 and 1973, and .70 between 1973 and 1982 for the older generation. The crucial figures here are the .57 for the younger generation and the .67 for the older generation. Now in their mid-30s, the younger generation is approaching the level of attitudinal stability their parents had in their mid- to late 40s.

Table 10–2 presents the bivariate associations between party identification and vote choice for each presidential election. Several things are evident from these data. For example, except for 1964, Strong Republicans have been more likely to support their candidates than Strong Democrats. The dominant finding, though, is the close association between party identification and presidential vote. The relationship was a little weaker in 1964 (when a fair number of Republicans voted for Lyndon Johnson) and in 1972 (when a larger number of Democrats voted for Richard Nixon). But a "weaker" association in this case means that Kendall's Tau-c correlation dropped to "only" .62 in 1964 and .54 in 1972. Even including these figures, the series of correlations is .72, .75, .77, .62, .77, .54, .70, .72, and .77 for the presidential elections from 1952 through 1984. The association has been quite strong and uncommonly stable in view of the variety of candidates and circumstances that have characterized these elections.

Three Questions

Satisfying as these data are in demonstrating the importance of party identification, they also raise some questions. As you run your eye across the percentages in the party identification categories in Table 10–2 and compare them to the row totals, you can see the patterns of vote by identification category that lead to the very high measures of association. But notice the votes cast by the Weak Partisans. In 1956, 1960, 1964, 1972, 1976, and 1984, more Weak Democrats defected to the Republican candidate than did Independent Democrats. And in 1960, 1964, 1968, and 1976, more Weak Republicans defected than did Independent Republicans. Remember that the Weak Partisans identify with a party rather than with independents when answering the first party identification question. What is going on here? In particular, *what are the party identification questions measuring* that would account for this behavior?

A second paradox arises out of the strong bivariate correlations between party identification and vote. It is nice to know that the correlation has dropped below .7 only twice in three decades and even then has shown a very substantial relationship. Standing alone, this doesn't raise any question. But remember what we learned about party attitudes in Chapter 9. The data in Figure 9–2 (and elsewhere) showed that attitudes about parties were less important in the vote decision than they had been. How can party identification be of continuing importance while attitudes about parties are becoming less consequential? Specifically, *how does party identification interact with other attitudes in vote choice?* And how can such interaction explain this paradox?

Third, we saw in Table 10–1 that the 1950s and the decade between 1972 and 1982 have been periods of stability in the aggregate distribution of party identification. Aggregate stability, however, may result *either* from individual stability *or* from an equilibrium condition. Let's assume a population of 500 is made up of 300 Democrats and 200 Republicans. If no Democrats switch to

TABLE 10–2
Association between Party Identification and Presidential Choice

Year and Candidate	Strong Democrat	Weak Democrat	Independent Democrat	Independent	Independent Republican	Weak Republican	Strong Republican	Total
1952								
Stevenson	84%	62%	61%	20%	7%	7%	2%	42%
Eisenhower	16	38	39	80	93	93	98	58
Tau–c = .72								
1956								
Stevenson	85	63	67	17	7	7	1	40
Eisenhower	15	37	33	83	93	93	99	60
Tau–c = .75								
1960								
Kennedy	89	72	89	47	13	18	1	50
Nixon.	11	28	11	53	87	82	99	50
Tau–c = .77								
1964								
Johnson.	95	82	90	77	25	43	10	68
Goldwater	5	18	10	23	75	57	90	32
Tau–c = .62								
1968								
Humphrey	92	68	64	30	5	11	3	46
Nixon.	8	32	36	70	95	89	97	54
Tau–c = .77								
1972								
McGovern	73	49	61	30	13	9	3	36
Nixon.	27	51	39	70	87	91	97	64
Tau–c = .54								
1976								
Carter	92	75	76	43	14	22	3	51
Ford.	8	25	24	57	86	78	97	49
Tau–c = .70								
1980								
Carter	89	65	60	26	13	5	5	44
Reagan	11	35	40	74	87	95	95	56
Tau–c = .72								
1984								
Mondale	89	68	79	28	7	6	3	42
Reagan	11	32	21	72	93	94	97	58
Tau–c = .77								

Data source: 1952 through 1984 Election Studies, Survey Research Center/Center for Political Studies.

the Republican party and if no Republicans switch to the Democratic party, the party balance remains 300 Democrats and 200 Republicans. Here aggregate-level stability results from individual-level stability. Alternatively, if 25 Democrats switch to the Republican party and 25 Republicans switch to the Democratic party, the party balance still remains the same. In this case, aggregate-level stability results from an equilibrium condition in which movements in opposite directions cancel each other out.

Now let's say that over a given time period, 35 Republicans switch to the Democratic party and only 25 Democrats switch to the Republican party. There is a considerable difference in the rate of change among those switching parties: 58 percent moving in the Democratic direction and only 42 percent moving in a Republican direction. This would result in a population of 310 Democrats and 190 Republicans. In terms of overall balance between the parties, there would be only a 2 percent shift. The nature of equilibrium processes is such that *it takes a very great difference in the rate of change at the individual level before you notice anything at the aggregate level.* Consequently, aggregate-level stability (especially when it is as approximate as that in Table 10–1) tells you very little about individual-level stability. To say anything more, we must ask: *How stable is party identification at the individual level?*

We shall address these three questions—What is party identification measuring? How does party identification interact with other attitudes in vote choice? How stable is party identification?—in the balance of this chapter.

MEASUREMENT PROBLEMS

The question, "Generally speaking, do you think of yourself as a Republican, a Democrat, an independent, or what?," was first used by Warren E. Miller in a local Ann Arbor study in 1951. The question worked quite well, but in order to increase its explanatory power, two follow-up questions were added during pretests preceding the first major national study in 1952. One asked Republicans and Democrats whether they thought of themselves as strong or weak partisans. The other asked independents whether they were closer to the Republicans or Democrats.

When the resulting data were published in 1954, emphasis was placed on the then novel idea of psychological attachment to a party. The idea that groups exercised influence over their members was familiar enough to social psychologists; but most political scientists at that time thought of belonging to a political party either in terms of voting for that party or as being registered as a Republican or a Democrat. So rather than discuss the details of scale construction, the authors of *The Voter Decides* underscored the role of parties as groups that were sources of influence.

> The sense of personal attachment which the individual feels toward the group of his choice is referred to . . . as identification, and, with respect to parties as groups, as *party identification.* Strong identification is equated with high signifi-

> cance of the group as an influential standard . . . . [It is assumed] that most Americans identify themselves with one or the other of the two major parties, and that this sense of attachment and belonging is predictably associated with their political behavior. (Campbell, Gurin & Miller, 1954, pp. 88–89, 111)

The authors were clear in their own minds that the basic classification was a threefold division between Republicans, Independents, and Democrats. They saw the subdivisions (Strong Republicans, Weak Republicans, Independent Republicans, and so on) as devices to allow them to capture additional variance, but they did not say this in print. The original investigators were also aware that Weak Partisans were sometimes more likely to defect than Independent Partisans.[2] They published data showing this and made their data available so other scholars could conduct independent investigations, but they did not offer any explanations of why this should or should not occur.

By the 1970s, with literally hundreds of scholars sifting through the party identification data, a number of persons became uncomfortable with the accumulating findings. A lively exchange took place in the literature (Petrocik, 1974; Brody, 1977; Wolfinger et al., 1977; Miller & Miller, 1977; Fiorina, 1977; Shively, 1977, 1979; Valentine & van Wingen, 1980; Weisberg, 1980; Dennis, 1981; Miller & Wattenberg, 1983). The principal questions concerning the categories of party identification were:

1. Why do Weak Partisans sometimes defect at rates greater than Independent Partisans?
2. What does being an Independent mean?
3. Are the Independent Partisans more like the Weak Partisans or the Independents?

One of the most interesting suggestions was that party identification could not be properly conceived as a single dimension (Van Wingen & Valentine, 1978; Weisberg, 1980). The traditional view placed Strong Democrats and Strong Republicans at the opposite end of the scale. This implied that if you were a Strong Democrat, you were attracted toward the Democratic party *and* repelled from the Republican party, with the opposite implication if you were a Strong Republican. If you were an Independent, you were midway between these positions and not atttracted to either party. But the basic question— "Generally speaking, do you think of yourself as a Republican, a Democrat, an independent, or what?"—invokes the respondent's self-image and perceptions of Republicans, Democrats, and independents. The traditional conception was that *one* of these political groups would serve as a reference group (that is, a positively valued source of cues). But if you admit the possibility of *multiple* reference groups or the possibility that *none* of the political reference groups was positively evaluated, then how respondents see themselves with

---

[2] I first noticed this myself when analyzing 1964 data. When I showed the data to Warren Miller, his comment was, "Oh, yes, the W curve. That's very familiar."

respect to Republicans, Democrats, and Independents becomes a more complex matter.

The 1980 Election Study contained some evidence supporting the more complex view. Two of the questions asked separately about support for parties and independence. The party item asked: "Do you think of yourself as a supporter of one of the political parties or not?" The independence item asked: "Do you ever think of yourself as a political independent or not?" Table 10-3A shows a cross-tabulation of the answers to these questions. If the traditional interpretation is correct that being an Independent is the opposite of being a Strong Partisan, then all the cases ought to be in either the upper right-hand cell (as party supporters who are not independents) or the lower left-hand cell (as independents who are not party supporters). The data suggest that this traditional interpretation applies to a majority of citizens, but it does not to a substantial minority. Nearly 15 percent (the upper left-hand cell) report both parties and independents as reference groups, and double that proportion (the lower right-hand cell) are not accepting cues from either parties or independents.

Those who regard themselves as both partisans and independents do not

TABLE 10–3
The Complexity of Party Identification, 1980

A. Party Support by Independence

Party Supporter?	Independent?	
	Yes	No
Yes	14.8%*	26.2%
No	28.9	30.0

B. What Is Traditional Identification Question Measuring?

Traditional Strength Component

Party Supporter or Independent	Strong Partisan	Weak Partisan	Inde- pendent Partisan	Inde- pendent	Total
Party supporter .... (upper right-hand cell)	62.1%†	23.9%	4.1%	0.5%	26.2%
Supports party and independent.......... (upper left-hand cell)	18.2	14.8	16.8	6.2	14.8
Neither................. (lower right-hand cell)	15.5	44.0	15.6	33.5	30.0
Only independent .... (lower left-hand cell)	4.2	17.3	63.4	59.3	28.9
Tau–*b* = .32					

* The cell entries are percentages of the total.
† The cell entries are column percentages.
Data source: 1980 Election Study, Center for Political Studies.

pose much of a problem to party identification except as they require conceiving of multiple reference groups. These citizens are getting some of their cues from at least one party and other information from candidate and issue cues, as do independents. But those who reject both partisanship and independence are more difficult to handle. They appear to resemble the "no-preference nonpartisans" identified by Arthur Miller and Martin Wattenberg,[3] and seen by those authors to be increasing as parties become less salient. "To these respondents parties are not perceived as relevant to the political process; therefore many of these citizens may not consider themselves to be Independents simply because in their minds there are no meaningful partisan objects to be independent from" (1983, p. 117).

In the face of these difficulties, what is the traditional party identification series measuring? Data on this question are shown in Table 10–3B, where the traditional strength component is cross-tabulated against the four categories from Table 10–3A. Most of the Strong Partisans are, in fact, party supporters. Most of the Independent Partisans and Independents do, in fact, think of themselves as independents. They are more similar to each other than either is to the Weak Partisans—although the Independent Partisan category has a larger proportion who think of themselves as both partisans and independents. The measurement problem comes primarily in the Weak Partisan category. This category contains a little bit of everything. Moreover, the largest number of the Weak Partisans consists of those who reject both parties and independence and are (from the standpoint of the underlying reference-group theory) unpredictable in their behavior.

Another series of questions on party identification was asked in the 1980 Election Study. Each respondent was asked: "Do any of these statements come close to what you mean when you say you think of yourself as an independent [or whatever the party identification category was]?" Then each was asked to agree or disagree with each of a series of 6 to 11 statements. The statements (such as "I dislike both parties" or "I don't know enough to make a choice," for independents) were all plausible interpretations of someone's view of what that party identification category meant. Unfortunately for the cause of certainty, majorities of the respondents *disagreed* with most of the statements.

Strong Partisans agreed with three statements: 65 percent said they "almost always support the Democratic [or Republican] candidates"; 60 percent agreed they were "enthusiastic about what the Democratic [or Republican] party stands for"; and 63 percent said, "Ever since I can remember, I've been a Democrat [or Republican]." Habitual voting seemed to be more of a Demo-

---

[3] The one difference is that the no-preference nonpartisans studied by Miller and Wattenberg are those classified (incorrectly, they argue) as either Independent Partisans or Independents. The largest proportion of those who reject both partisanship and independence in the 1980 sample (58 percent) are Weak Partisans.

cratic than a Republican tendency: 71 percent of the Strong Democrats agreed they'd been Democrats "ever since I can remember" compared to 56 percent of the Strong Republicans; and a majority of the Strong Democrats (55 percent) agreed with "My parents were Democrats and I am too," whereas only a minority of Republicans (44 percent) agreed with the comparable statement.

Only one statement was agreed to by Weak Partisans: 66 percent said they would "vote for the person, not the party." (A majority of Weak Republicans—56 percent—said they "usually prefer Republican candidates, but sometimes I support Democrats"; but only 44 percent of Weak Democrats assented to the comparable statement.) None of the statements read to Independent Partisans was agreed to by a majority.[4] Independents agreed with two statements: 70 percent said, "I decide on the person not the party," and 56 percent assented to "I decide on the issues not the party label."

The rejected alternatives were significant in setting aside some plausible interpretations. Substantial majorities of partisans said that they did not dislike the opposite party, and almost all Independents rejected statements that they disliked both parties. This undercuts a single-dimension interpretation. Being attracted to one political group does not mean being repelled by others. Majorities also said that their party identification did not depend on their views of Jimmy Carter or Gerald Ford. Thinking of oneself as "a Republican, a Democrat, an independent, or what" does not depend on short-term candidate cues.

The only substantive meaning that can be extracted from these responses comes from the Strong Partisans' agreement that they usually vote for the party, the Weak Partisans' statements that they usually vote for the person, and the Independents' agreement that they decide on the basis of the person or the issues. This is consistent with reference-group theory, which implies Strong Partisans are accepting cues from their parties, Weak Partisans are accepting voting cues from candidate sources, and Independents are accepting cues from candidate or issue sources but leaves open the question of what, if anything, is motivating voters who did not agree with these statements.

Finally, note the moderate association (Tau-b = .32) between the traditional party identification classification and that based on separate partisanship and independence questions. This means that the traditional classification is picking up some but not all of a more complex reality and is quite consistent with data that suggest that many but not all persons are correctly classified by the traditional scheme. It appears that some citizens have multiple (partisan and independent) reference groups, some have only one such reference group, and some have no such reference group. No one-dimensional taxonomy is going to capture all of this, but the traditional classification is a good first approximation.

---

[4] For whatever reason, only 6 statements were read to the Independent Partisans, compared to 8 to both Strong and Weak Partisans and 11 to Independents.

INTERACTION WITH OTHER ATTITUDES

The Extent of Cognitive Consistency

The extent to which citizens' political cognitions are consistent with one another has been a matter of considerable controversy among political scientists. This is not the place to review all the positions taken by various protagonists (for some of the leading arguments, see Lane, 1973; Nie & Andersen, 1974; Converse, 1975; Bennett, 1977; Sullivan, Piereson & Marcus, 1978; and Bishop, Tuchfarber & Oldendick, 1978), but one of the problems concerns how cognitive consistency should be measured.

Any measure of cognitive consistency has two aspects. One is the criterion by which consistency is judged. This criterion may be liberalism-conservatism, partisanship, rules of logic that imply a necessary connection between elements, or something else. If the criterion is, say, liberalism-conservatism and if all of a person's attitudes are what we have agreed to call liberal, then we would say that by this criterion the person has consistent attitudes. If some of the person's attitudes are liberal and others are conservative, then we would say that the person's attitudes are inconsistent.

It is important to know just what criterion is being used. Attitudes that are consistent by one criterion may be inconsistent by another. For example, if Republicans take a more liberal position than Democrats on foreign policy and a more conservative position on economics, then an individual Republican who held these attitudes could be judged consistent by a partisan criterion but inconsistent by a liberal-conservative criterion. *The criterion for consistency must be explicit* so we know how to judge each case.

The second aspect of measurement is whether the data concern a population of individuals or whether there is sufficient information about each individual to know if each person's own attitudes are consistent. This is essentially a levels-of-analysis problem. The two levels are individual and within-individual. The data determine what inferences can be properly drawn.

If the data concern a population of individuals, then the proper meaning of consistency is that attitudes are consistent across individuals. For example, if attitudes on civil rights and attitudes on jobs are correlated, then Person A, who favors government action to protect civil rights, is also likely to favor government action to provide jobs. Person B, who opposes government activity in the civil rights area, is also likely to think that people should find their own jobs without government help. The essential variation here is between A and B (and other members of the population being studied). These data do not demonstrate (although they do not rule out) any necessary relationship between civil rights and jobs in the thinking of either A or B.

On the other hand, if we can "get inside" each person's cognitive structure, we can make inferences about consistency within the individual. Suppose, for example, in an in-depth interview, the respondent has explained the relationship she or he sees between civil rights and jobs. Then the investigator can assert that these attitudes are consistent for that person. Or if we have survey data that include some criterion that can be applied to each individual, a similar conclusion can be reached. If a person claims to be a conservative and gives a conservative answer to questions on civil rights and jobs, then that person's attitudes may be said to be consistent. Since the concept of consistency is that there are links between elements of an individual's thought, *within-individual data are the proper ones to use.*

Table 10–4 gives the distributions for two measures of cognitive consistency that have been constructed using partisan criteria and within-individual data. The index of partisan issue consistency is based on proximity measures of issues. To measure proximity, one question asks where a respondent stands on an issue. A second asks what the respondent's perception is of the candidate's stand on the same issue. With this information, we can determine the distance (proximity) between the respondent's preference and perception of the candidate's position. The index of partisan attitude consistency is based on the same series of questions we used in Chapter 8 to measure information level and in Chapter 9 for the probit model of presidential vote choice.

Partisan criteria were used for assessing consistency with both indexes. If the respondents were Republicans, they were regarded as consistent if they perceived the Republican candidate's position to be closer to their own when answering the proximity questions or if they expressed pro-Republican or anti-Democratic attitudes when answering the series of questions quoted at the outset of Chapter 8. If they were Democrats, they were regarded as

TABLE 10–4
Distribution of Cognitive Consistency by Two Indexes*, 1972

Cognitive Consistency Score†	Percent of Electorate Falling within Range	
	Partisan Issue Consistency	Partisan Attitude Consistency
1.0.	16.3%	5.8%
.81–.90	13.4	4.1
.71–.80	13.2	10.7
.61–.70	11.4	17.2
.51–.60	7.3	17.4
.5	15.3	18.3
.40–.49	4.1	12.9
.30–.39	3.4	8.5
.20–.29	8.1	2.8
.10–.19	1.8	0.8
0	5.7	1.5

* For details on the construction of these indexes, see Appendix A–10.1.
† A higher consistency score indicates more consistent attitudes.
Data sources: Partisan Issue Consistency Index, 1972 Hofstetter Survey of General Public; Partisan Attitude Consistency Index, 1972 Election Study, Center for Political Studies.

consistent if they perceived the Democratic candidate's position to be closer to their own when answering the proximity questions or if they expressed pro-Democratic or anti-Republican attitudes when answering the longer series of questions. Details about the construction of the two indexes may be found in Appendix A–10.1, but the essential point to bear in mind when examining Table 10–4 is that a high score on either index means greater cognitive consistency.

The cognitive consistency indexes show that most people experienced a moderate degree of partisan inconsistency.[5] The distributions on the two indexes are not identical (nor would they be expected to be since the two indexes were differently constructed), but they are in agreement on three basic points.

1.   Only a relatively small proportion of the total population has completely consistent attitudes.
2.   Both of the distributions have bulges at the .5 mark, meaning that there are citizens whose attitudes are equally balanced between the two major parties.[6]
3.   By far the most important, the largest proportion of citizens (45 percent on the partisan issue consistency index and 49 percent on the partisan attitude consistency index) have scores between .6 and .9.

This means that the majority of their attitudes favor their own party but they can see some favorable aspects about the opposing party.

Think back to the St. Louis immigrant and the woman living in Bellingham, Washington, whose interviews you read at the beginning of Chapter 8. These two respondents' information levels were very high and high, respectively, but they were reasonably typical so far as cognitive consistency was concerned. The St. Louis woman certainly favored the Democrats but did say that there were some good progressive Republicans. The Washington housewife leaned toward the Republicans but liked Democratic plans to check tax loopholes and approved of Jimmy Carter's Christianity. To understand how such persons make their vote choices, we need a theory that will explain decisions made in the face of a moderate amount of inconsistent information.

Party Identification as Arbiter

Attitude conflict is one of the most familiar findings in the voting field. After analyzing data gathered in the first major voting study, Paul Lazarsfeld and his colleagues (Lazarsfeld, Berelson & Gaudet, 1944) devised a theory of

---

[5] See Figure 11–2 for the distributions of the partisan attitude consistency index for two other years.

[6] This is of interest because all Independents were excluded from these indexes. (A partisan criterion of consistency could not be applied to them.) Hence, some Strong Partisans, Weak Partisans, or Leaners must be equally divided in their attitudes.

cross-pressures to deal with such conflict. Cross-pressures are simply the forces (the citizen's own attitudes, peer influences, or whatever) pulling a person in opposite directions in an election situation. The more cross-pressured a person is, the more likely that person is to delay the voting decision or to try in some similar way to avoid the cross-pressures.

More recently, Peter Sperlich has introduced some qualifications to this straightforward theory: "First . . . attitudinal conflicts which are not at least of a certain minimum importance to the person are not likely to produce cross-pressure effects. Second . . . the more important the conflict, the stronger will be the behavioral effect" (1971, p. 90). When he speaks of importance, Sperlich is referring to centrality (about which more shortly), but his propositions hold if we understand importance to refer to the extent of partisan inconsistency, and the behavioral effect resulting from this inconsistency to be defection to the opposite party in voting.

Figure 10–1 shows a plot of voting defection by partisan issue consistency. Both of the effects predicted by Sperlich's cross-pressure theory are present. The data points for consistency above .6 are depicted by dots, and the relationship between these consistency scores and the likelihood of defection are shown by the solid line. (Both the dots and the solid line appear in the lower left corner of the figure.) The consistency scores from .6 down to 0 are depicted by x's and the relationship between these scores and the likelihood of defection by the dashed line. (The x's and the dashed line begin in the lower part, somewhat to the left of center, and proceed to the upper right of the figure.)

Now notice that the solid line is nearly parallel to the bottom of the figure. This means that as one increases inconsistency (that is, as the consistency scores decrease), there is very little effect on the probability of defection. Voters, only two thirds of whose attitudes favor their party, are just as likely to support their party as voters whose attitudes are completely consistent. To repeat Sperlich's words, "attitudinal conflicts which are not at least of a certain minimum importance to the person are not likely to produce cross-pressure effects." In 1972, the magnitude of inconsistency necessary before much defection took place was a score of about .6.

In contrast, the dashed line representing the relation between inconsistency and defection for low-consistency scores moves upward and to the right. This means that once one has reached a certain threshold (the .6 score in this instance), the more a voter agrees with the opposition, the greater the likelihood the voter will defect. After the threshold is reached, there is a strong relationship between inconsistency and defection.

This relationship appears to be quite robust. That is, one can vary the strength of party identification, interest in the campaign, concern with the outcome of the election, education, newspaper usage, and national television usage—all variables that affect information level and political activity—and obtain roughly the same relationships. ***Until one reaches a given threshold,***

FIGURE 10–1
Partisan Defection by Issue Consistency, 1972

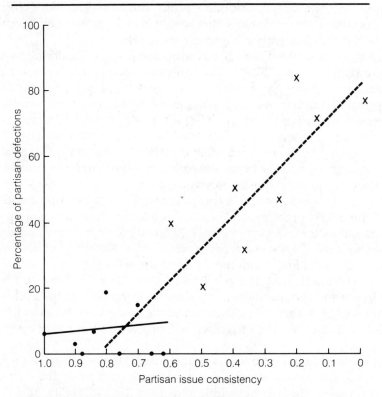

The dots represent defection rates for partisan consistency scores of .6 or higher. The x's represent defection rates for consistency scores of .6 or lower. The regression lines, the lines that represent the prediction one makes about the dependent variable (partisan defection) from knowledge of the independent variable (cognitive consistency) have been calculated by weighting the data points in this figure for the number of cases they represent. For consistency scores higher than .6, represented by the solid line, there is little relation between consistency scores and defection rate: $r = .17$. For consistency scores of .6 or lower, represented by the dashed line, there is a very strong relation: $r = .83$.

there is little relation between partisan inconsistency and vote defection. After that threshold is reached, there is a strong relationship.[7]

All this implies that party identification interacts with other attitudes to affect presidential vote choice in two ways.[8] First, as we saw in the proportion of high-consistency scores in Table 10–4, most of the identifiers' perceptions

---

[7] For a demonstration of similar results with 1968 data, see Norman Fogel (1974).

[8] Party identification has a different effect on votes for other offices. Among other reasons for this, once you shift from the presidency to subpresidential offices, the voters know less about the candidates and so are less likely to need an arbiter to resolve attitude conflicts (see Hinckley, Hofstetter & Kessel, 1974, pp. 143–45).

favor their own party. Second, as we saw in Figure 10–1, party identification appears to act as if it were an arbiter in the face of the moderate cognitive inconsistency that most people experience. Attitude conflicts tend to be resolved in favor of one's own party. Therefore, most identifiers vote for their own party's candidate.

Party Identification as Central

Party identification, acting both directly and indirectly through more specific attitudes, appears to exercise a strong effect on presidential vote choice; it continues to do so even at a time when attitudes about parties are less consequential. In 1972, the year from which the data for our analysis of cognitive consistency came, party attitudes made up less than 10 percent of the total and were not significantly related to vote choice. How can this paradox of inconsequential party attitudes and very consequential party identification be resolved?

First, party identification is much more likely to be a central attitude. Attitude objects are said to possess centrality when they are of enduring concern to the individual; they are more important than others in the individual's cognitive structure. For those with some degree of interest in politics, the attitude objects in the party identification question are more likely to be of enduring concern (and hence, central) than other political objects. If the individual is very interested in politics and regards more than one of the political groups (that is, Republicans, Democrats, or independents) as reference groups, then the question would focus both on the self and on multiple reference groups. This would produce a complex attitude but certainly a central one. If only one political group is a positive reference group for the person, then the likelihood is that there would be a strong affective tie between the person and the party with which that person identified. For persons unconcerned with politics, the situation is more problematical. For example, if their inclusive values were religious, their reference groups would be more likely to be their churches rather than any political groups.[9] In the first two cases, though, party identification would be the most likely of a person's political attitudes to be central and so exercise some influence over other attitudes.

Questions that simply ask about political parties, on the other hand, do not have any special standing. They tap attitudes about objects that are wholly external to the individual. Hence, these attitudes about various aspects of parties will not occupy central positions in a person's cognitive structure, but party identification will. The centrality of party identification thus resolves our paradox of the declining importance of party attitudes and the continued importance of party identification. Even if attitudes about parties as such

---

[9] In this last case, again assuming a church as a reference group, specific attitudes might be judged according to how they fit into a denominational outlook. For further discussion of centrality, see Judd and Krosnick (1982); Krosnick (1986).

were to disappear entirely, party identification could continue to act as an arbiter in the face of conflicting attitudes about candidates and issues.

INDIVIDUAL–LEVEL STABILITY

How Stable Is Party Identification?

If party identification is a central attitude, it ought to be a stable attitude. The argument from centrality is that since other attitudes are arrayed around the central attitude, there are greater psychological costs to changing a central attitude (with consequences for a whole cluster of associated attitudes) than to altering one of the peripheral attitudes. We have already seen that party identification has been relatively stable on the aggregate level, especially in the 1950s and the 1970s. Now, how stable is party identification on the individual level?

In what has been recognized as a classic analysis, Philip Converse (1964) demonstrated that *party identification was more stable on the individual level than were other attitudes*. In spite of Converse's careful statements, many seemed to think that he (and his coauthors in *The American Voter*) were claiming that party identification was absolutely stable. This was not their intent.[10] In fact, Converse was busy studying the extent of longitudinal change in party identification. As he put the matter in a 1966 letter:

> Naturally, we never intended to say that nobody ever changes, and any excla-
> mations over stability are entirely relative. The Tau-*b* [correlation] for the full
> party identification measure over a four-year period in the panel was .68. How
> stable this is, of course, depends on one's expectations and other information
> cast in comparable form. Party identification is less stable than sex and religious
> creed, but about the same level of stability as things like occupation, union
> membership, and so forth. What is most impressive, perhaps, is that there are
> no other measures of political attitudes of any type which are even within rough
> shooting distance of this degree of stability.

More recent findings have added to our understanding in very important ways. One of these was the 17-year study by Kent Jennings and his colleagues (discussed earlier in this chapter) showing that the indentification of the younger generation tends to be more independent than that of their parents. Another was John Jackson's (1975) and Morris Fiorina's (1981, chap. 5) use of nonrecursive models to show that party identification can be affected by more specific attitudes concerning issues and candidates. But the central insight—that party identification is more stable than other political attitudes though not absolutely so—remains as Converse stated it in the 1960s.

---

[10] The major reason for this lack of understanding was that complex findings tend to be simplified as they pass into the accepted body of thought in any discipline. But there were two specific reasons as well. The first data from the 1956–58–60 panel study were *just* becoming available when *The American Voter* was going to press and so were not discussed in that influential book. And Philip Converse was busy with so many other scholarly projects that his findings were not published until his relatively short book, *The Dynamics of Party Support*, appeared in 1976.

TABLE 10–5
Stability of Political Attitudes, 1972–1976

Attitude	Tau–b Correlation	Percent of Respondents Changing Position*	Mean Change*
Party identification......	.69	· 50.2%	−.10
Neoisolationism........	.31		
Foreign aid............	.27		
Cut military spending ...	.36		
Government handling of economy..........	.27		
Tax rate	.26	67.8	.14
Federal power	.28		
Standard of living	.36	67.5	.17
Health insurance	.42	66.2	.15
Civil rights too fast?	.44		
Aid minority groups.....	.38	67.3	.23
School integration	.41		
Busing	.42	35.4	−.15

* The percent of respondents changing positions and the extent of the mean change are reported only for those attitudes measured on seven category scales, because a respondent is more likely to select a different answer when given more to choose among. The mean percent of persons reporting changes on seven category scales is 60.4; on three category scales, 40.7; on two category scales, 30.4. The seven category scales provide the appropriate comparison for party identification.

Data source: 1972–1976 Panel Study, Center for Political Studies. (No 1974 data were used. This analysis was based on only the two time points.)

Table 10–5 presents data on this point from 1972 respondents who were reinterviewed in 1976. Three measures of stability are given: Kendall's Tau-*b* correlations for 1972 and 1976, the proportion of respondents who changed positions between the two time points, and the mean extent of change along the underlying scale. The table compares the stability of party identification with specific attitudes from four policy areas. From top to bottom, they are international involvement, economic management, social benefits, and civil liberties. The attitudes about civil liberties appear to be the most stable of the policy attitudes, but the correlation between the two time points is far higher for party identification.

Both of the other measures confirm this impression of stability. In all but one case (busing[11]), fewer respondents shifted position on party identification than did so on other attitudes. The average extent of change on party identification was also less than it was for any of the specific attitudes.

---

[11] Busing was unusual because both the 1972 and 1976 distributions were skewed due to the strong opposition to busing. Of the 64.6 percent with stable attitudes on this topic, 90 percent were persons who were strongly opposed to busing in both 1972 and 1976.

When changes did take place on party identification, two thirds of the changers moved only one category along the seven-category party identification scale. The largest number of changers consisted of 1972 Weak Democrats who said they were Strong Democrats in 1976; the second largest number was made up of 1972 Strong Republicans who said they were Weak Republicans in 1976. Given what we know (from Table 10–3B) about the jumbled nature of the Weak Partisan category, this does not represent much of a change.

Information Level, Cognitive Consistency, and Party Identification

Specific attitudes (such as those about issues or candidates) can influence the stability of party identification in two ways. First, the specific attitudes provide informational support. The more citizens know about politics, the more likely they are to know why they are Republicans or Democrats. Because of this, their party identifications are better anchored in a bed of specific attitudes. Second, the other attitudes support party identification if they are consistent with it. We have already seen that one can tolerate a certain amount of cognitive inconsistency without defecting in voting. Probably, the same thing applies in party identification. The specific attitudes change rather easily. As long as only a few of the attitudes in the cluster associated with party identification are inconsistent, this can be tolerated. When a substantial number of other attitudes become inconsistent with one's party identification, then the probability of changing party identification becomes much greater.

In Table 10–6, we see what happens to the stability of party identification when we vary the properties of information level and cognitive consistency. In general, the data support the argument in the preceding paragraph. When either information level or cognitive consistency is low, then the correlations (.49 and .56, respectively) are also relatively low. This tells us that party identification is less stable when information or partisan consistency is low. As we move into the average-minus and the average-plus categories, the

TABLE 10–6
Stability of Party Identification by Cognitive Properties, 1972–1976

Cognitive Property in 1972	Level			
	Low	Average Minus	Average Plus	High
Information level	.49	.67	.70	.59
Partisan attitude consistency	.56	.60	.73	.63

* Entries are Kendall's Tau–*b* correlations between party identification in 1972 and 1976 for respondents in the category. The correlation for all respondents was .69.
Data source: 1972–1976 Election Study, Center for Political Studies.

correlations rise. This tells us that party identification becomes more stable as information increases and as other attitudes become more consistent. So far, so good. But notice what happens as we move from the average-plus category to the high category. The correlations decline, meaning that party identification is less stable in the high categories.

Why should this be so? The reason is found in the lack of association between information level and partisan consistency.[12] The best-informed citizens are likely to have attitudes that are inconsistent with their party identifications. Recall the free-lance photographer from Philadelphia. She was the best informed of the seven respondents, and she could certainly see good points about the Republicans and the Democrats. Persons who know this much are open to change because of conflicting attitudes. Citizens with the most consistent attitudes, on the other hand, are not likely to know very much. Recall the beer-can worker from Findlay, Ohio. His attitudes were almost completely pro-Republican, but he was not very well informed. Persons of this kind are open to persuasion of the opposite party—if anyone can get their attention—because they don't have enough information for their attitudes to be very well anchored.

The apparently irregular results can be reconciled with the general argument about the stabilizing effects of greater information and attitudinal consistency. Close examination finds the expected effects of more information and more consistency. It is just that there are very few people who are both well informed and completely consistent in their attitudes.

SUMMARY

In this chapter, we have seen something of the complexity of party identification, its relation to presidential vote choice, and its stability. As to complexity, there is evidence that some have multiple partisan reference groups, some have one, and some have none. The traditional measure of party identification can properly categorize those who get their cues from a single source but not those with multiple reference groups or no partisan reference group at all. As to presidential vote choice, we saw a strong association at the bivariate level and later examined this in light of the centrality of party identification when it interacts with more specific attitudes. On stability, party identification was relatively stable on the aggregate level during the 1950s and the 1970s, and much more stable at the individual level than other attitudes whatever the time period. Also, its stability could be increased with enhanced information and greater cognitive consistency.

---

[12] The relation varies a bit depending on the year and the measure of partisan consistency used. I have plotted information level against partisan attitude consistency for 1952, 1972, and 1976. I have also plotted information level against partisan issue consistency for 1972. In every case, the slope was very close to 0, meaning that information level and partisan consistency were independent of each other.

In this part of the book, we covered the concepts of internal structure, external structure, and time as they applied to citizen activity in presidential elections. Internal cognitive structure was analyzed with respect to information level and the salience, partisan valence, consistency, and centrality of attitudes. Internal structure was very much dependent on external structure because of the content of the informational environment as affected by media characteristics and campaign strategies and because of the citizen's involvement with the informational environment. The citizen's activity in the political environment, specifically presidential vote choice, was shown to be highly predictable from the nature of the citizen's attitudes. Temporal effects were shown, both in the modest increase in the "average" citizen's information level in the course of a campaign, and in the variation from one campaign to another of both specific attitudes and party identification.

As we saw in earlier parts of the book, campaign strategists are not free to choose just any strategy. They are limited by the internal composition of their supporting coalition and by the external support they are trying to obtain. Similarly, citizens are unlikely to respond in just any way. They are limited by the matrix of attitudes that exists at the beginning of the campaign. But just as we have seen a variety of strategies followed by different coalitions with different goals, the response of the electorate also varies from one campaign to the next. For if the matrix of attitudes is relatively stable in the very short term, it is rather more flexible in the longer term. And the reaction of the electorate in the next election will be determined by the modification of those attitudes as a result of what the administration does in office over the next four years, by the strategy its opposition chooses to use to challenge it, and by the strategy with which it chooses to defend its record.

Part Five

Conclusion

Chapter 11

Continuity and Change in Presidential Parties

WHAT'S HAPPENING TO THE PARTIES?

Presidential parties are alive and playing a dynamic role in American politics. After all the material covered to this point, this should hardly be a surprise. Yet, this is not the only view of American political parties.

Many scholars, especially those writing in the 1970s, claimed that political parties were passing from the American scene. Walter Dean Burnham asserted:

> The American electorate is now deep into the most sweeping transformation it has experienced since the Civil War. . . . This critical realignment . . . is cutting across older partisan linkages between the rulers and the ruled. The consequence is an astonishingly rapid dissolution of the political party as an effective intervenor between the voter and the objects of his vote at the polls. (1975, p. 308)

Everett Carll Ladd claimed that the "series of strange electoral performances [in the 1960s and 1970s] is chiefly the result of the pronounced weakening of American political parties that has taken place in recent decades—a process that has by now brought them to the point of virtual death as organizations" (1982, p. 51). One did not have to look far to find visions of crape; writings about political parties were filled with "decomposition," "dealignment," "disarray," "decay," and other mournful nouns.

A second view reflects an opinion, long held by some American scholars, that parties *ought* to be stronger than they are. "England and France," Woodrow Wilson wrote a century ago, "recognize and support simple, straight-forward, inartificial party government . . . whilst we . . . permit only a less direct government by party majorities. . . . The English take their parties straight—we take ours mixed" (1884, pp. 97–98). Wilson's current intellectual heirs are more realistic about the limits to reform, but their views are to some degree affected by what William Crotty has called the "seductive myth of the perfect party: cohesive, policy oriented, representative, and disciplined" (1980b, p. 34). Some (Pomper, 1980) simply think parties are important and should be stronger. Others (Harmel & Janda, 1982, p. 117) see hints that movement in that direction may have begun.

My own view is closer to the clear-eyed, moderate posture taken in a fine new book by Leon Epstein. He does not

> express gloom and doom about the future of a democracy whose parties disinte-grate. I have doubts about both the extensiveness of party decline and the earlier glories of American parties. And I do not envision or advocate the transforma-tion of American parties into strikingly new and powerful institutions. (1986, p. 3)

I agree with this and would add one further element: the prior obligation of a scholar to understanding. This does not mean that I oppose advocacy. Scholars, after all, are citizens and have every right to speak out. But if one wishes to speak with authority, then comprehension of the subject matter must come first. Political parties are complex institutions. With any such entity, changes are almost always taking place, but most are microchanges. Some of them weaken the institution; others strengthen it. Some reinforce one another; others cancel each other out. Therefore, simple statements about overall institutional change—"the Democratic party has virtually died" or "the presidency has become preeminent"—almost never capture the under-lying reality.

The Availability of Evidence

The collection of data concerning political parties has been quite uneven. As you could tell from the analysis of citizen activity, richly detailed surveys of the electorate have been conducted regularly for some time. We also have good time-series data on legislative parties because of the roll-call votes re-corded for all members of the House and the Senate. Given these data, there has been a great deal of work on voting behavior and legislative politics, and theories of these forms of politics are well articulated.

On the other hand, the 1972 Hofstetter data set is still the only national study of electoral activists, and good data about the presidency remain diffi-cult to come by. Partly because of the unevenness of data collections and partly because many scholars specialize in only one or two subjects, it has not been generally understood that one cannot collect data on only one institu-tional domain and then make generalizations about "political parties."

Table 11–1 summarizes the most complete, simultaneously collected data available about Democrats and Republicans in several different institutional

TABLE 11–1
Positions of Various Party Groupings by Policy Area, 1972

Party Grouping	International Involvement	Economic Management	Social Benefits	Civil Liberties
	Policy Area*			
Democratic representatives	Moderate	Liberal	Liberal	Moderate
Democratic electoral activists	Moderate liberal	Moderate	Liberal	Liberal
Democratic citizens	Moderate	Moderate	Moderate liberal	Moderate conservative
Republican citizens	Moderate	Moderate	Moderate	Moderate conservative
Republican electoral activists	Moderate	Moderate	Moderate	Moderate conservative
Republican White House staff	Moderate conservative	Moderate conservative	Moderate conservative	Moderate conservative
Republican representatives	Conservative	Conservative	Moderate conservative	Moderate conservative

* For discussion of the scores that determine the positions in the policy areas, see Appendix A–11.1.
   Data sources: Electoral activists and citizens, 1972 Hofstetter study; White House staff, interviews with Domestic Council staff members; congressional data courtesy of Aage R. Clausen.

domains. We do not have measures on those involved in nomination politics that year (1972), but we do have identical questions that were addressed to citizens, electoral activists, and members of the White House staff and votes of members of the House of Representatives in the same policy areas.

There is considerable variation as one moves across the several sets of actors. In the case of economic management, the variation goes across the full ideological spectrum from liberal to conservative. In general, citizens take moderate positions, Democratic activists take more liberal positions, and Republican activists take more conservative positions. In general, the more involved the activists are with policy questions, the farther out they are along the ideological spectrum. There are a couple of exceptions to this liberal-to-conservative ordering. Representatives tend to take more conservative positions in international involvement, and Democratic electoral activists are more liberal on civil liberties (especially busing) than representatives who had to run for reelection.

Since the data come from a single year, we ought to be quite cautious in interpreting this pattern. What is clear, however, is that *moving from one institutional setting to another does make a difference.* Most scholars have been very careful to recognize that *findings about political parties are time specific.* (In other words, one does not assume that attitudes that were important in 1984 voting decisions are also important in 1988 voting decisions until one has a chance to test this by looking at 1988 data.) What also needs to be understood is that *findings about political parties are institution specific.*

One major message of this book is that one cannot make verifiable statements about political parties as a whole. No one can observe the entire Democratic party or the entire Republican party. What can be observed is a particular coalition in a particular institution, or sets of persons who think of themselves as Democrats or Republicans. Therefore, we cannot describe "the Democratic party" or "the Republican party" except as an abstraction. But we can say what the Reagan coalition has been doing at the Republican National Convention or what a group of Strong Democrats thinks about Jesse Jackson, and independent observers can inspect the evidence to determine if our assertions are true. It follows that such questions as "Whither political parties?" are inherently unanswerable so long as the question refers to entire parties. In order to ask about continuity and change, the general question must be decomposed into answerable segments.

Some Answerable Questions

In this chapter, we want to examine evidence on change in the areas covered in this book. What about coalition formation? What about the structure and temporal pattern of nomination politics? What about the structure and temporal pattern of electoral politics? What about the information level and consistency of citizens' perceptions? What about the relation of attitudes to citizens' voting choices? What about the informational environment?

We shall restrict our attention to the time period covered in this book: 1952 to the present. To the extent that evidence is available, we want to ask whether recent data show a pattern that is new or significantly different since 1952. We want to distinguish between election-to-election variations and those that suggest longer-run change. And we want to ask whether any changes that have occurred have tended to weaken or strengthen national political coalitions.

COALITION COMPOSITION

Coalition building, of course, has been going on for a very long time. One can analyze the election of John Quincy Adams in 1824 as a result of the maneuvering of the four protocoalitions supporting Adams, Andrew Jackson, William H. Crawford, and Henry Clay (Riker, 1962, chap. 7). For that matter, coalition building among the English barons preceded the issuance of the Magna Charta, so coalition building is hardly unique to American politics or a development of recent decades.

The Convention Delegates

A limited change has taken place in the identity of the actors involved in nomination politics. Calls for party reform go back a long way (Ranney, 1975), but the Democrats' McGovern-Fraser Commission took unusually aggressive action in this direction. For the 1972 convention, they called for quotas for hitherto underrepresented population categories: women, blacks, and young persons. More recent Democratic commissions have softened these requirements and moved to increase the role of party leaders. The Mikulski Commission opted for an affirmative action program for the 1976 convention. The Winograd Commission recommended that each state's delegation to the 1980 convention be increased by 10 percent and that these seats be filled by party leaders and elected state officials. The Hunt Commission created a bloc of 550 delegate seats to the 1984 Democratic convention to be filled by party officials uncommitted to any candidate. The Fairness Commission, chaired by Donald Fowler, made minimal changes in the Democratic delegate selection rules for 1988.

Republican committees (the DO Committee, the Rule 29 Committee, and the Rules Review Committee) have limited themselves to encouraging state parties to send more female, black, and youthful delegates. The net of all this has been a marked increase in female delegates. Women have increased from 13 percent of the Democratic delegates in 1968 to 42, 53, and 51 percent in 1972, 1980, and 1984, respectively; women were 16 percent of the Republican delegates in 1968, were just under one third of the delegates in 1972 through 1980, and constituted 46 percent of the GOP delegates in 1984. Blacks and "under 30s" were 24 percent and 16 percent of the 1972 Democratic delegates but fell to 18 percent and 8 percent, respectively, in 1984. Blacks and young delegates have remained very small proportions of the Republican delegates (Farah, 1984; Farah, Jennings & Miller, 1982; Mitofsky & Plissner, 1980; Ranney, 1978, p. 232; Roberts, 1984).

The delegates also continue to come from the upper socioeconomic strata. In 1984, 35 percent of the Republican delegates and 51 percent of the Democratic delegates had postgraduate degrees; 57 percent of the Republican delegates and 42% percent of the Democratic delegates had incomes over $50,000; virtually all came from white-collar occupations. "Domination of the presidential elite by a skill-based middle class was even more complete in 1972 than it was in 1948–52," concluded Jeane Kirkpatrick (1976, p. 65) after a study of those delegates. Her conclusion remains true today.

The views of Democratic delegates from 1972 through 1984 were more liberal than views of citizens who thought of themselves as Democrats; and 1980 and 1984 GOP delegates were much more conservative than citizen Republicans (Kirkpatrick, 1976, chap. 10; Ladd, 1978, p. 65; Mitofsky &

Plissner, 1980; Roberts, 1984). These attitudes, of course, have consequences in the type of platforms adopted and the type of candidates nominated by the conventions. But differences between activists and citizens are not new. In 1956 and 1964, Republican activists had attitudes that were unrepresentative of Republican citizens (McClosky, Hoffman & O'Hara, 1960; Jennings, 1966); the Democrats were unrepresentative in 1972 and 1976; and both parties managed to be simultaneously unrepresentative in 1980 and 1984.

A Continuing Interest in Issues

What about the activists' interest in issues? We saw in Chapter 2 that members of nomination coalitions had a strong interest in issues, and in Chapter 3 that the same thing was true of electoral activists. But is this new? In the absence of hard evidence, this question cannot be answered with complete certainty. What we do know is that as soon as political scientists began asking activists if they were interested in issues, the answer was yes.

The question was not asked directly in the first survey of convention delegates in 1956, but Democratic delegates agreed at levels that "suggested unanimity within the sample" with regard to taxes on small and middle income, slum clearance, social security, and minimum wages; Republicans agreed for government regulation of business, business taxes, regulation of trade unions, and minimum wages. Members of both parties' coalitions agreed on issues important to their constituents (McClosky et al., 1960, pp. 424–25). There is no evidence that nomination or electoral activists were uninterested in issues at any point in the time period under consideration, and many instances can be cited of earlier issue-oriented behavior—for example, the positions on civil rights taken by then Minneapolis Mayor Hubert Humphrey and the Dixiecrats at the 1948 Democratic convention.

Within the two parties' nomination coalitions, there appears to have been two reversals of characteristic attitudes. Because of an historic split in the Republican party between internationalist and isolationist wings, Democrats were more willing than Republicans to favor military alliances and defense spending in 1956 (McClosky et al., 1960, p. 415). By the 70s, though, Republicans were more likely than Democrats to favor reliance on military means where necessary (Kirkpatrick, 1976, pp. 181–85). Because of a North-South split in the Democratic party, Republicans were more liberal on civil rights. Since 1964, Republicans have become the more conservative party on this issue (Carmines & Stimson, 1981). Otherwise, the parties' relative postures have remained the same.

Anne Costain reports an increase in ideological voting in contests between winning and losing coalitions at Democratic conventions. The "balance of left factional and nonleft factional voting noted in the Humphrey, McGovern, and Carter votes is less likely to indicate the emergence of a new consensus . . . than a continuing struggle between a vital left bloc in the convention and all the other groups which must join together in order to defeat the left" (1978, p. 110). This parallels Republican contests throughout this period, in which all nonright groups had to coalesce to defeat an increasingly active right coalition before it finally overwhelmed them in 1980 and 1984.

Continuing Nationalization

There is some evidence that both nomination and electoral coalitions have become more national in character. The most liberal groups in earlier Democratic nomination coalitions were all from the West and Midwest. The most conservative groups in earlier Republican nomination coalitions were all southern, with the exception of Ohio (which was simply being loyal to Senator Taft) and Illinois (Munger & Blackhurst, 1965). By 1976, the liberal Democratic coalition included groups from every region except the South, and the conservative Republican coalition included groups from every region except the East (Costain, 1978). In 1980, the liberal Kennedy coalition was unable to wrest much southern strength from a southern-based Carter coalition, but the conservative Reagan coalition attracted a number of groups from the East.

In Chapter 3, we saw that the issue groups making up the Republican and Democratic electoral coalitions were drawn from every region. Without comparable earlier data, we must be cautious in interpretation; but we do know that earlier authorities, such as V.O. Key and Arthur Holcombe, placed great stress on sectionalism. Therefore, it would seem that the current composition of nomination and electoral coalitions reflects the continuing nationalization of American politics.

In short, coalition building goes on apace. More women are involved; the majority of actors comes from the skill-based middle class. Because of the activists' interest in issues, the coalitions are formed around groups that take similar issue positions, with the principal ideological thrust coming from conservatives in the Republican party and from liberals in the Democratic party. These coalitions are increasingly nationwide in scope.

NOMINATION POLITICS

The pattern of first-ballot nominations was well established by the 1950s. There have been only three conventions since 1936 that did not have first-ballot nominations.[1] The Republicans picked Wendell Willkie on the sixth ballot in 1940 and Thomas E. Dewey on the third ballot in 1948; and the Democrats nominated Adlai Stevenson on the third ballot in 1952. The typical

---

[1] Until 1936, the Democrats had a rule that a two-thirds majority was necessary for nomination. Woodrow Wilson was nominated on the 46th ballot in 1912, James M. Cox on the 44th ballot in 1920, John W. Davis on the 104th ballot in 1924, and Franklin D. Roosevelt on the 6th ballot in 1932. Other factors besides the two-thirds rule were involved in these long contests. The relative strength of urban and rural groups in the Democratic party was changing, and poor preconvention communication made multiple ballots valuable as signals of the probable success of various coalitions.

pattern since 1936, though, has been that of a first-ballot ratification of a decision made in preconvention activity.

A Longer Nomination Process

The nomination process lasts much longer now than it did in the 1950s. Among the factors contributing to this were the victories of George McGovern in 1972 and Jimmy Carter in 1976. Unlike earlier aspirants who were well known before the primaries (such as Eisenhower, Kennedy, or Goldwater), both McGovern and Carter had been discounted as serious contenders. But both began very early, both captured the nomination, and together they solidified a pattern of earlier activity that others have followed.

Other considerations have worked in the same direction. The Federal Election Campaign Act of 1974 made it necessary to set up a committee to raise early money in order to qualify for federal matching funds. Party reforms stipulating that more delegates are to be elected at the district (rather than the state) level have also led to more organization. And the heavy press coverage of the first glimmerings of strength—polls reflecting strength in New Hampshire, surveys of delegates likely to attend Iowa caucuses, and the beginnings of the Michigan Republican caucus process in 1986—has placed a premium on a good initial showing. This, of course, requires a lot of effort in the states where these events are being held. For all of these reasons, the nomination process has been pushed well back into the incumbent president's term.

Consequences of an Increasing Number of Primaries

The proportion of delegates chosen in primaries increased very sharply in the 1970s, reaching a peak in 1980. In 1952, 39 percent of both Republican and Democratic delegates were so selected,[2] and the proportion remained fairly stable through 1968. But the Democratic percentage jumped to 61 percent in 1972, 73 percent in 1976, and 75 percent in 1980, while the Republican proportion rose to 53 percent in 1972, 68 percent in 1976, and 74 percent in 1980. The Democratic percentage declined to 53 percent and the Republican proportion to 61 percent in 1984 (Arterton, 1978, p. 7; Ranney, 1981, p. 369; Ranney, 1985, p. 333).

The first clear implication of a high proportion of primaries to conventions was to further handicap late entrants. With many delegates chosen before their entrances into the race, their hope of building a winning coalition depended on groups of uncommitted delegates being picked. An uninstructed delegation is more likely to come from a state convention: political activists attending a convention are more likely than citizens to think of the strategic advantages of joining a coalition at the opportune moment, while citizens

---

[2] Fifty-nine percent of Republican delegates, and 54 percent of Democratic delegates were elected by primaries in 1916. From that point on, the popularity of primaries declined until only 36 percent of both parties' delegates were so chosen in 1948.

voting in primaries tend to opt for the most attractive candidate in preference to "none of the above."

A second consequence of more primaries is to strengthen aspirants—as long as they are equipped to come into a state and run an effective primary campaign—at the expense of state party leaders. This is not new. In California in 1952, for example, "many Democrats, dissatisfied with [the state party] leadership, rallied behind [Senator Estes] Kefauver, whose slate of delegates soundly trounced the so-called 'uninstructed' slate to the national convention" that was made up of party officials (Shields, 1954, p. 674). Increasing the number of primaries simply increases the number of opportunities for coalition leaders to act independently of party leaders, which in turn increases the likelihood that an outsider can capture the party's nomination. This is not new either. The authors of a comprehensive review of the nomination process from the 1830s through 1956 concluded:

> It is in the nature of presidential nominating contests that new men are always under consideration and must sometimes be nominated. The Republican choice in 1940, for example, lay mainly between three men whose fame had not yet matured: Dewey, a defeated first-time candidate for governor; Taft, a junior senator of two years' standing; and Willkie, a public utility magnate who had never held public office. (David, Goldman & Bain, 1960, p. 161)

So, presidential aspirants—some of whom are outsiders—gain power at the expense of state and local party leaders. And since one of these aspirants is ultimately elected president, the process tends to produce presidents who are less beholden to these party leaders.

A third concomitant of the growing number of primaries has been the establishment of party rules as clearly superior to state law. The McGovern-Fraser guidelines gave states a choice between primaries and conventions that adhered to certain criteria. Many states opted for primaries. These rules were tested in a case growing out of the seating of a reform delegation from Illinois at the 1972 Democratic National Convention in place of an elected delegation led by Chicago Mayor Richard J. Daley. When the case reached the U.S. Supreme Court, Justice Brennan held, for the Court: "The convention serves the pervasive national interest in the selection of candidates for national office, and this national interest is greater than any interest of an individual state." This led the leading scholar of party reform to conclude that "the national party organs' power to make rules governing presidential nominating processes is, both in political reality and legal principle, at its highest peak by far since the early 1820s" (Ranney, 1978, p. 230).

Challenging Incumbent Presidents

Yet another change in nomination politics has been the increasing number of challenges to incumbent presidents. Perhaps the most significant were George Wallace's 1964 campaign in the primaries and the 1972 challenges of liberal Republican Representative Pete McClosky of California and conservative Republican Representative John Ashbrook of Ohio. They were significant because incumbents Lyndon Johnson and Richard Nixon were both certain of renomination, yet both sitting presidents were challenged from within their own parties. And politically vulnerable presidents—Johnson in 1968, Ford in 1976, and Carter in 1980—faced much more serious challenges. Lively nomination politics is no longer confined to the party out of power.

To sum up, the basic pattern of nomination politics was established by the beginning of our time period. What we have seen is an expansion of this pattern. There are now many more primaries; nomination politics lasts quite a bit longer; real contests often take place within the in party. The national parties and the leaders of nomination coalitions have been strengthened at the expense of state political leaders by the spread of this modern pattern.

ELECTORAL POLITICS

Professionalization of Campaigns

As we saw in Chapter 4, the origins of professional campaign staffs came a generation earlier than the 1950s. Expertise was brought to the Democratic National Committee when national chairman John Raskob hired Charles Michelson to handle publicity in the late 1920s and Republican national chairman John D. M. Hamilton began a tradition of party civil service in the 1936–40 period.

One could argue that professionalization has continued since 1952. There are certain slots on a campaign staff that are usually filled by those with appropriate professional backgrounds. Professionalism, Christopher Arterton has reminded us, has been most successful in those areas of campaign behavior that demand a level of expertise, such as polling and computer services. Even more important in their impact on campaign strategy has been the incorporation of professionals in the strategy groups that make basic campaign decisions. John Deardourff, Stuart Spencer, Robert Teeter, and Richard Wirthlin have been making many of the basic Republican decisions; Jerry Rafshoon, Pat Caddell, and Peter Hart have been ranking strategists on the Democratic side.

But the case for spreading professionalism since the 1950s should not be pressed too far, because its antecedents are so clear. Campaign management firms were organized well before the 1950s, especially in California. Persons coming from public relations or newspaper backgrounds who were involved in the 1952 Eisenhower campaign included Robert Humphreys, James C. Hargerty, Murray Chotnier, and Robert Mullen. Batten, Barton, Durstein, and Osborn as well as the Kudner, Ted Bates, and Whitaker and Baxter firms were all working on the campaign (Kelley, 1956, chaps. 5, 6). The 1952 Republican campaign plan "outlined basic strategy, organization, appeals, types of speeches, literature, advertising, television and radio programs, the relative weight to be given to various media, the kinds, places, and times of campaign trips and rallies, and the areas in which efforts were to be concentrated" (Kelley, 1956, p. 1). This makes it hard to argue that expertise and experience were lacking at the beginning of our three-decade time period.

The National Committees

The Republican National Committee has taken on a number of new activities. Credit for this belongs to Mary Louise Smith, national chair during the Ford administration, and particularly to William Brock, who guided the committee from 1977 until 1981. One important Brock innovation was national commit- tee agreement during 1977–78 to pay the salary for an organizational director for each state party. This was subject to some conditions; for instance, the person chosen had to be acceptable to the national committee. But the pro- gram meant that every state committee had a trained staff director. In addi- tion, there were 15 field directors, who maintained liaison with state party organizations in two- to six-state areas, such as Michigan and Pennsylvania; Indiana, Kansas, Kentucky, and Missouri; or Arkansas, Louisiana, Missis- sippi, and Texas.

A Local Election Campaign Division of equal size focused on state legisla- tive elections across the country in 1978. Their efforts included some 75 cam- paign seminars, $1 million in direct cash grants to GOP candidates, and help with surveys, radio and TV spots, and scheduling. A Computer Services Division conducted analyses for state parties that installed terminals and paid telephone line charges. In 1978, all this cost some $3 million in direct contribu- tions and the salaries of organizers and consultants and was in addition to the normal operations of the national committee that were carried forward at the same time (Republican National Committee Chairman's Report, 1979).

The Democratic National Committee has made efforts to develop similar strength during the 1980s. But it must be said that they were much weaker than the Republicans. One reason was the much stronger financial base estab- lished by the GOP. An even more important reason was a lack of concern with the national committees during the presidencies of Lyndon Johnson and Jimmy Carter.

John Bibby (1980) makes an important distinction between procedural re- form and organizational reform and argues that the two parties have followed different paths toward nationalization. The Democrats have stressed rule changes through the activities of the McGovern-Fraser, Mikulski, Winograd, Hunt, and Fairness Commissions. The Republicans have stressed organiza- tion. While it could be said that the GOP activity strengthens both state and national parties, the ability of the national party to provide cash and cam- paign services to the states certainly gives the national committee more lever- age in state affairs than hitherto.

There has been a move away from a "unified" campaign structure in which presidential campaigns are conducted through the national committee. From

1952 through 1968, at least one of the party campaigns in each election was run by the national committee staff, and both were organized this way in 1956 and 1964. From 1972 through 1984, though, the campaign headquarters were located in separate presidential campaign committees, and the Federal Election Campaign Act of 1974 makes it likely that this will continue to be the case. Gerald Ford had given a speech as vice president saying that campaigns should be run through the national committee. Ford wanted to run his 1976 campaign that way but was told that the new campaign finance law required a separate committee (Ford, 1979, p. 275). (President Ford was misinformed about this. There is a provision that allows a candidate to designate the national committee as the agent to spend public funds.) In any case, the effective location of power to make decisions about national campaign strategy will reside with those persons authorized to act by the presidential candidate. The effect of the 1974 statute is to reduce the candidate's opportunity to concentrate that authority in the national committee if he wishes to do so.

Increasing Technology and Escalating Costs

One of several changes in campaign technology has been the move from the campaign train to the campaign plane. The train is now used for nostalgia and the special circumstance of several medium-sized cities that are more conveniently accessible by rail. Otherwise, the campaign moves by jet in order to appear in a number of different media markets the same day. This moves the candidate about more rapidly, of course, but it hasn't affected the relative power of national and state parties very much.

Changes have taken place in the communications used to reach the voters and to find out what they are thinking. The first year in which extensive use was made of television was 1952. At that time, it was just one of several media employed, but it soon moved to a position of dominance in the media campaign. Polling was employed in the 1950s, but it was intermittent and focused on high-reliability estimates of candidate standing. Three decades later, the information flow was continuous, and there were some instances of very sophisticated analysis. These shifts have moved influence from the state to the national level. Heretofore, state leaders could claim special knowledge of the situations in their states. Now, national leaders armed with computer printouts may have better data, both on the views of citizens in a given state and on the media outlets that should be used to reach them.[3]

The changes in communication techniques have also shifted power on the national level away from generalists and into the hands of specialists. It is sometimes said that these technological changes have diminished the influence of politicians. A better interpretation would be that power has shifted to

---

[3] Remember our finding in Chapter 3 that the county campaign leaders' perception of views in their community was no better than one would expect by chance. This means that the use of polls is improving politicians' understanding of citizens' thinking.

different types of politicians—those who have mastered the use of media and polling.[4]

The use of jets, polls, and particularly television has made presidential campaigning much more expensive. Even ignoring the orgy of spending in the 1972 Nixon campaign, the cost of major party general election campaigns rose 335 percent from 1952 through 1968. In cost per vote cast, expenditures rose from 19 cents to 60 cents over the same time period (Alexander, 1972, pp. 6–7).

Two important developments in campaign funding occured during this time period. One was the Republican sustaining membership campaign begun in 1962. In 1964, the program brought in some $2 million in average contributions of $10 each. By 1979, there were over 600,000 contributors, and the average Republican contribution was approximately $26. After the 1980 Reagan campaign, the Republicans had 1.5 million contributors, and the number continues to grow.

The second development was federal funding at a level of $20 million in 1974 dollars; $47.3 million in 1984. This direct funding has at least three effects. First, it allows campaigns to escape destitution such as the Humphrey campaign experienced in September 1968. Second, the act guarantees the national committees a minor role (they were authorized to spend $6.9 million in 1984), but it makes it less likely that the campaigns will be run through them. Third, the tight limits—in constant dollars, about 70 percent of the amount spent in 1968—will compel some hard decisions about the best use of the available funds.

Taken together, the conflicting effects of the several developments in electoral politics are not easy to summarize. They certainly tend to favor national party leaders rather than state leaders because they point to centralized decision making. One of the national committees, the Republican, is providing a range of services throughout the country and has developed a mass financial base, but the authority of both national committees has been reduced by provisions of the Federal Election Campaign Act of 1974. Modern modes of transportation and communication have made presidential campaigns much more expensive and have shifted influence toward politicians who under-

---

[4] If we go back to the 1950s, we find Joseph Napolitan active in Springfield, Massachusetts, politics, and we find John Deardourff on the staff of Representative Jessica McC. Weis of New York. Napolitan came into national politics when his Springfield friend, Lawrence O'Brien, was a leader in the Kennedy campaign; Deardourff was on Nelson Rockefeller's staff. Napolitan became a leading Democratic campaign consultant, and Deardourff a leading Republican consultant.

Comparing contemporary parties to those of the 19th century, Arterton points out that while the function—communication with the voters—has remained the same, there has been a shift from personal to impersonal modes. "During the nineteenth century, political communications depended primarily on face-to-face contact. The wardheeler's job was to be personally acquainted with as many voters as possible within his territory. . . . [Now] precinct captains and wardheelers have been supplanted by telephones, mass media, computer-assisted direct mail and targeting, and polling" (1984, p. 7).

stand these techniques. But in spite of the shifts brought on by technology, the presidential candidate and his advisors still face the central problem of deciding which voters they wish to appeal to and how they are going to do so successfully.

CITIZEN ATTITUDES AND ACTION

Levels of Information

There is no evidence that American citizens know substantially more or less about politics than they did three decades ago. The information levels for 1952, 1976, and 1984 are shown in Figure 11–1. By comparing the curves, it can be seen that the distributions of information across the three decades are very similar. There were a few more people falling into the higher information categories in 1952 and 1984, and a few more people falling into the lower information categories in 1976. But the differences between the means are not significant, and the shapes of the curves are similar.

Using the Media

There have been a few changes in the composition of the media since 1952. In 1952, television sets were in 34 percent of U.S. homes; by 1976, television was

FIGURE 11–1
Citizen Information Levels, 1952, 1976, 1984

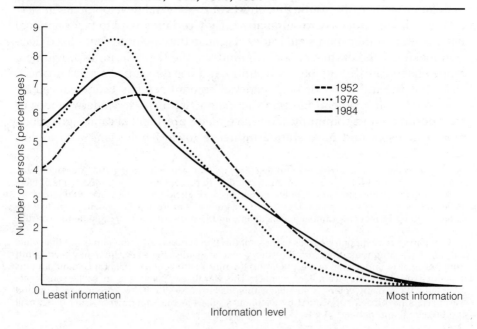

available in 97 percent of the homes. The average number of hours per day spent watching TV also increased from 4.85 in 1955 to 6.43 in 1975. Total circulation of magazines and newspapers increased; but when adjusted for population growth, magazine circulation went up and newspaper circulation dropped. Daily newspaper circulation per 100 adults declined from 48.2 to 38.2 during this time period, while magazine circulation rose from 142.2 per 100 adults to 157.3 over the same years (Sterling & Haight, 1979).

When asked to identify their sources of information about the campaign, the respondents' answers showed parallel changes. Only half said they learned about politics through television in 1952, but this figure rose to 86 percent in 1984. Use of print media declined slightly over the same time period. Newspaper reading slipped an insignificant 2 percent (from 79 to 77 percent), and magazines dropped from 41 to 35 percent. The pattern that had become established was one of nearly universal television use, wide newspaper reading, and use of magazines by the more literate part of the population.

Media and Information Levels

When we turn from the use of various media to their impact on citizens' information levels, we see something different. Table 11–2 gives measures of association between use of a given medium and the level of information that a respondent has. In 1952 (when there was a mixed pattern of media use), magazines, newspapers, and television all had the same effect on how much a respondent knew. By 1976, however, we have the pattern that we already saw in Table 8–2. The higher measure of association between magazines and information level and the lower measure of association between television and information level mean that use of the more demanding print medium was producing more information whereas television was transmitting less information.

TABLE 11–2
Association between Information Level and Informational Environment, 1952, 1976, and 1984

	Measure of Association (Kendall's Tau-c)		
	1952	1976	1984
Medium used			
Magazines	.28	.39	.35
Newspapers	.27	.23	.28
Television	.30	.16	.17
Involvement with informational environment			
Education	.28	.28	.32
Political interest	.43	.40	.39

Data source: 1952, 1976, and 1984 Election Studies, Survey Research Center/Center for Political Studies.

While the effects of obtaining information from one medium or another seem to have changed, the effect of simply being involved with the informational environment has hardly changed at all. Two of the three questions related to citizens' seeking out information (which were reported in Table 8–5) were also asked in 1952. As you can see from Table 11–2, the association between seeking out information and knowing about politics was essentially the same whether measured in 1952, 1976, or 1984.

Issues and Candidates

As we saw in Chapter 9, there were few long-term changes in the salience of citizens' attitudes about issues and candidates. Attitudes about issues were quite salient in every single election. Indeed, they were the most salient category in every election except 1956 and 1976, when candidate attitudes were more prominent. Candidate attitudes have been a strong second, constituting more than a third of all attitudes in every election except 1984. Attitudes about political parties have declined in salience since 1972, but parties were considerably less visible than issues or candidates throughout the whole period.[5]

The partisan valence of attitudes, of course, varied from election to election. When considering only the three broad categories, attitudes about candidates usually favored the Republicans, and attitudes about issues more often than not favored the Democrats. There are many exceptions to this when the more detailed set of attitudes is considered; but overall, the Republicans had the more attractive candidate every year except 1964, and Democrats profited more from issues save for 1968, 1972, and 1980.

When citizens' attitudes are related to their voting decisions, there has been variation from election to election but little indication of long-term change. Attitudes about parties were very important in the 1950s, important in 1960, 1968, and 1984, but less consequential in the intervening elections. Candidate attitudes were very important in every election save 1952. Because of the role of vague general attitudes, all issue voting is increased when there is greater ideological distance between the candidates. Specific-issue voting is increased when voters are able to judge the record of an incumbent president. Overall, however, issue voting has been very important in every single election. Probit analysis relating all the attitudes to presidential choice has consistently predicted between 85 and 90 percent of the cases.

Party Identification

There have been two related changes in party identification. The first was a sharp decline in the mid-60s in the proportion of persons who thought of themselves as Strong Partisans: 38 percent were either Strong Democrats or

---

[5] Whether there ever was a time when attitudes about parties were as salient as attitudes about candidates or issues cannot be determined with these data. Without pre-1952 evidence, we don't know one way or the other.

Strong Republicans in 1952; 29 percent so regarded themselves in 1984. The second has been a gradual growth in the proportion of Independents who do not see themselves as closer to either party. Only 5 percent fell into this category in 1952; 13 and 11 percent did so in 1980 and 1984, respectively.

It is important that the effect of these changes be neither overestimated nor underestimated. The decline in the number of Strong Partisans and the increase in the number of Independents opens the possibility of wider fluctuation from one election to the next. Hence, the 1984 election results are not as reliable a guide to the 1988 election outcome as the 1952 results were to the 1956 outcome.

At the same time, citizens have not been departing from the political parties in very massive proportions. Ninety-one percent of citizens could be classified as Strong, Weak, or Independent Partisans in 1952; 87 percent could be so classified in 1984. The advantage enjoyed by the Democrats over the Republicans as a consequence of party identification was 57 percent to 34 percent in 1952, and 52 percent to 33 percent in 1980. This Democratic advantage dropped to 48 to 39 percent in 1984, but it is still too early to know if this represents a permanent change or a response to short-term forces. For the time being, the fluctuations are still on either side of the same center of political gravity.

It is also important that this relative stability on the aggregate level not be confused with stability on the individual level. The relative stability of party identification types in the population results from an equilibrium condition in which individual changes in one direction are canceled out by individual changes in the opposite direction. When we move to the individual level, it turns out that attitudes are neither more nor less stable in the 1970s than they were in the 1950s.

Two panel studies provide data on individual-level stability and change. One was from 1956 through 1960. The second, which provides the data reviewed in Chapter 10, was from 1972 through 1976. When results of the two studies were compared, party identification was just as stable in the 1970s as it was in the 1950s. And "where more specific issues can be directly matched, continuity values seem amazingly stationary across the two panels" (Converse & Markus, 1979, p. 43).

Cognitive Consistency

The extent of cognitive consistency does not seem to have changed over our time period, at least when consistency is measured against a partisan criterion on the individual level. Figure 11–2 charts the distributions for partisan attitude consistency for 1952 and 1976, showing some variation from election to election. In 1972, probably because George McGovern was perceived to be taking stands that were inconsistent with the preferences of many Democrats, the proportion of completely consistent attitudes was much lower. But as a comparison of the 1952 and 1976 lines shows, the proportions of consistent and inconsistent attitudes over a longer time period are virtually the same.

FIGURE 11–2
Distribution of Cognitive Consistency, 1952 and 1976

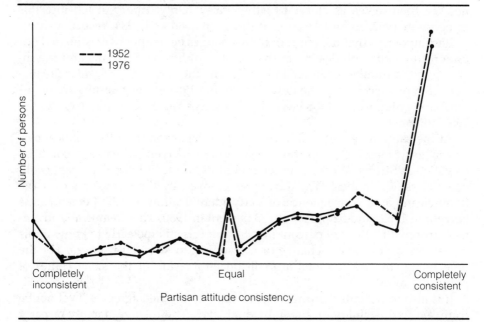

In sum, there are changes in the available media and in the use that is made of them. There has been a decline in the salience of attitudes about political parties and in the proportion of citizens who think of themselves as Strong Partisans. However, there have not been any changes in citizens' information levels, in the relation between information level and involvement with the informational environment, in the temporal stability of attitudes, in cognitive consistency, in the partisan advantage resulting from the distribution of party identification, in the salience or importance of attitudes about candidates or issues, or—most important of all—in the relation between these attitudes and the presidential choice made by citizens.

CONCLUSION

Continuity and Change

There is, as always, an amalgam of continuity and change. Let's take the elements of continuity first. The actors who are recruited to nomination and electoral politics continue to be, in Jeane Kirkpatrick's nice phrase, the "skill-based middle class." As far back as we have reliable data, activists have been interested in issues. The underlying purposes of coalition building persist: A coalition must recruit delegates to win the nomination and must persuade voters to win an election. This means there must be a national campaign organization, some means of moving the candidate and his entourage around the country; speeches that explain the candidate's positions, material released in a form that the media can use, funds raised, and so forth. Many of these activities are carried on by professionals and have been during the period under review.

Most of the cognitive elements underlying citizen response have been quite stable. The amount of information known by the electorate, the partisan consistency of their attitudes, the salience and importance of attitudes about both candidates and issues, and the relation of these attitudes to presidential choice have shown little variation.

What elements have changed? There are now more women among convention delegates. The coalitions formed in nomination and electoral politics are more national in character. Nomination politics now lasts much longer; national party rules are now recognized as superior to state law; there has been a considerable increase in the proportion of delegates selected in primaries; incumbent presidents have been challenged with some regularity.

There have been a number of essentially technological innovations in the conduct of election campaigns. Jet aircraft, television, continual opinion surveys, and computers have become part of campaigns just as they have become part of much of American life in the late 20th century. Professionals who know how to unite this technology with politics now play a larger role in strategy decisions.

All this is expensive, and campaigns now cost many times what they did. The Republican party has developed a very successful mass finance drive, and federal funding for presidential campaigns has been available since 1976. At the same time that there has been this increased organizational activity, fewer citizens think of themselves as Strong Partisans, and attitudes about the parties have become even less salient.

Presidential Parties: Weaker or Stronger?

Whether any organizational entity has become weaker or stronger depends, of course, on one's point of view. What strengthens one entity may weaken another. Since our concern in this book is with presidential politics, we want to know whether the nomination and electoral coalitions—and the institutions in which they transact their business—have been weakened or strengthened.

To answer this question, we want to focus on the changes just listed. The continuities in organization and citizens' cognitions mean that parties are *not* disappearing, but that is a slightly different point. So, which changes have weakened, and which have strengthened?

I think three changes have weakened presidential parties. The first is the frequency with which presidents are challenged for their own party's nomination, and the length of nomination politics. Strictly speaking, this does not affect nomination or electoral politics as much as it does executive politics. When a president and his immediate assistants have to divert time and resources from executive leadership to protect the president's political base, it distracts the administration from its prime responsibility of governing.

Second, the Federal Election Campaign Act of 1974 has not helped national parties. It does lessen the parties' dependence on interest groups, and it means that the national parties do not have to wait for state parties to meet their quotas in national fund drives. But the act largely removes the national committees from financial decisions about presidential campaigns and inhibits presidential candidates from conducting their campaigns through the national committees even if they want to do so.

Third is the decline in salience of attitudes about parties in citizens' presidential choices and, more importantly, the reduced number of Strong Partisans in the electorate. To be sure, how one sees this depends on whether it is viewed from the perspective of the majority or minority party. From a minority perspective, the increased independence could be seen as giving the minority party a better chance to appeal successfully to enough majority party voters to win. But from the perspective of either party, the smaller number of Strong Partisans means that there is a smaller deliverable vote.

At the same time, a number of changes have strengthened presidential parties relative to state and local entities. The increased number of primaries means that an effectively organized nomination coalition can go into states and win delegates without being beholden to state leaders. The coalitions that are being formed in both nomination and electoral contexts are moving steadily from a regional to a national character. National party rules have been held superior to state law. The Republican party has achieved an independent base of small contributors and now offers a wide range of services. Professionals now have better information about citizens' views and are taking part more frequently in basic strategy decisions. All these changes have tended to produce more nationalized, more professionalized parties.

When I was a very small boy, I could watch airplanes from nearby Wright Field as they maneuvered overhead. Usually they were biplanes, but now and again I saw a triplane. When I was slightly older, one of the events that marked late morning was the arrival of the horse-drawn bakery truck. It was full of good smells and was a source of curiosity as to how the horse knew where to stop even though the deliveryman was sometimes away from the truck giving a housewife the products she had ordered. I haven't seen many triplanes or horse-drawn bakery trucks lately, but I do not believe this means the end of the aviation or baking industries. Similarly, I have not read much lately about urban party bosses such as E. H. Crump of Memphis, Edward J. Flynn of the Bronx, Tom Prendergast of Kansas City, Frank Hague of Jersey City, or others who were in power during the 1930s, but I do not take this as evidence of the disappearance of political parties. Today, we have presidential parties.

Appendix

Indexes and Measures

A–3.1 Difference Scores

The statement in the interview schedule preceding the six party norms was: "Now let's consider party work. Would you say you feel a *strong* obligation or *some* obligation *to do* each of the following—or to *avoid* doing each of the following in the conduct of political affairs?" Then each respondent was read statements such as "Hold strong personal beliefs about a number of different issues" and "Weigh prior service to the party very heavily in selecting candidates for nomination." The answers to these items formed a five-magnitude scale: Strong Obligation to Do, Some Obligation to Do, No Obligation to Do or Avoid, Some Obligation to Avoid, Strong Obligation to Avoid. With Republican activists, for example, the distributions of responses to the two quoted items were:

	Obligation to Do		No Obligation	Obligation to Avoid	
	Strong	*Some*	*Obligation*	*Some*	*Strong*
Have personal beliefs....	56.5	28.8	12.0	0.5	2.1
Weigh party service	28.8	33.2	30.5	3.7	5.8

A difference score is simply the difference between the proportion who report a strong obligation to do whatever action is mentioned and the proportion who say they have a strong obligation to avoid that action. This provides a summary measure that can be used in place of the full distribution. In the example, the difference score for Republican activists was 54.4 for holding strong personal issue beliefs and 23.0 for weighing party service in selecting nominees. Having single numbers facilitates comparisons between parties and between norms. Difference scores of this kind were used by Arthur Miller (1974).

A–3.2 Agreement Scores

The agreement scores between activists were based on responses to 15 attitude items. The items were printed on cards, and each respondent placed the card containing the statement on a sort board that was divided into seven categories: Strongly Agree, Agree, Slightly Agree, Not Sure, Slightly Disagree, Disagree, Strongly Disagree. The items, classified by policy area, were:[1]

> International involvement
> > We must bring all American troops back from foreign countries.*
> > We must have peace in Vietnam.*
> > The government should help countries all over the world.
> > America should spend whatever is necessary to have a strong military force.
> Economic management
> > Wages and prices should be controlled by the government.*
> > Government spending should be cut.*
> > The federal government is getting too powerful.
> Social benefits
> > Welfare payments ought to be increased.*
> > Social security benefits ought to be increased.*
> > The government ought to help pay everyone's medical bills.
> Civil liberties
> > Busing should not be used to desegregate schools.*
> > The police ought to be given more authority.*
> > I favor letting Negroes move into white neighborhoods.
> Natural resources
> > The government should act to stop pollution.*
> Agriculture
> > Farmers should be guaranteed a good income.*

Each of these items reflected a central dimension in the policy area in question, and some were worded negatively to guard against response-set bias. Each answer was given a score ranging from 7 for Strongly Agree to 1 for Strongly Disagree. Each person's set of responses then was written

---

[1] Asterisks denote 10 items for which there were citizen responses from the counterpart mass survey.

as a row vector with 15 components. For example, the vector (7,7,7,7,7,4,4,4,4,4,1,1,1,1,1) would correspond to Strongly Agree answers to the first five items, Not Sure answers to the next five items, and Strongly Disagree answers to the last five items.

Vector subtraction (taking absolute differences) was used to begin to calculate an observed attitude distance between each pair of persons. If a person had Not Sure responses (that is, scores of 4) to every item, the attitude distance between this person and the example given in the preceding paragraph would be:

$$(7,7,7,7,7,4,4,4,4,4,1,1,1,1,1)$$
$$\underline{(4,4,4,4,4,4,4,4,4,4,4,4,4,4,4)}$$
$$(3,3,3,3,3,0,0,0,0,0,3,3,3,3,3)$$

The sum of the components in the vector of absolute differences is used to obtain an observed attitude distance. In this example, the observed attitude distance would be 30. This procedure assumes that the measurement is accurate enough to permit subtraction (a very strong assumption in view of the measurement method used) and that each attitude is of equal importance, but it avoids any other assumption about the spatial location of the components with respect to each other.

The formula for a raw agreement score is:

$$\text{Agreement score} = \left(1 - \frac{\text{Observed attitude distance}}{\text{Maximum attitude distance}}\right)$$

Since the maximum attitude distance in this case is 90 (6 units along each of 15 scales), the raw agreement score in the example would be $(1 - 30/90)$, or .67. The raw agreement scores have the property of varying between a value of 1.0 when both persons give identical responses to every item and a value of 0 when both persons are located at the opposite ends of every single scale. The agreement scores reported in Chapter 3 have been corrected, so the 0 point is set at the level that would be obtained with randomly distributed responses. This follows a suggestion by Herbert Weisberg (1978) that a measure should represent percentage improvement over chance. A value of 1.0 represents complete agreement with both the raw agreement scores and the corrected agreement scores.

Agreement scores were also calculated between activists and citizens living in their home counties. These were based on 10 items for which we also had citizen responses from the counterpart mass survey. The 10 items are marked with asterisks in the list above.

For the agreement scores denoting attitudinal similarity, the responses of each activist were matched against the mean responses of citizens interviewed in the activist's county.

In the case of agreement scores for perceptual accuracy, the stimulus items given the activists were adapted to begin with the phrase, "Voters in this area favor . . ." (For example, "Voters in this area favor cutting government spending.") The agreement scores were then calculated between each activist's responses to these perceptual items and the mean responses for the citizens interviewed in the activist's county.

A–3.3 Use of Cluster Procedure to Isolate Issue Groups

The first step was the calculation of agreement scores between each pair of Republican activists and each pair of Democratic activists, following the procedure explained in Appendix A–3.2. After deleting those activists with missing data, we had a 181-by-181 matrix of agreement scores for the Republicans and a 182-by-182 matrix of agreement scores for the Democrats. These matrixes were used as input to an OSIRIS CLUSTER program that had been modified to handle matrixes this large.

The OSIRIS CLUSTER program accepts similarities data (for example, correlations or, in this case, agreement scores) and groups the cases with the closest relations to each other in the same cluster. There are three parameters that must be set in the program: STARTMIN, ENDMIN, and STAYMIN. All three stipulate minimum cutoff values that stop the clustering procedure. STARTMIN denotes a minimum score to start a cluster. The clustering procedure begins with the pair of cases having the highest value with respect to each other. As long as there is a pair of cases whose score is higher than STARTMIN when the previous cluster has been assembled, another cluster is begun with the two unclustered cases having the highest score with respect to each other. If there is no pair with a score higher than the stipulated START-MIN, the clustering procedure terminates. (This is the operational meaning of being an isolate with respect to the issue groups. In addition to being excluded from other groups by the ENDMIN and STAYMIN parameters, there exists no other activist for whom the isolate has an agreement score above the stipulated STARTMIN.)

Once a cluster is begun, the case with the highest average score with respect to the two clustered cases is added to form a three-case cluster. Then the case with the highest average score with respect to the three clustered cases is added to form a four-case cluster. This process continues until there is no unclustered case whose average score with the cases already in the cluster is above ENDMIN. The STAYMIN parameter causes deletion of any case whose average score has fallen below the STAYMIN level (because of the addition of other cases after it was already in the cluster).

Since the procedure considers only unclustered cases when forming new clusters, it has a tendency to inflate earlier clusters at the expense of those formed later. (A later cluster might provide a better fit for a case than the cluster to which it was already assigned, but the case would not be considered for the second cluster.) Therefore, the standard OSIRIS CLUSTER program was modified to check the average score of each case with every existing cluster after all the clusters were formed. Each case with a higher score with another cluster would be moved to it. These moves would, of course, change all the average scores somewhat, so another check would be made, and cases would again be reassigned. The modified program will go through as many iterations of this kind as the user chooses. This is controlled by selecting an ITER parameter. By selecting an appropriately high number, the user can ensure that each case ends up in the cluster with which it has the highest average score.

In the analysis runs that isolated the issue groups, the STARTMIN, END-MIN, and STAYMIN parameters were set at .9, .7, and .7, respectively, for raw agreement scores. The ITER parameter was set at 30. This produced the four Republican issue groups and 65 isolates and the seven Democratic issue groups and 22 isolates.

To this point, the procedure was entirely blind. We did not make any assumptions about the probable character of the groups beyond the definitional stipulation that members of the same group should have common attitudes and the operational assumption that the clustering procedure would lead to groups with common attitudes. (We avoided any assumption that all liberals, or all Roman Catholics, or all Southerners, or all of any category would belong to the same group.) Once group membership (or the lack of it in the case of isolates) was determined, a new variable denoting the issue group to which each activist belonged was created and was added to the data set.

The addition of this information as an attribute of each activist made possible the determination of the attitudinal and demographic characteristic of the groups. The median scores, the discussion of group attitudes on individual issues, the demographic characteristics, and other findings about the issue groups are based on this procedure.

The integrity of the issue groups was tested in two ways. First, random scores were generated (and tested for sequential dependency) and were used as data for a hypothetical population. Agreement scores were calculated on the basis of these "attitudes," and the matrix of agreement scores thus derived was used as input to the CLUSTER program. The STARTMIN, END-MIN, and STAYMIN parameters were again set at .9, .7, .7. No clusters were formed. This meant three things. The level of agreement within our issue groups was above random chance; the procedure used to correct the agreement scores so they would reflect percentage improvement beyond chance was valid; and the issue groups were not just artifacts created by use of the software.

Second, we looked at the within-group and between-group agreement scores of the issue groups. (These data are shown in A–3.5.) The average corrected within-group score was .49 for Republican groups and .51 for Democratic groups. The average corrected between-group score was .35 for Republican groups and .30 for Democratic groups. The average corrected agreement score for all Republican activists was .29; it was .30 for all Democratic activists. Thus we could be sure that we had a higher rate of agreement within the issue groups than among other possible combinations.

While the CLUSTER program was used in this instance to isolate issue groups from the larger populations of activists, it can also be used to observe how the groups combine into coalitions. This can be done by gradually lowering the parameters and thus determining which cases (and, by inference, which groups) move together. If done in small steps, the stages of coalition formation show in something of the same manner that time-lapse photography allows one to observe the opening of a flower. Although only a footnote reference was made to this in the text, the processes of coalition formation among Republican and Democratic activists were studied in this way. Essentially, the results substantiated the analysis presented in the text.

A–3.4 Multidimensional Scaling

Multidimensional scaling is an analytical technique that accepts similarities data (such as correlations or agreement scores) and provides a geometric plot of the data points, such that the most similar cases are located closest together and the most dissimilar cases are located farthest apart. Imagine three data points, a, b, and c. Assume that the ab correlation is .9, that the bc correlation is .1, and that the ac correlation is also .1 If these data points were analyzed by multidimensional scaling, a and b should be located quite close together in the resulting plot (because of the high correlation between them), while c should be located equidistant from a and b (because c has the same correlation with both) and much farther away (because the correlation between c and a or b is so low). Achieving such a plot becomes more difficult as the number of data points goes up, but the goal remains that the more closely associated the data, the closer the data points should be to each other. The degree to which this goal is achieved is determined by a measure of the goodness of fit called stress. A stress value of 0 means that the goal has been achieved with every pair of data points; a stress value of 1 means that the configuration is the worst possible.

Multidimensional scaling is a data reduction technique similar to factor analysis or cluster analysis in that it assumes that there is some simpler underlying pattern to the multiple relationships in a large data matrix. If this assumption is correct in a given case, then one should be able to achieve a solution with low stress and low dimensionality. In such a case, the resulting geometric plot can be studied, and the observer's knowledge of the cases may permit an intuitive interpretation of the meaning of the dimensions. For example, if there were a two-dimensional solution in which liberal Democrats appeared in the upper left quadrant, liberal Republicans in the upper right quadrant, conservative Democrats in the lower left quadrant, and conservative Republicans in the lower right quadrant, then the horizontal axis could be interpreted as a Democrat-Republican dimension and the vertical axis could be interpreted as a liberal-conservative dimension. (For further discussion of the technique itself, see Kruskal & Wish, 1978; Rabinowitz, 1975.)

Multidimensional scaling could not be used for direct identification of the electoral activists' issue groups. For one thing, the plot is of individual cases, and with 181 Republican activists and 182 Democratic activists, the resulting plot would be so dense that it would be difficult to read and almost impossible to tell where one group ended and another began. Since the identity of the issue group members was determined in a cluster analysis, however, multidimensional scaling could be used to develop a spatial analysis that might suggest the relationship of the issue groups to each other.

Figures 3–1 and 3–2 were developed with the aid of multidimensional scaling but are not based exclusively on that technique. Rather than trying to analyze all of the cases, five cases were chosen from each of the seven Democratic issue groups, and six cases were chosen from each of the four Republican issue groups. The cases selected from each group were those with the highest average agreement scores with other members of their groups. After this selection, a 35-by-35 matrix of agreement scores was constructed for the Democrats, and a 24-by-24 matrix was constructed for the Republicans. These were used as input to the OSIRIS MDSCAL program (the Shepard-Kruskal multidimensional scaling program).

Two analysis runs were made with the data for each party. The first began with three dimensions, the second with six. The Stress values associated with given numbers of dimensions in each solution are shown in Table A–1. The results suggested several things. The similarity of pattern between the parties (leaving aside the single instance of very high stress for the Democrats) strongly substantiated the argument in the book that the internal structures of the two electoral parties are quite similar. The number of dimensions and high stress values meant that the structures in both parties were multidimensional and the best MDSCAL solution would have five dimensions. And the lack of a two-dimension solution with a low stress value meant that no two-dimensional plot would provide more than an approximate guide to the location of the groups with respect to each other in an issue space.

The plot that provided the basis for Figure 3–1 came from the four-dimensional Republican solution with Dimension 2 as the horizontal axis and Dimension 3 as the vertical axis. The plot that provided the basis for Figure 3–2

TABLE A–1

Number of Dimensions	Stress	
	Republicans	Democrats
Run 1		
1	.63	.65
2	.50	.49
3	.41	.38
Run 2		
1	.63	.85
2	.52	.55
3	.38	.36
4	.31	.26
5	.24	.20
6	.25	.21

came from the two-dimensional Democratic solution (in the three-dimension analysis run). Dimension 1 is the horizontal axis, and Dimension 2 is the vertical axis. The circles in Figures 3–1 and 3–2 have nothing to do with multidimensional scaling. The MDSCAL plot gave locations for individual group members. I simply assumed that the center of the space defined by the five Democratic or six Republican cases could be taken as the central location of the group in an issue space and then drew circles proportionate to the size of the groups. The cases belonging to different groups did plot separately in all but one instance. The Dominant Democratic group was located more or less on top of the Thrifty Liberals. I moved the Thrifty Liberals a short distance to an unoccupied area that was consistent with the Thrifty Liberals' proximity to the other Democratic groups.

The *approximate* utility of Figures 3–1 and 3–2 should be emphasized for two reasons. First, the stress values tell us that the Republican plot gives us only part of a fair solution and the Democratic plot part of a poor solution (even before I moved the Thrifty Liberals). Second, the size of the circles is a useful device to convey an impression of the relative size of the groups, but some of the individual members would be located outside the area suggested by the circles. Tables 3–3 and 3–4 contain more accurate information. Figures 3–1 and 3–2 are visual devices that convey some of this information.

A–3.5 Within– and Between–Group Agreement Scores

The agreement scores in Table A–2 have been corrected so that 0 corresponds to the degree of agreement expected by chance, and 1.0 corresponds to complete agreement. The figures may therefore be interpreted as the percentage improvement over chance.

A–3.6 Consensus Scores

The consensus score is another measure of agreement. Whereas the agreement score is derived from a comparison of individual responses, the consensus score is based on an analysis of the distribution of responses for the group in question. It rests on two assumptions. The first is that if consensus does exist in a group, responses should tend to fall into a modal category. The second is that measurement error will cause some of the consensual responses to fall into the categories immediately adjacent to the "true" modal category.

Therefore, one is justified in comparing the number of responses actually falling into the mode and two adjacent categories with the number that would be expected to do so if there was an equal distribution of answers in each magnitude of the scale. This leads to the formula:

$$\text{Consensus} = \left(\frac{\text{Frequency observed} - \text{Frequency expected}}{N - \text{Frequency expected}} \right)$$

TABLE A–2
Within- and Between-Group Agreement Scores

Republican Groups	Dominant Group	Conservative Libertarians	Economic Managers	Republican Moderates	Isolates
Dominant group	.51	.43	.32	.40	.24
Conservative libertarians		.46	.31	.33	.18
Economic managers			.45	.30	.20
Republican moderates				.49	.19
Isolates					.12

Democratic Groups	Dominant Group	Liberal Pacifists	Liberal International- alists	Cautious Liberals	Thrifty Liberals	Democratic Moderates	Coercive Individ- ualists	Isolates
Dominant group	.53	.43	.41	.35	.36	.38	.19	.17
Liberal pacifists		.52	.28	.31	.33	.29	−.01	.12
Liberal internationalists			.51	.40	.35	.23	.19	.15
Cautious liberals				.49	.36	.32	.29	.21
Thrifty liberals					.52	.32	.22	.17
Democratic moderates						.47	.27	.17
Coercive individualists							.44	.14
Isolates								.04

The consensus score takes on values bounded by +1.0 and

$$\left(\frac{n - f_e}{N - f_e}\right)$$

where n is the minimum number of responses that could be in a modal category. A value of +1.0 occurs when there is complete consensus—that is, when all the responses fall into the mode and two adjacent categories. A value of 0 occurs when the number of cases in the mode and two adjacent categories is just that expected if the answers were equally distributed among all categories. Negative values occur when there is disagreement. This would take place if one subgroup agreed with a statement while another subgroup disagreed, thus causing a bimodal rather than a unimodal distribution.

TABLE A–3

Information-Level Category	Number of Responses	Percent of Electorate
Low........................	0–1–2	17.5%
Average minus.................	3–4–5–6–7	41.2
Average plus	8–9–10–11–12	25.5
High	13–14–15–16–17	11.7
Very high	18–19–20–21–22	3.2
Extremely high................	23 through 31	0.9

A–8.1 Information–Level Measure

The measure of information level is a simple count of the number of responses given to the series of open-ended questions about parties and candidates. The Center for Political Studies usually codes up to 10 responses (that
is, 5 likes and 5 dislikes) for each party and candidate. This gives the measure
a theoretical range from 0 to 40. The actual range in 1976 was from 0 to 31.

The 1976 distribution of the measure is portrayed in Figure 8–1, and the
data are presented in Table A–3. The mean value is 7.1, and the standard
deviation is 5. The categories for Table 8–1 (and subsequent cross-tabulations)
started at the mean value. A new category began at each standard deviation
(except for the highest, where there were very few cases).

This measure makes the same assumption that is made for open-ended
questions: that the better informed person will say more about a topic than a
less informed person. It is open to the challenge that a garrulous person will
say more than a taciturn person even though the latter may know more. In
order to check the validity of this information-level measure, correlations
were run between it and a host of other variables with which it might be
related. The highest correlation (Tau-c = .44) was with the interviewer's own
estimate of the respondent's level of political information. Other high correlations are shown in Table A–4. Since all of these variables should be correlated
with a true measure of political information, this measure appears to be valid.

TABLE A–4

Related Variable	Kendall's Tau–c
Interest in the campaign	.40
Reads about national politics in newspapers...........	.40
Reads magazines................................	.39
Follows public affairs.............................	.37
Tries to influence another person's vote	.35
Reads about international affairs in newspapers	.35
Interviewer's estimate of respondent's intelligence	.34

A–9.1 Probit Analysis

Probit analysis was a technique first developed in biology and then extended to economics. It was introduced in political science by Gerald Kramer (1965, 1971) and more recently has been employed by a number of others (McKelvey & Zavonia, 1969; Aldrich & Cnudde, 1975; Rosenstone & Wolfinger, 1978; Fiorina, 1981). It was developed to handle the problem of a dichotomous dependent variable. It has since been extended to other applications, but the dichotomous dependent variable makes it particularly appropriate for voting analyses.

The problem can be visualized with a single independent and a single dependent variable. If both are free to vary, then a relationship is shown by drawing a regression line that minimizes the distance of any data point from the line. If the relationship is as shown in the figure ($y = bx + u$, where $b = 1$), then one would say that the two variables are related because a unit change in x would be associated with a unit change in $y \pm$ an error term, u.

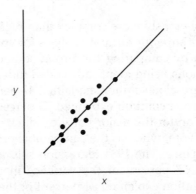

Now consider what happens if y, the dependent variable, can take on just two values. No matter what kind of straight line one draws, as in (A) or (B), many of the data points are going to be far from the line. A line also "predicts" that many of the data points should fall in the middle of the two values or outside of the values. Since the dependent variable is restricted to the two values, this is impossible. If, however, one draws an S-curve, as in (C), then a great many of the data points are going to be located close to the curve, and few "impossible" predictions will be made.

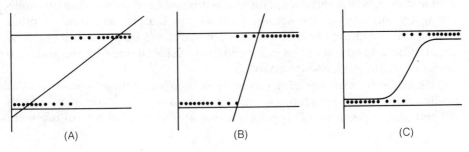

(A)   (B)   (C)

There are several functions in the mathematical literature that produce an S-curve of the desired form. All of these rely on some assumed underlying distribution. If the two values are 1 and 0, then the basic model is

$$P = \text{Prob}(Y_i = 1) = F(\beta'X_i) \text{ and } P = \text{Prob}(Y_i = 0) = 1 - F(\beta'X_i)$$

One of the functions that can be used to estimate these probabilities is to assume that $F(\beta'X_i)$ has a cumulative normal distribution. In this case, a change in one unit of the independent variable will produce a change in the probability that $Y_i = 1$ by an amount that is directly proportional to $\beta'F(\beta'X_i)$. Unlike simple linear regression, these equations cannot be solved. They can only be estimated. Therefore, the interpretation is altered from a statement that a unit change in x will produce a change of so many units in y to a maximum likelihood estimate that a unit change in X_i will produce a change in the *probability* that Y_i will take on one value rather than the other. (The word *probit* in probit analysis is an abbreviation for "probability unit." It is also sometimes called "normit" by way of reference to the cumulative normal distribution.)

Probit analysis is obviously more complex than regression analysis, but its assumptions make it a superior form of analysis for voting data. Its increased power can be shown by comparing the probit solutions used in Chapter 9 with regression solutions using identically coded independent variables. Using 1976 data, the regression solution explained 47 percent of the variance in the vote, while the probit solution explained 73 percent of the variance. The 1980 regression solution for the major party candidates explained 51 percent of the variance in the vote, whereas the comparable probit solution explained 80 percent of the variance. The 1984 regression solution for the major party candidates explained 57 percent of the variance in the vote, whereas the comparable probit solution explained 84 percent of the variance. (For further information about probit analysis, see Aldrich & Cnudde, 1975; Aldrich & Nelson, 1984; Fiorina, 1981, Appendix A; Hanushek & Jackson, 1977, chap. 7; and Nelson & Olson, 1978.)

The maximum likelihood estimates in Chapter 9 were reported as MLE* to denote the fact that they had been standardized. The computer program written (and kindly made available) by Richard McKelvey does not contain any standardization. Indeed, some scholars question if this should be done at all. The computer program does supply the sample variance for the independent and dependent variables. This made it possible to standardize by multiplying by the ratio of the square roots of the sample variances. In other words, the maximum likelihood estimate is standardized by multiplying it by the standard deviation of the independent variable divided by the standard deviation of the dependent variable.

The reason for standardizing can be seen from an example. The maximum likelihood estimates for economic management and agriculture in 1976 were .29 and .52, respectively. This suggests that attitudes about agriculture were more important in 1976 than attitudes about economics. Now recall that a unit change in any independent variable produces a change in the probability that the dependent variable will take on one value rather than the other. This is important because the variance for economic management was 3.52 and the variance for agriculture was .05. This means that attitudes on economics vary across more units than do attitudes on agriculture, and they therefore have more opportunities to affect vote. It is this consideration that is taken into account when standardizing. In this example, standardization increases the maximum likelihood estimate for economics from .29 to 1.10 and decreases the MLE for agriculture from .52 to .25, thereby reflecting the much greater range through which economic attitudes vary and the restricted range for attitudes on agriculture.

Another reason for standardizing this way is related to a goal of the analysis. By controlling for the effects of variance, standardization allows a better comparison between the effects of the attitude components in a given election. But we also want to be able to make comparisons across elections—and it happens that the variance for vote has been remarkably stable (see Table A–5). The variance was slightly depressed in the one-sided elections of 1964 and 1972; but even including those years, the variance in the dependent variable (i.e., vote) has been relatively steady. When one uses this method of standardization for any one election, the denominator of the ratio is quite similar for other years. This allows us to make comparisons across elections.

TABLE A–5

Year	Sample Variance for Vote
1952	.244
1956	.241
1960	.250
1964	.219
1968	.248
1972	.230
1976	.250
1980	.246
1984	.243

A–9.2 Attitude Categories for Voting Analyses

The Center for Political Studies master code categories in 1976 are shown in Table A–6. The master codes in the seven candidate categories, the two party categories, and the seven issue categories were simply combined for the three broad attitude categories.

Parallel coding decisions were made for the other years.

TABLE A–6

Category	Master Codes
Candidates	
General	0009, 0036, 0201, 0223–0224, 0427–0430, 0443–0455, 0457, 0497–0498, 0505, 0701–0711, 0721–0722, 0797
Record and incumbency	0217, 0553, 0554, 0611
Experience	0211–0212, 0215–0216, 0218–0221, 0297, 0313, 0314, 0425–0426, 0456
Management	0311–0312, 0407–0408, 0601–0602, 0605–0610, 0612, 0697, 0841–0842
Intelligence	0413–0422
Trust.	0213–0214, 0307–0308, 0309–0310, 0401–0404, 0431, 0432, 0603, 0604, 1010–1020
Personality.	0301–0306, 0315–0320, 0411–0412, 0423–0424, 0433–0442, 0459–0460
Parties	
People in party	0001–0008, 0010–0035, 0037–0097, 0502–0504, 0508, 0541–0542
Party affect	0101–0197, 0500–0501, 0506, 0507, 0597
Issues	
General	0509–0512, 0515–0518, 0531–0536, 0551–0552, 0720, 0801–0828, 0843–0897, 0900, 0934–0935, 0997, 1297
International involvement	0513–0514, 0519–0520, 1101–1172, 1175–1177, 1179–1197
Economic management	0901–0904, 0911–0913, 0926–0933, 0936–0941, 0952–0958, 1007–1009, 1201–1214
Social benefits	0905–0910, 0914–0925, 0965–0967, 0994–0996, 1001–1003, 1219, 1222, 1227–1228, 1233–1234
Civil liberties.	0405–0406, 0946–0951, 0968–0993, 1173–1174, 1178, 1217–1218, 1223–1226, 1229–1232
Natural resources	0959–0964, 1004–1006
Agriculture.	0942–0945, 1215–1216
Missing data.	9001–9002, 9996–9999, 0000

A–9.3 Multivariate Analyses of Causes of Issue Voting

The independent variables were issue distance, incumbency, and time. The measure of issue distance used was derived from Steven Rosenstone's estimates of candidate positions on the social welfare dimension. He obtained these by asking scholars to score the candidates' actual positions "the way an insightful political observer of the day would have evaluated the actions and positions of the candidate prior to the election." Rosenstone took the judgments of 37 election scholars whose assessments were very highly correlated with each other and, after a process of standardization to remove idiosyncratic tendencies, accepted an average of the 37 scores as indicating the relative liberalism or conservatism of each candidate. (For further details, see Rosenstone, 1983, pp. 172–78.)

The issue distance is simply the difference between the score of the Republican candidate and that of the Democratic candidate in each election. The Pearsonian correlation between these social welfare distance measures and the maximum likehood estimates for social benefits is quite substantial, .60. The issue distance measures are used to indicate the candidates' overall issue tendencies because the correlation between issue distance and the MLEs for all issues is even higher, .77.

The dependent variables were standardized maximum likelihood estimates for the election in question. The MLEs for all issue voting were those reported in Figure 9–2. The MLEs for specific-issue voting were weighted averages of the MLEs for each policy area. In 1984, for example, the salience of international involvement was 12.6, that for economic management was 23.0, and the salience for all six policy areas was 54.4. Therefore, the MLE for international involvement was weighted .23 (12.6 divided by 54.4), and that for economic management was weighted .42 (23.0 divided by 54.4) in calculating the MLE for specific-issue voting.

It was difficult to find any statistically significant relationships. With three independent variables and nine data points, there were only five residual degrees of freedom in the multiple regressions. This meant that any relationship had to be very close before it would be statistically significant.

When all issue voting was the dependent variable, issue distance was significant, and incumbency and time were not. The beta for issue distance was .68, and R^2 adjusted for the small number of cases was .45. When incumbency and time were dropped from the equation, the beta for issue distance went up to .77, and R^2 increased to .77. The t-test was 3.2; and with seven degrees of freedom, this meant the relationship could be accepted at a .99 confidence level.

When specific-issue voting became the dependent variable, problems with autocorrelation were encountered. When corrected for autocorrelation and with issue distance as the only independent variable in the regression, the relationship still did not reach the .95 condidence level necessary for statistical significance. There was, however, a t-test of 1.43. With seven degrees of freedom, the relationship can be accepted at the .90 confidence level. If this is not quite statistical significance, it still shows a strong effect.

Incumbency did not show any significant effects until three elections (1952, 1980, and 1984) were dropped from the analysis. With analysis reduced to only six cases, incumbency did show a significant relationship with specific-issue voting. When incumbency was the only independent variable in the regression, it had a beta of .80. The adjusted R square was .56, and with a t-test of 2.69 and four degrees of freedom, the relationship could be accepted at the .95 confidence level. The question is whether one wishes to accept a relationship between incumbency and specific-issue voting when the evidence comes from only six selected cases.

A–10.1 Indexes of Partisan Issue Consistency and Partisan Attitude Consistency

Both of the indexes were based on the assumption that partisans would have more favorable perceptions of their own party than of the opposition. Strong Republicans, Weak Republicans, and Independent Republicans were regarded as consistent if they evaluated the Republican party more highly than the Democratic party. The opposite convention applied to Strong Democrats, Weak Democrats, and Independent Democrats. Independents were excluded from these scales.

The index of partisan attitude consistency was constructed from the responses to five issue items and the associated perceptions of the candidates. The issue items included were:

> Welfare payments ought to be increased.
> The police ought to be given more authority.
> America should spend whatever is necessary to have a strong military force.
> We must have peace in Vietnam.
> Busing should not be used to desegregate schools.

Each respondent reacted to these statements by placing a card containing the statement in one of seven positions on a sort board ranging from Strongly Agree to Strongly Disagree. Each of the five items was adapted so the respondents could similarly indicate their perceptions of the two presidential candidates. For example:

> McGovern as president would increase welfare payments.
> Nixon as president would increase welfare payments.

For each item, respondents were given a score of 1 if their own party's candidate was perceived as being closest to their preferred position, a score of 0 if the opposition candidate was perceived as being closest to their preferred position, and a score of .5 if the candidates were perceived as being equidistant from their preferred position. The respondent's score on the index of partisan issue consistency was the average of these item scores for the items on which the respondent expressed a preference and reported perceptions of both presidential candidates.

The index of partisan attitude consistency is based on the open-ended questions that were used to analyze information level and presidential vote choice. A score of +1 was assigned to each comment that favored the respondent's own party or criticized the opposition party. A score of −1 was assigned to each comment that criticized the respondent's own party or favored the opposition party. The sum of these scores was divided by the total number of comments. This produced a raw index that varied between +1 for complete partisan consistency and −1 for complete partisan inconsistency. The raw scores were then adjusted to bounds of 1 for complete consistency and 0 for complete inconsistency so as to be comparable to the index of partisan issue consistency.

A–11.1 Median Positions of Various Party Groupings

Responses to card-sort items were used to calculate median scores for electoral activists, citizens, and members of the White House staff. Items and policy areas in which they were grouped in this analysis were:[2]

>International involvement
>>The government should help countries all over the world.
>>We should bring all American troops back from foreign countries.*
>>America should spend whatever necessary to have a strong military force. (R)
>>We must have peace in Vietnam.*
>Economic management
>>Wages and prices should not be controlled by the government.(R)
>>Government spending should be cut.(R)
>>The government should act to stop pollution.
>>The federal government is getting too powerful.(R)
>Social benefits
>>The government ought to help pay everyone's medical bills.
>>Welfare payments ought to be increased.
>>Social security benefits ought to be increased.*
>Civil liberties
>>I favor letting Negroes move into white neighborhoods.*
>>Busing should not be used to desegregate schools.(R)
>>The police ought to be given more authority.(R)

All 14 of the items were given to citizens and to the electoral activists. Ten of the items were included in the interviews with members of the White House Domestic Council staff. The four that were omitted from the Domestic Council interviews are indicated with asterisks. There were some minor variations in wording in four of the stimulus items given to the Domestic Council staff members. The most important of these concerned foreign aid and busing. These were phrased "The United States should help countries all over the world" and "Busing should not be used to achieve a racial balance in schools" in the White House interviews.

In computing the scores by policy area, strong agreement was given a score of 7 (that is, most liberal) and strong disagreement was given a score of 1 (that

---

[2] Asterisks denote items omitted from the White House Domestic Council interviews. (R) denotes items with reversed scoring: strong agreement = 1; strong disagreement = 7.

TABLE A–7
Median Scores

Party Grouping	Policy Area			
	International Involvement	Economic Management	Social Benefits	Civil Liberties
Democratic representatives	3.6	6.0	6.7	4.2
Democratic electoral activists	4.9	4.4	5.9	6.0
Democratic citizens	4.2	3.9	4.7	3.3
Republican citizens	4.1	3.5	4.1	2.9
Republican electoral activists	4.0	3.8	3.6	3.5
Republican White House staff...............	3.4	3.1	3.3	3.1
Republican representatives	1.7	2.4	2.6	2.5

is, most conservative) with eight items. With the other six items, all indicated by an (R), the scoring was reversed, so that strong agreement was given a score of 1 and strong disagreement a score of 7.

The scores for the representatives were based on roll-call votes cast in each policy dimension and were arrayed on scales ranging from 10 to 30 by Aage R. Clausen. Professor Clausen kindly made these scales available, and they were converted to a 1 to 7 range for purposes of comparability. It is appropriate to use these to compare with the attitude scores in the other institutional domains, because members of Congress are customarily judged by their behavior. One would also expect that representatives would have more extreme scores because of institutional tendencies (Republicans voting with Republicans and Democrats voting with Democrats) toward bifurcation.

The median scores underlying Table 11–1 are shown in Table A–7.

Bibliography

Abramson, Paul R. (1983) *Political Attitudes in America: Formation and Change.* San Francisco: W. H. Freeman.

Abramson, Paul R., Aldrich, John H., and Rhode, David W. (1986) *Change and Continuity in the 1984 Elections.* Washington, D.C.: Congressional Quarterly Press.

Adams, William C. (1985) "Convention Coverage." In Michael J. Robinson and Austin Ranney, eds., *The Mass Media in Campaign '84.* Washington, D.C.: American Enterprise Institute, pp. 18–23.

Aldrich, John H. (1980a) *Before the Convention: A Theory of Campaigning for the 1976 Presidential Nomination.* Chicago: University of Chicago Press.

_____. (1980b) "A Dynamic Model of Pre-Convention Campaigns." *American Political Science Review* (September), pp. 651–669.

Aldrich, John H., and Cnudde, Charles. (1975) "Probing the Bounds of Conventional Wisdom: A Comparison of Regression, Probit, and Discriminant Analysis." *American Journal of Political Science* (August), pp. 571–608.

Aldrich, John H., Gant, Michael, and Simon, Dennis. (1978) "To the Victor Belong the Spoils: Momentum in the 1976 Nomination Campaigns." Paper prepared for the 1978 Meeting of the Public Choice Society.

Aldrich, John H., and Nelson, Forrest D. (1986) *Linear Probability, Logit and Probit Models.* Sage University Series on Quantitative Applications in the Social Sciences, 07-045. Beverly Hills, Calif: Sage Publications.

Alexander, Herbert E. (1972) *Political Financing.* Minneapolis: Burgess.

_____. (1976) *Financing the 1972 Election.* Lexington, Mass.: D. C. Heath.

_____. (1984a) *Financing Politics: Money, Elections, and Political Reform,* 3d ed. Washington, D.C.: Congressional Quarterly Press.

_____. (1984b) "Making Sense about Dollars in the 1980 Presidential Campaign." In Michael J. Malbin, ed., *Money and Politics in the United States: Financing Elections in the 1980s.* Chatham, N.J.: Chatham House.

_____. (1985) "American Presidential Elections since Public Funding, 1976–

1984." Paper prepared for delivery at the XIIth World Congress of the International Political Science Association, Paris, France, July 15–20.

Allsop, Dee. "Election Year Fluctuations in Party Identification." Ph.D. diss., Ohio State University.

Allsop, Dee, and Weisberg, Herbert F. (1986) "Measuring Change in Party Identification in an Election Campaign." Paper prepared for delivery at the 1986 Annual Meeting of the Midwest Political Science Association, Chicago, April 10–13.

Apple, R. W., Jr. (1976) "The Ethnics Vote in the States that Really Count." New York Times (October 10), p. E1.

Arrington, Theodore S. (1975) "Some Effects of Political Experience on Issue Consciousness and Issue Partisanship among Tucson Party Activists." American Journal of Political Science (November), pp. 695–702.

Arterton, F. Christopher. (1984) Media Politics: The News Strategies of Presidential Campaigns. Lexington, Mass.: Lexington Books.

Asher, Herbert B. (1984) Presidential Elections and American Politics: Voters, Candidates and Campaigns since 1952, 3d ed. Chicago: Dorsey Press.

Axelrod, Robert. (1972) "Where the Votes Come From: An Analysis of Electoral Coalitions, 1952–1968." American Political Science Review (March), pp. 11–20.

———. (1986) "Presidential Election Coalitions in 1984." American Political Science Review (March), pp. 281–284.

Barber, James David, ed. (1974) Choosing the President. Englewood Cliffs, N.J.: Prentice-Hall.

———, ed. (1978) Race for the Presidency: The Media and the Nominating Process. Englewood Cliffs, N.J.: Prentice-Hall.

Barnes, Samuel H., and Petrescu, Octavian. (1986) "Dimensions of Political Sophistication and Party Images: A Three-Nation Panel Study," Paper prepared for delivery at the 1986 Meeting of the American Political Science Asso-

ciation, Washington, D.C., August 28–31.

Barnett, Marguerite Ross. (1983) "The Strategic Debate over a Black Presidential Candidacy." PS (Summer), pp. 489–491.

Beck, Paul Allen. (1974) "Environment and Party: The Impact of Political and Demographic County Characteristics on Party Behavior." American Political Science Review (September), pp. 1229–1244.

Bennett, W. Lance. (1977) "The Growth of Knowledge in Mass Belief Systems: An Epistemological Critique." American Journal of Political Science (August), pp. 465–500.

Bibby, John F. (1980) "Party Renewal in the National Republican Party." In Gerald M. Pomper, ed., Party Renewal in America: Theory and Practice. New York: Praeger Publishers.

Bibby, John F., Cotter, Cornelius P., Gibson, James L., and Huckshorn, Robert J. (1982) "Parties in State Politics." In Herbert Jacob and Virginia Gray, eds., Politics in the American States, 4th ed. Boston: Little, Brown.

Bishop, George E., Tuchfarber, Alfred J., and Oldendick, Robert W. (1978) "Change in the Structure of American Political Attitudes: The Nagging Question of Question Wording." American Journal of Political Science (May), pp. 250–269.

Bonafede, Dom. (1983a) "Democratic State Party Leaders See Race Even as Glenn Gains on Mondale." National Journal (July 16), pp. 1484–1489.

———. (1983b) "Democratic State Party Leaders See Mondale Pulling Away from Glenn." National Journal (December 17), pp. 2612–2616.

Bone, Hugh A. (1971) American Politics and the Party System. New York: McGraw-Hill.

Brams, Steven J. (1978) The Presidential Election Game. New Haven, Conn.: Yale University Press.

Brams, Steven J., and Fishburn, Peter C. (1978) "Approval Voting." American Political Science Review (September), pp. 831–847.

————. (1983) *Approval Voting*. Cambridge, Mass.: Birkhauser Boston.

Broder, David S. (1970) "Reporters in Presidential Politics." In Charles Peters and Timothy J. Adams, eds., *Inside the System*. New York: Praeger Publishers.

————. (1984a) "The Generation Issue." *Washington Post*, National Weekly Edition (March 12), p. 4.

————. (1984b) "Hart's Hurdles." *Washington Post*, National Weekly Edition (June 4), p. 4.

————. (1984c) "A Contest of Unequals." *Washington Post*, National Weekly Edition (November 5), p. 4.

————. (1986) "Democratic Kudzu." *Washington Post*, National Weekly Edition (March 24), p. 4.

Brody, Richard A. (1977) "Stability and Change in Party Identification: Presidential to Off-Years." Paper prepared for delivery at the 1977 Annual Meeting of the American Political Science Association, Washington, D.C., September 1–4.

Burnham, Walter Dean. (1970) *Critical Elections and the Mainsprings of American Politics*. New York: W.W. Norton.

————. (1975) "American Politics in the 1970's: Beyond Party?" In William N. Chambers and Walter Dean Burnham, eds., *The American Party Systems: Stages of Political Development*, 2d ed. New York: Oxford University Press, pp. 308–357.

Caddell, Patrick, and **Wirthlin, Richard.** (1981) "Face Off: A Conversation with the Presidents' Pollsters." *Public Opinion* (December–January), pp. 2–12, 63–64.

Campbell, Angus, Converse, Philip E., Miller, Warren E., and **Stokes, Donald E.** (1960) *The American Voter*. New York: John Wiley & Sons.

Campbell, Angus, Gurin, Gerald, and **Miller, Warren E.** (1954) *The Voter Decides*. Evanston, Ill.: Row, Peterson.

Cannon, James M., ed. (1960) *Politics, U.S.A.: A Practical Guide to the Winning of Public Office*. Garden City, N.Y.: Doubleday Publishing.

Cannon, Lou. (1982) *Reagan*. New York: G. P. Putnam's Sons.

Carmines, Edward G., and **Stimson, James A.** (1981) "Issue Evolution, Population Replacement, and Normal Partisan Change." *American Political Science Review* (March), pp. 107–118.

————. (1986) "On the Structure and Sequence of Issue Evolution." *American Political Science Review* (September), pp. 901–920.

Cattani, Richard J. (1983) "The 'Big Bang' Theory of '84 Politics." *Christian Science Monitor* (February 17), pp. 1, 9.

Chester, Lewis, Hodgson, Godfrey, and **Page, Bruce.** (1969) *An American Melodrama: The Presidential Campaign 1968*. New York: Viking Press.

Clarke, James W. (1970) Personal communication.

Clausen, Aage R. (1973) *How Congressmen Decide: A Policy Focus*. New York: St. Martin's Press.

Clausen, Aage R., and **Cheney, Richard B.** (1970) "A Comparative Analysis of Senate and House Voting on Economic and Welfare Policy: 1953–1964." *American Political Science Review* (March), pp. 138–152.

Clymer, Adam. (1984) "The 1984 National Primary." *Public Opinion* (August–September), pp. 52–53.

Coleman, Milton. (1984) "When the Candidate is Black Like Me." *Washington Post*, National Weekly Edition (April 23), pp. 8–9.

Comparative State Election Project. (1973) *Explaining the Vote: Presidential Choices in the Nation and the States*. Chapel Hill, N.C.: Institute for Research in Social Science.

Converse, Philip E. (1964) "The Nature of Belief Systems in Mass Publics." In David E. Apter, ed., *Ideology and Discontent*. New York: Free Press.

————. (1966) Letter to author dated March 4.

————. (1975) "Public Opinion and Voting Behavior." In Fred I. Greenstein and Nelson W. Polsby, eds., *Handbook of Political Science*. Vol. 4.

Reading, Mass.: Addison-Wesley Publishing.

————. (1976) *The Dynamics of Party Support: Cohort Analyzing Party Identification.* Beverly Hills, Calif.: Sage Publications.

Converse, Philip E., and Markus, Gregory B. (1979) "Plus ça Change. . .: The New CPS Election Study Panel." *American Political Science Review* (March), pp. 32–49.

Corwin, Edward S. (1948) *The President Office and Powers, 1787–1948: History and Analysis of Practice and Opinion,* 3d rev. ed. New York: New York University Press.

Costain, Anne N. (1978) "An Analysis of Voting in American National Nominating Conventions, 1940–1976." *American Politics Quarterly* (January), pp. 375–394.

Cotter, Cornelius P., Gibson, James L., Bibby, John F., and Huckshorn, Robert J. (1984) *Party Organizations in American Politics.* New York: Praeger Publishers.

Cotter, Cornelius P., and Hennessy, Bernard C. (1964) *Politics without Power: The National Party Committees.* New York: Atherton.

Crotty, William J. (1980a) *The Party Symbol: Readings on Political Parties.* San Francisco: W.H. Freeman.

————. (1980b) "The Philosophies of Party Reform." In Gerald M. Pomper, ed., *Party Renewal in America: Theory and Practice.* New York: Praeger Publishers.

Crotty, William J., and Jacobson, Gary C. (1980) *American Parties in Decline.* Boston: Little, Brown.

Curry, George E. (1984) "Jackson a Dilemma for Black Reporters." *Chicago Tribune* (April 2), pp. 1, 4.

David, Paul T., Goldman, Ralph M., and Bain, Richard C. (1960) *The Politics of National Party Conventions.* Washington, D.C.: Brookings Institution.

Dennis, Jack. (1981) "On Being an Independent Partisan Supporter." Paper prepared for delivery at the 1981 Annual Meeting of the Midwest Political Science Association, Cincinnati, Ohio, April 16–18.

Dillin, John. (1984) "Democrats Take On Bitter Tone of Ford-Reagan in '76." *Christian Science Monitor* (April 3), pp. 1, 34.

Downs, Anthony. (1957) *An Economic Theory of Democracy.* New York: Harper & Row.

Drew, Elizabeth. (1977) *American Journal: The Events of 1976.* New York: Random House.

————. (1981) *Portrait of an Election: The 1980 Presidential Campaign.* New York: Simon & Schuster.

Edsall, Thomas B. (1986) "Maybe the Democrats Should Use a Tin Cup." *Washington Post,* National Weekly Edition (March 3), p. 11.

Edwards, George C., III. (1983) *The Public Presidency: The Pursuit of Popular Support.* New York: St. Martin's Press.

Eldersveld, Samuel J. (1964) *Political Parties: A Behavioral Analysis.* Chicago: Rand McNally.

————. (1982) *Political Parties in American Society.* New York: Basic Books.

Endicott, R. Craig. (1985) "P & G Retains Advertising Crown." *Advertising Age* (September 26), pp. 1–2.

Epstein, Leon D. (1974) "Political Parties." In Fred I. Greenstein and Nelson W. Polsby, eds., *Handbook of Political Science.* Vol 4. Reading, Mass.: Addison-Wesley Publishing.

————. (1986) *Political Parties in the American Mold.* Madison: University of Wisconsin Press.

Everson, David H. (1980) *American Political Parties.* New York: New Viewpoints.

Farah, Barbara G. (1982) "Political Ambition: An Enduring Quest among Political Activists." Paper prepared for delivery at the 1982 Annual Meeting of the American Political Science Association, Denver, September 2–5.

————. (1984) "Delegate Polls: 1944 to 1984." *Public Opinion* (August–September), pp. 43–45.

Farah, Barbara G., Jennings, M. Kent, and Miller, Warren E. (1982) *Report to Respondents: The 1980 Convention Delegate Study.* Ann Arbor, Mich.: Institute for Social Research.

Fiorina, Morris P. (1981) *Retrospective Voting in American National Politics.* New Haven, Conn.: Yale University Press.

Fishel, Jeff. (1977) "Agenda Building in Presidential Campaigns: The Case of Jimmy Carter." Paper prepared for delivery at the 1977 Annual Meeting of the American Political Science Association, Washington, D.C., September 1–4.

Flanigan, William H., and Zingale, Nancy H. (1983) *Political Behavior of the American Electorate,* 5th ed. Boston: Allyn & Bacon.

Fogel, Normal J. (1974) "The Impact of Cognitive Inconsistency on Electoral Behavior." Ph.D. diss., Ohio State University.

Ford, Gerald R. (1979) *A Time to Heal.* New York: Harper & Row.

Fortune (1935) "The Democratic Party" (April), p. 136. Cited in Pendleton Herring, *The Politics of Democracy: American Parties in Action.* New York: Holt, Rinehart & Winston, 1940, p. 265.

Gatlin, Douglas. (1973) "Florida." In Comparative State Election Project, *Explaining the Vote: Presidential Choices in the Nation and the States, 1968.* Chapel Hill, N.C.: Institute for Research in Social Science.

Germond, Jack W., and Witcover, Jules. (1985) *Wake Us When It's Over: Presidential Politics of 1984.* New York: Macmillan.

Gerston, Larry N., Burstein, Jerome S., and Cohen, Stephen S. (1979) "Presidential Nominations and Coalition Theory." *American Politics Quarterly* (April), pp. 175–197.

Gibson, James L., Cotter, Cornelius P., Bibby, John F., and Huckshorn, Robert J. (1981) "Assessing Institutional Party Strength." Paper prepared for delivery at the 1981 Annual Meeting of the Midwest Political Science Association, Cincinnati, Ohio, April 16–18.

———. (1982) "Whither the Local Parties? A Cross-Sectional and Longitudinal Analysis of Party Organizations." Paper prepared for delivery at the 1982 Annual Meeting of the Western Political Science Association, San Diego, California, March 25–27.

Goldman, Peter, and Fuller, Tony. (1985) *The Quest for the Presidency 1984.* New York: Bantam Books.

Graber, Doris A. (1976) "Press and TV as Opinion Resources in Presidential Campaigns." *Public Opinion Quarterly* (Fall), pp. 285–303.

———. (1980) *The Mass Media and Politics.* Washington, D.C.: Congressional Quarterly Press.

———. (1982a) "Hoopla and Horse-Race in 1980: Campaign Coverage: A Closer Look." Paper prepared for delivery at the 1982 Annual Meeting of the Midwest Association for Public Opinion Research, Chicago, November 19–20.

———, ed. (1982b) *The President and the Public.* Philadelphia: Institute for the Study of Human Issues.

Greeley, Andrew M. (1974) *Building Coalitions: American Politics in the 1970's.* New York: Franklin Watts.

Greenstein, Fred I. (1974) "What the President Means to Americans." In James David Barber, ed., *Choosing the President.* Englewood Cliffs, N.J.: Prentice-Hall.

Guylay, L. Richard. (1960) "Public Relations." In James M. Cannon, ed., *Politics, U.S.A.: A Practical Guide to the Winning of Public Office.* Garden City, N.Y.: Doubleday Publishing.

Hanushek, Erik A., and Jackson, John E. (1977) *Statistical Methods for Social Scientists.* New York: Academic Press.

Harmel, Robert, and Janda, Kenneth. (1982) *Parties and their Environments: Limits to Reform?* New York: Longman.

Hart, Gary W. (1973) *Right from the Start: A Chronicle of the McGovern Campaign.*

New York: Quadrangle/New York Times.

Hart, Peter, and **Wirthlin, Richard.** (1985) "Moving Right Along: Campaign '84's Lessons for 1988." *Public Opinion* (December–January), pp. 8–11, 59–63.

Harwood, Richard, ed. (1980) *The Pursuit of the Presidency.* New York: Berkley Books.

Heard, Alexander. (1960) *The Costs of Democracy.* Chapel Hill: University of North Carolina Press.

Herring, Pendleton. (1940) *The Politics of Democracy: American Parties in Action.* New York: Holt, Rinehart & Winston.

Hershey, Marjorie R. (1977) "A Social Learning Theory of Innovation and Change in Political Campaigning." Paper prepared for delivery at the 1977 Annual Meeting of the American Political Science Association, Washington, D.C., September 1–4.

—————. (1984) *Running for Office: The Political Education of Campaigners.* Chatham, N.J.: Chatham House.

Hinckley, Barbara. (1981) *Coalitions and Politics.* New York: Harcourt Brace Jovanovich.

Hinckley, Barbara, Hofstetter, Richard, and **Kessel, John H.** (1974) "Information and the Vote: A Comparative Election Study." *American Politics Quarterly* (April), pp. 131–158.

Hoagland, Henry W. (1960) "The Advance Man." In James M. Cannon, ed., *Politics, U.S.A.: A Practical Guide to the Winning of Public Office.* Garden City, N.Y.: Doubleday Publishing.

Hofstetter, Richard. (1976) *Bias in the News: Network Television Coverage of the 1972 Election Campaign.* Columbus: Ohio State University Press.

Holcombe, Arthur N. (1950) *Our More Perfect Union: From Eighteenth Century Principles to Twentieth Century Practice.* Cambridge, Mass.: Harvard University Press.

Howell, Susan E. (1976) "The Psychological Dimension of Unity in American Political Parties." Paper prepared for delivery at the 1976 Annual Meeting of the American Political Science Association, Chicago, September 2–5.

Huckshorn, Robert J. (1976) *Party Leadership in the States.* Amherst: University of Massachusetts Press.

—————. (1984) *Political Parties in America,* 2d ed. Monterey, Calif.: Brooks/Cole Publishing.

Ivins, Molly. (1976) "Liberal from Goldwater Country." *New York Times Magazine,* (February 1), pp. 12–33.

Jackson, John E. (1975) "Issues, Party Choices, and Presidential Votes." *American Journal of Political Science* (May), pp. 161–185.

Jennings, M. Kent. (1966) Personal communication.

Jennings, M. Kent, and **Markus, Gregory B.** (1984) "Partisan Orientations over the Long Haul: Results from the Three-Wave Political Socialization Panel Study." *American Political Science Review* (December), pp. 1000–1018.

Jennings, M. Kent, and **Niemi, Richard G.** (1981) *Generations and Politics.* Princeton, N.J.: Princeton University Press.

Jennings, M. Kent, and **Zeigler, Harmon,** eds. (1966) *The Electoral Process.* Englewood Cliffs, N.J.: Prentice-Hall.

Johnson, Loch K., and **Hahn, Harlan.** (1973) "Delegate Turnover at National Party Conventions, 1944–68." In Donald R. Matthews, ed., *Perspectives on Presidential Selection.* Washington, D.C.: Brookings Institution.

Johnson, Lyndon B. (1971) *The Vantage Point.* New York: Popular Library.

Jones, Charles O. (1981) "Nominating 'Carter's Favorite Opponent': The Republicans in 1980." In Austin Ranney, ed., *The American Elections of 1980.* Washington, D.C.: American Enterprise Institute.

Jordan, Hamilton. (1982) *Crisis: The Last Year of the Carter Presidency.* New York: G.P. Putnam's Sons.

Judd, Charles M., and **Krosnick, Jon A.** (1982) "Attitude Centrality, Organization, and Measurement," *Journal of Per-*

sonality and Social Psychology (March), pp. 436–447.

Keech, William R., and **Matthews, Donald R.** (1976) *The Party's Choice.* Washington, D.C.: Brookings Institution.

Kelley, Stanley, Jr. (1956) *Professional Public Relations and Political Power.* Baltimore: Johns Hopkins University Press.

Kelley, Stanley, Jr., Ayers, Richard E., and **Bowen, William G.** (1967) "Registration and Voting: Putting First Things First." *American Political Science Review* (June), pp. 359–377.

Kelley, Stanley, Jr., Collat, Donald S., and **Rogowski, Ronald.** (1981) "The End Game in Presidential Nominations." *American Political Science Review* (June), pp. 426–435.

Kessel, John H. (1974) "The Parameters of Presidential Politics." *Social Science Quarterly* (June), pp. 8–24.

———. (1975) *The Domestic Presidency: Decision-Making in the White House.* North Scituate, Mass.: Duxbury.

———. (1977) "The Seasons of Presidential Politics." *Social Science Quarterly* (December), pp. 418–435.

Key, V. O., Jr. (1949) *Southern Politics in State and Nation.* New York: Alfred A. Knopf.

———. (1964) *Politics, Parties, and Pressure Groups,* 5th ed. New York: Crowell.

Kirkpatrick, Jeane. (1976) *The New Presidential Elite: Men and Women in National Politics.* New York: Russell Sage Foundation and Twentieth Century Fund.

Kramer, Gerald H. (1965) "Decision Theoretic Analysis of Canvassing and other Precinct Level Activities in Political Campaigning." Ph.D. diss., Massachusetts Institute of Technology.

———. (1971) "The Effects of Precinct-Level Canvassing on Voter Behavior." *Public Opinion Quarterly* (Winter 1970–71), pp. 560–572.

Kraus, Sidney, ed. (1962) *The Great Debates: Kennedy vs. Nixon, 1960.* Bloomington: Indiana University Press.

———, ed. (1979) *The Great Debates: Ford vs. Carter, 1976.* Bloomington: Indiana University Press.

Krosnick, Jon A. (1986) "Policy Voting in American Presidential Elections: An Application of Psychological Theory to American Politics." Ph.D. diss., University of Michigan.

Kruskal, Joseph B., and **Wish, Myron.** (1978) *Multidimensional Scaling.* Sage University Series on Quantitative Applications in the Social Sciences, 07-011. Beverly Hills, Calif.: Sage Publications.

Ladd, Everett Carll. (1982) *Where Have All the Voters Gone? The Fracturing of American Political Parties,* 2d ed. New York: W.W. Norton.

Ladd, Everett Carll, and **Hadley, Charles D.** (1978) *Transformations of the American Party System,* 2d ed. New York: W. W. Norton.

Lamb, Karl A. (1966) "Under One Roof: Barry Goldwater's Campaign Staff." In Bernard Cosman and Robert J. Huckshorn, eds., *Republican Politics: The 1964 Campaign and Its Aftermath.* New York: Praeger Publishers.

Lane, Robert E. (1973) "Patterns of Political Belief." In Jeane M. Knutson, ed., *Handbook of Political Psychology.* San Francisco: Jossey-Bass.

Lazersfeld, Paul F., Berelson, Bernard, and **Gaudet, Hazel.** (1944) *The People's Choice.* New York: Duell, Sloan and Pearce.

Lelyveld, Joseph H. (1976a) "The Selling of a Candidate." *New York Times Magazine* (March 28), pp. 16–17, 65–71.

———. (1976b) "President's New TV Commercials." *New York Times* (October 29), p. 22.

———. (1976c) "Iowa Woman, 79, Who Met a 'Nobody' in '75, Is Tickled by Carter Victory." *New York Times* (November 4), p. 51.

Lengle, James I., and **Shafer, Byron E.** (1976) "Primary Rules, Political Power, and Social Change." *American Political Science Review* (March), pp. 25–40.

———. (1983) *Presidential Politics: Read-*

ings on Nominations and Elections, 2d ed. New York: St. Martin's Press.

Levin, Eric. (1977) "How the Networks Decide What Is News." *TV Guide* (July 2), pp. 4–10.

Levinson, Daniel J. (1977) *The Seasons of a Man's Life.* New York: Alfred A. Knopf.

Light, Paul C., and **Lake, Celinda.** (1985) "The Election: Candidates, Strategies, and Decisions." In Michael Nelson, ed., *The Elections of 1984.* Washington, D.C.: Congressional Quarterly Press.

Lydon, Christopher. (1972) "How McGovern Rose to Top in Long Campaign." *New York Times* (June 11), p. 40.

Malbin, Michael J. (1981) "The Conventions, Platforms, and Issue Activists." In Austin Ranney, ed., *The American Elections of 1980.* Washington, D.C.: American Enterprise Institute.

Maraniss, David. (1984) "Tracing the Roots of Gary Hart's Ideas." *Washington Post,* National Weekly Edition (April 30), pp. 8–10.

Markus, Gregory B. (1982) Political Attitudes during an Election Year: "A Report on the 1980 NES Panel Study." *American Political Science Review* (September), pp. 538–560.

Marvick, Dwaine. (1973) "Party Organizational Behavior and Electoral Democracy: The Perspectives of Rival Cadres in Los Angeles from 1963 to 1972." Paper prepared for delivery at the Ninth World Congress, International Political Science Association, Montreal, Canada, August 19–25.

Matthews, Donald R, ed. (1973) *Perspectives on Presidential Selection.* Washington, D.C.: Brookings Institution.

————. (1978) "Winnowing: The News Media and the 1976 Presidential Nominations." In James David Barber, ed., *Race for the Presidency: The Media and the Nominating Process.* Englewood Cliffs, N.J.: Prentice-Hall.

Matthews, Donald R., and **Prothro, James W.** (1966) *Negroes and the New Southern Politics.* New York: Harcourt Brace Jovanovich.

McClosky, Herbert, Hoffman, Paul J.,

and **O'Hara, Rosemary.** (1960) "Issue Conflict and Consensus among Party Leaders and Followers." *American Political Science Review* (June), pp. 406–427.

McGinniss, Joe. (1969) *The Selling of the President 1968.* New York: Trident Press.

McKelvey, Richard, and **Zavonia, William.** (1969) "A Statistical Model for the Analysis of Legislative Behavior." Paper prepared for delivery at the 1969 Annual Meeting of the American Political Science Association, New York, September 1–8.

Michelson, Charles. (1944) *The Ghost Talks.* New York: G. P. Putnam's Sons.

Miller, Arthur H., and **Miller, Warren E.** (1977) "Partisanship and Performance: 'Rational' Choice in the 1976 Elections." Paper prepared for delivery at the 1977 Annual Meeting of the American Political Science Association, Washington, D.C., September 1–4.

Miller, Arthur H., and **Wattenberg, Martin P.** (1983) "Measuring Party Identification: Independent or No Partisan Preference?" *American Journal of Political Science* (February), pp. 106–121.

Miller, Warren E., and **Jennings, M. Kent.** (1986) *Parties in Transition: A Longitudinal Study of Party Leaders and Party Supporters.* New York: Russell Sage Foundation.

Miller, Warren E., and **Levitin, Teresa E.** (1976) *Leadership and Change: Presidential Elections from 1952 to 1976.* Cambridge, Mass.: Winthrop Press.

Mitofsky, Warren J., and **Plissner, Martin.** (1980) "The Making of the Delegates, 1968–1980." *Public Opinion* (October–November), pp. 37–43.

Moley, Raymond E. (1960) "Collaboration in Political Speech Writing." In James M. Cannon, ed., *Politics, U.S.A.: A Practical Guide to the Winning of Public Office.* Garden City, N.Y.: Doubleday Publishing.

Moore, Jonathan, ed. (1981) *The Campaign for President: 1980 in Retrospect.* Cambridge, Mass.: Ballinger.

Moore, Jonathan, and Fraser, Janet, eds. (1977) *Campaign for President: The Managers Look at '76.* Cambridge, Mass.: Ballinger.

Munger, Frank J., and Blackhurst, James. (1965) "Factionalism in the National Conventions, 1940–1964: An Analysis of Ideological Consistency in State Delegation Voting." *Journal of Politics* (May), pp. 375–394.

Naughton, James M. (1976) "Ford Hopes Linked to Catholic Vote." *New York Times* (September 5), pp. 1, 26.

Neisser, Ulrich. (1976) *Cognition and Reality.* San Francisco: W.H. Freeman.

Nelson, Forrest D., and Olson, Lawrence. (1978) "Specification and Estimation of a Simultaneous-Equation Model with Limited Dependent Variables." *International Economic Review* (October), pp. 695–709.

Nie, Norman H., and Andersen, Kristi. (1974) "Mass Belief Systems Revisited: Political Change and Attitude Structure." *Journal of Politics* (August), pp. 540–591.

Nie, Norman H., Verba, Sidney, and Petrocik, John R. (1976) *The Changing American Voter.* Cambridge Mass.: Harvard University Press.

Niemi, Richard G., and Jennings, M. Kent. (1969) "Intraparty Communication and the Selection of Delegates to a National Convention." *Western Political Quarterly* (January), pp. 29–46.

Niemi, Richard G., and Weisberg, Herbert F, eds. (1984) *Controversies in American Voting Behavior,* 2d ed. Washington, D.C.: Congressional Quarterly Press.

Nimmo, Dan, and Savage, Robert L. (1976) *Candidates and Their Images: Concepts, Methods and Findings.* Santa Monica, Calif.: Goodyear Publishing.

Ogden, Daniel M., and Peterson, Arthur L. (1968) *Electing the President,* rev. ed. San Francisco: Chandler.

Ornstein, Norman, Mann, Thomas E., Malbin, Michael, Schick, Allen, and Bibby, John F., eds. (1984) *Vital Statistics on Congress,* 1984–1985 ed. Washington, D.C.: American Enterprise Institute.

Orren, Gary R. (1978) "Candidate Style and Voter Alignment in 1976." In Seymour Martin Lipset, ed., *Emerging Coalitions in American Politics.* San Francisco: Institute for Contemporary Studies.

———. (1985) "The Nomination Process: Vicissitudes of Candidate Selection." In Michael Nelson, ed., *The Elections of 1984.* Washington, D.C.: Congressional Quarterly Press.

Page, Benjamin I. (1978) *Choices and Echoes in Presidential Elections: Rational Man and Electoral Democracy.* Chicago: University of Chicago Press.

Page, Benjamin I., and Brody, Richard A. (1972) "Policy Voting and the Electoral Process: The Vietnam War Issue." *American Political Science Review* (September), pp. 979–995.

Parry, James M. (1977) "AMDAHL Speaks: Carter Really Won the Election." *National Observer* (February 12).

Patterson, Thomas E. (1978) "Assessing Television Newscasts: Future Directions in Content Analysis." In William Adams and Fay Schreibman, eds., *Television Network News: Issues in Content Research.* Washington, D.C.: George Washington University.

Patterson, Thomas E., and McClure, Robert D. (1976) *The Unseeing Eye: The Myth of Television Power in National Politics.* New York; G. P. Putnam's Sons.

Petrocik, John R. (1974) "Intransitivities in the Index of Party Identification." *Political Methodology* (Summer), pp. 31–48.

———. (1981) *Party Coalitions: Realignments and the Decline of the New Deal Party System.* Chicago: University of Chicago Press.

Polsby, Nelson W., and Wildavsky, Aaron. (1984) *Presidential Elections,* 6th ed. New York: Charles Scribner's Sons.

Pomper, Gerald M. (1979) "New Rules and New Games in the National Conventions." *Journal of Politics* (August), pp. 784–805.

————. (1980) "The Contribution of Political Parties to American Democracy." In Gerald M. Pomper, ed., *Party Renewal in America: Theory and Practice.* New York: Praeger Publishers.

————. (1981) *The Election of 1980: Reports and Interpretations.* Chatham, N.J.: Chatham House.

————. (1985) *The Election of 1984: Reports and Interpretations.* Chatham, N.J.: Chatham House.

Pomper, Gerald M., and **Lederman, Susan S.** (1980) *Elections in America: Control and Influence in Democratic Politics,* 2d ed. New York: Dodd, Mead.

Price, David E. (1984) *Bringing Back the Parties.* Washington, D.C.: Congressional Quarterly Press.

Rabinowitz, George B. (1975) "An Introduction to Non-Metric Multidimensional Scaling." *American Journal of Political Science* (May), pp. 343–390.

Ranney, Austin. (1975) *Curing the Mischiefs of Faction: Party Reform in America.* Berkeley: University of California Press.

————. (1978) "The Political Parties: Reform and Decline." In Anthony King, ed., *The New American Political System.* Washington, D.C.: American Enterprise Institute.

————, ed. (1981) *The American Elections of 1980.* Washington, D.C.: American Enterprise Institute.

————, ed. (1985) *The American Elections of 1984.* Durham, N.C.: Duke University Press.

Raskin, A. H. (1972) "All Over Lot in '72 Campaign." *New York Times* (August 20), pp. E1–E2.

Republican National Committee Chairman's Report. (1979) Washington, D.C.: Republican National Committee.

Republican National Committee Chairman's Report. (1980) Washington, D.C.: Republican National Committee.

Riker, William H. (1962) *The Theory of Political Coalitions.* New Haven, Conn.: Yale University Press.

Roberts, Steven V. (1984) "Delegates 'Feel Good' about Candidate." *New York Times* (August 24), p. 10.

Robinson, Michael J. (1976) "Television News and the Presidential Nominating Process: The Case of Spring." Unpublished manuscript.

Robinson, Michael J., and **Ranney, Austin,** eds. (1985) *The Mass Media in Campaign '84.* Washington, D.C.: American Enterprise Institute.

Rosenstone, Steven J. (1983) *Forecasting Presidential Elections.* New Haven, Conn.: Yale University Press.

————. (1985) "Explaining the 1984 Presidential Election." *Brookings Review* (Winter), pp. 25–32.

Rosenstone, Steven J., and **Wolfinger, Raymond E.** (1978) "The Effect of Registration Laws on Voter Turnout." *American Political Science Review* (March), pp. 22–45.

Rubin, Richard L. (1976) *Party Dynamics: The Democratic Coalition and the Politics of Change.* New York: Oxford University Press.

Safire, William. (1975) *Before the Fall: An Inside View of the Pre-Watergate White House.* Garden City, N.Y.: Doubleday Publishing.

Schlesinger, Joseph A. (1975) "The Primary Goals of Political Parties: A Clarification of Positive Theory." *American Political Science Review* (September), pp. 840–849.

Schram, Martin. (1977) *Running for President 1976: The Carter Campaign.* New York: Stein and Day.

Sears, David O. (1977) "The Debates in the Light of Research: An Overview of the Effects." Paper prepared for delivery at the 1977 Annual Meeting of the American Political Science Association, Washington, D.C., September 1–4.

Sears, David O., and **Chaffee, Steven H.** (1979) "Uses and Effects of the 1976 Debates: An Overview of Empirical Studies." In Sidney Kraus, ed., *The Great Debates: Ford vs. Carter, 1976.* Bloomington: Indiana University Press.

Shanks, J. Merrill, and **Miller, Warren E.** (1985) "Policy Direction and Performance Evaluation: Complementary Explanations of the Reagan Elections." Paper prepared for delivery at the 1985 Annual Meeting of the American Political Science Association, New Orleans, Louisiana, August 29–September 1.

Shafer, Byron E. (1983a) "Continuity and Change, Predictability and Change, in the Politics of Presidential Selection." *PS,* (Fall), pp. 648–655.

————. (1983b) "Projecting the Outcome in 1984." *PS,* (Fall), pp. 689–694.

Shields, Currin V. (1954) "A Note on Party Organization: The Democrats in California." *Western Political Quarterly* (December), pp. 673–683.

Shively, W. Phillips. (1977) "Information Costs and the Partisan Life Cycle." Paper prepared for delivery at the 1977 Annual Meeting of the American Political Science Association, Washington, D.C., September 1–4.

————. (1979) "The Development of Party Identification in Adults." *American Political Science Review* (December), pp. 1039–1054.

Simon, Herbert. (1952) "Comments on the Theory of Organizations." *American Political Science Review* (December), pp. 1130–1152.

Smith, Hedrick. (1979) "Carter's Race against Time." *New York Times Magazine* (September 2), pp. 12–15, 26, 28.

Smith, Richard Norton. (1983) *Thomas E. Dewey and His Times.* New York: Simon & Schuster.

Sorauf, Frank J. (1984) *Party Politics in America,* 5th ed. Boston: Little, Brown.

Sorenson, Theodore. (1965) *Kennedy.* New York: Bantam Books.

Soule, John W., and **Clarke, James W.** (1970) "Amateurs and Professionals: A Study of Delegates to the 1968 Democratic National Convention." *American Political Science Review* (September), pp. 888–898.

Soule, John W., and **McGrath, Wilma E.** (1975) "A Comparative Study of Presidential Nominating Conventions." *American Journal of Political Science* (August), pp. 501–517.

Sperlich, Peter W. (1971) *Conflict and Harmony in Human Affairs: A Study of Cross-Pressures and Political Behavior.* Chicago: Rand McNally.

Sperling, Godfrey, Jr. (1972) "Steelworkers Wary on McGovern." *Christian Science Monitor* (September 20), p. 3.

Stein, Herbert. (1985) *Presidential Economics: The Making of Economic Policy from Roosevelt to Reagan and Beyond,* rev. ed. New York: Simon & Schuster.

Sterling, Christopher, and **Haight, Timothy.** (1979) *The Mass Media: Aspen Institute Guide to Communication Industry Trends.* Queenstown, Md.: Aspen Institute.

Stevenson, Robert L. (1978) "The Uses and Non-Uses of Television News." Paper prepared for the International Society of Political Psychology Meeting, New York, September 1978.

Stokes, Donald E., Campbell, Angus, and **Miller, Warren E.** (1958) "Components of Electoral Decision." *American Political Science Review* (June), pp. 367–387.

Sullivan, Dennis G., Pressman, Jeffrey L., Page, Benjamin I., and **Lyons, John J.** (1974) *The Politics of Representation: The Democratic Convention 1972.* New York: St. Martin's Press.

Sullivan, John L., Piereson, James E., and **Marcus, George E.** (1978) "Ideological Constraint in the Mass Public: A Methodological Critique and Some New Findings." *American Journal of Political Science* (May), pp. 250–269.

Taylor, Paul. (1984) "Mondale Has Decided Not to Write Off California." *Washington Post,* National Weekly Edition (August 27), p. 11.

Truman, David B. (1971) *The Governmental Process,* 2d ed. New York: Alfred A. Knopf.

Valentine, David C., and **van Wingen, John R.** (1980) "Partisanship, Independence, and the Partisan Identification

Index." *American Politics Quarterly* (April), pp. 165–186.

Verba, Sydney, and **Nie, Norman H.** (1972) *Participation in America: Political Democracy and Social Equality.* New York: Harper & Row.

Weinraub, Bernard. (1984a) "Mondale Wins Kennedy's Endorsement." *New York Times* (June 26), p. 44.

————. (1984b) "Mondale Shifting Focus from Deficit." *New York Times* (October 18), p. 16.

Weisberg, Herbert F. (1978) "Evaluating Theories of Congressional Roll Call Voting." *American Journal of Political Science* (August), pp. 554–577.

————. (1980) "A Multidimensional Conceptualization of Party Identification." *Political Behavior* (no. 1), pp. 33–60.

————. (1985) "The Electoral Kaleidoscope: Political Change in the Polarizing Election of 1984." Paper prepared for delivery at the 1985 Annual Meeting of the American Political Science Association, New Orleans, Louisiana, August 29–September 1.

West, Darrell M. (1984) *Making Campaigns Count: Leadership and Coalition-Building in 1980.* Westport, Conn.: Greenwood Press.

White, F. Clifton. (1967) *Suite 3505: The Story of the Draft Goldwater Movement.* New Rochelle, N.Y.: Arlington House.

White, Theodore H. (1973) *The Making of the President 1972.* New York: Atheneum.

————. (1982) *America in Search of Itself: The Making of the President 1956–1980.* New York: Harper & Row.

Wilcox, W. Clyde. (1985) Personal communication.

Williams, Daniel C., Weber, Stephen J., Haaland, Gordon A., Mueller, Ronald H., and **Craig, Robert E.** (1976) "Voter Decisionmaking in a Primary Election." *American Journal of Political Science* (February), pp. 37–49.

Wilson, Woodrow. (1884) *Congressional Government,* Meridian Edition. New York: Meridian Books, 1956.

Wirthlin, Richard, Breglio, Vincent, and **Beal, Richard.** (1981) "Campaign Chronicle." *Public Opinion* (February–March), pp. 43–49.

Witcover, Jules. (1977) *Marathon: The Pursuit of the Presidency.* New York: Viking Press.

Wolfinger, Raymond E., and others. (1977) "The Myth of the Independent Voter." Paper prepared for delivery at the 1977 Annual Meeting of the American Political Science Association, Washington, D.C., September 1–4.

Wooten, James T. (1976) "Carter Strategy from the Start: 1976 Was the Year for a Gambler." *New York Times* (June 10), p. 42.

Yarnell, Steven. (1975) "The Measurement of Perceptual Accuracy: A Methodological Note." Ohio State University. Typescript.

Index

About the Author

After receiving his Ph.D. from Columbia University in 1958, John H. Kessel taught at Amherst and Mount Holyoke Colleges and the University of Washington. He became Arthur E. Braun Professor of Political Science at Allegheny College in 1965. Since 1970, he has been Professor of Political Science at The Ohio State University.

Mr. Kessel's other books include *The Goldwater Coalition, The Domestic Presidency*, and *Presidential Parties.* His articles have appeared in the *American Political Science Review, American Journal of Political Science, Social Science Quarterly,* and other professional journals. He has been a member of the Council of the American Political Science Association, editor of the *American Journal of Political Science,* and president of the Midwest Political Science Association.

A Note on the Type

The text of this book was set in 10/12 Palatino using a film version of the face designed by Hermann Zapf that was first released in 1950 by Germany's Stempel Foundry. The face is named after Giovanni Battista Palatino, a famous penman of the 16th century. In its calligraphic quality, Palatino is reminiscent of the Italian Renaissance type designs, yet with its wide, open letters and unique proportions it still retains a modern feel. Palatino is considered one of the most important faces from one of Europe's most influential type designers.

Composition by Bi-Comp, Inc., York, Pennsylvania

Printed and bound by Malloy Lithographing, Inc., Ann Arbor, Michigan